REMEMBERING THE JAGIELLONIANS

Remembering the Jagiellonians is the first study of international memories of the Jagiellonians (1386–1596), one of the most powerful but lesser known royal dynasties of Renaissance Europe. It explores how the Jagiellonian dynasty has been remembered since the early modern period and assesses its role in the development of competing modern national identities across Central, Eastern and Northern Europe.

Offering a wide-ranging panoramic analysis of Jagiellonian memory over five hundred years, this book includes coverage of numerous present-day European countries, ranging from Bavaria to Kiev, and from Stockholm to the Adriatic. In doing so, it allows for a large, multi-way comparison of how one shared phenomenon has been, and still is, remembered in over a dozen neighbouring countries. Specialists in the history of Europe are brought together to apply the latest questions from memory theory and to combine them with debates from social science, medieval and early modern European history to engage in an international and interdisciplinary exploration into the relationship between memory and dynasty through time.

The first book to present the Jagiellonians' supranational history in English, *Remembering the Jagiellonians* opens key discussions about the regional memory of Europe and considers the ongoing role of the Jagiellonians in modern-day culture and politics. It is essential reading for students of early modern and late medieval Europe, nineteenth-century nationalism and the history of memory.

Natalia Nowakowska is a Fellow and Associate Professor in History at Somerville College, University of Oxford, and Principal Investigator of the European Research Council (ERC) funded project 'Jagiellonians: Dynasty, Memory & Identity in Central Europe'. Her previous publications include *King Sigismund and Martin Luther: The Reformation before Confessionalization* (2018) and *Church, State and Dynasty in Renaissance Poland: The Career of Cardinal Fryderyk Jagiellon (1468–1503)* (2007).

Remembering the Medieval and Early Modern Worlds

Also in this series

Remembering the Crusades and Crusading
Edited by Megan Cassidy-Welch

Forthcoming titles

Remembering Early Modern Revolutions
Edited by Edward Vallance

REMEMBERING THE JAGIELLONIANS

Edited by Natalia Nowakowska

LONDON AND NEW YORK

First published 2019
by Routledge
2 Park Square, Milton Park, Abingdon, Oxon OX14 4RN

and by Routledge
711 Third Avenue, New York, NY 10017

Routledge is an imprint of the Taylor & Francis Group, an informa business

© 2019 selection and editorial matter, Natalia Nowakowska; individual chapters, the contributors

The right of Natalia Nowakowska to be identified as the author of the editorial material, and of the authors for their individual chapters, has been asserted in accordance with sections 77 and 78 of the Copyright, Designs and Patents Act 1988.

All rights reserved. No part of this book may be reprinted or reproduced or utilised in any form or by any electronic, mechanical, or other means, now known or hereafter invented, including photocopying and recording, or in any information storage or retrieval system, without permission in writing from the publishers.

Trademark notice: Product or corporate names may be trademarks or registered trademarks, and are used only for identification and explanation without intent to infringe.

British Library Cataloguing in Publication Data
A catalogue record for this book is available from the British Library

Library of Congress Cataloging in Publication Data
Names: Nowakowska, Natalia, 1977- editor.
Title: Remembering the Jagiellonians / edited by Natalia Nowakowska.
Description: London ; New York : Routledge, 2018. | Includes bibliographical references and index.
Identifiers: LCCN 2018002058| ISBN 9781138562394 (hardback : alk. paper) | ISBN 9781138562400 (pbk. : alk. paper) | ISBN 9780203709788 (ebook)
Subjects: LCSH: Jagellon dynasty—Influence. | Poland—History—Jagellons, 1386-1572. | Europe, Eastern—Kings and rulers—History. | Nobility—Europe, Eastern—History. | Collective memory—Europe, Eastern.
Classification: LCC DJK46 .R46 2018 | DDC 943.8/023—dc23
LC record available at https://lccn.loc.gov/2018002058

ISBN: 978-1-138-56239-4 (hbk)
ISBN: 978-1-138-56240-0 (pbk)
ISBN: 978-0-203-70978-8 (ebk)

Typeset in Times New Roman
by Keystroke, Neville Lodge, Tettenhall, Wolverhampton

CONTENTS

List of illustrations vii
Map of Jagiellonian Europe ix
Jagiellonian family tree x
Acknowledgements xiii
Notes on contributors xv

    Introduction: time, space and dynasty 1
    Natalia Nowakowska

1 Our foreign traitors and redeemers: remembering
  Jagiellonians in Lithuania 28
  Giedrė Mickūnaitė

2 An ambiguous golden age: the Jagiellonians in Polish
  memory and historical consciousness 49
  Natalia Nowakowska

3 The memory of the Jagiellonians in the Kingdom of Hungary,
  and in Hungarian and Slovak national narratives 71
  Stanislava Kuzmová

4 Did Bohemian Jagiellonians exist? 101
  Ilya Afanasyev

5 Remembering Jagiellonians in German-speaking lands 121
  Dušan Zupka

6 Remembering a past princess: Catherine Jagiellon and the construction of national narratives in Sweden and Finland 141
Susanna Niiranen

7 The Jagiellonians in Belarus: a gradual release of memory 162
Simon M. Lewis

8 The Jagiellonians in Ukrainian traditions 183
Tetiana Hoshko

9 The Jagiellonian dynasty in Russian historiography and memory 205
Olga Kozubska-Andrusiv

Bibliography 224
Index 258

ILLUSTRATIONS

Figures

Map of Jagiellonian Europe (c.1500)		ix
Jagiellonian family tree		x
1.1	Landscape of Jagiellonian ruins, Jan Rustem (c. 1820)	30
1.2	Two oil paintings by Žygimantas Augustinas (2016)	42
2.1	Etching from Kamsetzer's *Gabinet Marmurowy* (1784)	54
2.2	Model for the sculpture *Procession to the Wawel* (1911)	57
3.1	*The Discovery of the Corpse of King Louis II*, Bertalan Székely (1860)	80
4.1	Jagiellonian genealogical table by Bohuslav Balbín (1687)	108
4.2	Czech cartoon depicting Jagiellonian rulers (1979)	113
5.1	Painting of the 1475 wedding, Landshut town hall (1883)	133
6.1	Engraving of Catherine Jagiellon's tomb, Johan Litheim	146
6.2	Tapestry of Catherine Jagiellon and Duke John (1961)	151
7.1	Monument to Sophia of Halshany (c. 2005)	176

Table

5.1	The Jagiellonian princesses and their marriages into the Holy Roman Empire	122

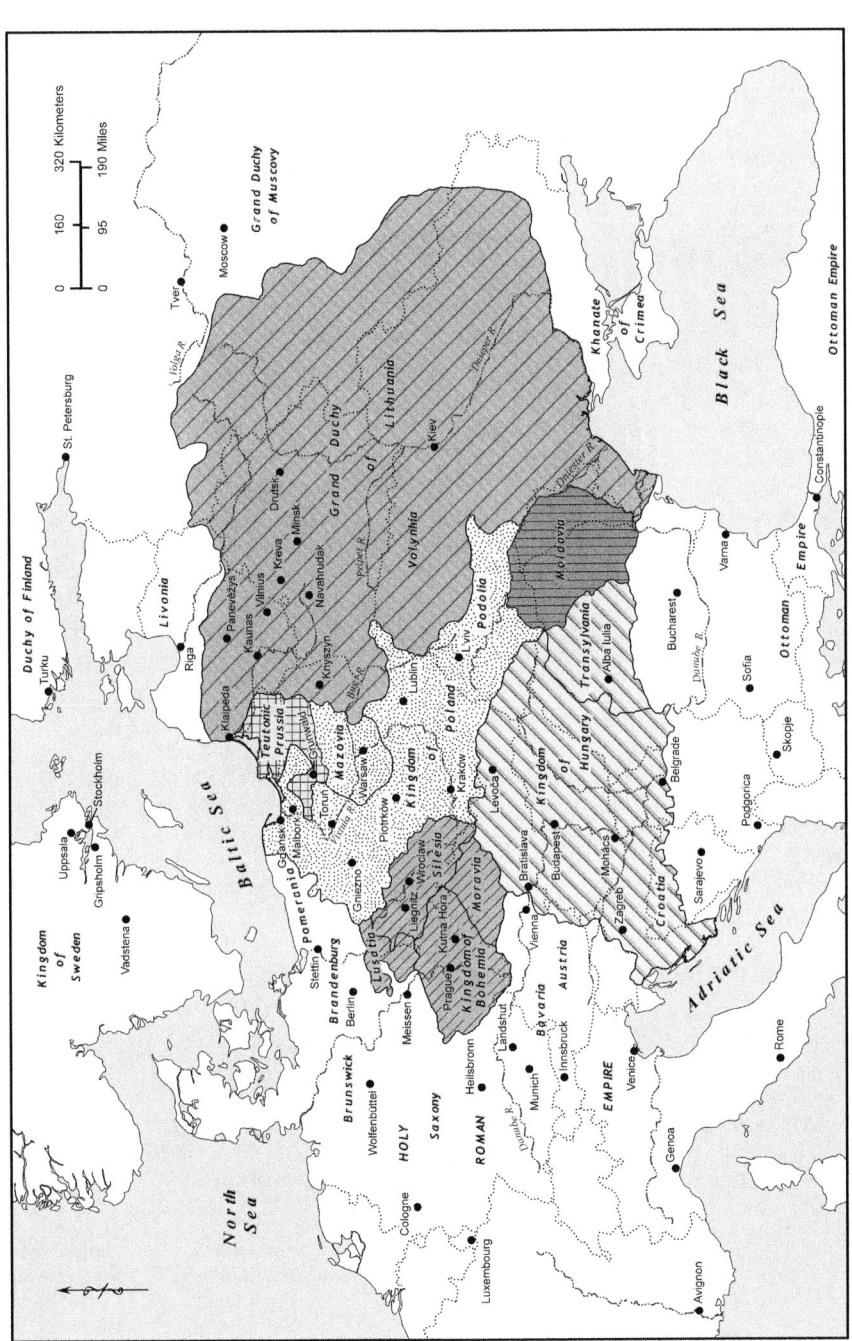

Jagiellonian Europe (c.1500), © Gordon Thompson

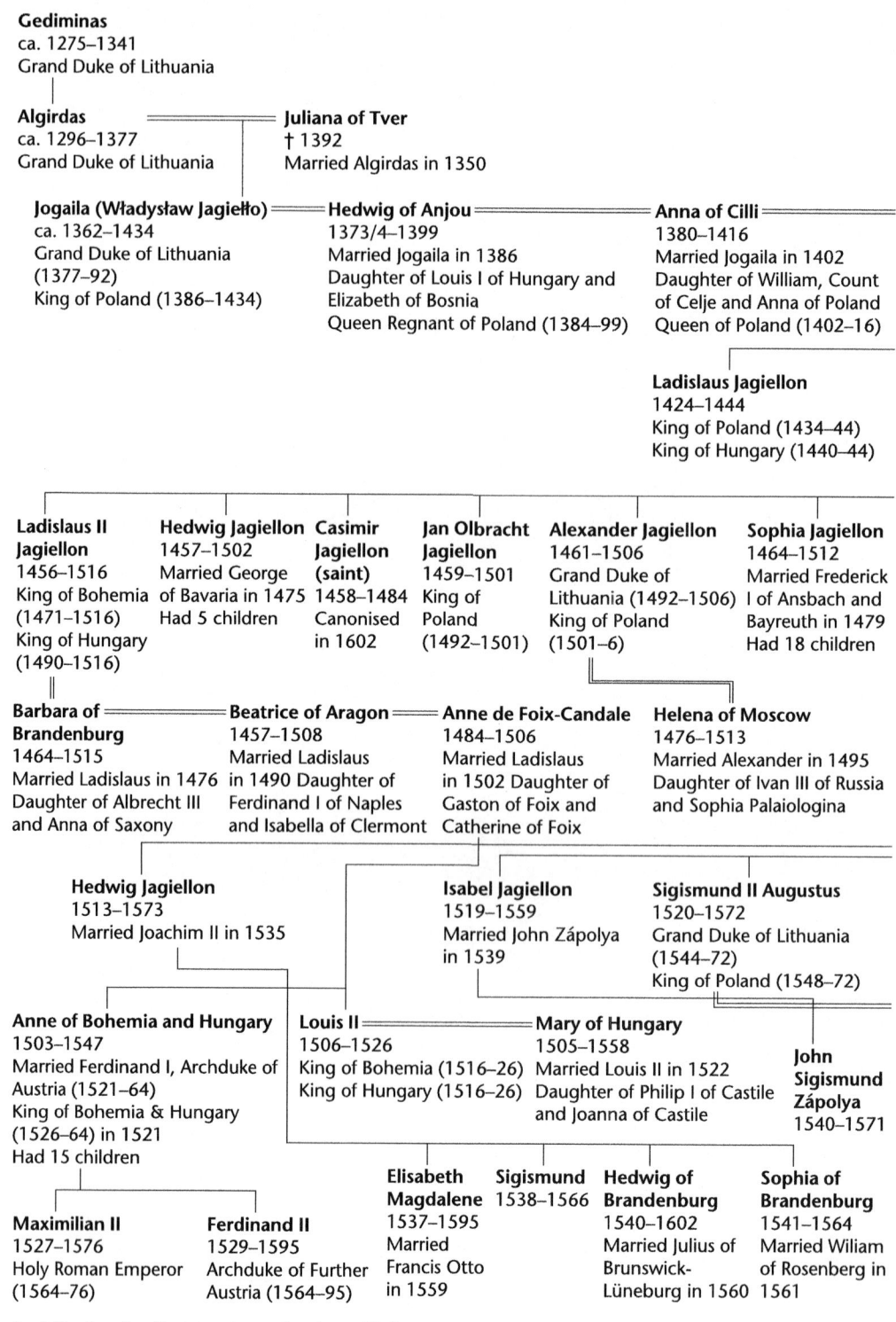

Jagiellonian family tree, drawn by Artur Kula

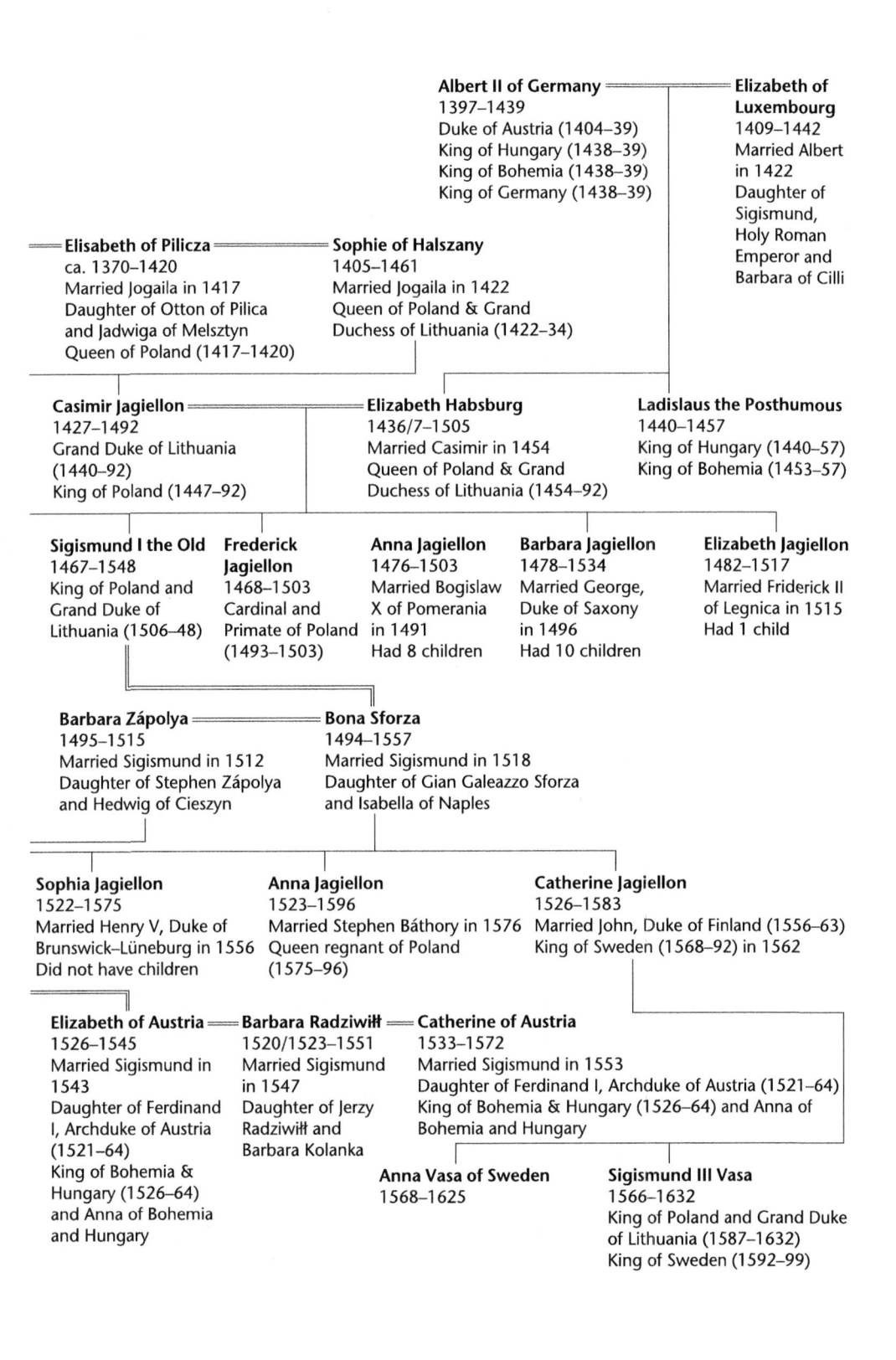

Albert II of Germany ══════ **Elizabeth of Luxembourg**
1397–1439
Duke of Austria (1404–39)
King of Hungary (1438–39)
King of Bohemia (1438–39)
King of Germany (1438–39)

1409–1442
Married Albert in 1422
Daughter of Sigismund, Holy Roman Emperor and Barbara of Cilli

══ **Elisabeth of Pilicza** ══ **Sophie of Halszany**
ca. 1370–1420
Married Jogaila in 1417
Daughter of Otton of Pilica and Jadwiga of Melsztyn
Queen of Poland (1417–1420)

1405–1461
Married Jogaila in 1422
Queen of Poland & Grand Duchess of Lithuania (1422–34)

Casimir Jagiellon ══════════ **Elizabeth Habsburg** **Ladislaus the Posthumous**
1427–1492
Grand Duke of Lithuania (1440–92)
King of Poland (1447–92)

1436/7–1505
Married Casimir in 1454
Queen of Poland & Grand Duchess of Lithuania (1454–92)

1440–1457
King of Hungary (1440–57)
King of Bohemia (1453–57)

Sigismund I the Old **Frederick Jagiellon** **Anna Jagiellon** **Barbara Jagiellon** **Elizabeth Jagiellon**
1467–1548
King of Poland and Grand Duke of Lithuania (1506–48)

1468–1503
Cardinal and Primate of Poland (1493–1503)

1476–1503
Married Bogislaw X of Pomerania in 1491
Had 8 children

1478–1534
Married George, Duke of Saxony in 1496
Had 10 children

1482–1517
Married Friderick II of Legnica in 1515
Had 1 child

Barbara Zápolya ══════ **Bona Sforza**
1495–1515
Married Sigismund in 1512
Daughter of Stephen Zápolya and Hedwig of Cieszyn

1494–1557
Married Sigismund in 1518
Daughter of Gian Galeazzo Sforza and Isabella of Naples

Sophia Jagiellon **Anna Jagiellon** **Catherine Jagiellon**
1522–1575
Married Henry V, Duke of Brunswick–Lüneburg in 1556
Did not have children

1523–1596
Married Stephen Báthory in 1576
Queen regnant of Poland (1575–96)

1526–1583
Married John, Duke of Finland (1556–63)
King of Sweden (1568–92) in 1562

Elizabeth of Austria ══ **Barbara Radziwiłł** ══ **Catherine of Austria**
1526–1545
Married Sigismund in 1543
Daughter of Ferdinand I, Archduke of Austria (1521–64)
King of Bohemia & Hungary (1526–64) and Anna of Bohemia and Hungary

1520/1523–1551
Married Sigismund in 1547
Daughter of Jerzy Radziwiłł and Barbara Kolanka

1533–1572
Married Sigismund in 1553
Daughter of Ferdinand I, Archduke of Austria (1521–64)
King of Bohemia & Hungary (1526–64) and Anna of Bohemia and Hungary

Anna Vasa of Sweden **Sigismund III Vasa**
1568–1625

1566–1632
King of Poland and Grand Duke of Lithuania (1587–1632)
King of Sweden (1592–99)

ACKNOWLEDGEMENTS

Producing *Remembering the Jagiellonians* has been an ambitious undertaking, involving multiple countries, languages, alphabets and scholars, and as such has drawn on the support of a wide number of institutions and people. The principal debt and acknowledgement is to the European Research Council (ERC). The research published in this book was entirely funded by the ERC under the European Union's Seventh Framework Programme (FP7/2007-2013) as ERC grant agreement number 335814, as part of the Starting Grant Project *Jagiellonians: Dynasty, Memory and Identity in Central Europe* (www.jagiellonians.com). The ERC's grants have had, and continue to have, a transformative effect on Humanities research in the UK and far beyond, enabling scholars to ask new questions in new ways. Comparative memory work on this scale would not have been possible without an ERC grant, and my own intellectual debt to the ERC will certainly long outlive this five-year project. I thank the team who worked as Research Associates on the project for engaging with its research questions with precision, energy and rigour: Ilya Afanasyev, Dr Stanislava Kuzmová, Dr Giedrė Mickūnaitė, Dr Susanna Niiranen and Dr Dušan Zupka. Briony Truscott, our Project Administrator, has done so much to keep this show on the road in the past four years, for which I am sincerely grateful. Thanks to the History Faculty at the University of Oxford, Somerville College, and the Oxford Research Centre in the Humanities (TORCH), which have supported this project in multiple ways.

For this memory strand of the project's research, I also wish to warmly thank scholars who wrote background papers for us on Jagiellonian historiography in other ex-Jagiellonian countries: Tomislav Matić on Croatia, János Incze on Romania, and Miloš Ivanović on Serbia. Even though there was not room to include all these papers in the final volume, I draw attention to their key findings in the Introduction. Thanks to those who gave papers at the Jagiellonians project workshop on 'Regional Memory' in Oxford in spring 2015: Joanna Wawrzyniak

(Warsaw), Barak Kushner (Cambridge), Patrick Clibbens (Oxford), Leyla Neyzi (Sabancı University), Christine Allison (Exeter), Gai Jorayev (UCL), Félix Krawatzek (Oxford), Monika Baár (Leiden), Kamil Činátl (Prague), Andrea Purdeková (Oxford) and Natalya Vince (Portsmouth). Discussing problems of regional memory in this highly interdisciplinary group gave a boost to our own project's research. I would also like to thank very warmly Marcin Jarząbek and Gregor Fiendt for inviting me to speak on Jagiellonian and European memory at the Fifth Congress of Foreign Researchers of Polish History, in Krakow in 2017 – their feedback, and questions from the panel audience, were most stimulating. Dr Johannes Wolf has provided excellent editorial assistance in preparing the final text of this volume. Artur Kula kindly drew the family tree. I would also like to thank Laura Pilsworth at Routledge for her interest in this research from a very early stage, and both Laura and Morwenna Scott for their supportive, friendly and highly professional input at every stage. Thanks to the three anonymous peer reviewers, who gave valuable feedback on what to clarify, and further emphasise, in the volume. Louise Berglund gave me plenty of good and morale-boosting advice on how to edit a collected volume during her spell as an Academic Visitor in Oxford. Finally, I would like to thank all the contributors for their good humour, hard work and patient replies to every query over several years. Hopefully, this book will underscore the new perspectives which can emerge when historians and scholars from right across Europe – from Oxford to Lviv – join forces to tell neglected stories.

A note on spelling

In Hungarian scholarship, the monarch who ruled from 1490 to 1516 is usually called 'Wladislaus'. However, for consistency in this volume, with its coverage of multiple territories and traditions, the spelling 'Ladislaus' has been adopted throughout.

CONTRIBUTORS

Ilya Afanasyev is a Research Fellow at the Birmingham Research Institute for History and Cultures, University of Birmingham. He is interested in the construction of collective identifications, the long history of ethnicity and nationhood, 'dynasty' and, increasingly, the history of debt. He specialises in both medieval and early modern history of Western and Central Europe and is trying to work at the intersections of intellectual history and political economy. Between 2014 and 2016, he was a Research Associate on the ERC *Jagiellonians* project at Oxford, responsible for research on Bohemia. He has published articles in *Historical Research*, *Anglo-Norman Studies* and *The Journal of Medieval History*.

Tetiana Hoshko is an Associate Professor in the Department of Classical, Byzantine & Medieval Studies at the Ukrainian Catholic University in Lviv, and a postdoctoral researcher in the Department of History of Central and Eastern Europe at the Taras Shevchenko National University of Kyiv. Her studies deal mainly with the urban history of Poland and Lithuania (including Ruthenian lands) in the fourteenth to seventeenth centuries. She is the author of *Narysy istorii magdeburz'koho prava v Ukraini XIV – pochatku XVII st.* [Essays on the History of Magdeburg Law in Ukraine, 14th – Early 17th Century] (2002) and *Khrestomatiia istorii Ukrainy lytovs'ko-pol's'koi doby* [A Reader on the History of Ukraine: The Polish-Lithuanian Period] (2011). She has recently published articles in *Kwartalnik Historii Kultury Materialnej* (2014), *Ukrains'kyi istorychnyi zhurnal* (2017) and *Ukraina v Tsentral'no-Skhidnii Yevropi* (2017).

Olga Kozubksa-Andrusiv received her MA in Art History (Ukrainian Academy of Art, Kyiv) and in Medieval Studies (Central European University, Budapest). Her PhD degree was awarded by the Department of Medieval Studies (Central European University, Budapest). Her research interests include the history of medieval art and religious architecture, urban studies, history and historiography of the mendicant orders, and uses and abuses of the Middle Ages in the nineteenth to twenty-first centuries.

Stanislava Kuzmová is currently a researcher at the Faculty of Arts, Comenius University in Bratislava (Department of Slovak History). She earned her PhD in Medieval Studies at the Central European University in Budapest, where she worked as postdoctoral researcher before joining the Jagiellonians project in Oxford in 2014–16. Her book based on her doctoral dissertation, *Preaching Saint Stanislaus: Medieval Sermons on St. Stanislaus of Cracow, His Image and Cult* (2013), was awarded the Stefan Krzysztof Kuczyński Prize for best publication in historical sources and auxiliary sciences in Poland in 2014. Her research interests include cults of saints, hagiography and sermon studies, and medieval religiosity.

Simon M. Lewis is a DFG Research Fellow at the University of Potsdam. He has held research posts at Freie Universität Berlin, the University of Oxford and the University of Warsaw, and completed a PhD in Slavonic Studies in 2014 at the University of Cambridge. Lewis's academic interests include cosmopolitanism, transnational history and cultural memory. He has published articles on memory, postcolonialism and trauma in the literature and culture of Belarus and Poland, and he is a co-author of the collective monograph *Remembering Katyn* (2012). His monograph *Belarus – Alternative Visions: Nationhood, Memory and Cosmopolitanism* is forthcoming with Routledge.

Giedrė Mickūnaitė holds a PhD in Medieval Studies from the Central European University in Budapest (2002). In 2014–16 she worked as Research Associate for the ERC project *Jagiellonians: Dynasty, Memory, Identity in Central Europe* at the University of Oxford. Currently, she is Professor of Art History at the Vilnius Academy of Arts. Her research enquires into the relation of pictorial and textual imagery, asking about the vocabulary of visual experience and the temporal dimension of images. She also explores the work of memory in providing cultural legacy and argues that oblivion is a means for ordering the past. Mickūnaitė publishes regularly in the Lithuanian and international scholarly press and also acts as an exhibition curator.

Susanna Niiranen is a Senior Researcher in the Department of History and Ethnology, University of Jyväskylä, Finland. Her publications concern various aspects of medieval and early modern literature, medicine, gender, vernacularisation and transmission of knowledge. In 2015–16 she worked for the ERC project *Jagiellonians: Dynasty, Memory and Identity in Central Europe*, at the University of Oxford, where she investigated Catherine Jagiellon as a member of the Jagiellonian dynasty in Sweden. She is currently participating in an international book historical project working on late medieval and early modern libraries.

Natalia Nowakowska is an Associate Professor in Early Modern History at the University of Oxford, and a Fellow of Somerville College. She is Principal Investigator of the ERC project *Jagiellonians: Dynasty, Memory and Identity in Central Europe* (2013–18, www.jagiellonians.com). Natalia is the author of two monographs which set late medieval and early modern Polish history within its wider European context – *Church, State and Dynasty in the Career of Cardinal Fryderyk Jagiellon, 1468–1503* (2007; co-winner of the Kulczycki Prize) and *King Sigismund of Poland and Martin Luther: The Reformation before Confessionalization* (2018). Natalia also publishes on crusading, the printing revolution and the late medieval church, with articles in *Past & Present* and *Historical Research*.

Dušan Zupka, PhD in History, is a lecturer in the General History Department, Comenius University in Bratislava. He is a historian of medieval and early modern Europe focusing on cultural and political history, and author of the monograph *Ritual and Symbolic Communication in Medieval Hungary under the Árpád Dynasty, 1000–1301* (2016). He has also published several articles on power, rulership and communication in medieval Central Europe. He worked as a Research Associate with the ERC Jagiellonians project in Oxford, looking at Jagiellonian princesses and their legacies in the Holy Roman Empire and Austria.

INTRODUCTION

Time, space and dynasty

Natalia Nowakowska

This volume makes an experimental intervention at the intersection of three fields: the study of medieval and Renaissance Europe, the history of the modern world, and memory studies in present-day social sciences. Our volume takes as its mnemonic subject the Jagiellonians – one of the most spectacular royal houses seen in Renaissance Europe, yet a dynasty entirely unfamiliar to (or 'forgotten' by) many scholars and students of European history. In their heyday, the Jagiellonians (c.1386–c.1572) ruled vast tracts of Europe – the Grand Duchy of Lithuania, the medieval and early modern elective kingdoms of Poland, Bohemia and Hungary, and the principality of Transylvania, lands stretching from Zagreb on the Adriatic coast, to Kiev on the Eurasian steppe. Jagiellonian princesses married into the ruling houses of Scandinavia, the Holy Roman Empire and Austria.[1] Reconfigured into the language of twenty-first-century geography, the lands formerly ruled by the Jagiellonians today encompass twelve polities, and over 25 per cent of European Union member states. They include (all, or parts of) the Czech Republic, Slovakia, Hungary, Romania, Croatia, Serbia, Poland, Lithuania, Latvia, Belarus, Ukraine and the (westernmost) Russian Federation (see map). Jagiellonian royal females, meanwhile, have left further legacies in Austria, Sweden, Finland and right across the Federal Republic of Germany. As such, the potential canvas for memories of this profoundly international royal house – comparable, in their own day, only to the Habsburgs – is vast.[2] This book represents the very first attempt to analyse memories of the Jagiellonians, right across the many European territories in which they were once present.[3]

Studies of memory, particularly for Central Europe, have overwhelmingly focused on *current* memories of *recent* (above all twentieth-century) events.[4] Yet the Jagiellonians, although a medieval and Renaissance phenomenon, speak directly to two live debates in memory studies – a debate about space, and a debate about time. They are also pertinent to the issue of European memory, raising the question of how such a large-scale dynasty can have passed out of wider European cultural, pedagogical, political and scholarly memory – of why we have 'remembered' the Tudors, Bourbons, Habsburgs and Medici, yet 'forgotten' the Jagiellonians. This Introduction will first situate the Jagiellonians within current theoretical debates in memory studies, before offering a brief account of their rise and fall (1380s to 1590s), and the very first comparative, panoramic sketch of the evolution of Jagiellonian memory in Europe (from the 1590s to the present day). This account, which posits three principal phases of Jagiellonian memory since the sixteenth century, is a bird's eye, editor's synthesis and interpretation of the essays in this volume, collating the research findings of our nine contributors. This Introduction asks, finally, how far Jagiellonian memories travel through space and time, whether or not they constitute a 'regional' memory, and the wider lessons this royal family and its memorialisation can offer – to historians of the Middle Ages and early modern period, to scholars of modern nationalism, and to those debating methods and theories in memory studies today.

Theories: memory, time, space

It is now a truism that memory studies has swept like a wave through humanities and social science since the 1980s. Research on memory is conducted in multiple disciplines: sociology, literature, political science, anthropology, history and cultural/media studies. Its study has become so pervasive that it has been described as a 'polylogue', the 'new critical conjunction of history and theory'.[5] So great is its success in attracting researchers, that accounting for the popularity of memory studies has become a research question in itself.[6] Distinct from (but influenced by) models of human memory operating in psychology and neuroscience, this vast field of what is variously called 'cultural', 'collective', or 'social' memory studies how the past is subsequently represented in society. As the forefather of memory studies, the French sociologist Maurice Halbwachs (d.1945), put it, 'the past is not preserved, but is reconstructed on the basis of the present'.[7] Astrid Erll (2010) defines collective memory as 'the question of how the past is created and recreated within socio-cultural contexts', thereby generating 'socially shared versions of history'.[8] For Wulf Kansteiner, collective memory is 'a complex process of cultural production and consumption'.[9] Memory thus involves intent: making others 'remember', in a particular way, historical events which they as individuals could not literally remember (such as a fifteenth-century king). In this volume, some contributors suggest that we can describe these invocations of the past using not the catch-all term 'memory', but alternative formulations such as 'historical culture', 'historical representations', or 'historical consciousness'.[10]

Memory studies is currently engaged in a far-reaching debate about space, as the field moves from its original national focus, towards the international, transnational and supra-national. On what spatial plane, or geographical level, should memory properly be studied? Much early work explored memory solely within the parameters of the nation-state, as the most active and natural creator, and container, for narratives about the historic past. Rousso's (1987) research on French memories of the Vichy regime serves as a classic example.[11] Since the 2000s, however, there has been a growing reaction against studying individual national memory cultures in isolation. As scholarship has developed an increasingly sophisticated understanding of national memory narratives as constructed, part mythical, and relatively recent creations (from the nineteenth and twentieth centuries), memory scholars in turn have become sensitised to the risk of amplifying, or sanctioning, these grand national narratives in their own work. The anxiety is that, by studying these national tales on their own terms, as unique, self-evident, and self-contained stories, the scholar becomes a servant of these nationalisms, and not simply their observer.[12] This is what Ilya Afanasyev in this volume terms 'the methodological nationalism so inherent in memory studies', and what Pestel et al. recently called 'the implicit nationalising bias' of memory research.[13] Globalisation, and a turn towards global history, have instead led scholars to claim that memory does not stop at borders, but travels past them.[14] At present, there are at least three 'spatial' models for studying memory beyond the individual nation-state. In a 'national-comparative' approach, national memory regimes are contrasted with one another, in a search for patterns, e.g. in Troebst's analysis of East European memories of World War II.[15] Alternatively, some scholars emphasise the trans-national dimensions of memory, i.e. the transmission, cross-fertilisation and entanglement of particular memories between different societies.[16] Finally, others investigate authentically supra-national forms of remembering, 'discursive arenas of memory that are above the level of the nation-state' whether at a global, European, or regional level.[17] The question of whether post-Soviet Central Europe constitutes a distinctive 'region of memory' has, for example, been intensively studied.[18]

The Jagiellonians are a fruitful case study to bring to these debates about memory and space, because they were unique among Renaissance dynasties in the geographical character of their hegemony. Whereas houses such as the English Tudors (1485–1603) or Portuguese Aviz (1385–1580) governed just one European kingdom, and the Habsburgs ruled a plethora of scattered lands (Netherlands, Castile, Naples), the Jagiellonians alone governed a neighbouring set of polities, thereby forming a concentrated geographical 'bloc'– creating a common historical thread and the potential for shared memory. Whereas the Habsburgs, for example, permit the study of international, comparative-national memory, such as in Dixon and Fuchs's study of *The Histories of Charles V*, the Jagiellonians enable us to go further – to pose questions about regional memory (trans-national, and supra-national) across polities, societies and peoples in immediate physical proximity to each other.[19] One can ask whether there exists (or has existed) a shared 'regional memory' of the Jagiellonians, without necessarily subscribing to the much-debated idea of 'Central Europe' as a historical constant or entity in its own right.[20]

This sprawling Renaissance dynasty also speaks to a debate in memory studies about time: about the age of the social memories we observe in action. Halbwachs himself has been classified as a 'presentist', as believing that memory was entirely shaped by and in the present, with no real relationship to the actual past it claimed to depict/relate.[21] However, there is a growing conviction that memory is not assembled from purely contemporary materials, but has deep roots and history of its own, its form dictated by 'long historical processes'.[22] This is often referred to as re-mediation, i.e. stories travelling long distances across time. This comes as no real novelty to historians: in the 1970s, for example, Philippe Joutard found that local stories of World War II resistance in the Cévennes were verbatim re-tellings of seventeenth-century local tales of Protestant insurrection.[23] Social scientists in this field are increasingly attuned to the remediation of memory. Michael Bernhard and Jan Kubik's (2014) comparative investigation of how ex-Communist societies commemorated the twentieth anniversary of 1989 identified different types of 'memory regime' in Central Europe, for example, but could account for this variation only by speculating that these memories were in fact re-performances of much older local, hard-wired traditions (or memory scripts), perhaps dating back in Poland to the Partition period of the nineteenth century, or in Hungary to anti-Habsburg risings of the seventeenth.[24] Some theorists now identify the entanglement of memories across time as a definitive methodological and conceptual problem – as the issue which will shape a 'third wave' of interdisciplinary memory studies. Feindt, Hadler, Pestel et al. have since 2014 published diagrams and equations illustrating this problematic dimension of memory: that what we see today are probably memories of memories, in a deep echo chamber.[25]

Here too, the Jagiellonians provide a useful case study, as a phenomenon located far back in time – dating to the fourteenth century – which enables us to observe the evolution, and re-mediation, of memory over the long term. Many studies of historic memory have a dual-period design, e.g. Pollmann's examination of seventeenth-century memories of the sixteenth-century Dutch revolt, or Eiden's study of seventeenth- to twentieth-century memories of the medieval Piast rulers of Silesia.[26] Studies tracing memory across the *longue durée* are, however, rarer.[27] This volume sketches the main features of Jagiellonian memory from the Renaissance period to the present, across epochs, but crucially also (where possible) takes this story right back to the royal line's own day, to the original discourses, texts, sources and iconographies surrounding them. As such, it actively links up historical study of a subject itself (the Jagiellonians) with the study of its subsequent memory. Many of our contributors are medievalists, versed in fifteenth- and sixteenth-century sources on the Jagiellonians, and well placed to recognise echoes of these first traditions in subsequent centuries. This volume thus aims to offer a 360-degree view of Jagiellonian memory, plotted across two dimensions, in space and time – across multiple neighbouring polities/societies, from the 1380s to the 2010s. Before explaining how this book tackles such a daunting task, let us first look more closely at who the Jagiellonians were, and are.

Jagiellonians: rise and fall (1380s to 1570s)

The royal line known to us as 'Jagiellonians' originated as rulers of the Grand Duchy of Lithuania, the last pagan polity in late medieval Europe, and also its largest. This Grand Duchy encompassed Baltic territories, as well as swathes of present-day Belarus, Ukraine and western Russia, as a successor state to the glittering polity of Kievian Rus' (ninth to thirteenth centuries), and the retreating Mongols of the Golden Horde (1240s–c.1500). The Grand Duchy's hegemony over these Christian Orthodox towns and peoples south of Lithuania was consolidated under Vytenis (d.1316) and his brother Gediminas (d.1341), after whom the grand ducal dynasty is sometimes named, 'Gediminids'.[28] Gediminas's grandson Jogaila (Jagiełło, Iagel), grand duke from 1377, finding himself under intense military pressure from the crusading Teutonic Knights of Prussia, in 1385–86 converted to Roman Christianity, married the queen-heiress of Poland (Hedwig of Anjou, r.1384–99), signed the first treaty of union between Poland and the grand duchy at Kreva, and took up residence in Kraków as a Catholic Latin king (Ladislaus, Władysław), in a remarkable act of political and cultural self-reinvention.

Retaining the title of supreme duke of Lithuania, Jogaila named his powerful cousin Vytautas 'the Great' as the grand duchy's ruler (r.1392–1430).[29] At the Battle of Grunwald/Tannenberg in 1410, one of the biggest pitched battles of the late Middle Ages, the cousins' combined Polish, Lithuanian, Ruthene and Tartar forces inflicted a famous and crippling defeat on the Teutonic Knights.[30] Jogaila's stature in Europe grew: he emerged as a powerful partner-rival to the Holy Roman Emperor Sigismund of Luxembourg (d.1437), was offered the crown of religiously-dissident Bohemia, and asserted his influence to the south in Moldavia (present-day Moldova-Romania). But throughout his four-decade career as a mighty Catholic king, Jogaila was no traditional dynast. It was only with his fourth marriage, to the young Orthodox noblewoman Sofia of Halshany, that the ageing Jogaila unexpectedly became father to two sons in the 1420s (see Jagiellonian family tree).[31]

When Jogaila died in 1434, these princes were small children, but they too were to emerge as ambitious, multi-polity rulers: one briefly, one for many decades. The eldest, Ladislaus III (1424–44), survived a chaotic and dangerous minority as king of Poland, and was in 1440 elected king of Hungary. Medieval Hungary was a far bigger, richer kingdom than Poland, covering present-day Hungary, Slovakia and Croatia, as well as parts of Serbia and Romania. Travelling to Buda, Ladislaus prosecuted a brief civil war against his Habsburg rivals for the crown, before turning his military attention to the Ottomans, with the encouragement of Rome.[32] In 1444, at the Black Sea town of Varna, in today's Bulgaria, Ladislaus I's great crusading army suffered a catastrophic defeat at the hands of Sultan Murad II: the Polish-Hungarian king's body was never found.[33] This was a moment of near-eclipse for Jogaila's fledgling royal line. The Hungarian crown passed to a Habsburg prince, the Polish monarchy witnessed a prolonged and destabilising interregnum, and only in Vilnius did Jogaila's line retain power, in the person of his 17-year-old surviving son, grand duke Casimir (1427–92).

After years of terse negotiations, grand duke Casimir was crowned king of Poland in 1447, like his father and brother. His reign marked the start of a decisive new phase in the family's international influence. Casimir IV's marriage to Elizabeth Habsburg (1454) was one of the most fertile royal matches in late medieval Christendom, producing six sons and five (surviving) daughters. The peripatetic Casimir IV stabilised his rule in the Polish monarchy and the grand duchy, conquered a chunk of Prussia from the Teutonic Knights (1454–66), tried to defend his Lithuanian patrimony against the rising power of Muscovy, and as his children reached adulthood saw them fan out across the courts of Europe. In 1475, his oldest daughter Hedwig married George the Rich of Bavaria at Landshut, in a wedding so lavish it has passed into legend. Hedwig's sister Sophie married the Margrave of Brandenburg (1479), her sister Anna the Duke of Pomerania (1491), her sister Barbara the duke of Saxony (1496), and her sister Elizabeth the duke of Leignitz (1515). The offspring of these Polish princesses were so numerous that the printer Hieronymous Wietor and historian Jodocus Ludovicus Decius struggled to fit them on a double-page 'Jagiellonian' family tree in 1521, an image peopled chiefly with German princelings.[34]

Yet it was to the south, and not within the Holy Roman Empire, that Jogaila's grandchildren made their most dramatic geopolitical impact at the turn of the fifteenth and sixteenth centuries. Casimir IV's oldest son, Ladislaus (1456–1516), was elected king of Bohemia in 1471, where he presided over a biconfessional Utraquist-Catholic religious settlement, and started to rebuild the royal citadel of Prague after the Hussite wars.[35] In 1490, having triumphed in a bitter succession war, Ladislaus II also won the Hungarian crown once worn by his namesake uncle, forging an ambitious dual Hungarian-Bohemian monarchy. Though both elective, he claimed these kingdoms through the maternal line, via Elizabeth Habsburg. In Buda, he inherited the splendid Renaissance castle of his mighty predecessor, and his father's great nemesis, King Matthias Corvinus (r.1458–90). Ladislaus II faced down the 1514 peasant rising which shook Hungary, strived via crusades and border fortifications to protect the monarchy from Ottoman encroachments, and in 1502 made a match with the French royal family, marrying their cousin Anne de Foix (1484–1506).[36] The children of this union, Anna (1503–47) and Louis (1506–26), represented a new Prague-Buda branch of Jogaila's royal line. In a much-debated attempt to secure peace in Central Europe at a summit in Vienna in 1515, King Ladislaus II engaged his children to the Habsburg heirs of the Holy Roman Emperor Maximilian I, in a double-wedding treaty.

Following his father Casimir's death in 1492, Ladislaus II sought to establish himself as the senior member and leader of his royal house. However, despite ambitious dynastic summits such as the one held at Levoča (in present-day Slovakia) in 1494, his brothers – King John Albert of Poland (r.1492–1501), Cardinal Frederick of Poland (1468–1503) and Alexander (grand duke of Lithuania from 1492, and king of Poland from 1501) – repeatedly subverted their eldest brother's authority. John Albert challenged the Hungarian king with a Polish military expedition into Moldavia (1497), Frederick manoeuvred to deny Ladislaus the Polish crown in the election of 1501, while Alexander was distracted with his own affairs in the grand duchy, where even his wedding to Helena of Muscovy did not bring a cessation of warfare with her father Ivan III.[37] The dream of a grand alliance of Casimir IV's sons, a great arc of royal power stretching from Vilnius to Belgrade and protecting Christendom's eastern flank, failed to materialise.

As John Albert (d.1501) and Alexander (d.1506) died one after another without heir, the Polish crown, and the grand duchy, fell to a prince who had never expected to wear it: Casimir's fifth son, Sigismund (aged 40), who had spent his youth dallying at Ladislaus II's court and ruling minor duchies in Silesia. Ladislaus II himself was deeply anxious about his own son's succession in Hungary and Bohemia – he died in 1516, having begged the Emperor Maximilian, King Sigismund and the Hungarian nobles to recognise Louis as his heir. While Louis II did succeed, his reign was brief. His life closely echoed the fate of Ladislaus of Varna (d.1444). Presiding over a cosmopolitan court in Buda with his wife Mary Habsburg, aged 20 Louis led a crusading army against the Ottomans. This time, battle was joined not on the Black Sea littoral, but in eastern Hungary itself, near the town of Mohács. In August 1526, in a rout, King Louis II of Hungary and Bohemia was killed, his Austrian queen widowed, and the great medieval kingdom of Hungary plunged into a vicious and protracted civil war.[38] Ferdinand Habsburg (1503–64), Austrian archduke, through his wife Anna Jagiellon claimed her dead brother's two crowns. The royal pair were elected rulers of Bohemia, but in Hungary their succession was opposed by a large part of the nobility, who instead elected John Zapolya (1487–1540) as their king. Zapolya carved out for himself a small 'independent' Hungarian kingdom centred on Transylvania, under Ottoman protection.

All this, King Sigismund of Poland and the grand duchy watched with dismay. Although Louis II's closest male relative, he chose not to contest the Bohemian and Hungarian crowns. Indeed, the leitmotif of Sigismund I's rule in the Polish monarchy and Lithuania was the pursuit of peace: he concluded peace treaties with the Teutonic Order and the Ottoman sultan. In Prague and Buda, Jagiellonians lived on only in the person of Queen Anna (d.1547), who often resided in Prague, and bore Ferdinand ten children. In the Polish monarchy, Sigismund's reign brought a celebrated Golden Age of Renaissance culture and, with his marriage in 1518 to the Milanese-Neapolitan princess Bona Sforza of Bari, a new Jagiellonian heir, Sigismund Augustus (1520).[39] The Polish court made a sudden intervention in the Habsburg-Zapolya civil war in Hungary in 1539, projecting their influence south once more, when Sigismund I's oldest daughter, Isabella, was married to King John Zapolya. With Zapolya's death, and the birth of a posthumous heir (1540), Isabella found herself at the heart of the Hungarian civil war, brokering deals with the sultan and Habsburgs, eventually securing for herself and her son John Sigismund (1540–71) rule of the principality of Transylvania.

As this spirited Polish-Hungarian prince grew up in Transylvania, Jagiellonian rule in Poland and the grand duchy itself entered its closing phase. The cosseted and glamorous Sigismund Augustus (1520–72), who succeeded his father in 1548, experienced serious marital travails. Neither his marriages to two Habsburg archduchesses, Elizabeth (d.1545) and Catherine (d.1572), nor his scandalous marriage to the Lithuanian noblewoman Barbara Radvilaitė/Radziwiłł (d.1551), gave him an heir. Sigismund Augustus, who spent long periods in Vilnius, oversaw Polish expansion into Livonia (present-day Latvia and Estonia) in the 1560s, spent lavishly on tapestries and new palaces, and backed a major reform campaign by the lower nobility.[40] In 1569, estranged from his third wife and despairing of a divorce, Sigismund Augustus forced through the Union of Lublin, a settlement which legally fused Poland and the grand duchy, a preparation for a post-Jagiellonian joint future. When his nephew John Sigismund Zapolya died in Alba Iulia (today's Romania) in 1571, Sigismund Augustus made his own will, in which he acknowledged that his successor was unknown; in summer 1572 he died at Knyszyn castle.

This was, however, not quite the end of Jogaila's line. The name itself lived on, initially, in the late king's three surviving sisters: Sophie, duchess of Brunswick-Luneburg (1522–75); Anna, unmarried princess of Poland (1523–96); and Catherine, queen of Sweden (1526–83), who had been married to Duke John of Finland (1537–92) in 1562, only to be imprisoned for five years in Gripsholm castle by John's enraged brother King Eric. In the Polish-Lithuanian interregna which followed Sigismund Augustus's death (1572–3, 1574–5, 1585–7), it was these sisters who were able to successfully present themselves as heirs to Jogaila.[41] Anna Jagiellon was elected queen of Poland in 1575, alongside Stephen Batory (r.1575–86) as king. And at Batory's death, the Polish nobility elected as their next monarch the Swedish prince Sigismund (b.1566), son of Catherine Jagiellon, as the 'Jagiellonian' heir. In effect, the direct geopolitical successors to 'Jagiellonian Europe' would be (via Anna Jagiellon, d.1547) the Habsburg monarchy of Austria-Hungary-Bohemia (1526–1918), and (via Catherine Jagiellon, d.1583) the Polish-Lithuanian Commonwealth (1572–1795) – ruled at first by Swedish-descended Vasa kings (1587–1668), and later by a plethora of foreign and native rulers. While historians traditionally date the end of the Jagiellonian dynasty to 1572, it would be a key claim made by their descendants and successors in these female lines that the dynasty had in fact never ended. Jagiellonian history, and Jagiellonian memory, were thus closely elided, with no neat dividing line between the two.[42]

Jagiellonian narratives: history and memory (1580s–2010s)

In the first phase of Jagiellonian memory, occupying the early modern period (sixteenth to eighteenth centuries), the primary agents of the family's memorialisation were their princely descendants in the Polish-Lithuanian Commonwealth, in Austria-Hungary-Bohemia, and (likewise via female lines) in principalities throughout the Holy Roman Empire. Across those lands, elaborate funerary monuments were erected for Jagiellonians by their kin and political successors, often decades after their deaths. In Alba Iulia, in the principality of Transylvania, Isabella Jagiellon's successor Stefan Batory is thought to have been the guiding figure behind the erection of her tomb monument in the 1580s.[43] In Uppsala cathedral, between 1584 and 1591, King John of Sweden erected a splendid monument to his late wife Catherine Jagiellon, in one of the most prestigious royal sites in Scandinavia.[44] In Wolfenbüttel's Marienkirche, the dukes of Brunswick-Lüneburg erected a fine carved effigy of their stepmother, Princess Sophie of Poland.[45] In the nave of Prague cathedral, Queen Anna's Habsburg sons commissioned from Alexander Colyn a marble necropolis (1566–90), depicting their mother, who had died in 1547.[46] As late as 1626–36, Sigismund III of Poland-Lithuania ordered construction of the baroque Saint Casimir chapel in Vilnius cathedral, to honour his newly beatified princely kinsman, the late medieval prince Casimir (d.1484).

Jagiellonian ancestors were also invoked, and honoured, in a variety of other media by early modern courts. At Ambras castle, outside Innsbruck, a painted panel depicts the Habsburgs' assorted princely ancestors, Jogaila among them.[47] In Warsaw Palace's Marble Room, created as a prestige audience chamber for King Ladislaus IV of Poland-Lithuania in the 1640s, the Dutchman Peter Danckers de Rij painted for its walls a series of Jagiellonian ancestor portraits.[48] From the sixteenth to the eighteenth century, printed genealogical diagrams demonstrated with scholarly precision the presence of Jagiellonian blood in reigning monarchs in Bohemia, Sweden and across the Holy Roman Empire, for example, the 1588 genealogy of the Pomeranian dukes, or a 1716 Saxon genealogy which made the case for Augustus III as future king of Poland-Lithuania.[49] One purpose of this 'remembering' and honouring of the Jagiellonians was surely to legitimise reigning princes – to stress descent from Jogaila's mighty house was to convey a message of continuity, lineage and prestige, all sources of political authority in early modern polities.

There was, however, an alternative set of early modern memory discourses about the Jagiellonians among the elites of their former lands. This we might term the 'national kings' model, whereby Jogaila's kin were invoked not primarily with reference to any particular royal lineage, but instead with reference to their office – as individual kings who formed links in the great chain of a kingdom's or duchy's history. This approach was pronounced, for example, in chronicles, which set out to tell the centuries-long story of a people and a crown, in ways which flatten or suppress kings' individual familial identities. Fifteenth- and sixteenth-century kings (to us, 'Jagiellonians') are slotted into this schema, for example, in histories by Jan Dubravius (1522), Václav Hájek (1541) or Maciej of Miechów's *Chronica Polonorum* (1521).[50] These crown-focused mnemonic-historical narratives were also expressed in visual form, as *icones regum* (chronologically arranged portrait cycles of national kings). An *Icones ducum regeumque Bohemiae* was printed in 1544, in Poland multiple *icones regum poloniae* were on sale from the 1560s, and painted series of historic national kings were found on the walls of Prague castle (sixteenth century), in Prussian town halls (1640s), and in the Pauline monastery of Częstochowa (eighteenth century).[51] Whether 'dynastic' or 'regnal', what united both these strands of early modern memories about the Jagiellonians was of course their focus on the institution of monarchy itself.

Memories of the Jagiellonians entered a second, pivotal phase in the long nineteenth century, as most of the ex-Jagiellonian lands found themselves locked into imperial-style formations. The kingdoms of Bohemia and Hungary had been ruled by Habsburg Austria from 1526, but Czechs and Magyars regularly rebelled against this situation (1707, 1848). The Commonwealth of Poland-Lithuania was obliterated outright when it was territorially partitioned by Prussia, Habsburg Austro-Hungary and tsarist Russia in 1795. Finland, with its own Jagiellonian connections, was likewise Russian-ruled from 1809. And, in a different way, many of the principalities associated with the Jagiellonians found themselves in a united Germany from 1871. If in the early modern period, the Jagiellonians had embodied sovereignty, in the long nineteenth century they came instead to represent lost sovereignty. A narrative of lost kingdoms and lost countries came to dominate 'remembering' of the Jagiellonians. It was expressed principally (but not exclusively) in the new master narratives of national history created by an emerging class of professional historians.[52] These scholars, armed with new nationalist ideologies, related what Mazower calls 'the story of the rendezvous of a chosen people with the land marked out for them'.[53] The precise role which Jogaila's royal house played in these new narratives of national loss varied. Attitudes ranged from celebration to demonisation, but with the negative end of that spectrum clearly predominating. In a twist, many national memory cultures now started to define their identity *against* the Jagiellonians.

To borrow Bernhard and Kubik's language of 'mnemonic regimes', the most positive such regimes regarding the Jagiellonians in the long nineteenth century were found in Bavaria and Finland.[54] In King Ludwig II's (r.1864–86) Bavaria, part of the German Reich from 1871, the 1475 wedding of George the Rich of Bavaria with Princess Hedwig of Poland became a focal point of local memory. From 1882, the town hall of Landshut was decorated with a major fresco scheme depicting the glorious events of 1475, and from 1902 locals started to organise large-scale wedding re-enactments (which continue to this day). In Bavaria, we see a local, urban, carnivalesque memory of Jagiellonian figures.[55] In Finland, meanwhile, the brief sojourn of Catherine Jagiellon in Turku castle in the 1560s became important in narratives of national history, as the moment when Finland was brought into contact with the full splendour of the Renaissance, the Polish princess a key agent of Europeanisation. Catherine and Duke John's court at Turku inspired leading cultural figures, such as the composer Sibelius (*Scènes historiques*, 1899) and poet Eino Leino.[56] In Bavaria and Finland alike, Jagiellonian women were remembered as bringing to the urban/national community both Renaissance splendour and a certain historic dignity.

In a second and larger group of countries, however, the Jagiellonians were by contrast associated specifically and powerfully with the loss of national political independence. In Lithuania, Poland and Hungary, this royal line was blamed for each nation's unique political calamity. New national narratives now identified the nation's Golden Age as coming immediately before Jagiellonian rule, thus casting the Jagiellonians as heralds or agents of decline: the Gedimin or Vytautas period for Lithuania (thirteenth century to 1430s), the Hussite Revolution for Bohemia (1409–), or the reign of Matthias Corvinus for Hungary (1458–90). In Lithuanian tradition, the gently elegiac treatment of Jogaila's line seen in printed albums of Jagiellonian ruins produced by Napoleon Orda and others had, by 1906, given way to more hostile judgements. The *History of Lithuania* penned by Jonas Maironis was among the first to condemn the Jagiellonians explicitly, as un-Lithuanian, absentee, negligent lords who had done little to protect the nation from Polonisation, or Muscovite encroachment.[57] In Hungarian-Magyar historical-national thought, the death of King Louis II Jagiellon at Mohács in 1526 became a defining moment, marking the fall of the medieval kingdom to Ottomans and Habsburgs. The emotional pitch around Louis–Mohács was intense from the late eighteenth century onwards, as seen in Imhre Ihászi's five-act tragedy *Mohács* (1795), iconic paintings by Petrics (1850) and Székely (1860, see Figure 3.1), and political essays entitled simply *Mohács*. As Stanislava Kuzmová shows, Louis II here functioned both as a Pieta-like allegory for the death of Hungary herself, and as the worthless, incompetent author of calamity and 'national decay', who had squandered Hungarian sovereignty.[58] Polish nineteenth-century memory of the Jagiellonians was more ambiguous, because these rulers were now identified as the authors both of the kingdom's Renaissance Golden Age, *and* of the later disaster of the Partitions. From the 1870s, leading historians such as Michał Bobrzyński (Kraków) and Ksawery Liske (Lwów) blamed the Jagiellonians in vituperative terms for the Partitions; yet simultaneously, people from that very Galician elite milieu raised significant funds for the restoration of Jagiellonian tombs and chapels on Wawel hill, as a living monument to the glorious Polish past. This paradox was perhaps best captured in the paintings of the celebrated artist Jan Matejko, who painted Jagiellonians obsessively for over three decades (1860s–90s), with splendour, melancholia and bitterness mingling in his canvases.[59]

Further east, in a third type of nineteenth-century mnemonic regime, the Jagiellonians were blamed not for throwing away national independence, but for wickedly stifling it in the first place. In emerging Ukrainian and Belorusian master narratives, imperialist Poles were cast as the nation's historical nemeses, with Jagiellonians condemned as agents of Polish influence and interests. In the first Belarusian-language history, by Vatslau Lastouski (1910/18), Belarusian identity (rooted for him in Orthodox Christianity, Ruthene history and language) was juxtaposed with the Jagiellonians, who stifled national development and presided over decline, as 'invaders'.[60] Mykhailo Hrushevsky (1866–1934), the father of Ukrainian national historiography, was even more forthright in his multi-volume *History of Ukraine-Rus'*. Hrushevsky described the centuries of Jagiellonian rule as a dark age of 'statelessness', in which Ukrainians had been enslaved by Polish kings, 'a passive subject of foreign rule and of foreign law formed on foreign foundations'.[61] In Ukrainian master narratives, it was the Cossacks and rural populace who formed the true nation in the late medieval and early modern period, not their rulers.

In a final type of long nineteenth-century mnemonic regime, the Jagiellonians were identified as rival empire-builders, and a national nemesis guilty of distorting history itself. In tsarist Russia, which had annexed so much of the former

Polish-Lithuanian Commonwealth, historians such as Sergey Soloviev, in his twenty-nine-volume *History of Russia from Ancient Times* (1851–), characterised the Jagiellonians as illegitimate western imperialists, who had diverted Slav Eastern Europe (Belarus, Ukraine, western Russia, Lithuania, Poland) from its true historical destiny of rule from Muscovy. In the wake of the anti-tsarist 1863 Uprising in the former Commonwealth, Russian thinkers distilled these ideas into the 'West Russia' thesis, which asserted that the bulk of the former Grand Duchy of Lithuania had in fact always been properly, and historically, Russian. As Olga Kozubska-Andrusiv shows, Jogaila emerged as a traitor of Russian peoples, and the 1795 Partition as simply a natural historical correction to, and undoing of, the 1386 Polish-Lithuanian union of Krewo.[62] These readings of the Jagiellonians as cynical empire-builders also found echoes in early twentieth-century Romanian scholarship, in the works of Nicolae Iorga (1871–1940), who cast these royals as a threatening Other – claiming that the dynasty's aim c.1500 had been to build a vast European empire stretching from Moscow to Venice.[63]

It was also the case that in certain lands once ruled by the Jagiellonians, new nationalist histories were able to virtually ignore the dynasty, as a subject of minimal interest. Romanian scholarship, identifying the principality of Moldavia (rather than Hungarian-ruled Transylvania) as a historic, independent Romanian state in the fifteenth and sixteenth centuries, saw the Jagiellonians chiefly as external aggressors, for example in King Jan Olbracht of Poland's 1497 Moldavian military expedition.[64] Likewise, although parts of modern Serbia (including Belgrade) lay within the Jagiellonian-ruled kingdom of Hungary, Serbian national scholarship from the nineteenth century saw its own historic statehood not within that monarchy, but outside it, for example in Đurađ Branković's Despotate of Serbia (1402–59).[65] Croatia too, an integral part of the medieval Hungarian monarchy, produced a modern historiography in which the Croatian lands were the main focus (or even presented as essentially separate from Hungary), with Buda and its kings viewed somewhat from afar.[66] In this way, the geographical contortions of the nationalist imagination could neatly remove the Jagiellonian dynasty from the canvas of memory altogether, as necessary.

Two developments in long nineteenth-century Jagiellonian memory can perhaps be distilled from this: Othering, and fragmentation. These royals underwent a clear Othering, because in the age of nationalism the Jagiellonians were identified in almost all their former lands as (bad) foreigners.[67] Fragmentation and diversification occurred as new historical interpretations, in a much wider range of languages, written from increasingly incompatible vantage-points, arose (as the four premodern Jagiellonian-ruled polities fractured into a dozen separate nationalisms).[68] The crucial context, or condition, for all this was of course the absence of an imperial Jagiellonian successor state in modern Europe. The Bohemian-Hungarian lands had become a long-term Habsburg sphere, and the Polish-Lithuanian Commonwealth so lauded by Sigismund Augustus in his will had become one of Europe's great failed states.[69] Put differently, no great European power, and no great nationalism, of the nineteenth century claimed the Jagiellonians as its totem and origin story (even Poles embracing them only hesitantly, with Polish opinion sharply divided). Memory of the Jagiellonians as a great European royal house, so long cherished by early modern princes, had in a sense been orphaned.

The twentieth and twenty-first centuries represent both a hiatus and a curious third phase of Jagiellonian memory, and its gradual eclipse. After 1918, many of the ex-Jagiellonian lands (re)acquired independence (as the republics of Poland, Lithuania, Czechoslovakia, Hungary, Finland, Yugoslavia, Romania), albeit not always in quite the ways nationalists had dreamed of. The master narratives of national loss honed in the nineteenth century proved remarkably durable, and in the interwar years of 1918–39 they simply hardened further. Poland's annexation of Vilnius in 1920 spurred new attacks by Lithuanian writers on Jogaila as 'an eternal enemy' of the nation.[70] The 1920 Treaty of Trianon, which broke up the historic kingdom of Hungary, was also read in Magyar nationalisms as a new disaster, a 'second Mohács' and further partition.[71] In the Polish Second Republic, a certain longing for (and coveting of) the former Commonwealth lands to the east was epitomised in Oskar Halecki's famous 1937 article on 'the Jagiellonian idea' – the dynasty here as shorthand for Polish hegemony to the east.[72]

Even the massive re-drawing of borders c.1945, and the inclusion of most ex-Jagiellonian lands within the Soviet bloc (Poland, Czechoslovakia, Hungary, Romania) or the USSR itself (Lithuania, Ukraine, Belarus), did not displace the core nationalist narratives of the previous century. In Soviet Russia, the re-acquisition of Lithuania and western Ukraine in the wake of World War II simply re-activated the old tsarist-era 'West Russia' thesis, for example.[73] While Marxist scholarship behind the Iron Curtain certainly marginalised the Jagiellonians as a feudal dynasty, the royal line's underlying function in narratives of national history did not change, remaining intact throughout the Communist period until 1989.[74] When fresh, revisionist, and even rehabilitative historical scholarship was produced on the Jagiellonians in the 1990s – by Gudavičius in Lithuanian, Tibor Neumann in Hungarian, or by Dumin, who saw the dynasty as a model for a democratic, open Slav world, in Russia – these works had no discernible effect on wider national narratives or social memories, in which the place of the Jagiellonians was already fixed.[75] A 2016 public survey in Hungary, for example, found that the election of Ladislaus II in 1490 is still ranked as one of the top ten errors in Hungarian history; in 2010, a Romanian poet could breathe life afresh into Iorga's 1904 imperial view of the Jagiellonians, describing King John Albert of Poland as imagining 'subdued peoples from the west and east shouting his name'.[76] It is thus not in historiography and scholarship per se that the real changes in Jagiellonian memory have occurred in the late twentieth and early twenty-first centuries; the real dynamism is elsewhere, and has largely occurred since 1989.

The post-1989 period has, for example, seen a wave of Jagiellonian monument building across Central Europe. These statues' messages vary from the national, to the very local. *The Dream of Gediminas* monument (1996), in Vilnius's cathedral square, for example, features Jogaila alongside other grand dukes, in a commemoration of Lithuanian historic statehood. Most of the new Jagiellonian statues have, however, been erected as local initiatives. The town of Mohács acquired a statue of Louis II by Irme Varga in 2006, for example, Drutsk in Belarus a statue of Jogaila's fourth wife Sofia of Halshany in 2010, and Lithuania's Panevėžys a statue of Alexander Jagiellon.[77] It is, however, principally in Polish towns that Jagiellonian statues have appeared – over a dozen since the 1990s, all stressing an individual royal's link with a community's local history.[78] Here we have a devolution of royal memory, to town councils and local historical associations, in a civil society memorialising of Jagiellonians.

A second area of contemporary dynamism lies in what we might term commercialised heritage memory, where the Jagiellonians feature as twenty-first-century popular entertainment. This phenomenon occurs in both traditional and new media, and Jagiellonian women hold a special appeal within it. A ballet entitled *Barbora Radvilaitė*, telling the story of King Sigismund Augustus's second marriage, was for example staged in Vilnius in 2011 and is regularly revived in Lithuania.[79] The musical *Sof'ia Gol'shanskaia'* premiered in Minsk in 2013, while Stockholm's Royal Armoury staged Eva Mattson's monologue-biopic of Queen Catherine Jagiellon in 2014.[80] Novels about Jagiellonian women have also been a growth area since circa 2000 – for example, in Germany Manfred Böckl's *Bride of Landshut* (2001), in Belarus Anatol Butevich's *The Queen Did Not Betray the King* (2010), or in Poland Alina Zerling-Konopka's *Isabella: Fate Decreed It* (2015).[81] It is also possible to engage in cultural consumption of Jagiellonians more directly. A dizzying array of Jagiellonian-themed merchandise is on sale at heritage sights: Princess Hedwig trinkets in Bavarian Landshut, Jagiellonian cookbooks (Jogaila's recipe for cucumbers and honey) and Sigismund Augustus chocolate in Lithuania, or Catherine Jagiellon tea in Finnish Turku.[82] The online world is also a rich hunting ground for Jagiellonian memorabilia – on Polish-language websites in particular, one can purchase a Sigismund Augustus board game, or intricately costumed Jagiellonian 'royal couples' dolls.[83]

Only in Belarus is this twenty-first-century cultural and material production about (female) Jagiellonians coordinated from the top, with a clear national message: state publications of the Lukashenko regime praise Sofia (born in present-day Belarus) as a true Belarusian patriot, the Belarusian mother of a dynasty which ruled swathes of Europe, the National Bank commemorating her with a special coin in 2006.[84] Elsewhere, the main impulse in telling stories of Jagiellonian women would appear to be a romanticising one. These queens and princesses are invoked in the twenty-first century not so much as a statement of national identity, but as stories of an individual's quest for romantic love. Thus Barbara Radvilaite, who in the Soviet period represented the martyrdom of Lithuania, now becomes in popular culture a martyr for love, as is argued in this volume.[85] Catherine Jagiellon's sixteenth-century motto 'Nemo nisi mors' ('only death [can part us]') has likewise become increasingly central to Finnish readings of her life as grand love story, her wifely devotion stressed in stained glass and tapestry (see Figure 6.1).[86] Giedrė Mickūnaitė suggests that, in such cases, Jagiellonians now simply function as 'celebrities', supplying 'intrigue and entertainment'.[87]

The effect of these Jagiellonian love stories, and material kitsch, across their former lands is to produce a potentially trivialising memory, quite different in tone from the solemn-patriotic tenor of nineteenth-century national-tragic remembrance. The softening, or even shallowness, of Jagiellonian memory in the twenty-first century has occurred, we might conjecture, precisely because this dynasty no longer sits on the first plane of national or social memory. It has been decisively displaced by the extreme traumas of Europe's twentieth century (World War II, genocide, totalitarianism). It is here that political hot, raw, tragic social memory, and its resulting memory wars, are now located instead.[88] Jagiellonian memory is now, typically, a medium for nostalgia and light diversion, rather than the focus of unresolved national and social trauma. It is this dethroning of Jagiellonian memory, now pushed into the background, which is the key development of the post-1945 period.

There are, nonetheless, hints of a possible repoliticisation of Jagiellonian memory in the 2010s. Czech far right anti-Muslim groups invoke Louis II and Mohács as a key moment in their narratives of a Christian Europe's fight against Islam.[89] In 2017, the Polish Foreign Ministry funded, as part of its public diplomacy programme, a research project entitled 'Jagiellonian Ideas', which promotes globally an image of Jagiellonian 'Poland' as a tolerant haven for Ukrainians, Belarusians and Lithuanians.[90] In today's sharply polarised Central European politics, Jagiellonians can serve both internationalist, cosmopolitan agendas and highly nationalist ones – as evidenced by Jogaila himself, depicted seated and serene in a sculpture erected in Budapest to celebrate Polish-Hungarian friendship within the EU, but as an aggressive anti-German warrior on T-shirts sold by a Polish retailer specialising in nationalist-military merchandise.[91]

Regional memory – memory across space?

Can one speak, then, in any meaningful way of a 'regional memory' of the Jagiellonians – of an evolving mnemonic system which is in some sense shared by, or connects, the ex-Jagiellonian lands today lying between France and Russia? Any conclusions about such a vast subject come with obvious caveats. Memories of the Jagiellonians are (and have always been) diverse; the intensity of their memorialisation ebbs and flows, and it always competes with other memories, both pre-modern and modern (Hussitism, totalitarianism), as one part of a much bigger mosaic of jostling stories about the past. On the basis of the research presented in this volume, some initial answers can be given. Yet, to address whether there exists a 'regional memory' of this medieval-Renaissance dynasty, we need to distinguish between the three possible meanings of 'regional memory' – national-comparative, trans-national and supra-national.

If we apply a national-comparative, compare-and-contrast, approach to the evidence presented here of long-term Jagiellonian memory, the pattern which emerges is a paradoxical one of 'parallel-but-separate'. Polities or societies have employed the same mnemonic media to invoke Jagiellonians to convey different messages. The vehicles, genres, ideologies and outer packing of memory are, in other words, largely shared across these ex-lands in any given period – the Renaissance tomb, the nineteenth-century history painting, the twenty-first-century heritage site souvenir. These templates for memory are part of a wider shared set of European or even global technological and ideological resources, and cultural practices, which are not specifically 'Central European'. The Tudors, Aviz or even Asian sixteenth-century royal lines are, at given moments, invoked in exactly the same media as the Jagiellonians: novels, spectacle, film.[92] Yet the actual messages conveyed are highly heterogeneous and locally specific – whether asserting the legitimacy of a seventeenth-century Polish king, or telling a twentieth-century story of Hungarian national destiny. Nationalist ideologies of course encapsulate this parallel-but-separate riddle: providing a common historical narrative (the nation and its struggle), which individual elites in Scandinavia or East and Central European nations could fill with their own distinctive story, adapting the Jagiellonians to their local ends. The painters who produced Jagiellonian-themed canvases in the mid-nineteenth century provide a useful illustration of parallel-but-separate memory. Hugo Salmson from Sweden, Bertalan Székely from Hungary, and Jan Matejko from Poland all painted Jagiellonian canvases in the 1860s, having trained in Bavaria under the same masters of the internationally celebrated Munich School – yet their Jagiellonian images were fitted solidly into national tragic narratives, from which they derived their meaning, in (purely) locally legible stories, such as Queen Catherine at Gripsholm castle (Sweden), Isabella Jagiellon fleeing Transylvania (Hungary), or the Battle of Grunwald (Poland).[93] Here, 'regional memory' of the Jagiellonians is like a seedling tray – the plants growing closely packed alongside one another, subject to the same environmental influences, but in their separate squares of soil. What the Jagiellonians reveal here, then, is a persistent pillarisation of European memory.

What of regional memory in its second sense, as trans-national memories? Cross-border, entangled memory is often implicitly presented as a feature of today's globally connected, mobile world, but this is perhaps to miss the point that in Central Europe nations themselves are hopelessly entangled, and thus their memories (including those of the Jagiellonians) are too.[94] The very creation of nineteenth-century nationalisms in this part of Europe first required the twelve would-be nationalities of the four ex-Jagiellonian pre-modern polities to disentangle their stories from one another. Czech, Slovak, Austrian, Croatian and Hungarian memories emerged from the (once shared) medieval kingdom of Hungary; Finnish and Swedish memories from the kingdom of Sweden; and Polish, Lithuanian, Latvian, Belarusian, Russian and Ukrainian narratives from the Polish-Lithuanian union (later Commonwealth). Thus when Croatian- and Hungarian-language scholarship alike share an anecdote about King Ladislaus II Jagiellon being so poor he had to buy his own wine at Buda taverns, these are not modern post-national, cross-fertilising stories (not 'travelling memory'), but memories which are essentially shared or congenitally joined, with a common point of origin.[95] The individuals who have shaped Jagiellonian memory were often themselves deeply entangled in overlapping traditions, identities and languages – such as Stankevich, writing about late medieval Jagiellonian history in Belorusian in Polish-ruled Vilnius in the 1920s.[96] The massively enmeshed nature of Jagiellonian national memory in Europe highlights how 'post-national' memory scholarship can risk essentialising (and reifying) 'national' memory, in the very act of stressing its cross-cultural dimensions, by presenting clear-cut national memory traditions as a normal state of affairs. Returning to our horticultural metaphor, these plants may appear to grow in separate containers, but beneath the surface their root systems are literally entangled.

National memories of Jagiellonian kings and queens are thus profoundly entangled structurally, but without being particularly in active dialogue or contact with one another. Cross-fertilisation is the exception, historically, rather than the norm. We do, for example, see cases of bi-lateral fostering of Jagiellonian memory between national governments. In 1933, the Polish state gave to Finland's Turku castle a copy of Cranach's portrait of the queen; in the 1970s in a major episode of détente diplomacy the Polish People's Republic lent 125 objects for a Catherine Jagiellon exhibition at Turku; and in 2014 it was again the Polish Embassy which supported the play about the Jagiellonian princess staged in Stockholm's Royal Armouries.[97] Similarly, Tibor Gerencsér's research has found that, as part of official 'joint' Hungarian-Polish commemorations of Stefan Batory in the interwar years by the two Foreign Offices and civil society groups, Poland presented the Hungarian government with a replica of the gold crown of Anna Jagiellon, Batory's queen.[98] Outright memory wars over Jagiellonians, meanwhile, are surprisingly rare in this volume. The most overt are the 1572–87 Polish-Lithuanian interregna, when Central European princes standing for election as king asserted their own exclusive Jagiellonian descent (over that of rival candidates) and, four centuries later, the interwar Polish-Lithuanian conflict over Vilnius, and thus over the ownership and nature of Jagiellonian figures such as Saint Casimir and Jogaila.[99] The search for cross-fertilising or dialogic Jagiellonian memories between ex-Jagiellonian lands is thus a surprisingly barren one. Monarchies, nations or states have tended to maintain mutually antagonistic memories of the Jagiellonians, but without mutual engagement. For the most part these different mnemonic traditions polemicise about each other (often in their own languages), rather than with each other. In that sense, Jagiellonian memory is akin to a series of people shouting in separate rooms. This is seen, for example, by memories of a key Jagiellonian signifier, the 1410 Battle of Grunwald, today claimed simultaneously by multiple countries as their national achievement – by the Poles in lavish re-enactments, by Ukrainians in a 2010 commemorative medal, in Belarusian scholarship, and by the state-funded Russian Military Historical Society which describes Grunwald as a Russian victory over the Germans.[100] These narratives tacitly exist alongside one another – 1410 is not actively fought over in modern memory wars, but simply claimed by each side, in its own (domestic) national and social remembering. Here, the quest for the trans-national, for connectedness, instead points us back towards the stubborn 'parallel-but-separate' model.

What of regional memory in perhaps its ultimate sense, of an over-arching Jagiellonian story which floats above national memory cultures, conferring a shared regional identity? First, we may note there is precious little by way of an available regional master narrative of the Jagiellonian past. The overwhelming majority of academic research on these royals still reads them squarely as part of a national past, focusing on the family's local activities within one kingdom – for example Macek's *The Jagiellonian Age in the Czech Lands* (1992), or *The Jagiellonians and Their World* (2016), a set of twenty-one essays in Polish edited by Piotr Węcowski, in which their world is, in effect, Poland.[101] The only pan-regional narrative of Jagiellonian history to date is Almut Bues's brief German overview, *Die Jagiellonen* (2011).[102] A bolder attempt to construct a regional narrative of Jagiellonian history was the international exhibition *Europa Jagiellonica: Art and Culture in Central Europe under the Rule of the Jagiellonians*, which showed in Kutná Hora, Warsaw and Potsdam, and which originated in a German-funded research project at the University of Leipzig (2000–5).[103] The exhibition's message was that the dynasty's rule across Central Europe produced (or coincided with) a Golden Age of artistic production which linked Prague, Vilnius, Buda and Kraków. Yet the difficulties encountered by the exhibition are testament to the serious obstacles to forging 'regional' memory – loans of art treasures from the Jagiellonian courts by national collections took almost a decade to negotiate, and even then many were pulled out at short notice by national authorities, leaving gaps in the display. These tangible Jagiellonian memories, in other words, were physically prohibited from crossing borders.[104] The low cultural and political capital of the Jagiellonians as a regional heritage is also seen, from a different angle, in political rhetoric – when post-1989 politicians launch multi-lateral regional initiatives, they do not invoke the slogan 'Jagiellonian Europe', but instead the 'Visegrad Group' or 'Three Seas', the Polish President Andrzej Duda's 2017 call to form an alliance of those EU countries located between the Adriatic, Baltic and Black Seas.[105] 'Jagiellonian Europe', as a supra-national story, historical unit or regional identity, thus belongs to Assmann's category of latent, un-activated or potential memory.

Even if the ex-Jagiellonian countries have developed no shared account of Jagiellonian history and its meanings, in one important respect these can be described as a set of regional memories – in that they are native to this specific part of Europe, and not readily legible beyond it. The *Europa Jagiellonica* exhibition revealed how unknown this leading Renaissance dynasty is in post-1945 Western Europe. A German reviewer, writing in *Die Zeit*, made the alien-ness, unfamiliarity and oblivion of the dynasty the subject of the review's very byline: 'Jagiellonians: who's heard of them?' In game-show style, the reviewer went on to ask their readers: 'For 250,000 Euros, are Jagiellonians a) a type of tropical fruit, b) a harmless type of virus, c) an Eastern European dynasty, d) lightweight elementary particles?'[106] *Die Zeit*'s joke reinforces arguments made by Pestel et al., that 'European' memory is often West European post-war 'hegemonic' memory, which since 1989 has had little space or use for stories which Central and East Europeans claim as their own, and as worthy of inscription into shared European memory.[107] Troebst too hypothesises that there are 'meso-regional divisions' in European memory.[108] The inability of Jagiellonian memory (unlike Habsburg, Borgia, Tudor memory) to travel and appeal internationally to European and global audiences speaks too to Tomasz Zarycki's arguments in his *Ideologies of Eastness*. Zarycki suggests that, in the modern era, this part of Europe has had narratives inscribed on it by external forces, i.e. western powers and imperial Russia, failing to generate its own successful, autonomous discourses.[109] The Jagiellonians thus form a 'regional' memory in so far as they are remembered (more or less, however variously) from Turku to Prague to Alba Iulia to Moscow, but remain totally absent from western and West European memories of Europe's Renaissance and medieval past. So, in this reading, the Jagiellonians are a particularly Central European kind of ghost, an unquiet spirit lurking beneath our familiar western textbook narratives of fifteenth- and sixteenth-century Christendom.

And what of memories travelling across time? As we have seen, researchers have become increasingly interested in the idea of re-mediation, of stories about the past which travel seemingly intact down the centuries. If the movement of Jagiellonian memory across space is halting, uneven and messy, the transmission of specific memories about these royals across time can show disconcerting consistency. Several of the essays in this volume find, as Stanislava Kuzmová puts it, that 'the image of the Jagiellonians over time is static overall', even if its functions might evolve. The long-term influence of fifteenth- and sixteenth-century chronicles of a kingdom's history in 'setting' or fixing judgements and anecdotes about Jagiellonian kings is remarkable – of texts such as Jan Długosz's *Annales Regni Poloniae* (c.1480), Stefan Brodarics's account of the Battle of Mohács, Jan Dubravius's (1552) Bohemian chronicle, or the work of Johannes Tomasic (1561).[110] The tales of Jagiellonian kings, deeds and characters set out by chroniclers provided the underpinnings of nineteenth-century national historiography of the Jagiellonians, which were in turn taken up in modern painting and fiction, and which still inform popular culture. As the essay on Bohemia in this volume shows, Dubravius's portrait of a weak King Ladislaus II who said 'yes, yes' to everything his courtiers asked is found, word for word, in Czech historical cartoons for children in the 2000s (see Figure 4.2) – and in a host of sources in between, century after century.[111] The essay on Poland too stresses how Jagiellonian memory has in the long term crystallised around particular motifs – *icones regum poloniae* portrait cycles, a Renaissance Golden Age, the Battle of Grunwald – which can be traced back directly to the fifteenth or sixteenth century, to printed tracts, royal letters, or Długosz's prose.[112] In other words, the Jagiellonians show how old many of the 'memories' we observe at work today are, still taking their shape from rhetoric about the Jagiellonians first penned by their own contemporaries. Here, 'remediation' of memory consists of the same stories recycled through time, with their actual content remarkably hard or impermeable, travelling bullet-like through centuries, from text to text to text. The essay on Poland suggests that the packaging of the Jagiellonian past into these constantly repeated and living stories (Jogaila on the battlefield at Grunwald, Louis II dying in a stream at Mohács, Hedwig arriving at the Landshut wedding) starts, in its very narrative structure and archetypal royal characters, to resemble the genre of the fairy tale.[113]

If the Jagiellonians and their memory can cast some light on how multi-polity early modern phenomena are remembered in subsequent centuries, across space and time, their story also comes with a sting in the tail. The Jagiellonians can teach us much about the nature of dynasty itself as a container or vehicle for memory (or historical representations), dynasty being one of the central units of traditional political history. A successful international dynasty (a trans-national phenomenon by definition) is, for example, a poor fit for historical narratives focused on a single polity. From the sixteenth century to the present day, historians across these lands have awkwardly squashed this enormous, supra-national royal house into local polity-focused narratives: just as Miechowita's *Chronica Polonorum* of 1519 had minimal interest in what the Jagiellonians did outside Poland, so the 2016 essay collection of the very latest Polish research on the dynasty is focused overwhelmingly on that kingdom, and Polish historians have long tried to downplay, delegitimise or shrug off the family's non-Polish involvements, especially in Bohemia and Hungary.[114] Czech historians too draw a line around the family's non-Bohemian exploits, casting domestic royal activity as good, but a king's political relationships with foreign Jagiellonian relatives as bad, and against the national interest.[115]

Yet more fundamentally, to select dynasty as the object of memory is to come up against one of the key findings of the wider ERC Jagiellonians project, of which this volume forms just one part, or output – that 'dynasty' is a very slippery idea indeed.[116] As some of our essays discuss, on the basis of the project's collective research, the very name 'Jagiellonian' has a complex history of its own, and should not be taken as a timeless given.[117] In the fifteenth century, the family were occasionally referred to as the 'house of Casimir [IV]', and the first recorded use of 'Jagiellonian' as a collective name for a royal line is found only in the 1516 poem *Bellum Prutenum*, a literary-humanist historicising invention printed 116 years after Jogaila was crowned king of Poland in Kraków. For much of the sixteenth century 'Jagiellonum' remained a term used rarely, confined to a courtly educated elite, in neo-Latin texts penned for royal ceremonies such as weddings and funerals. It only entered mainstream international political discourse, and was only used by the family itself (i.e. the sisters Catherine, Sophie and Anna), during the Commonwealth's interregna of the 1570s and 1580s. And it was only in the period of modern scholarship that 'Jagiellonian dynasty' became a natural, unquestioned shorthand – in eighteenth-century Hungarian encyclopaedias, or nineteenth-century Polish-language scholarship.[118]

Not only is the very terminology of 'Jagiellonians' largely retrospective, but the concept of a collective, unified 'dynasty' of that name is also far from a given. Sixteenth-century texts, for example, simply do not use 'dynasteia' in reference to this royal family, but 'domus' or 'familia'. Much of the 'Jagiellonian memory' or memorialising discussed above is not necessarily conscious evocation of a dynasty per se (although some of it is), but instead remembering of particular individuals or events which historical scholarship tends to label 'Jagiellonian'. The principal 'thing' being remembered might be not Jagiellonians, but instead the 'house of Sigismund [I]', the glorious crown of Bohemia, the Gediminids (stretching back far before Jogaila), or a Polish princess, or a battle, or the founding of a town. As Dušan Zupka writes in this volume, 'memories of the Jagiellonians in the German-speaking lands are anything but the memory of the Jagiellonian dynasty'.[119] If we are to trace the evolution and remediation of memory discourses over long periods of time, as proponents of a 'third wave' of memory studies advocate, the 'Jagiellonians' teach us that we need to be very alert not only to how a given 'thing' is remembered, but also to the language and concepts underpinning the mnemonic subject itself (i.e. whether it really is a 'thing'). Otherwise, we risk seriously misreading past memory regimes (and intentions), in anachronistic ways. Or, as Ilya Afanasyev sums it up in this volume, we often 'take our conceptual apparatuses for granted and treat them as reliable tools in our attempts to represent the past' – and our attempts to study memories of it.[120] The idea of dynasty, as it exists in modern historical scholarship, has a history of its own, which we need to excavate before we can fully understand the long-term memorialisation of what appear to us to be named dynasties.

The volume

The contributors to this volume include specialists on medieval Europe, the early modern period and Slavonic literature. The nine essays are divided into linguistic or 'national'/polity traditions, not to enshrine the nation-state as the only author of memory, but to trace evolutions (and discourse) within particular languages where possible. The essays take as their focus memories of Jagiellonian royalty, individually or collectively, and not the general word 'Jagiellonian' as a wider code or signifier – in the sense, for example, of the Jagiellonian University (in Kraków) or the 'Jagiellonian idea', that vast political and literary discourse about the nature of the former Commonwealth, as paternal/civilising/imperial/colonial.[121] This foray into the potentially enormous, but new, subject of international Jagiellonian memory is the most 'high risk' aspect of the ERC Jagiellonian project, due to challenges of both methodology and scope. It is, however, an invitation to further inter-disciplinary conversations in this field.

The collection opens with Giedrė Mickūnaitė's essay on Lithuania, which explores themes such as sites and dukes, saints and sins, stage and web, examining in particular how Jagiellonian memory acquires a 'ghostly' nature when key elements of its material heritage have disappeared. A trio of essays then tackle the three Central European kingdoms ruled by this line, for periods of between 200 and 50 years. Natalia Nowakowska's essay on Poland, a hot-spot of Jagiellonian memory, traces early modern mnemonic conflicts and the cultivation of emotionally intense, imagined Jagiellonian worlds in nineteenth-century Partitioned Polish culture, exploring that century's intermingling of the languages of statehood and fairy tale. Stanislava Kuzmová describes the emergence and divergence of

Hungarian and Slovak images of the Jagiellonians within the Austro-Hungarian monarchy (1526–1918) and beyond, with the Battle of Mohács enshrined for centuries as the dominant, catastrophic lens through which these rulers are viewed. Ilya Afanasyev, meanwhile, in his essay on Bohemia tests how far one can deconstruct the categories of 'Czech', 'Jagiellonian' and 'dynasty', tracing conceptual shifts from early modern printed texts, to present-day Czech schoolbooks.

We then travel to places where the memory of Jagiellonians is refracted almost entirely through royal women. Dušan Zupka, writing on the ten Jagiellonian princesses married to German and Austrian princes between 1475 and 1556, takes as his theme 'from hero to zero' – asking how the enormous prestige this royal family enjoyed within the fifteenth-, sixteenth- and seventeenth-century Holy Roman Empire has faded into a modern near-oblivion, with the curious exception of the Landshut wedding pageants. In the only essay (and only set of national memories) to focus on just one Jagiellonian figure, Susanna Niiranen compares Swedish and Finnish treatments of Queen Catherine Jagiellon (d.1583). With a particular focus on the northern *lieux de memoires* which are a feature of Catherine's memory, the essay suggests that Swedish tradition marginalises the Polish princess as Other, while in Finnish narratives her attraction has lain precisely in her exotic, foreign nature.

Our final essays explore three major traditions which have emerged out of the ex-Grand Duchy of Lithuania and its populations – Belarusian, Ukrainian and Russian. Simon M. Lewis shows the tussle, since the emergence of a self-conscious Belarusian nationalism and scholarship in the 1900s, over whether to see the Jagiellonian grand dukes as a Belarusian 'Us', or an oppressive Polish 'Them', exploring what he terms a 'gradual release of memory' seen especially since the 1990s. Tetiana Hoshko's essay on Ukrainian traditions explains how the master framework originally constructed by Hrushevsky has rendered the Jagiellonians an undisputed Other – although within this there are nuances in Ukrainian scholarship, on topics such as Orthodox-Latin relations or Jagiellonian diplomacy. She notes that these academic debates have not, however, produced any wider, popular Ukrainian memory of Jogaila's line. Finally, Olga Kozubska-Andrusiv guides us through the imperial, Soviet and post-Soviet historical-ideological phases of Russian memory of the Jagiellonians – with the Jagiellonian-ruled Grand Duchy of Lithuania occasionally offering an attractive or dangerous vision of an alternative western-facing Russian past (or future), but more often a tale of a historic enemy. So, the question of whom the Grand Duchy of Lithuania belongs to, and of who the Jagiellonians therefore were, has long touched on the nature of empire, statehood and nation in the former lands of Kievian Rus'; that being the memory which often sits behind memories of the Jagiellonians. We start, however, in Vilnius, the city where our historical-mnemonic story begins. It was from Vilnius castle that Jogaila from the 1370s ruled vast territories, and over that castle's excavated archaeological remains that in 2013 the Renaissance grand ducal palace was reconstructed, as a symbol of the Baltic republic of Lithuania's post-Soviet independence – memories, pasts and narratives literally stacked up on top of one another, in a microcosm of the trajectories of Jagiellonian memory.

Notes

1 For international overviews, see A. Bues, *Die Jagiellonen: Herrscher zwischen Ostsee und Adri*, Stuttgart, 2010; and M. Duczmal, *Jagiellonowie: Leksykon biograficzny*, Kraków, 1996.
2 For overviews of Habsburg history, as a point of comparison, see A. Wheatcroft, *Habsburgs: Embodying Empire*, London, 1995; and M. Rady, *The Habsburg Empire: A Very Short Introduction*, Oxford, 2017.
3 For a rare study of one aspect of Jagiellonian memory, see A. Nikžentaitis, *Witold i Jagiełło: Polacy i Litwini we wzajemnym stereotypie*, Poznań, 2000.
4 See, for example, M. H. Bernhard and J. Kubik, *Twenty Years after Communism: The Politics of Memory and Commemoration*, Oxford, 2014; U. Blacker, A. Etkind and J. Fedor, *Memory and Theory in Eastern Europe*, New York, 2013; M. Pakier and J. Wawrzyniak, eds, *Memory and Change in Europe: Eastern Perspectives*, New York, 2016.
5 A. Erll, 'Travelling Memory', *Parallax* 17, 4, 2011, pp. 4–18, at p. 4; K. Lee Klein, 'On the Emergence of Memory in Historical Discourse', *Representations*, 69, 2000, pp. 127–150, at p. 128.
6 Klein, 'On the Emergence of Memory'.
7 M. Halbwachs, *On Collective Memory*, trans. and ed. L. A. Coser, Chicago, 1992, p. 40.
8 A. Erll, 'Regional Integration and (Trans)cultural Memory', *Asia Europe Journal* 8, 2010, pp. 305–315, at pp. 305–306.
9 W. Kansteiner, 'Finding Meaning in Memory: A Methodological Critique of Collective Memory Studies', *History and Theory* 41, 2, 2002, pp. 179–197, at p. 179.
10 S. Niiranen, below, p. 143, and I. Afanasyev, below, p. 103.
11 H. Rousso, *Le syndrome de Vichy (1945–198..)* [sic], Paris, 1987.
12 On nationalism, see the classic B. Anderson, *Imagined Communities*: *Reflections on the Origin and Spread of Nationalism*, London, 1983.
13 Afanasyev, below, p. 103; F. Pestel, R. Trimçevb, G. Feindt and F. Krawatzek, 'Promise and Challenge of European Memory', *European Review of History* 24, 4, 2017, pp. 495–506, at p. 496.
14 Erll, 'Travelling Memory'; R. Crownshaw, 'Introduction', *Parallax* 17, 4, 2011, pp. 1–3.
15 S. Troebst, 'Halecki revisited: Europe's conflicting cultures of remembrance', in M. Pakier and B. Stråth, eds, *European Memory? Contested Histories of Politics and Remembrance*, New York, Berghahn, 2016, pp. 56–63; see also Bernhard and Kubik, *Twenty Years after Communism*.
16 Erll, 'Regional integration', pp. 312–313; G. Feindt, F. Krawatzek, D. Mehler, F. Pestel and R. Trimçev, 'Entangled Memory: Towards a Third Wave in Memory Studies', *History and Theory* 53, 2014, pp. 24–44.
17 Quote from 'Regions of Memory' Project conference website, Warsaw University, 2016, http://enrs.eu/en/news/1337-regions-of-memory-ii-memory-regions-as-discourse-and-imagination, accessed 5.11.17. See also Pakier and Stråth, *European Memory?*; D. Levy and N. Sznaider, *The Holocaust and Memory in the Global Age*, trans. A. Oksiloff, Philadelphia, Temple University Press, 2006.
18 Blacker et al., *Memory and Theory*; Pestel et al., 'Promise and Challenge'; Pakier and Wawrzyniak, *Memory and Change*.
19 C. Scott Dixon and M. Fuchs, eds, *The Histories of Emperor Charles V: Nationale Perspektiven von Persönlichkeit und Herrschaft*, Münster, 2005.
20 On this question, see in particular N. Berend, 'The Mirage of East Central Europe: Historical Regions in a Comparative Perspective', in G. Jaritz and K. Szende, eds,

Medieval East Central Europe in a Comparative Perspective: From Frontier Zones to Lands in Focus, Abingdon, 2016, pp. 9–23.
21 Coser, 'Introduction', *On Collective Memory*, pp. 25, 28.
22 Erll, 'Regional integration', p. 305.
23 P. Joutard, *La Légende des Camisards. Une sensibilité au passé*, Paris, 1977, discussed in J. Pollmann, *Early Modern Memory*, Oxford, 2017, pp. 5–6.
24 Bernhard and Kubik, *Twenty Years after Communism*, pp. 285–287.
25 Pestel et al., 'Promise and Challenge'; Feindt et al., 'Entangled Memory'; S. Hadler, 'Europe's Other? The Turks and Shifting Borders of Memory', *European Review of History* 24, 4, 2017, pp. 507–526.
26 'Tales of the Revolt. Oblivion, Memory and Identity in the Low Countries, 1556–1700' Project, led by Judith Pollmann, 2008–2013, https://vre.leidenuniv.nl/vre/tales/emm/tales-of-the-revolt/Pages/startPage.aspx, accessed 5.11.17; M. Eiden, *Das Nachleben der schlesischen Piasten: dynastische Tradition und moderne Erinnerungskultur vom 17. bis 20. Jahrhundert*, Cologne, 2012.
27 Exceptions include M. Brook, *Popular History and Fiction: The Myth of August the Strong in German Literature, Art and Media*, Bern, 2013.
28 For a recent overview, see D. Baronas and S. C. Rowell, *The Conversion of Lithuania: From Pagan Barbarians to Late Medieval Christians*, Vilnius, 2016.
29 G. Mickūnaitė, *Making a Great Ruler: Grand Duke Vytautas of Lithuania*, New York, 2005.
30 The terms *Ruthene* and *Rus'*, commonly used in Jagiellonian history, loosely refer to the peoples who had been part of the medieval polity of Kievian Rus'.
31 On Jogaila, see J. Krzyżaniakowa and J. Ochmański, *Władysław II Jagiełło*, Wrocław, 1990; and R. Frost, *The Oxford History of Poland-Lithuania*, vol. I, Oxford, 2015.
32 See S. Sroka, *Z dziejów stosunków polsko-węgierskich w późnym średniowieczu: szkice*, Kraków, 1995.
33 J. Jefferson, *The Holy Wars of King Wladislas and Sultan Murad: The Ottoman-Christian Conflict from 1438–1444*, Leiden, 2012.
34 J. L. Decius, *De Iagellonum Familia*, Kraków, 1521.
35 K. Baczkowski, *Walka Jagiellonów z Maciejem Korwinem o koronę czeską w latach 1471–1479*, Kraków, 1980; J. Macek, *Jagellonský věk v českých zemích, 1471–1526*, Prague, 1992.
36 See, for example, T. Neumann, 'II. Ulászló koronázása és első rendeletei (Egy ismeretlen országgyűlésről és koronázási dekrétumról)', *Századok* 142, 2, 2008, pp. 315–337; and M. Rady, 'Rethinking Jagiello Hungary, 1490–1526', *Central Europe* 3, 1, 2005, pp. 3–18.
37 For relations between these brothers, see N. Nowakowska, *Church, State and Dynasty: The Career of Cardinal Fryderyk Jagiellon (1468–1503)*, Basingstoke, 2007.
38 G. Perjés, *The Fall of the Medieval Kingdom of Hungary, 1526–41*, Boulder, 1989.
39 The most meticulous study of the reign is W. Pociecha, *Królowa Bona, 1494–1557: ludzie i czasy Odrodzenia*, 4 vols, Poznań, 1948–1959.
40 A. Sucheni-Grabowska, *Zygmunt August: król polski i wielki książę litewski: 1520–1562*, Warsaw, 1996.
41 A. Przeździecki, *Jagiellonki Polskie w XVI wieku*, 4 vols, Kraków, 1868–1878; Felicia Rosu, *Elective Monarchy in Transylvania and Poland-Lithuania, 1569–1587*, Oxford, 2017.
42 For close discussion of Jagiellonian memory and rhetoric in the late sixteenth century, see N. Nowakowska, I. Afansyev, S. Kuzmová, G. Mickūnaitė, S. Niiranen and D. Zupka, *Dynasty in the Making: The Idea of the Jagiellonians, c.1386–1640* (forthcoming).
43 For the latest research on Transylvanian monuments, see Dóra Mérai, 'Memory from the Past, Display for the future: Early Modern Funeral Monuments from the Transylvanian Principality', doctoral thesis, Central European University, 2017.
44 Niiranen, below, pp. 144–147.

45 D. Zupka, below, p. 124.
46 Zupka, below, pp. 123–124.
47 On display at Ambras Castle, Austria; a nineteenth-century painting, showing this image on display, is reproduced in C. Klapisch-Zuber, *L'arbre des familles*, Paris, 2003.
48 N. Nowakowska, below, pp. 51–52.
49 Niiranen, below, p. 145; Afanasyev, below, pp. 107–108; Zupka, below, pp. 126–129. For 'regnal' ways of discussing the Jagiellonians in the fifteenth and sixteenth centuries, see Nowakowska et al., *Dynasty in the Making*.
50 Afanasyev, below, p. 105.
51 Nowakowska, below, pp. 52, 62; Afanasyev, below, p. 106.
52 See M. Baár, *Historians and Nationalism: East Central Europe in the Nineteenth Century*, Oxford, 2010.
53 M. Mazower, *Salonica, City of Ghosts: Christians, Muslims and Jews, 1430–1950*, London, 2004, p. 474.
54 Bernhard and Kubik, *Twenty Years after Communism*.
55 Zupka, below, pp. 132–135.
56 Niiranen, below, pp. 152–154.
57 G. Mickūnaitė, below, p. 32.
58 Kuzmová, below, pp. 78–81.
59 Nowakowska, below, pp. 53–58.
60 S. Lewis, below, pp. 164–165.
61 Quoted and discussed by T. Hoshko, below, pp. 184–185.
62 See O. Kozubska-Andrusiv, below, pp. 206–207.
63 N. Iorga, *Istoria lui Ştefan cel Mare pentru poporul roman*, Bucureşti, 1904, pp. 221–222, 233–4. With thanks to János Incze.
64 See for example A. D. Xenopol, *Istoria românilor din Dacia Traiană*, Bucharest, 1888–1893; and for the wider context, Lucian Boia, *History and Myth in Romanian Consciousness* (Budapest, New York, Central European University Press, 2001). With thanks to János Incze.
65 See the work of Jovan Rajić, a leading figure in Serbian nineteenth-century historiography: J. Rajić, *Istorija raznih slavjanskih narodov, naipače Bolgar, Horvatov i Serbov*, Saint Petersburg, 1795. With thanks to Miloš Ivanović.
66 For example, Ivan Krstitelj Tkalčić, *Hrvatska povjestnica*, Dragutin Albrecht, Zagreb, 1861. With thanks to Tomislav Matić.
67 With the exception of Slovakia, where nineteenth-century Slovak scholars were pleased to identify that they had been ruled by fellow Slavs in the Jagiellonian kings; see Kuzmová, below.
68 For this process in the Commonwealth, see T. Snyder, *The Reconstruction of Nations: Poland, Ukraine, Lithuania, Belarus, 1569–1999*, New Haven, Yale University Press, 2003.
69 A. Franaszek, ed., *Testament Zygmunta Augusta*, Kraków, Ministry of Art and Culture, 1975.
70 Mickūnaitė, below, pp. 32–34.
71 Kuzmová, below, pp. 85–87.
72 Nowakowska, below, p. 59.
73 Kozubska-Andrusiv, below, p. 210.
74 Perhaps in Lithuanian scholarship a greater degree of evolution in the Soviet period is visible, with St Casimir and Barbara Radvillas emerging as codes for political resistance; see Mickūnaitė, below, pp. 36–38.
75 Mickūnaitė, below, p. 39; Kozubska-Andrusiv, below, p. 212.
76 C. Mănicută, 'Ştefan cel Mare – evocare istorică şi mit romantic', *Codrul Cosminului* 10, 2004, pp. 81–82, with thanks to János Incze; Kuzmová, below, p. 89.
77 'The Statue of King Louis II by Imre Varga', anon., https://www.kozterkep.hu/~/1126/II_Lajos_szobra_Mohacs_2006.html, accessed 5.11.17; Lewis, below, pp. 175–176; *City with Which My Heart Lies*, Panevėžys Tourism Centre, www.panevezysinfo.lt/upload/1204/files/PANEVEZYSknyga.pdf, accessed 5.11.17.

78 Nowakowska, below, pp. 60–61.
79 Mickūnaitė, below, p. 41.
80 Lewis, below, p. 179; Niiranen, below, p. 149.
81 Zupka, below, p. 130; Lewis, below, pp. 178–179; Nowakowska, below, p. 61.
82 For the cookbook, see Mickūnaitė, below, p. 42. Photographs of these objects, taken during fieldwork, have been posted on the @Jagiellonians project Twitter account (2013–).
83 Nowakowska, below, p. 61.
84 Lewis, below, pp. 175–176.
85 Mickūnaitė, below, pp. 38, 42.
86 Niiranen, below, p. 151.
87 Mickūnaitė, below, p. 40.
88 For example, E. Ochman, *Post-Communist Poland: Contested Pasts and Future Identities*, Abingdon, 2013.
89 Afanasyev, below, p. 116.
90 See the project's web-page, www.facebook.com/ideejagiellonskie/ (accessed 8.5.18).
91 For Visgrad Four ministers laying flowers at the statue in 2013, see the Polish Foreign Ministry press release, 'Western Balkans top of the agenda', www.msz.gov.pl/en/news/western_balkans_top_of_the_agenda_during_v4_ministers__meeting_in_budapest_, accessed 5.11.17. The website https://shop.spreadshirt.pl/koszulki-historyczne/ sells Jogaila images alongside those of Piłsudzki and the leading Polish nationalist thinker Roman Dmowski, and Polish military symbols.
92 J. de Groot, *The Historical Novel*, Abingdon, 2010; for 'romantic' memorialisation of Asian sixteenth-century royals, see for example the 2001 Thai film *The Legend of Suriyothai*. For Tudor-themed gifts retailed by British palaces, see www.historicroyalpalaces.com/giftcollections/historicroyalpalaces/hamptoncourtpalace.html, accessed 6.11.17.
93 Niiranen, below, p. 147; Nowakowska, below, p. 55; Kuzmová, below, pp. 80–81. For the Munich school, see C. Härtl-Kasulke, *Karl Theodor Piloty (1826–1886): Karl Theodor Pilotys Weg zur Historienmalarei, 1826–55*, Munich, 1991.
94 E.g. Snyder, *The Reconstruction of Nations*.
95 See Kuzmová, below, p. 73; R. Horvat, 'Rat kralja Vladislava II. na Lovru Iločkoga', *Vienac* XXVIII, 2, 1896, pp. 30–31, with thanks to Tomislav Matić.
96 Lewis, below, p. 167.
97 Niiranen, below, pp. 149, 151–152.
98 See B. Kossányi, *A Báthory-Sobieski emlékkiállítás katalogusa: Catalogue de l'exposition commémorative Báthory-Sobieski*, Budapest, 1933, with thanks to Tibor Gerencsér.
99 For interregnum speeches, see the chronicle of Ś. Orzelski, *Bezkrólewia ksiąg ośmioro, czyli, dzieje Polski od zgonu Zygmunta Augusta, 1572 aż do r. 1576*, Warsaw, 1980; Nikžentaitis, *Witold i Jagiełło*; Mickūnaitė, below, pp. 32–35.
100 Hoshko, below, p. 198; Nowakowska, below, p. 61; Kozubska-Andrusiv, below, p. 216.
101 Macek, *Jagellonský věk*; *Jagiellonowie i ich Świat*, ed. Piotr Węcowski, Kraków, 2016.
102 Bues, *Die Jagiellonen*. See also the work of Riga Regina Trimoniene, discussed by Mickūnaitė, below, p. 38.
103 *Europa Jagiellonica* website, https://research.uni-leipzig.de/gwzo/index.php?option=com_content&view=article&id=678&Itemid=567, accessed 6.11.17. The Leipzig University-based project has published a series of largely art historical works, with the series title *Studia Jagellonica Lipsiensia*. See also Zupka and Afanasyev in this volume, pp. 114, 131.
104 See the exhibition catalogue foreword by P. Mrozowski, 'Europa Jagiellonica – z warszawskiej perspektywy', *Europa Jagiellonica, 1386–1572. Sztuka i kultura w Europie Środkowej za panowania Jagiellonów*, Warsaw, 2012. On this point, see also Maciej Górny and Kornelia Kończal, 'The (Non-)Travelling Concept of les Lieux de Mémoire: Central and Eastern European Perspectives', in Pakier and Wawrzyniak, *Memory and Change*.

105 Nowakowska, below, p. 60; and Visegrad Group website, www.visegradgroup.eu/about, accessed 7.11.17.
106 M. Mesenhöller, 'Ein früher Traum von Europa', *Die Zeit*, 7 March 2013: 'Jagiellonen sind a) eine tropische Fruchtsorte, b) ein harmloser Virenstamm, c) eine osteuropäische Dynastie, d) leichte Elementarteilchen. Zu gewinnen wären 125.000, vielleicht 250.000 Euro.'
107 Pestel et al., 'Promises and Challenges'.
108 Troebst, 'Halecki Revisited', p. 58.
109 T. Zarycki, *Ideologies of Eastness*, London, 2014.
110 Nowakowska, below, pp. 50, 63–64; Kuzmová, below, pp. 73, 76; Afanasyev, below, p. 105. For Tomasich's chronicle, a key source for modern Croatian historiography of the Jagiellonian period, see I. Kukuljević Sakcinski, ed., *Chronicon breve Regni Croatiae. Joannis Tomasich Minoritae – Kratak ljetopis hrvatski Ivana Tomašića malobraćanina*, Arkiv za povjestnicu jugoslavensku, no. 9, 1868, pp. 1–34. With thanks to Tomislav Matić.
111 Afanasyev, below, pp. 113–114.
112 Nowakowska, below, pp. 61–63.
113 Nowakowska, below, p. 63.
114 Maciej of Miechów, *Chronica Polonorum*, Kraków, 1519; Węcowski, *Jagiellonowie i ich Świat*. For queasiness about Jagiellonian family agendas beyond Poland, see for example H. Łowmiański, *Polityka Jagiellonów*, ed. Krysztof Pietkiewicz, Poznań, 1999, p. 460; A. Sucheni-Grabowska, 'Jagiellonowie i Habsburgowie w pierwszej połowie XVI wieku, konflikty i ugody', *Śląski Kwartalnik Historyczny Sobótka* 38, 4, 1983, pp. 449–467.
115 Afanasyev, below, pp. 111–112.
116 For these findings, see the project's second book, N. Nowakowska, I. Afansyev, S. Kuzmová, G. Mickūnaitė, S. Niiranen and D. Zupka, *Dynasty in the Making: The Idea of the Jagiellonians, c.1386–1640* (forthcoming).
117 Discussed here by Mickūnaitė, below, p. 28; Nowakowska, below, p. 64; Afanasyev, below, pp. 101–102; Zupka, below, p. 135.
118 See Kuzmová, below, p. 74.
119 See Zupka, below, p. 135.
120 See Afanasyev, below, p. 101.
121 'History, Memory and Legacies of the Polish-Lithuanian Commonwealth' was the theme of the 5th International Congress of Foreign Historians of Poland, held in Kraków in October 2017.

1

OUR FOREIGN TRAITORS AND REDEEMERS

Remembering Jagiellonians in Lithuania

Giedrė Mickūnaitė

The Grand Duchy of Lithuania was the patrimony and political point of origin of the Jagiellonians, and was ruled by them as grand dukes from the fourteenth until the late sixteenth century. Having emerged as a short-lived kingdom under Mindaugas (d.1263), Lithuania was consolidated as a grand duchy under Vytenis (r.1295–1316), whose brother Gediminas (r.1316–41) gave his name to the Gediminid ruling house. Jogaila succeeded his father Algirdas (r.1345–77) to the grand ducal seat, only to be overthrown by his uncle Kęstutis in 1381–82. Having re-established himself as grand duke, Jogaila was elected king of Poland in 1386. This election resulted in Lithuania's conversion to Catholicism and Jogaila's residence in the kingdom of Poland. Having styled himself supreme duke of Lithuania, Jogaila transferred the grand ducal office to his cousin Vytautas (r.1392–1430), who later earned the epithet 'the Great'. The close association of Lithuania and Poland, which began with Jogaila's election, culminated in the establishment of the Commonwealth of both nations in 1569 during the reign of Sigismund Augustus (1544/8–72). However, it was only after all male heirs of Jogaila had died out in 1572 that the Jagiellonian name started to be exploited when claiming political power and royal prestige. Individual rulers continued to be referred to as lawgivers and authors of major deeds; thus the Jagiellonians remained symbolically present in the political thought and practice of the Polish-Lithuanian Commonwealth, even if physically extinct. After a brief glimpse into the consolidation of the Jagiellonian legacy in the seventeenth and eighteenth centuries, this essay concentrates on the period after the third partition of the Polish-Lithuanian Commonwealth in 1795. It traces developments in the Lithuanian remembrance of the Jagiellonians and discusses its manifestations from the establishment of the Lithuanian nation-state in 1918 and throughout the twentieth century to this day.

In 1603, Krzysztof Warszewicki's *Liber Parallelum* . . .[1] paired Jogaila and Sigismund Augustus as the two complementary biographies framing the Jagiellonian dynasty. The first represented potential, the second embodied decay. Warszewicki's view echoed opinions current in the later 1570s. Critical judgements about the reign of Sigismund Augustus and his mismanagement of the Commonwealth were expressed during the king's lifetime and exploded after his heirless death. The nobility mobilised to execute their right to elect the king, rather than approve the son of the deceased one, as had happened ever since the election of Jogaila. The newly elected king's reign was considered a contrast to that of the last Jagiellonian. Indeed, it exceeded these projections, although unfortunately not as expected: Henri Valois (r.1573–74) was late to assume royal office and, having arrived in the Commonwealth, stayed there for just four months before secretly escaping to France to take the inherited throne. The foreign king from far away appeared to be a profound failure. In parallel, disputes about the inheritance of Sigismund Augustus and arguments for the Commonwealth's debt to the Jagiellonians for two hundred years of prosperous rulership provided a favourable package for the Jagiellonians memorialised as a whole.[2] Hence Warszewicki's negative judgement in the 1603 paired biographies seemed anachronistic, as under the reign of Sigismund Vasa (1587–1632), who styled himself as a Jagiellonian and profoundly exploited his blood connection to the extinct dynasty, the Jagiellonians had come to be regarded in a highly positive light.

Although the negative reputation of Sigismund Augustus had expired by the turn of the sixteenth century and the memory of the Jagiellonians had begun the steep path towards rehabilitation, the contrasting evaluations of individual Jagiellonian kings remained marked. The split between collective lineage and individual personalities concerned only males and, moreover, only the crowned ones and St Casimir (d.1484), whose saintly reputation exceeded royal merits and situated him firmly on the 'good' end of the scale. With the election of Sigismund Vasa, Jagiellonians in the plural functioned as a currency of politics and prestige. Jagiellonian blood became the rhetorical trump card of Sigismund's election and the natural bond tying the Vasa kings to the Commonwealth.

While the grand ducal office guaranteed the Jagiellonians' symbolic presence in politics and legislation, the canonisation of Casimir in 1602 and the celebrations of his triumph in Vilnius in May 1604 opened an avenue for new memories of the Jagiellonians. During the first half of the seventeenth century, kings, magnates, and monastic orders promoted the saint's cult. Most importantly, the Church invested in and maintained devotion to St Casimir. The saint's lives always emphasised his status as prince of Poland and grand duke of Lithuania, and this repetition of ducal titles in text and iconography firmly sustained the Jagiellonian association.[3]

It was only after the dissolution of the Commonwealth (1795) that the Jagiellonians' active membership in political discourse expired and their name entered memory proper. In the absence of statehood, Jagiellonians personified the glorious past 'when our kings reigned' and symbolised the nascent Lithuanian and Polish nations, embodying both a shared history and increasingly distinct nationhoods. At the beginning of the nineteenth century, the Lithuanian nation was represented by the citizens of the former grand duchy and, in addition to Lithuanians, included Samogitians, Poles, Belarusians, Ukrainians, Tatars and other ethnic groups communicating mostly in the Polish language. Many of them were nostalgic for the lost state and cherished its heritage and history. Part of this history was naturally associated with the Jagiellonians, regarded as 'our natural lords'.

The fact that the Jagiellonians had held grand ducal and royal offices privileged them not only during their lifetime, but also in history and memory. Rather than be discovered, they had merely to be reshaped according to the needs and views of evaluators and their audiences. The latent presence of the Jagiellonians required only minor stimuli to be activated; their memory functioned as a kind of distorted echo where various deeds from the past were evoked to the tunes of the present. The selective work of memory also contributed towards concentrating memories of the Jagiellonians in Vilnius and around the framing personalities of the dynasty – Jogaila and his great-grandson Sigismund Augustus.

Sites

From the moment the grand duchy was annexed by the Russian Empire, the tsarist government started restricting access to the country's past, first by taking the state archive consisting of the books of Lithuanian Metrica to St Petersburg, and then

FIGURE 1.1 Landscape of Jagiellonian ruins. 'Vilna, View of the Jagiellon Royal Castle destroyed in 1802, and a part of the Cathedral', attributed to Jan Rustem (c.1820); pen and brush in grey and black, grey wash, on paper. National Museum in Krakow/Princes Czartoryski Museum. Image from the laboratory stock of the National Museum in Krakow

by reshaping the cityscape of Vilnius, which was turned into governor's seat.[4] In 1798, tsarist Governor Ivan Fryzel' ordered the demolition of the grand ducal palace, and by 1802 the 'dangerous wreck' was gone. The demolished palace deprived memories of the Jagiellonians of a tangible container. Without this palace, a much-needed substitute was found in visual art.[5] The drawing of the palace by Pietro de Rossi[6] from 1793, now lost, was copied extensively, with many of these copies bearing captions identifying the building as the Jagiellonian palace. The naming of the palace after the Jagiellonians can also be traced to town plans,[7] suggesting a topographical echo of oral tradition. During the first years under tsarist rule, the preservation of historic images was led by private initiatives, most of which have become anonymous today. In 1844 the wider public learned of Franciszek Smugliewicz's[8] water-colours with historic views of Vilnius from 1786.[9] The delayed public awareness of these images relates to a much broader movement that can be called 'the past in pictures', caused by the suppression of the anti-tsarist uprising of 1831 and the heavy censorship imposed on texts.[10] Napoleon Orda (1807–83) is the emblematic figure of this movement. Having returned from forced emigration in 1856, Orda decided to 'capture the shivers of our bygone civilisation'[11] by making thousands of drawings of historically charged sites in the former Commonwealth. Two hundred and sixty of his pictures were lithographed and published in fascicles of the *Album of Historic Views of Poland* (1873–83).[12] Of the twelve cityscapes representing Vilnius, three feature non-extant buildings copied from Rossi's drawings. Curiously, the picture of the grand ducal palace (without Jagiellonian captions) has been turned around while lithographing and thus reflects its own absence, making the entire site an almost unrecognisable dream space from the past.[13]

Stories

The search for, or rather construction of, a dream that could be claimed as real is a key characteristic of nineteenth-century historiography. Dependent on Albert Wivk Koiałowicz's (1609–77) academic *History of Lithuania* (1655–69),[14] historians accepted a past divided into the reigns of legendary and historic grand dukes. For Koiałowicz, Lithuanian history ended with the Union of Lublin (1569), when the grand duchy entered the Commonwealth. As the conclusion of the union almost coincided with the death of Sigismund Augustus and the end of Jagiellonian reign, the dynasty's name became virtually synonymous with that of the grand duchy. Nineteenth-century historians took this conclusion for granted and toiled to extend their narratives deeper into the past. Hence, Teodor Narbutt (1784–1864)[15] began the *Ancient Deeds of the Lithuanian People* (1835–41) with a distant mythological age and ended with the reigns of Sigismunds.[16] Ever since the time of its publication, scholars have disagreed as to the value of Narbutt's enterprise, most frequently accusing the author of forgeries and inventions.[17] Amateur and passionate storyteller as he was, Narbutt rendered the Romantic vision of history in words. Ending the *Deeds* with 1572, he concluded dramatically: 'the last of the sovereign monarchs of Lithuania and the last bearing the Jagiellonian arms, Sigismund Augustus, died . . . and I break my pen on his tomb'.[18] The *Deeds* represented the Jagiellonians as a sequence of individual rulers, who became a single whole, a dynasty, upon extinction. While opinions about particular individuals and evaluations of their reigns vary, the Jagiellonians in plural are considered good and beneficial for their subjects. Simonas Daukantas (1793–1864),[19] the very first historian to write in the Lithuanian language, follows the established periodisation and judgements in his *Samogitian History*.[20] Motiejus Valančius (1801–75) not only refers to Jagiellonian reigns in his *History of the Samogitian Bishopric* (1848),[21] but also observes the hierarchy of titles by placing the deeds of King Jogaila higher than those of the Grand Duke Vytautas.[22] The pioneers of Lithuanian national historiography, Narbutt, Valančius, and especially Daukantas, toiled to distinguish a specifically Lithuanian character and to provide Lithuanians with a special role in the past of the grand duchy. These amateur historians started constructing Lithuanian identity as difference, taking language as the prime feature of this distinction. Suppressed after the anti-tsarist uprising of 1863, the Lithuanian language functioned as a key identifier and platform for national resistance.[23] Banned in the Russian Empire, Lithuanian books were printed abroad and smuggled across the border. Although the publication of history books was rare, it was here that paganism was added as another distinctly Lithuanian feature.[24] Hence, national identity stemmed from the Lithuanian language, as a segment of contemporaneity, and the pagan faith, as a segment of historicity. As for the Jagiellonians, the grand ducal office secured them a permanent place in history; however, their reputation required some revision according to the new national criteria. The Catholic priest and celebrated poet Jonas Mačiulis-Maironis (1862–1932) was the first to alter the activities of the Jagiellonians. His *History of Lithuania* (1906)[25] evaluated every reign for its contribution towards Lithuanian-ness, which, when simplified, meant less Polishness. In the eyes of Maironis, the Jagiellonians were generally weak rulers who did not protect Lithuania from Polish dominance. Jogaila is credited for the country's conversion and his neglect of the motherland was compensated for by the great deeds of Vytautas. Other Jagiellonians failed in defending the country, lost huge territories to the Muscovites, and succumbed to Polish manners and language. The death of Sigismund Augustus 'ended . . . the grand dukes stemming from Jogaila'[26] and afterwards, united with Poland, Lithuania entered an almost entirely subdued state, which lasted until 1905. The history written by Antanas Alekna repeats Maironis's opinions and raises the question of language. According to Alekna, Jogaila knew and Casimir learned Lithuanian; however, he doubted whether other grand dukes of 'Jogaila's stem' spoke it.[27]

Grand dukes

The establishment of the Republic of Lithuania in 1918 and the Polish occupation of the Republic's capital Vilnius in 1920 reshaped interpretations of history. The conflict with Poland was projected onto the beginnings of the shared past personified by two Lithuanians: Jogaila and Vytautas.[28] The former was regarded as traitor, at fault for bringing Poles into the country and its capital, whilst the latter was seen as defender of the Lithuanian nation, despite Polish treasons and other dangers. The extent of the negative exploitation of Jogaila's image was described by Zenonas Ivinskis (1908–71) in 1934:

> On 31st May it will be exactly five hundred years since the death of the Grand Duke of Lithuania and King of Poland Jogaila, son of Algirdas. Nobody cares! Not a word in newspapers! It seems that Lithuania had no such duke at all. Why?
> We have a very dark image of Jogaila. Memory has preserved him as murderer of Kęstutis, eternal enemy of Vytautas and of Lithuania. A few years ago, it seems in Kaišiadorys, he was put on trial. After reading a long accusation blaming him for selling Lithuania to the Poles in exchange for the beautiful Hedwig, he was sentenced to 'capital punishment' which was afterwards replaced with 'exile from Lithuania'.[29]

According to Ivinskis, the revision of Lithuanian history must begin with the image of Jogaila,[30] and writing about his personality meant addressing the most acute problems of Polish and Lithuanian history.[31] While Ivinskis's thoughts were accepted, fiction artfully revealed the ambivalence in Jogaila's image. Balys Sruoga (1896–1947) sets his play *Under the Giant's Shadow* (1932)[32] in 1430, the year Vytautas – 'the giant' – died. Jogaila, the senile king, acknowledges his own misery, calls himself a captive of the Polish crown, and is portrayed as an old man manipulated by Polish lords. Jogaila's weakness is emphasised by the ascription to him of a feminine role: he comes to Poland to marry Hedwig and brings Lithuania as his dowry; throughout his reign, he is forced to keep his interests to himself and to obey Polish lords while Vytautas exercises true power and authority. Jogaila expresses his attitude towards the kingdom and kingship when the legitimacy of his sons is doubted. Asked what he would do were he not the father of Queen Sophia's sons, Jogaila replies that he would forgive the queen, recognise the children, and leave them reigning over wicked Polish heads.[33]

The *History of Lithuania* (1936) edited by Adolfas Šapoka (1906–61),[34] the official master narrative commissioned by the Ministry of Education, aimed to rediscover Lithuanians in Lithuanian history, but tried to remain balanced in its judgements. The ethnocentric Šapoka's *History*, as the volume is generally referred to, describes the rise of a pagan nation under Gediminas and its apogee, reached by entering Christendom, during the reign of Vytautas, with whom no other ruler could compete. The Jagiellonians are also made more Lithuanian by being referred to as Gediminids. Portrayed quite positively as individual rulers (except for Alexander, grand duke from 1492 to 1501, 'a man of no skill'[35]), they remain incomparable to their pure Lithuanian ancestors. As a rule, Jogaila and Sigismund Augustus are the two Jagiellonians whose deeds are commented on extensively. The former is said to have unintentionally 'opened the doors' for Lithuania's future

Polonisation.[36] The latter is praised for his love of Barbara Radziwiłł (Lithuanian, Barbora Radvilaitė, c.1523–51) and attachment to Vilnius, the two features that re-establish the weakened bond with the Lithuanian patrimony.[37] Šapoka's *History* concludes that after the extinction of those Gediminids who could claim the throne, and the brief reign of Stephan Bathory (r.1576–86), 'the last venerable ruler of Lithuania',[38] the Lithuanian nation entered a dormant state that lasted until the rebirth of the nation in the second half of the nineteenth century.

Interwar historiography endeavoured to match the past with the values of the nation-state. These efforts left the Jagiellonians marginalised in historical, and neglected in official, discourse. While the names of the 'pure Lithuanian' grand dukes Gediminas, Algirdas, Kęstutis and, above all, Vytautas were given to state awards, army regiments, public institutions, streets and squares, none of the (male) Jagiellonians were regarded as pure enough to enter consideration for official commemoration. Even the news of the discovery of royal burials in Vilnius was described in comments as Polish noise around a few graves.[39]

The 'noise' was provoked by the great flood of 1931, which seriously damaged Vilnius Cathedral.[40] In order to reinforce the foundations of the building, engineers had to enter its basements, in the words of a reporter, full of 'historically unimportant bones'.[41] This newspaper phrase hints at the expectation of finding bones of historical importance, chiefly those of Grand Duke Vytautas, the 500th anniversary of whose death was celebrated with great pomp in Lithuania a year before.[42] In contrast to expectations, no crypts were found beneath the Chapel of St Casimir,[43] but the search continued. On 21 September 1931, the architect Jan Peksza broke a brick wall and opened an unknown crypt containing the remains of King Alexander and the queens Elisabeth (d.1545) and Barbara (d.1551), the two spouses of Sigismund Augustus. The discoveries became major news and soon the police were summoned to guard the cathedral's entrances. On the same day Polish Radio reported the discovery, which soon turned into a media event.[44] Although numerous stories spread, based on the dissemination of reports by respected witnesses, measures were taken to prevent any circulation of 'inappropriate images'. As a result, the entire visual documentation of the crypt and the remains was entrusted to respected artists.[45] In 1933, the artistic production was exhibited first in Warsaw and then moved to Vilnius. A display in the sacristy accompanied the installation of the royal coffins in the Chapel of the Virgin Mary and Sts Andrew and Stanislas.[46] This discovery was to culminate in the 'restoration of historical justice' by constructing a royal mausoleum under the Chapel of St Casimir. In 1939, the mausoleum was ready, but details of the reburial remain obscured by the outbreak of World War II. The turmoil of war, which also included the return of the Vilnius region to Lithuania and Lithuania's subsequent Soviet, Nazi and further Soviet occupation, pushed the entire issue far into the periphery, but not entirely into oblivion.

Saint

The troubles and desperation of war prompted many to search for supernatural protection, bringing St Casimir into devotional immediacy. The sole Jagiellonian saint had never lacked devotees, and his veneration naturally intensified during troubled times. Suppressed under the tsarist regime, devotion to St Casimir became a sign of Lithuanian Catholicism in diaspora communities and grew in parallel with Lithuanian nationalism. Of course, St Casimir was also a Polish saint; and his sainthood was understandably expected to bridge the acute conflict between Poland and Lithuania.

When Polish forces occupied Vilnius in 1920, it became apparent that Lithuania's historical capital would be associated with Poland. In 1922, the Sejm declared the Vilnius Wojewodship to be an integral part of the Republic of Poland. It was within this context of political, national, and military tensions that the Jagiellonian saint was appealed to for intercession. Bishop Jurgis Matulaitis (in Polish, Jerzy Matulewicz, 1871–1927, r.1918–25) initiated the celebration of the 400th anniversary of Casimir's canonisation. Although by that time it was well known that the saint had been canonised in 1602, the bishop decided to celebrate the hypothetical bull allegedly granted by Pope Leo X in 1521, which was believed to have ordained the Jagiellonian prince as saint.[47] The jubilee was an extremely necessary invention, an attempt by the Church to appease two close nations divided by extreme hostility. The bishop's pastoral address stated that 'St Casimir, as prince of Lithuania and Poland, united in his loving soul both Vilnius and Krakow, Lithuania and Poland. We should pray to him for intercession that national and social conflicts are removed . . .'[48]

Regardless of the bishop's bilingual appeal, the staging of the celebration designed by Ferdynand Ruszczyc (1870–1936) represented the saint as a solely Polish prince.[49] Understandably, on the other side of the disputed border, the saint's Lithuanian nationality was never doubted. Pictures for private devotion and art works for churches featured Lithuanian arms and Gediminid columns (rather than the double cross of the Jagiellonians) among the saint's attributes.[50] Among visual productions, the interior decoration of the Christ the King Cathedral in Panevėžys offers a close-up look at the public representation of the saint. The composition, dating from 1931–33, occupies the vault of the cathedral's apse and shows St Casimir appearing in the sky above Lithuanian solders kneeling in prayer. As Giedrė Jankevičiūtė has observed, the painting represents no specific military miracle by the saint, but shows a blended view of St Casimir's support to the nation fighting against foreign invaders.[51] As such invasions were never lacking in countries under the saint's patronage, his intercession was continuously evoked and devotion recast according to changing needs. Hence in 1943, the competition for St Casimir's image was re-organised for the 340th anniversary of the Jagiellonian prince's canonisation.[52] The major achievement of the preparations was the rebuilding of the torch on the dome of St Casimir's Church in Vilnius. In 1754, the torch was topped with a dome in the shape of a grand ducal cap, demolished after 1864, when the church was seized by the Orthodox.[53] The rebuilding of the cap-shaped dome also meant the elevation of the grand ducal insignia above the old town of Vilnius. The sad paradox is that the Soviet regime kept the insignia, but turned the church into a Museum of Atheism (1961–88). This forced transformation was part of targeted Soviet activities against the 'religious superstitions' which prevented people from seeking communist ideals, and St Casimir was right in the centre of their crosshairs. In 1950, Vilnius Cathedral was nationalised and converted into a picture gallery, and the saint's relics were left inside the secularised building. It was only in 1952 that permission to transfer the relics into the functioning Church of Sts Peter and Paul was given. The political implications of the saint's cult were censored as restorers rendered the seventeenth-century Latin inscription, 'When St Casimir appeared in the sky as a leader, the army of the Grand Duchy of Lithuania defeated the Muscovites', illegible.[54] The suppression of St Casimir's cult hardly bore particularly Jagiellonian connotations; rather, it was part of an annihilation of religious devotion aimed especially at its nationally specific representations. St Casimir's veneration drifted from Jagiellonian prince to patron of Lithuania. However, looking at the Lithuanian response and contribution to the cult, it is clear that his grand ducal title and Lithuanian origins were exploited, while the Jagiellonian connections were silenced. Throughout the Soviet occupation, devotion to St Casimir was nourished by Lithuanians in exile. It was there that the only Jagiellonian (one may call it such for the sake of this essay) opera, *Dux Magnus* (1984), was composed, on the occasion of the 500th anniversary of the saint's death.[55]

Sins

The Soviet regime not only despised and fought against 'religious superstitions' as the obstacle towards a bright communist future, but also recast the past. Thus, nations were reduced to either the 'people', or 'masses', references to statehood or nation as polity were banned, and critical scholarly vocabulary was subordinated to the clichés of Moscow-centred Stalinism.[56] Preoccupied with class struggle and revolutionary movements, Soviet historiography prioritised the nineteenth and twentieth centuries, whilst previous epochs were reshaped to fit a Marxist-Leninist perspective.[57] Soviet-style sins had to be found for the Jagiellonians, who 'together with other feudal lords oppressed common people'. Hence, Jogaila sinned when in the 1380s he 'turned away from the nascent Russian and Lithuanian union'[58] and allied with the Poles. It must be kept in mind that in the Soviet understanding, only the 'great Russian nation' was exempt from nationalist evil.

The so-called Khrushchev thaw allowed certain liberties for history writing; however, a well-implemented auto-censorship prevented the revision of Stalinist standards, and encouraged intellectual escapism. Historians educated under the Soviet regime developed a camouflage vocabulary saturated with communist clichés and cautiously selected research topics. Understandably, the Jagiellonians were not an acceptable topic, with the sole exception of the wars against the Teutonic Knights, termed 'German feudal aggression supported by the Catholic Church'.[59]

Soviet interests are reflected proportionally in a synthesis of Lithuanian history from 1985:[60] one-third of the volume is dedicated to the long nineteenth century, ending with the Bolshevik Revolution of 1917. The description of the feudal period is a paradox of narration: it combines a hatred of rulers, who exploit the ordinary people, neglect the needs of the country for the sake of a lavish court, and tighten oppression of peasants-turned-serfs, with an appreciation of Renaissance architecture and sculpture (as a style that observes the principles of realism), commissioned either by the 'evil' rulers and nobility or the equally 'exploitative and greedy' Catholic Church. The Jagiellonians, referred to as Gediminids, are marginal figures in the background of social and economic developments. However, readers skilful in deciphering the messages obscured by Soviet camouflage could rely on illustrations featuring Jogaila's tomb in Krakow, a portrait of Sigismund August on the Lithuanian grosz from 1547, or a picture of the Lower Castle of Vilnius with the cathedral and the grand ducal palace.[61]

Stage

As images escaped Soviet censorship more often, the arts conveyed desired meanings. Paradoxically, of all Jagiellonians, Barbara Radziwiłł appealed most to artists. The story of Sigismund Augustus and Barbara, cast by nineteenth-century Polish fiction into a romantic tragedy with strong patriotic connotations,[62] was reframed to accommodate Lithuanian agendas. For Polish romantics Barbara personified Poland, Sigismund Augustus was a nationally-mixed personality split between love and the duties of kingship, and his mother Queen Bona (d.1557) embodied foreign evil. The Lithuanian version of the story focused on the love between two Lithuanians as well as Sigismund's fight 'for the rights of the human heart'.[63] During the interwar period, the discovery of Barbara's remains nourished the Polish version, which was adapted for film in 1936. The Lithuanian version matured on stage in the 1970s.

During the Soviet occupation, the theatre, where spoken word, artistic gesture and visual setting were joined together, held an exceptional place amongst the public arts. On stage the Lithuanian language was spoken publicly, conveying disguised messages that audiences were keen to decipher and elaborate. Spectators skilled in searching for added meanings became the collective witnesses and sharers of hidden ideas, mostly through allusions, transgressing the censored reality. Examining the dramatic repertoire through a Jagiellonian lens, it is easy to single out the staging of Juozas Grušas's (1901–86) play *Barbora Radvilaitė*,[64] directed by Jonas Jurašas at Kaunas Drama Theatre in 1972. Although censors forced Jurašas to resign before the premiere, the revised staging was performed for more than a decade,[65] transforming the well-known love story into a nationally-charged appeal. The versified text of the play centres on the vital choice between love, duty, and life. Typically for 1970s Lithuanian historical drama, the plot exposes the inevitable conflict between personal desires and higher social ideals, and the final sacrifice of the former.[66] Barbara not only follows this scheme, but as a female character in the dynamics of a misogynist society, personifies Lithuania. The drama of love against social standards becomes a struggle for a recognised existence. Barbara wins the struggle at the moment of her coronation, but Lithuania's worthy existence can be affirmed only through human sacrifice. Initially, the scene of Barbara's death was represented as a symbolic martyrdom, with the queen's dead body replaced by the celebrated image of the Virgin Mary of Vilnius's Dawn Gate[67] which, according to popular legend, portrayed Barbara.[68] Censors removed this 'religious allusion'; however, the triad of Barbara–Lithuania–Mary lived on in rumour[69] as audiences were keen to add desired meanings and construct political interpretations. Neither the staging of *Barbora Radvilaitė* in Klaipėda in 1973,[70] nor the TV performance from 1982[71] enjoyed as much popularity as the play in Kaunas. In the distorted Soviet reality, Barbara and her assumed sacrifice for Lithuania became a kind of secular saint and martyr, taking the place of St Casimir, with a plot expanded by themes of sanctity with ambivalence, deadly choices, deep emotions, and fragile femininity. Obviously, the Jagiellonian part is marginal; however, Barbara's sacrificial love for Sigismund Augustus binds the last Jagiellonian to his patrimony, making him Lithuanian again.

Web

The restoration of Lithuania's independence on 11 March 1990 once again placed statehood at the centre of attention and the topic quickly entered the agendas of historical research. In addition to the reprinting of studies from the interwar period and those of émigré scholars debarred during the Soviet occupation, the first Lithuanian history of the 1990s extended the existence of the grand duchy to the third partition of the Polish-Lithuanian Commonwealth in 1795.[72] If Šapoka's *History* searched for Lithuanians in Lithuanian history, the 1995 volume was 'aimed at writing the political history of the state created and for centuries nurtured by Lithuanians'.[73] Understandably, the personalities and activities of rulers, regarded as initiators or catalysts of economic, military, and legal reforms, were at the centre again. The criterion of statehood was decisive when evaluating individual reigns. The Jagiellonians were reproached for neglecting their Lithuanian patrimony in favour of royal titles, which made grand ducal authority nominal. However, the Jagiellonians were collectively presented as a Lithuanian dynasty, whose power stretched beyond Poland and Lithuania. Archaeological finds from the Lower Castle of Vilnius, which illustrated the 1995 volume, were chosen to demonstrate the 'European level' of the Jagiellonian court.

In addition to discovering the Lithuanian past in the history of the grand duchy, another imperative of the 1990s aimed at regaining the country's presence in Europe. These two aspirations got entangled and manifest together in Rita Regina Trimonienė's study *The Grand Duchy of Lithuania and Central Europe* (1996),[74] focusing on the Jagiellonian reigns in Bohemia, Hungary, Poland and Lithuania. Centred on the place and role of the grand duchy within Jagiellonian policies, Trimonienė observes the decline of Lithuania's importance as a dynastic patrimony during the reign of Alexander and its rise with the birth of Sigismund Augustus. This research into political history is the first thorough attempt in Lithuanian historiography to look at Jagiellonians beyond Lithuania and Poland.

The *History of Lithuania* (1999) by Edvardas Gudavičius[75] focuses on the grand duchy under the Jagiellonians, whose reigns are considered decisive for the country's cultural transformation. Gudavičius regards Western Europe as an exception to, rather than the dominating pattern of, the medieval world order. Employing the binary opposition of a despotic Orient versus Western monarchies in which the estates had a say and role in government, Gudavičius ascribes fourteenth-century Lithuania, a country owned by the grand duke, to the despotic Orient. In the fifteenth century, this ownership gradually transforms into a monarchy with estates living on and from heritable land. Having succeeded his father, Grand Duke Jogaila embodied and represented the grand duchy, but decided to redirect the path that his country would follow. Later Jagiellonian reigns are presented as continuously pushing Lithuania westwards with the support of the highest nobility, whose share in government and economic power grows. The Jagiellonians are seen not as Lithuania's export to the kingdoms of Central Europe (as in Trimonienė's study), but as rulers bringing European culture and political practices to the grand duchy. Ending his volume with the Union of Lublin, Gudavičius concludes that during the reign of the Jagiellonians Lithuania managed to catch up with the Western tradition, at least superficially. The episodes when grand dukes resided in Vilnius (Alexander in 1492–1501; Sigismund Augustus in 1544–48) made the court a focal point for the reception and promotion of European culture and fashions. The result of this was that, from the late sixteenth century onwards, Lithuania became an active contributor to Western civilisation.

The reversed Eurocentrism of Gudavičius prompted revisions in history writing. Alfredas Bumblauskas worked to rethink the practice of national historiography,[76] altering the historical and spatial boundaries of Lithuanian history and offering a framework composed of facts rather than stories.[77] His *History of Old Lithuania, 1009–1795* (2005) presents and discusses topics from the country's past in the layout of a photograph album, suggesting that readers can opt for a DIY narrative. Over-reliant on visual material, Bumblauskas offers a set of issue-impressions about Lithuanian history. The period from 1387 to 1569 is termed the Europeanisation of Lithuania, with the Jagiellonians, identified as a Polish branch of the Gediminids, in the background of this cultural process.[78] The Jagiellonians are implicitly considered a native dynasty, in contrast to the Vasas, labelled as 'rulers of foreign origin'.[79] Bumblauskas is perhaps the first Lithuanian historian to look at Jagiellonian women as cultural and sometimes political actors, providing a brief description for every adult member of the family.[80]

The historiography of the 1990s had two principal messages – Lithuania is an integrated part of Europe and heir of the grand duchy – which had to be conveyed to the larger public. Lithuanians had to be taught how to inherit the multicultural legacy of the grand duchy and to see themselves not as an exception to, but a constituent part of, Western culture. National TV was instrumental in forging this twofold identity. The talk show *Secrets of the Past*, formatted as a dialogue between historians Edvardas Gudavičius and Alfredas Bumblauskas, became an exceptional media phenomenon, lasting from 1993 to 2004[81] and receiving the National Culture and Arts Prize in 1998. Focusing on Lithuania as part of Europe, the show emphasised the cultural homogeneity of Latin Christianity. Such a perspective not only rehabilitated Jogaila, but recast him as a *Kulturträger* of the last pagan nation. Visual evidence supported these arguments as reportages from abroad tracked down Lithuanian iconography, much of which was related to the Jagiellonians. Jagiellonian kings and their spouses demonstrated high status and were considered proof of Lithuanian prestige across Europe, and provided a curative message for people coping with shabbiness and shortage on a daily basis.

Retold to accommodate the concerns of the twenty-first century, Lithuanian history provided a tradition for democracy, tolerance, women's rights and other issues on today's agenda; however, it could hardly compete with other topics in terms of entertainment value. Past realities have been reduced to the genre of the 'true story', the truthfulness of which is attested to by intrigue, personal and political dramas, celebrities and, of course, secrets. These components shape the scenarios of the TV show *Detectives of History*,[82] first broadcast in 2013. Inclusive of all periods and aspects, the show prioritises neither the grand duchy, nor the Jagiellonians. However, some of them, recast into celebrities, are occasionally addressed and commented on.

Intrigue and entertainment are the structural principles of the popular history site 'Orbis Lituaniae'.[83] This scholarly contribution towards public impact offers a mosaic of stories, consciously avoiding a coherent narrative and focusing on the larger society of the past rather than its rulers. Hence, under the heading of personalities one finds only queens Sophia[84] and Barbara,[85] Alexander Jagiellon[86] and the description of the marriage of Catherine Jagiellon and John III Vasa.[87] The entry on the Jagiellonian and Habsburg meeting of 1515 focuses on the Lithuanian nobility in Sigismund's entourage.[88] Again, 'Orbis Lituaniae' is a DIY platform that encourages the finding of differences and playing with past identities. In such a game, the grand ducal persona cedes to mundane women and men, doctors and teachers, the devout and the adventurous.

Concrete

Physical reality offered a vivid parallel to the broadcast one. Since the mid-1980s, archaeological investigations of the Lower Castle of Vilnius have revealed numerous objects, many with heraldic signage and portraiture.[89] The restoration of independence prompted the rebuilding of the palace, regarded as the architectural embodiment of statehood purposefully demolished by the tsarist regime. The law outlining the reconstruction and function of the palace was passed by the Seimas (parliament) in 2000.[90] The National Museum Palace of Lithuanian Grand Dukes opened to visitors in 2013; however, further construction works continue. The museum's exhibition is twofold: the unearthed basement of the original palace houses archaeological finds, and the newly built storeys display the master narrative of Lithuanian greatness. The Jagiellonians, finally composed of both women and men, receive most attention in a display constructed of copies and associative objects, exhibited within imaginary interiors shaped as a pastiche of major artistic styles. The rebuilding of the palace and the establishment of the museum have been highly controversial: unearthed foundations and important finds are juxtaposed with a fantasy-historical structure, which having neither adequate architectural evidence, nor authentic contents to display, functions like a theme park.[91]

Retold

Debates in historiography, advances in research techniques, the adoption of new methodologies, and better access to primary sources made writing the twelve-volume *History of Lithuania* (2005–) a necessity. The three volumes covering the reign of the Gediminids from Vytenis to Sigismund Augustus[92] discuss Lithuania's place in world history and reflect on the social identities of ruling houses. The Gediminids are introduced as a clan, bound together by the sharing of supreme power, a sense of common origins and the heritable arms of the *Vytis*.[93] Jogaila and his heirs cherished the royal title; however, the identity of the Jagiellonians was created during the long reign of Casimir Jagiellon. The fact that Casimir's death was not followed by a fight over inheritance suggests that the clan had become a dynasty.[94] The dynastic self-consciousness of the Jagiellons manifested itself through 'the usage of Jogaila's sign – the double cross, which emerged together with the inheritable Jagiellonian name'.[95] The first Lithuanian Statute (1529) strengthened this dynastic identity by providing a hereditary grand ducal office.[96]

In line with historiographical tradition, the personalities of Queen Bona, Sigismund Augustus and Barbara Radziwiłł received extensive commentary and evolved into a discussion on the family relations of the last Jagiellons, where Bona is ascribed her malevolent role.[97] The death of Sigismund Augustus in 1572 ends the discussion on the Jagiellonian dynasty in Lithuanian historiography. Historians do not ascribe female Jagiellons active dynastic membership.

Woman

Fiction fills the feminine gap, cultivating and elaborating on the image of Barbara, making the Radziwiłł lady the most celebrated Jagiellon. The mausoleum and 'secret crypt' of Vilnius Cathedral containing Barbara's remains function as a pseudo-pilgrimage site. The story of Barbara and Sigismund Augustus continues to be exploited on various stages. While Barbara's image has been transformed into a personification of love rather than of nation, the scenography of a ballet from 2011[98] revived the Soviet-banned, and therefore enforced, association between the queen and the image of the Virgin Mary of the Dawn Gate. Today's performances still rely on the topos of mutually sacrificial love, as Barbara accepts being despised by the court and her royal in-laws, whilst Sigismund Augustus risks his crown for his beloved. Presented as drama[99] or musical,[100] the 'true story' triggers emotions, exposes passions, and contrasts illicit ties and erotic fascination with social order, public duties and official opinions. Barbara, whose coffin lies in the mausoleum under the Chapel of St Casimir,[101] is venerated as love's martyr, an image charged with greater appeal than the relics of the Jagiellonian saint.[102]

Ghosts

In today's Lithuania, the memory of the Jagiellonians is maintained from the top down. It is passed on as historical knowledge in schools, researched by scholars, appropriated by towns,[103] institutions and cookbooks,[104] broadcast by the media, recycled in fiction,[105] and staged as drama. Although this essay has no means by which to estimate the reception of the Jagiellonians among the broader public, an example from the visual arts reveals aptly how the memory of the Jagiellonians is activated. Painter Žygimantas Augustinas, whose first name coincides with, and surname differs just with the suffix '-in-' from, that of Žygimantas Augustas, the Lithuanian spelling of Sigismund Augustus, decided to put this annoying coincidence into a particular visual regime under the title 'The Case of *IN*'.[106] The artistic project undertakes a meticulous, almost forensic anthropometric investigation of surviving Jagiellonian portraits and remakes them by 'dressing' Jagiellonian bodies in the painter's own flesh. The project goes further in creating a conditional reality by making the re-skinned and modernised Jagiellonians inhabit their reconstructed palace in Vilnius. The interplay of fictional, physical and artistic realities involves the viewer, who has some knowledge of virtual lives and catches the Jagiellonian implications at a glance. Prompted by an almost Freudian slip in names, this artistic project offers a puzzling recognition, combining the 'high' knowledge and medium of painting with a transpersonal and transtemporal reality. Far from a typical approach, it represents the memory of the Jagiellonians

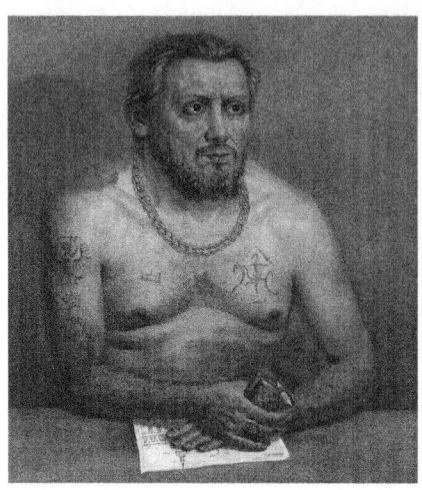

FIGURE 1.2 Žygimantas Augustinas, (a) 'The Pater of Ž. August(in)as' and (b) 'The Mater of Ž. August(in)as' (details of project 'IN'), oil on canvas, 90 x 100 cm each, 2016, Raulinaitis collection

in a nutshell. Jagiellonians are present in memory like fleshless ghosts, ready to assume the bodies and roles offered by various narratives. In their latent state they are reduced to the grand ducal office and Barbara's great love. If activated, they can be easily turned into political currency, tokens of Europeanness, protagonists of tolerance and multicultural practices, patrons of arts, and protectors or traitors of the homeland. Nearly all of these roles are male and all are fleshless. Conditional bodies, however, can be provided by the needs of the present, including the ghostly inhabitants of the fake grand ducal residence.

Echoes

At a very early stage, Lithuanian nationalism turned Warszewicki's juxtaposition on its head: Jogaila was labelled the nation's traitor, while Sigismund Augustus became regarded as the redeemer of Jagiellonian treason. However, Lithuanian linguistic nationalism had to negotiate the Lithuanian-ness of its rulers, the majority of whom neither spoke Lithuanian, nor resided in their patrimony. Redeemed, neglected, discovered, and exploited, the memory of the Jagiellonians has always been present and easily answers the calls of today. Whenever it becomes necessary to ground something in the past or accept invention as tradition, the Jagiellonians dutifully serve their Lithuanian patrimony, present as a celebrated ghost ready to be dressed in verbal clothes. Their appearances are functional and prestigious, but episodic; the Jagiellonians are quickly turned into a message, but cannot, even as historical figures, become fully fleshed bodies.

Notes

1 Ch. Varsevicius, *Caesarum regum et principum, unius et eiusdem, partim generis at nominis, partim etiam imperii ac dominationis, vitarum paralellum libri duo*, Krakow, Jacob Sibeneyher, 1603; herein quoted after Ch. Varsevicius, *Speculum analogiae et metamorphosis aliquot Magnatum. Hoc est: Caesarum regum et principum, unius et eiusdem, partim generis at nominis, partim etiam imperii ac dominationis, vitarum paralellum libri duo*, Frankfurt, 1608.
2 On Jagiellonian memory after the death of Sigismund Augustus, see N. Nowakowska et al., *Dynasty in the Making . . .* (forthcoming).
3 For the sources on the saint's life and cult see M. Čiurinskas, ed., *Šv. Kazimiero gyvenimo ir kulto istorijos šaltiniai / Casimiriana. Fontes vitae et cultus S. Casimiri, Fontes ecclesiastici historiæ Lithuaniæ* 3, Vilnius, Aidai, 2003; M. Čiurinskas, ed., *Ankstyvieji šv. Kazimiero 'Gyvenimai' / Casimiriana II. Vitae antiquiores S. Casimiri, Fontes ecclesiastici historiæ Lithuaniæ* 4, Vilniusi, 2004; J. Okoń et al., eds, *Żywot Świętego Kazimierza królewicza polskiego i książęcia litewskiego w Wilnie Roku 1606 przez Mateusza Chryzostoma Wołodkiewicza przełożony*, Warsaw, 2016. On the saint's iconography see S. Maslauskaitė, *Šventojo Kazimiero atvaizdo istorija XVI–XVIII a.*, Vilnius, 2010, and the exhibition catalogue – N. Markauskaitė and S. Maslauskaitė, eds, *Šventojo Kazimiero gerbimas Lietuvoje*, Vilnius, 2009; for the history of devotion to the saint in the nineteenth and twentieth centuries, see P. Subačius, ed., *Šventasis Kazimieras istorijos vyksme: įvaizdis ir refleksija*, Vilnius, 2006.
4 On Vilnius's St George (today, Gediminas) Avenue, see I. Tamošiūnienė, *Šv. Jurgio prospektas: nuo vizijos iki tikrovės*, Vilnius, 2012.

5 The fact that the palace acquired its final shape in the 1630s, that is, more than half a century after the death of the last Jagiellonian king, did not prevent the structure being associated with the Jagiellonians; see R. Janonienė, 'Vilniaus Žemutinės pilies ikonografiniai šaltiniai', in R. Ragauskienė, ed., *Vilniaus Žemutinė pilis XIV a.–XIX a. pradžioje. 2002–2004 m. istorinių šaltinių paieškos*, Vilnius, 2006, pp. 11–43.

6 Pietro de Rossi (c.1760–1831, active in Vilnius from c.1786 to 1811); A. Paliušytė, ed., *Lietuvos dailininkų žodynas*, vol. 2, *1795–1918*, Vilnius, 2012, p. 334.

7 Pehaps the most curious example is the early nineteenth-century map of the castle territory titled 'Plan pałacu X. Jagiełow. Z przyległymi budowlami w roku 1794', preserved in the National Library in Warsaw; Janonienė, 'Vilniaus Žemutinės pilies ikonografiniai šaltiniai', p. 29, fig. 10.

8 Franciszek Smugliewicz / Pranciškus Smuglevičius (1745–1807), Paliušytė, *Lietuvos dailininkų žodynas*, vol. 2, pp. 374–7.

9 Based on circumstantial evidence, Smugliewicz's water-colours are dated to 1797; they became more widely known from an article by Michał Homolicki (1791–1861), *Wizerunki i roztrząsania naukowe, Poczet nowy drugy*, Vilnius, 1844, vol. 24, pp. 269–84. The original album containing twenty pictures has been preserved in the National Museum of Krakow; Janonienė, 'Vilniaus Žemutinės pilies ikonografiniai šaltiniai', p. 30.

10 E. Aleksandravičius and A. Kulakauskas, *Carų valdžioje: XIX amžiaus Lietuva*, Vilnius, 1996, pp. 125–39.

11 This is how Orda described his project in the letter to Ignacy Domejko in 1876. V. Levandauskas and R. Vaičekonytė-Kepežinskienė, *Napoleonas Orda: senosios Lietuvos architektūros peizažai*, Vilnius, 2006, p. 30.

12 N. Orda, *Album widoków historycznych Polski*, Warsaw, 1873–83.

13 Ibid., ser. 2, no. 75; see Levandauskas and Vaičekonytė-Kepežinskienė, *Napoleonas Orda*, fig. 67, p. 90.

14 A. Wiivk Koialowicz, *Historiae Lithuaniae*, 2 vols, Gdansk, 1655; Antwerp, 1669.

15 T. Narbutt, *Dzieje starożytne narodu litewskiego*, 9 vols, Vilnius, 1835–41.

16 The plural of the names originated in the sixteenth century when the reigns of Sigismund the Old and Sigismund Augustus were joined together as co-rulers and later as two successive periods.

17 For an overview of the discussion, see A. Ragauskas, 'Ar istorikas Teodoras Narbutas (1784–1864) buvo istorijos šaltinių falsifikuotojas?', *Acta humanitarica universitatis Saulensis*, 9, 2009, pp. 324–35.

18 'Ostatni z udzielnych Monarchow Litwy i ostatni po mieczu z Jagellonów, Zygmunt August umarł . . . i, ja pióro moje na jego grobowcu kruszę'; T. Narbutt, *Dzieje narodu litewskiego*, vol. 9, *Panowania Zygmuntów*, Vilnius, 1841, p. 492. Narbutt did write a tenth volume of the *Deeds*, the supplement to the entire project; however, the volume has never been published and is known from fragmented drafts only; 'Dzieje narodu litewskiego przez Teodora Narbutta. Tom dziesiąty. Część 1-sza. Dodatki, poprawy, odmiany, autorowie i dzieła przytoczone, tudziej i regestr układowy, z ryciną, Wilno, 1842', Wroblewski Library of the Lithuanian Academy of Sciences, Manuscript Department, F. 18, B. 206/2/7.

19 S. Daukantas, *Istorija žemaitiška*, 2 pts, B. Vanagienė, ed., *Lituanistinė biblioteka*, Vilnius, Vaga, 1995. During his lifetime, Daukantas, under the pseudonym Jokūbas Laukys, published an outline of Lithuanian history, character and customs: *Budą senowęs-lėtuwiû kalnienû ir žamajtiû iszrasszcę pagał senowęs rasztû Jokyb's Łaukys*, St. Petersburg, 1845; for critical edition see S. Daukantas, *Raštai*, vol. 1, *Būdas senovės lietuvių kalnėnų ir žemaičių*, B. Vanagienė, ed., *Lituanistinė biblioteka* 16, Vilnius, 1976.

20 The piece remained in manuscript until the 1890s, when it was first published as S. Daukantas, *Lietuvos istorija*, 2 vols, Plymouth, 1893–7.

21 M. Valančius, *Žemajtiu wiskupistę aprasze k. Motiejus Wołonczewskis (1413–1841 m. istorija)*, 2 pts, Vilnius, J. Zawadzki, 1848. For critical editions see M. Valančius, *Raštai*, B. Vanagienė, ed., vol. 2, Lituanistinė biblioteka 12, Vilnius, 1972.
22 Valančius, *Raštai*, vol. 2, pp. 45–51.
23 On the uprising and so-called Lithuanian philological nationalism see Aleksandravičius and Kulakauskas, *Carų valdžioje*, pp. 283–95.
24 *Trumpa senosios Lietuvos istorija*, Tilsit, 1864.
25 J. Maironis, *Lietuvos istorija. Su kunigaikščių paveikslais ir žemėlapiais*, St Petersburg, 1906.
26 Ibid., p. 176.
27 A. Alekna, *Lietuvos istorija*, Šv. Kazimiero draugijos leidinys Nr.106, Kaunas, 1911, p. 68.
28 For the juxtaposition of the two images in Lithuania and in Poland see A. Nikžentaitis, *Vytauto ir Jogailos įvaizdis Lietuvos ir Lenkijos visuomenėse*, Vilnius, 2002.
29 Z. Ivinskis, 'Jogaila Lietuvos istorijoje ir mes. Jo mirties 500 metų proga', *Naujoji Romuva*, 171, 1934, p. 313.
30 Ibid., pp. 313–15.
31 Z. Ivinskis, 'Jogaila valstybininkas ir žmogus', in A. Šapoka, ed., *Jogaila*, Kaunas, Švietimo m-jos knygų leidybos komisija, 1935, p. 311.
32 B. Sruoga, *Milžino paunksmė: trilogiška istorijos kronika*, Kaunas, 1932.
33 Ibid., p. 68.
34 A. Šapoka, ed., *Lietuvos istorija*, Kaunas, Šviesa, 1936.
35 Ibid., p. 201.
36 Ibid., p. 176.
37 Ibid., pp. 212–13, pp. 228–9.
38 Ibid., p. 294.
39 'Triukšmas dėl karališkų karstų atradimo Vilniuje', *Mūsų Vilnius*, 28, 1931, p. 671.
40 For an in-depth discussion of the discovery, visual representation and the reburial of the royal remains see A. Andriulytė, 'Karališkųjų palaikų atradimas Vilniaus Arkikatedroje 1931 m.: atvaizdų kolekcija', *Acta Academiae Artium Vilnensis*, vol. 65/66, *Lietuvos kultūros karališkasis dėmuo: įvaizdžiai, simboliai, reliktai*, Vilnius, 2012, pp. 327–60.
41 Sulimczyk, 'W Bazylice Wileńskiej', *Słowo*, 14 August 1931, no. 193, p. 3. Andriulytė, 'Karališkųjų palaikų atradimas', p. 331.
42 On the celebrations see D. Mačiulis, 'Vytauto Didžiojo metų (1930) kampanijos prasmė', *Lituanistica*, 2, 2001, pp. 54–75.
43 Sulimczyk, 'W Bazylice Wileńskiej', p. 3.
44 For the thorough chronology of events, see Andriulytė, 'Karališkųjų palaikų atradimas', pp. 332–5.
45 Initially the team consisted of photographer Jan Bułhak and painters Ferdynand Ruszczyc, Liudomir Slendzinski and Kazimierz Kwiatkowski, to be later joined by painter Jerzy Hoppen and sculptor Bolesław Balzukiewicz; see Andriulytė, 'Karališkųjų palaikų atradimas', pp. 339–54.
46 The chapel was founded by King Casimir Jagiellon in 1484 as the burial place of his son Casimir, to be canonised saint in 1602. The same year that chapel was given to Bishop Eustachy Wołłowicz / Eustachijus Valavičius (1572–1630) in exchange for the place for St Casimir Chapel founded by King Sigismund Vasa. On exhibition and the display of coffins see Andriulytė, 'Karališkųjų palaikų atradimas', p. 331.
47 For a detailed account of the documents related to the celebration see G. Gustaitė, 'Šv. Kazimiero 400 metų kanonizavimo sukakties minėjimas 1922', *Lietuvių katalikų mokslų akademijos metraštis*, 21, 2002, pp. 388–406.
48 The pastoral letter was published in Polish: 'List pasterski. Jerzy Matulewicz . . .', *Nasza ziemia*, 21 May 1922, no. 16, pp. 3–4; and in Lithuanian: 'Jurgis Matulevičius, Dievo ir Apaštalų Sosto malone . . .', *Vilniaus garsas*, 28 May 1922, no. 19, pp. 2–3.
49 For a thorough discussion of the visual side of celebration see A. Andriulytė, 'Šv. Kazimiero relikvijų pagerbimas Vilniuje 1922 metais', in Subačius, *Šventasis Kazimieras istorijos vyksme*, pp. 66–74.

50 See G. Jankevičiūtė, 'Šv. Kazimiero atvaizdas XX a. Lietuvos dailėje ir 1943 m. konkursas', in Subačius, *Šventasis Kazimieras istorijos vyksme*, pp. 75–84.
51 G. Jankevičiūtė, *Dailės gyvenimas Lietuvos Respublikoje 1918–1940*, Kaunas, 2003, p. 263.
52 See Jankevičiūtė, 'Šv. Kazimiero atvaizdas XX a. Lietuvos dailėje', pp. 75–84.
53 On the torch see N. Markauskaitė, 'Lietuvos jėzuitų provincijos statybinė veikla: Vilniaus profesų namų Šv. Kazimiero bažnyčia XVII–XVIII amžiais', unpublished PhD dissertation, Vilnius, 2004, p. 67.
54 'S(ANCTO) CASIMIRO APPARENTE IN AERE QUASI DUCE EXERCITUS M(AGNI) D(UCATUS) L(ITHUANIAE) VICIT MOSCOS'; W. Appela and E. Ulčinaitė, eds, *Inscriptiones eccleasiarum Vilnensium / Inskrypcje z Wileńskich kościołów / Vilniaus bažnyčių įrašai*, vol. 1, Vilnius, 2005, p. 195. On the exile of St Casimir's relics see P. Vaičekonis, 'Šv. Kazimiero palaikų tremtis Vilniaus Šv. Apašt. Petro ir Povilo bažnyčioje (1952–1989)', in Subačius, *Šventasis Kazimieras istorijos vyksme*, pp. 157–64; on the restored inscription, see Vaičekonis, 'Šv. Kazimiero palaikų tremtis Vilniaus', p. 160.
55 *Dux Magnus*, composed by Darius Lapinskas, libretto by Kazys Bradūnas, English translation by John G. Paton Chicago, 1984. The opera was premiered in Toronto, 1984; Chicago, 1986; Vilnius, 1989; Markauskaitė and Maslauskaitė, *Šventojo Kazimiero gerbimas Lietuvoje*, no. 26, p. 249.
56 J. Žiugžda, ed., *Lietuvos TSR istorija. Nuo seniausių laikų iki 1861 metų*, pt 1, Vilnius, 1953; 2nd edn, 1957.
57 On Soviet historiography, see M. Górny, *The Nation Should Come First: Marxism and Historiography in East Central Europe*, Antoni Górny, trans., Aaron Law, ed., *Warsaw Studies in Contemporary History* 1, Dariusz Stola and Machteld Venken, eds, Frankfurt am Main, 2013.
58 Yu. Zhyugzhda, ed., *Istoria Litovskoi SSSR*, pt 1, *S drevneishykh vremen do 1861 g.*, Vilnius, 1953, p. 154.
59 E. Gudavičius and A. Nikžentaitis, eds, *Popiežių bulės dėl kryžiaus žygių prieš prūsus ir lietuvius XIII a.*, Vilnius, 1987; E. Gudavičius, *Kryžiaus karai Pabaltijyje ir Lietuva XIII amžiuje*, Vilnius, Mokslas, 1989.
60 B. Vaitkevičius, M. Jučas and V. Merkys, eds, *Lietuvos TRS istorija*, vol. 1, *Nuo seniausių laikų iki 1917 metų*, Vilnius, 1985.
61 Vaitkevičius et al., *Lietuvos TRS istorija*, pp. 78, 103, 105.
62 A. Feliński, *Barbara Radziwiłłówna: tragedya w 5 aktach*, Krakow, 1820; A. E. Odyniec, *Barbara Radziwiłłówna czyli Początek panowania Zygmunta-Augusta: poema dramatyczne w sześciu aktach, z prologiem*, Vilnius, 1850. Contemporary historiography tried to offer source evidence and elucidate controversies, but it also followed the romantic mode; see M. Baliński, *Pamiętniki o królowej Barbarze, żonie Zygmunta Augusta*, 2 vols, Warsaw, 1837–40.
63 Z. Ivinskis, 'Karalienės Barboros Radvilaitės drama', *Naujoji Vaidilutė*, 10, 1935, p. 380.
64 J. Grušas, *Barbora Radvilaitė*, Vilnius, Vaga, 1972.
65 On the staging in Kaunas see I. Aleksaitė, ed., *Lietuvių teatro istorija*, bk 3, *1970–1980*, Vilnius, 2006, pp. 162–5.
66 This scheme of personality split by 'higher' social demands and ultimately sacrificing one's human needs has been most thoroughly exploited in the trilogy of plays by Justinas Marcinkevičius, *Mindaugas* (1968), *Mažvydas* (1976) and *Katedra* (1970); see J. Marcinkevičius, *Raštai*, vol. 3, *Poemos, dramos*, Vilnius, 1982, pp. 110–413.
67 For the display of the image see Aleksaitė, *Lietuvių teatro istorija*, bk 3, p. 165. On history of the image, see M. Kałamajska-Saeed, *Ostra Brama w Wilnie*, Warsaw, 1990.
68 On Barbara's images see M. Matušakaitė, *Karalienė Barbora ir jos atvaizdai*, Vilnius, 2008.
69 For an excerpt from the 1973 performance, see 'Prisiminkime. J. Grušas "Barbora Radvilaitė"', www.lrt.lt/mediateka/irasas/14304, accessed 7.12.16.

70 Aleksaitė, *Lietuvių teatro istorija*, bk 3, p. 507.
71 *Barbora Radvilaitė*, director Vidmantas Bačiulis, pt 1, www.lrt.lt/mediateka/irasas/11144; pt 2, www.lrt.lt/mediateka/irasas/11145, accessed 7.12.16.
72 J. Kiaupienė, Z. Kiaupa and A. Kuncevičius, *Lietuvos istorija iki 1795 m.*, Vilnius, 1995; English translation: *The History of Lithuania before 1795*, Vilnius, 2000.
73 Kiaupienė et al., *Lietuvos istorija . . .*, p. 11.
74 R. R. Trimonienė, *Lietuvos Didžioji Kunigaikštystė ir Vidurio Europa XV–XVI a. sandūroje*, Šiauliai, 1996.
75 E. Gudavičius, *Lietuvos istorija*, vol. 1, *Nuo seniausių laikų iki 1569 metų*, Vilnius, 1999.
76 A. Bumblauskas, *Lietuvos istorijos modeliai XIX–XX a. istoriografijoje*, Vilnius, 2007.
77 A. Bumblauskas, *Senosios Lietuvos istorija, 1009–1795*, Vilnius, 2005.
78 Ibid., pp. 172–9.
79 Ibid., pp. 294–7. Importantly, the reigns of Henri Valois (1574) and Stephan Bathory (1576–1586) are not considered foreign.
80 Ibid., pp. 176–7.
81 *Būtovės slėpiniai* (1993–2004); the digital archive of 125 shows is accessible at www.lrt.lt/paieska/#/content/Būtovės slėpiniai, accessed 3.11.16; part of the show has been published in a book format: E. Gudavičius and A. Bumblauskas, *Būtovės slėpiniai*, A. Švedas, ed., vol. 1, *Nuo Netimero iki . . .*, vol. 2, *Užmiršta Lietuva*, Vilnius, 2014–16. For a scholarly discussion of the show see R. Šermukšnytė, 'Audiovizualinės istoriografijos atvejis Lietuvoje: televizijos laida "Būtovės slėpiniai"', *Lietuvos istorijos studijos*, 20, 2007, pp. 85–99.
82 For the digital archive of 147 shows visit 'Istorijos detektyvai', *LRT Mediateka*, www.lrt.lt/mediateka/irasai#/program/171, accessed 3.11.16.
83 'Orbis Lithuaniae. Lietuvos Didžiosios Kunigaikštystės istorijos', www.ldkistorija.lt, accessed 3.11.16.
84 R. Petrauskas, 'Karalių motina ir senelė: Sofija Alšėniškė', www.ldkistorija.lt/#karaliu-motina-ir-senele-sofija-alseniske_fact_294, accessed 5.11.16.
85 R. Ragauskienė, 'Mitai apie Barborą Radvilaitę', www.ldkistorija.lt/#mitai-apie-barbora-radvilaite_fact_265, accessed 5.11.16; R. Jankauskas, 'Barboros Radvilaitės kūno rekonstrukcija – antropologinės charakteristikos šaltinis', www.ldkistorija.lt/#barboros-radvilaites-kuno-rekonstrukcija-antropologines-charakteristikos-saltinis_fact_244, accessed 5.11.16.
86 R. Petrauskas, 'Paskutinis valdovas Vilniuje: Aleksandras Jogailaitis', www.ldkistorija.lt/#paskutinis-valdovas-vilniuje-aleksandras-jogailaitis_fact_302, accessed 5.11.16.
87 R. Ragauskienė, 'Iškilmės Vilniuje: 1562 m. Kotrynos Jogailaitės ir Suomijos kunigaikščio Jono III vestuvės', www.ldkistorija.lt/#iskilmes-vilniuje-1562-m-kotrynos-jogailaites-ir-suomijos-kunigaikscio-jono-iii-vestuves_fact_1564, accessed 5.11.16.
88 R. Ragauskienė, 'LDK didikai 1515 m. Jogailaičių ir Habsburgų susitikime Vienoje', www.ldkistorija.lt/#ldk-didikai-1515-m-jogailaiciu-ir-habsburgu-susitikime-vienoje_fact_495, accessed 5.11.16.
89 The most important finds were published in *Vilniaus Žemutinės pilies rūmai*, 5 pts, Vilnius, LII, 1989–2003.
90 Lietuvos Respublikos Lietuvos Didžiosios Kunigaikštystės valdovų rūmų atkūrimo ir paskirties įstatymas, 17 October 2000, no. VIII-2073, https://e-seimas.lrs.lt/portal/legal Act/lt/TAD/TAIS.111863, accessed 8.11.16.
91 The controversial aspects of the building and museum have been discussed in A. Bumblauskas, ed., *Lietuvos Didžiosios Kunigaikštystės valdovų rūmų atkūrimo byla. Vieno požiūrio likimas*, Vilnius, 2006.
92 J. Kiaupienė, ed., *Lietuvos istorija*, vol. 3, A. Dubonis, ed., *XIII a. – 1385 m.: valstybės iškilimas tarp Rytų ir Vakarų*; vol. 4, J. Kiaupienė, ed., *Nauji horizontai: dinastija, visuomenė, valstybė. Lietuvos Didžioji Kunigaikštystė 1386–1529 m.*; vol. 5, J. Kiaupienė, ed., *Veržli Naujųjų laikų pradžia. Lietuvos Didžioji Kunigaikštystė 1529–1588 metais*, Vilnius, 2011, 2009, 2013.

93 R. Petrauskas, 'Valdančioji dinastija: iškilimas, išnykimas, vidiniai konfliktai ir jų sprendimas', in Kiaupienė, *Lietuvos istorija*, vol. 3, p. 355.
94 R. Petrauskas, 'Lietuvos Didžiosios Kunigaikštystės valdymo struktūra ir institucijos', in Kiaupienė, ed., *Lietuvos istorija*, vol. 4, pp. 254–5.
95 Ibid., p. 256.
96 J. Kiaupienė, 'Lietuvos Didžiosios Kunigaikštystės kaitos laikas – 1529–1588 metai', in Kiaupienė, *Lietuvos istorija*, vol. 5, p. 129.
97 Ibid., p. 156.
98 *Barbora Radvilaitė*, Anželika Cholina, dir. and choreographer, Lithuanian National Opera and Ballet Theatre, 2011.
99 *Barbora Radvilaitė*, Jonas Jurašas, dir., Kaunas National Drama Theatre, 2014.
100 *Žygimanto Augusto ir Barboros Radvilaitės legenda*, Anželika Cholina, dir., Kipras Mašanauskas, comp., premiered in December 2014, Ach Theatre production on various stages, www.ach.lt/lt/spektakliai/carmen-22/#home, accessed 14.12.16.
101 For an overview of the exhibits, see S. Maslauskaitė, ed., *Vilniaus katedros požemiai. Vadovas*, Vilnius, 2013, p. 76.
102 The relics of St Casimir were translated back to the chapel on 4 March 1989; on the translation see Vaičekonis, 'Šv. Kazimiero palaikų tremtis Vilniaus', p. 163.
103 E.g. Panevėžys styles Alexander the town's founder based on the fact that the town's name is first mentioned in Alexander's letter from 7 September 1503; J. Fijałek and W. Semkowicz, eds, *Codex diplomaticus Ecclesiae Cathedralis necnon dioeceseos Vilnensis / Kodeks dyplomatyczny Katedry i diecezji Wileńskiej*, vol. 1, *1387–1507*, Krakow, 1948, no. 564, pp. 676–9. In 2003, the sculpted monument of Alexander by Stanislovas Kuzma was erected in the town square.
104 R. Laužikas, *Istorinė Lietuvos virtuvė. Maistas ir gėrimai Lietuvos Didžiojoje Kunigaikštystėje*, Vilnius, Briedis, 2014.
105 E.g. G. Viliūnė, *Vilniaus Madona*, Vilnius, Alma Littera, 2014, a detective novel centred on the marriage of Alexander Jagiellon and Helena of Muscovy.
106 Žygimantas Augustinas, 'The Case of *IN*', www.augustinas.lt/in_atvejis_en.html, accessed 26.1.17.

2

AN AMBIGUOUS GOLDEN AGE

The Jagiellonians in Polish memory and historical consciousness

Natalia Nowakowska

In a book published in Poznań in 1946, in the immediate aftermath of World War II, the historians Maria and Zygmunt Wojciechowski wrote:

> The times of the Sigismunds are and will remain a golden age of our past. When children want to learn about Poland, we direct their first steps to the Sigismund Chapel and to the courtyard of the Wawel castle ... Here, we experience unforgettable moments of joyful wonder.[1]

In Poland (broadly conceived), we find a particularly dense hotspot of Jagiellonian memory – multiple layers, centuries deep, in a dizzying range of media, depicting and interpreting what has established itself as arguably Poland's most iconic royal dynasty.[2] From the coronation of the pagan grand duke of Lithuania, Jogaila (Jagiełło) (d.1434), as king of Poland in Kraków cathedral in 1386, to the burial of his great-grandson Sigismund Augustus without heir in that same building in 1573, this family produced seven Polish monarchs.[3] The subject of Polish cultural memory of the Jagiellonian rulers is vast, relatively unmined, and this foray into it will inevitably be selective, subjective and preliminary. Venturing into this enormous panorama, this essay has two aims. First, it seeks to map the long-term patterns of Jagiellonian memory in Poland, and identify their evolving social-political functions, for the first time.[4] It identifies distinct phases, or modes, of Jagiellonian memory from the sixteenth century to the twenty-first: the discourses and images already in circulation during the long Jagiellonian period itself (1380s–1570s); early modern 'genealogical' memory cultivated by successor dynasties (1580s–1660s); a competing early modern 'national monarchy' memory popular among local elites (1570s–1790s); an elegiac nineteenth-century 'national' memory during the Partitions in which Jagiellonians embodied lost sovereignty (1800s–1918); state-directed memory (1918–), with Jagiellonians deployed as a Polish tool in Central

European geopolitics; and finally civic-commercial memory (c.1989–), in which Jagiellonians provide pleasant entertainment and nostalgia, having been pushed well into the background of Polish cultural memory by the brutal events of the twentieth century and their ongoing memory wars.[5]

The essay's second purpose is to probe the mutual relationship between these different memory regimes. How far are memories of the Jagiellonians in one period shaped by, or recycled from, earlier memories? Where is, say, eighteenth-century memory of the Jagiellonians in Poland deriving its content from? This, as we saw in the volume Introduction, is currently a moot point in the interdisciplinary field of memory studies. Judith Pollmann has stressed how far historic memory is remediated – showing, for example, how in Leiden during medieval famine, the privations of the Dutch Revolt, and food shortages in 1945, the same distinctive local story about herrings and bread pops up again and again, presenting itself as a true recent anecdote.[6] Feindt et al., in a series of major articles, have called on social scientists to recognise that memories are entangled across time as well as space, and for the historic dimension of cultural memory to form the focus of a new 'third wave' of memory research.[7] The second part of this essay will therefore highlight the remediation of Jagiellonian memory in Polish tradition by identifying a handful of motifs or codes which pop up century after century, from medieval chronicle, to Romantic painting, to Communist stamp, to twenty-first-century historical re-enactment. In this way, it looks at what Pestel et al. call 'the diachronic and synchronic dimensions of memory'.[8] The discussion concludes by addressing the challenges posed by dynasty as a container for memory, and their wider implications for how we might investigate and conceptualise deep historic memory.

The evolution of 'Jagiellonian' memory

In keeping with the volume's aim of linking up original material from the late medieval or early modern past with memories or renditions of it in subsequent centuries, let us start by outlining the rich but bifurcated local traditions about these kings already in circulation when Sigismund Augustus died at Knyszyn Castle in 1572. First, a highly critical discourse existed around these kings and their rulership – found in early texts such as an animal-fable satire composed circa 1417 on Jogaila, but most influentially expressed in the major chronicles of Jan Długosz (d.1480) and Miechowita (d.1523), who recounted scandalous tales of the royal family, questioned the legitimacy of its children, and lambasted examples of poor kingship.[9] Moral and political denunciations persisted throughout the sixteenth century: King Sigismund Augustus (1548–72), for example, generated a virtual sub-genre of polemical writing in his own right.[10] Alongside this, however, the Polish royal court produced a considerable body of panegyric material about the ruling family, including dozens of orations for royal weddings, funerals and diplomatic meetings, and a three-volume praise-chronicle by the royal secretary Jodocus Ludovicus Decius in 1521.[11]

It is also worth noting that the royal family's own artistic self-representation functions as a kind of original vanishing point for the many later depictions of

Jagiellonians in visual media. The Jagiellonian era produced three principal image-types of these royals: printed family trees, sculpted royal tombs, and collective portrait representations, such as Lucas Cranach the Younger's series of Jagiellonian miniatures (1550s), or the medal cycles produced by Padovano (1532) and Cornelius van Herwijck (1561).[12] As a political phenomenon which unfolded over several generations rather than a single event such as, say, a battle, this ruling house had thus already generated a complex set of memories and messages within the Polish monarchy well before it technically died out in 1572. These were the diverse, contradictory, 'raw materials' available to those creating subsequent Jagiellonian memory.

A powerful early mode of Jagiellonian memory, crystallising soon after their political extinction in 1572, was what we might term the 'genealogical-dynastic' memory cultivated by their cousins and successors on the Polish throne, the Vasas. After a period of turbulent interregna, in 1587 the Poles elected as their king the Swedish prince Sigismund Vasa (1566–1632), son of Princess Catherine Jagiellon of Poland (d.1583). Sigismund III established a line which would rule Poland-Lithuania for some eighty years (1587–1668), and for whom insistent invocation (and memorialisation) of their maternal Jagiellonian ancestors became central to claims regarding royal power, legitimacy and identity.[13] A printed festival book of 1587, *Sigismundi III Cracoviam ingressus*, can be read as a kind of opening master-text for Vasa dynastic memory of the Jagiellonians.[14] It describes the triumphal entry of the newly-elected Sigismund III into his royal capital of Kraków. Jagiellonians were adopted as the dominant theme of this *ingressus*. Reaching the city's suburbs, we are told, the new king came to an arch depicting 'the Jagiellonians, his ancestors'.[15] At each of the seven subsequent stops on the ceremonial route, a different Jagiellonian king 'spoke' to Sigismund III, acknowledging him as kin. The festival book reproduces the procession's 'images' and 'effigies' of the Jagiellonian kings in a series of full-page woodcuts. These represent the largest concentration of Jagiellonian images printed in a single volume in Poland since 1521. The book's anonymous author explicitly invokes memory and political pseudo-resurrection, writing that the Jagiellonians 'truly are worthy of memory, and it is not unjoyful for students of the past to depict those effigies as if alive, as far as possible . . .'[16] The *ingressus* serves as a reminder of the historic layering of memory – a work printed to commemorate an ephemeral event, which was itself a commemoration of past kings.

The genealogical imperative in Vasa-led memory of the Jagiellonians can also be seen in a series of striking seventeenth-century examples. In the 1640s, Sigismund III's son King Ladislaus IV (1632–48) commissioned the so-called Marble Room in the castle in Warsaw, the Polish-Lithuanian Commonwealth's new capital. Designed by the Italian architect Giovanni Battista Gisleni, this was to be the most splendid reception room in the complex.[17] It was decorated with inlaid coloured marbles, a fountain-stove, scenes depicting Ladislaus IV's military triumphs, and a series of twenty-two octagonal portraits of the king's ancestors by Peter Danckers de Rij, hung around the walls of the chamber like a frieze. This portrait cycle included Sforza and the Habsburg queens of Poland, but its main subjects were Jagiellonians, with Jogaila himself (the earliest figure depicted) presented as the original founder-ancestor of Ladislaus IV's line. Jerzy Lileyko argued that the purpose of the Marble Room was to assert the succession and electoral claims of Ladislaus IV's infant son, by functioning as a virtual family mausoleum for the Jagiellonians. The Danckers panels, he points out, match the funerary portraits popular among Polish nobles at the time in shape and size.[18] The Vasa kings did indeed invoke the Jagiellonians in their own mourning and self-memorialisation. The new royal (or 'Vasa') burial chapel constructed in Kraków cathedral from 1655 was modelled directly on the Jagiellonian chapel adjacent to it, a mirror image, and its black marble plaques carried gilded inscriptions which explicitly identified Sigismund III and his line as descendants of the Jagiellonians.[19] In the mid-seventeenth century, Jagiellonians as blood ancestors thus still formed a core plank of the self-presentation of Polish kings — indeed, following his abdication in 1668, John Casimir, the last Vasa monarch, organised the completion of the Vasa chapel, with its genealogical claims, as one of his last acts upon leaving Kraków for exile in France. He would also leave money for this purpose in his will in 1672.[20]

However, in the early modern period, the Jagiellonians could also be recalled in a rather different mode by poets, historians and artists — not as a self-contained family or distinct dynastic subset of royals, but rather as part of a much bigger, glorious, and (allegedly) unbroken continuum of Polish kings stretching back to the mythical founder Lech. In this 'national monarchy' mode, invocation of the Jagiellonians served principally to celebrate the broader institution and political community of the Polish monarchy itself. This approach is encapsulated in the popular sixteenth- and seventeenth-century genre of the *icones regum Poloniae* — catalogues of the historic kings of Poland, consisting of verses and/or woodcuts. Klemens Janicki's *Vitae Regum Polonorum elegiaco carmino descriptae* (1563), for example, was followed by the *Icones* of Jan Głuchowski (1605), Salomon Neuberger (1620), and many more.[21] In 1588 the polymath Tomasz Treter produced his influential *icones* woodcut, in which portraits of all Poland's kings were arranged to form the kingdom's heraldic eagle.[22] In this type of narrative, or visualisation, the Jogaila-descended kings who ruled from 1386 to 1572 occupy only a small part of the crowded historical stage of the Polish past. Of the forty-four kings depicted in Głuchowski's 1605 *Icones*, for example, only seven are 'Jagiellonians', and only three directly given that appellation.[23] The *icones* were not confined to the printed page. In the 1640s, the burghers of Thorn (Toruń) commissioned for their town hall a series of eighteen portraits of the kings of Poland, from Boleslaus the Bold (d.1025) to Ladislaus IV.[24] The Warsaw Marble Room and the Thorn gallery — created in the same decade, in the same medium — therefore juxtapose these two different ways of invoking the Jagiellonians in Polish early modernity, as personal kin of the reigning king, versus as a few bricks in the much bigger edifice of the immortal institution of the Polish monarchy.

It was this latter tradition which triumphed after the 1660s, when the kings of Poland-Lithuania no longer had any Jagiellonian blood ties to plausibly claim.

After the Vasas, the polity's electors chose kings from an array of new families, such as Jan Sobieski (1674–96), the Electors of Saxony August II and August III Wettin (1697–1763), and Stanisław August Poniatowski (1763–95). The royal-genealogical mode of recalling Jagiellonians fell away, and the Crown itself also started (along with its subjects) to invoke those fifteenth- and sixteenth-century rulers within the *icones regum poloniae* mode. The Jagiellonians were now presented by the Crown as venerable figures who glorified the monarchy and its elected incumbents as predecessors, not ancestors. This shift is epitomised by the wholesale remodelling of the Warsaw Marble Room in the years 1769–91, on the orders of King Stanisław August Poniatowski. Marcello Bacciarelli was commissioned to produce an entirely new set of portraits for the room, which effectively transformed the Vasa 'Jagiellonian mausoleum' into a splendid *icones regum Poloniae* cycle. He ejected all portraits of queens-consorts, included only kings of Poland, and pushed back the series' starting point by three centuries to commence with Boleslaus the Brave (d.1025). Jagiellonian kings deemed historically (not genealogically) significant were included – Bacciarelli, for example, painted Jogaila and Sigismund I prominently in victor's laurels, for the 1410 Battle of Grunwald and the 1519–21 Prussian war respectively.[25] The mnemonic purpose of these monarchs within Bacciarelli's Marble Room is to act as royal exemplars, not forefathers. The title of the new ceiling fresco made this very point: *Fame announcing the memorable deeds of Polish monarchs*.[26] This artistic project glorified in particular the monarchy's current incumbent. Stanisław August's coronation portrait was the largest image in the room, and Adam Naruszewicz's poem praising the chamber stressed the 'splendid league' of kings who looked down from heaven to bless the reign of the current ruler.[27] Johann Christian Kamsetzer's drawings of the room's interior (1784) show visitors admiring (only) the portrait of the reigning king himself. The Jagiellonians thus became useful background extras in a room which enshrined Stanisław August as its principal hero (see Figure 2.1). In the early modern period, then, we can trace a divergence or distinction between 'dynastic' and 'royal' memory of the Jagiellonians, with both ultimately legitimising the Crown, albeit from different angles. What happened, however, after the demise of the monarchy itself with the abdication of Stanisław August in 1795?

The long nineteenth century saw a wholesale recalibration of Jagiellonian memory in Polish culture, in the highly charged context of the Partitions. In 1795, Russia, Prussia and Austria-Hungary conducted their third and final Partition, or annexation, of Poland-Lithuania. The Polish monarchy ceased to exist as both territory and institution. In the European age of nationalism, Poland thus became a nation without a nation-state and 'Poland' itself a memory.[28] Polish cultural memory of the Jagiellonians in the nineteenth century had specific characteristics – the sheer outpouring of material about the dynasty; an intense cross-fertilisation between different media, such as scholarship, art and fiction; and an emphasis on the imagination, with the Jagiellonians' inner mental worlds, dress, political and private dramas reconstructed on a scale, and at an emotional pitch, not yet seen in

FIGURE 2.1 Etching from Kamsetzer's *Gabinet Marmurowy* (1784) showing contemporary viewers in the Marble Chamber, with portraits of King Stanisław August Poniatowski and earlier Polish kings. Photo: University of Warsaw Library © The Print Room of the University of Warsaw Library, Inw.zb.d. 8542

Poland. In the Partitions era, the Jagiellonians (dead for almost 400 years) became a vehicle for debating the destiny of the Polish nation. These royals, who had stood at the fulcrum of the polity's rise and fall, thus functioned in the nineteenth century as a powerful if ambiguous cipher for lost Poland itself. Here, we will consider in turn several interlocking elements of this mnemonic system – historical scholarship, history-painting, historical fiction, preservation of material heritage, and the 1910 ceremonies to mark the quincentenary of Jogaila's victory at the Battle of Grunwald (1410).

The founding of the first university posts in History (in Lwów and Kraków), and of the prestigious historical journal *Kwartalnik Historyczny* (f.1887), led to a surge of nineteenth-century publications on Polish history, a phenomenon which has been closely studied by Monika Baár and others. The important role played by the Jagiellonians in this scholarship can only be sketched here.[29] Meticulous studies of fifteenth- and sixteenth-century kings appeared, the fruits of decades of research: they included thick monographs on the reigns of Jogaila (d.1434) and Casimir IV (d.1492), or multi-volume source editions from the reign of Sigismund I (d.1548).[30] Such works, in addition to being scientifically pioneering, intervened in painful political debates about the causes of the Partitions. The epic *Poland and*

Her History (published from 1858), by the father of Polish historiography Joachim Lelewel (1786–1861), here offered a powerful master narrative of Polish history, imagining Poland as a suffering, innocent Christ among nations, preyed upon by wicked forces.[31] However, from the 1860s the so-called Kraków history school rejected this view, instead blaming the disaster of the Partitions on centuries of Polish political error, with the Jagiellonian kings identified as particular culprits.[32] Michał Bobrzyński, in his landmark *Sketch of Polish History* (1879), attacked these rulers for their short-sightedness, anarchy and weakness, while the Lwów professor Ksawery Liske portrayed them as gullible fools who in terrible sixteenth-century miscalculations had permitted the rise of the future Partitioning powers of Habsburg Austria and Prussia.[33] The Jagiellonians thus started to occupy a highly ambiguous place in modern Polish historical narrative – authors of both the country's Renaissance Golden Age and its later demise.

Arguably the most influential creator of Polish Jagiellonian memory in the nineteenth century was however not a university scholar, but an artist. Jan Matejko (1838–93), Director of the Kraków Academy of Fine Arts (from 1872), was one of the foremost cultural figures in Austrian-ruled Poland, and its most celebrated painter.[34] Throughout his long career he took as his chief subject scenes from the national past, and in particular the Jagiellonians. Matejko made his debut at a Kraków exhibition in 1856 with the painting *Władysław-Jagiełło Praying before the Battle of Grunwald*.[35] At least a third of his canvases over the next forty years featured Jagiellonians – fourteen paintings, some of them gigantic, plus many additional drawings of the dynasty.[36] While contemporaries such as Józef Simmler (d.1868) or Wojciech Gersson (d.1901) painted Jagiellonian subjects occasionally – particularly the tragic story of Queen Barbara Radziwiłł (d.1551) – nobody painted them as insistently as Matejko.[37] His canvases, though mocked by some critics as garish, were exhibited in Warsaw, Berlin, Vienna and Paris (where they won a gold medal in 1865), and were distributed in lithographic form to the 3,000 members of the Kraków Society of Friends of Fine Arts (1870s).[38] Matejko's history-painting was also in direct dialogue with the disaster of the Partitions. In common with Kraków historians such as Bobrzyński, Matejko placed the Jagiellonian kings and queens in the central frame of Polish national history, offering a vision of these rulers which was at once melancholic, nostalgic and critical. This can be seen in one of his most famous works, *The Prussian Homage* (3.8 x 7.8 metres), undertaken in 1879, the year of Bobrzyński's *Sketch*. *The Prussian Homage*, which depicts King Sigismund I taking a vow of fealty from the Grand Master of the Teutonic Order in 1525, thereby creating the Prussian state, is ambivalent in its very composition. In this crowded pageant, there is no Polish hero or central protagonist: not the gilt-clad King Sigismund, or Queen Bona, or the infant prince Sigismund, or the huge crowd of anxious noble and burgher onlookers. Instead, the figure positioned to catch the eye is Matejko himself, as the prophesying royal jester Stańczyk, in meditative-melancholic pose at the king's feet. Through works such as these, Matejko's vivid images and historical judgements of the Jagiellonians would burn themselves into the Polish cultural imagination for well over a century to come.

Jagiellonians were also energetically re-imaged in long nineteenth-century Polish fiction. Leading literary figures were drawn to them – the prolific and best-selling Józef Kraszewski (d.1887) penned multiple novels about Poland's Renaissance royalty; Lucjan Rydel (d.1918) and Stanisław Wyspiański (d.1907) wrote plays about the love affairs of King Sigismund August; while the Nobel prize-winning Henryk Sienkiewicz's 1910 masterpiece *The Teutonic Knights* recounted Jogaila's victorious 1410 military campaign.[39] This corpus of Jagiellonian historical fiction shared certain features. It was patriotic-didactic in tone, intent on imagining the Jagiellonians as fully as possible, and heavily indebted to (and in dialogue with) contemporary historical scholarship. Sienkiewicz, for example, wrote that historical fiction served society by 'illuminating and supplementing' knowledge of the national past, resurrecting figures from the gloomy twilight of the tomb and rendering them present again: here we have fiction as (patriotic) necromancy.[40] Kraszewski's novel *Infantka* (1884), on Princess Anna Jagiellon (d.1596), displays many of the traits of Polish historical fiction of this period. It offers a fine-grained, three-dimensional picture of the dying King Sigismund August's doctors, courtiers and mistresses, contemporary fears and rumours, the architecture, and daily routine of the royal court – all precisely rooted in the sixteenth-century sources recently published by the historian Aleksander Przeździecki.[41] The emotional timbre of *Infantka*, like Matejko's contemporary canvases, is one of bathos, calamity and bitter-sweetness. Kraszewski presents the last Jagiellonian king as magnificent but flawed, and the sixteenth-century courtiers bewailing the 'catastrophe', 'doom' and 'mess' of the country are, of course, in some sense also talking about the Partitions. The Jagiellonians are here indelibly associated with national loss.

This peculiar nineteenth-century Polish admixture of elegy and patriotic activism was also seen in campaigns to restore Kraków's Wawel hill, another key element in Jagiellonian myth-making. The Wawel, a castle-cathedral royal complex dating back to at least the tenth century, from the 1870s inspired a movement to reclaim, restore and revitalise the site for the Polish nation.[42] Restoration of the cathedral took place from 1891, led by the architect Sławomir Odrzywolski, diocesan authorities, Jan Matejko, Kraków City Council, and a local bank.[43] A 'Fund for the Royal Tombs' was administered by the Polish Academy of Sciences, and a restoration 'cent-collection' fund was organised by Aleksandra Ulanowska, whose tins circulated at aristocratic balls and in rural parishes alike.[44] Renovation of the Wawel was, to a large degree, Jagiellonian memory by another name: the celebrated Renaissance castle had been built by these kings, and a majority of the revered medieval royal tombs in the cathedral were of Jogaila's line.[45] The chapels of Sigismund I (d.1548), Casimir IV (d.1492) and Jogaila's queen Sophia (d.1461) were the first to be restored. In 1903, Antoni Madeyski was commissioned to design a tomb monument for King Ladislaus, who had vanished at the Battle of Varna (1444). Jogaila's tomb sculpture was moved, so that along with Madeyski's neo-gothic creation, two Jagiellonian kings could now flank the approach to the altar-shrine of St Stanisław, Poland's patron.[46] These activities reached an apogee with Wacław Szymanowski's (unrealised) design for a monument to be placed at the Wawel hill entrance. *Procession to the Wawel* (1907–11, see Figure 2.2), an epic

FIGURE 2.2 Model for the unrealised sculpture *Pochód na Wawel* (Procession to the Wawel) by Wacław Szymanowski (1911). Now in the National Museum in Kraków, inventory nr. II-rz-1688. Photograph courtesy of laboratory stock, National Museum in Kraków

rendition of Polish history, featured fifty-two figures led by Fate, including ten key kings and queens (3.5 metres high), of whom seven were Jagiellonians and their wives. Critics declared of the design that 'future generations will teach their children our history in the shadow of the cathedral, at the foot of *The Procession*'.[47] Szymanowski's *Procession* was an (unconscious?) echo of Sigismund III's 1587 *ingressus*, in which 'effigies' of Jagiellonian monarchs, arranged in historical order, had guarded the entrance to the royal spaces of Kraków. If Wojciech Baluś argues that the Wawel was in the nineteenth century definitively established as a place of metaphysical significance in the Polish cultural-national imagination through the three topoi of a readable text (speaking stones), ecclesiastical-historical shrine, and Polish (royal) pantheon, to this we might add that the memories of Jagiellonian kings formed a cornerstone of this vision.[48]

In a final twist in Partition-era memory, on the eve of World War I the Jagiellonians suddenly came into sharper, edgier political focus, with the 500th anniversary of Jogaila's victory at the Battle of Grunwald/Tannenburg (1410). In 1910, a Polish king's defeat of Prussia's Teutonic Knights was a highly resonant medieval event, given both official repressions against Poles in Prussia/Germany, and Kaiser Wilhelm II's enshrining of the Teutonic Knights' castle at Marienburg as a key site of German imperial-nationalist memory from 1902.[49] In Kraków, the church, city council, novelist Sienkiewicz, musician Ignacy Paderewski, and the Falcons youth movement organised commemorations on a massive scale. In July 1910, 150,000 people, including foreign journalists, attended three days of events – sporting/martial displays on Błonie field, a six-hour procession, and the unveiling of a new Grunwald monument near the city centre, at a ceremony complete with full orchestra, folk displays, singing, and speeches.[50] Poles from beyond Galicia participated: a woman from Bydgoszcz, in Prussian-ruled Poland, offered to bring tins of soil from the northern battlefield to the Kraków celebrations.[51] In 1910, Jogaila himself came, briefly if forcefully, to the very forefront of Polish historical memory – as a hero personifying the nation at the moment of its greatest military victory. Antoni Wiwaldski's Grunwald monument in Kraków took the form of a four metre high equestrian sculpture of the king.[52] Delegations laid wreaths the size of cartwheels decked with Polish flags at Jogaila's tomb in Kraków cathedral.[53] Kraków's leading cultural institutions organised a major exhibition on Jogaila and his times.[54] A one-hundred-page souvenir brochure (*księga pamięci*, literally 'book of memory') of the commemorations was dominated by images of Jogaila: his seal, tomb, bust, woodcuts.[55] It is less well known that the 1910 anniversary also held resonances well beyond Kraków, as across the Austrian-ruled province of Galicia small towns commissioned their own more modest busts or statues of Jogaila, mounted on columns or civic buildings, for example in Nowy Sącz, Mrzygłód, Przeworsk and Dynów.[56] These became enduring, charged sites of national memory in a local setting. These towns relate on their websites today the attempted destruction of the Jogaila statues by invading German forces in 1939 – claiming, from oral tradition, that locals smuggled bits of the king to safety in a cellar, or disguised his statue as that of a saint.[57] In 1910 therefore, after a century of partitions, Polish public, state-less memory thus briefly galvanised around Jogaila, not just as a soft-focus representative of a lost romantic past, but specifically as a leader of Polish anti-German armed struggle.

In all these ways, at the turn of the nineteenth century the now self-consciously national or nationalist Polish memory of the Jagiellonians merged the two main memory regimes of the early modern period – embracing the (genealogical) idea of Jagiellonians as a special, distinctive, named royal dynasty, while simultaneously taking from the *icones* tradition a sense of these people (as kings) as a powerful embodiment of Polish statehood.

With the recreation of a Polish state in the twentieth century (Second Republic, 1918–45; Polish People's Republic, 1945–89; Third Republic, 1989–), a new mode of Jagiellonian memory can be detected, a cipher for debating Poland's place within Central European geopolitics. An interwar golden age of Jagiellonian scholarship at Polish universities, led by figures such as Fryderyk Papeé (1856–1940), Ludwik Kolankowski (1882–1956) and Władysław Pociecha (1893–1958), took place in an atmosphere in which the Second Republic's relationship with its eastern neighbours was intensively debated in scholarship, politics and diplomacy.[58] The head of state Marshal Józef Piłsudzki, having annexed Vilnius and fought a major war against Boleshevik Russia, and facing a restive Ukrainian minority, argued for a union of Central European states led by Poland, looking to the Jagiellonian monarchs (who had yoked together so many peoples and states of the region) as his model.[59] The definitive formulation of this idea was expressed by the historian and diplomat Oskar Halecki in a hugely influential and controversial 1937 article entitled 'The Jagiellonian Idea'. Halecki argued that the Jagiellonians had realised Poland's true historical destiny – one of paternal, civilising, Catholic tutelage over its Lithuanian, Ukrainian and Belarusian neighbours. Newly independent Poland, he wrote, 'is seeking a new guiding idea, and intuitively turns to the old, yet eternally fresh Jagiellonian ideal'. Jagiellonians function here as code for de facto Polish hegemony in interwar Eastern Europe.[60]

If the Second Republic's leaders had invoked the Jagiellonians to look east, from 1948 the Communist regime instead used them to look west. In general, the Polish People's Republic and its Marxist ideology had limited use for Renaissance kings: the 1960 celebrations of the 150th anniversary of the Battle of Grunwald, for example, dispensed with Jogaila altogether, their speeches and statues instead presenting 1410 as a victory of the united Slav masses.[61] However, the Jagiellonians could be usefully pressed into the service of one key domestic and international message of the government: that the formerly German territories acquired by Poland in 1945 (Prussia, Pomerania, Silesia) were historically, authentically, and now permanently Polish. The Jagiellonians' fifteenth- and sixteenth-century rule, conquests, and presence in the Baltic littoral were emphasised in state-sponsored scholarship, and in concrete and sandstone.[62] In 1966, the city of Elbląg renamed its central square after King Casimir IV and placed a modernist statue of him outside the House of Culture, celebrating the 1466 treaty which had placed the town under Polish royal rule.[63] In 1974, a statue of Princess Anna Jagiellon (d.1503) was erected in Szczecin to assert Pomerania's historic links with the Polish Crown – Anna had been married to the duke of Pomerania.[64] Here, Jagiellonian memory could be deployed to legitimise the post-World War II redrawing of European borders.

In the twenty-first century, the Jagiellonians continue to haunt Polish foreign policy. A rhetoric, or shorthand, has developed to describe two competing visions of Poland's place in European geopolitics: a 'Piast' western-facing orientation, versus a 'Jagiellonian' stance projecting influence instead to the east.[65] Thus in 2009, the Minister of Foreign Affairs Radek Sikorski expressed support for the 'Jagiellonian idea', defining this as the promotion of stability and European culture among Poland's eastern neighbours, which could find new expression in Poland's support for further eastwards expansion of the European Union.[66] The political commentator Jakub Wojaś too concluded that 'if Poland succeeds in creating an eastern wing of the EU, it is possible that in the near future we will regain the international position enjoyed by Jagiellonian Poland'.[67] Here, the enlarged EU is in essence presented as the Jagiellonians' natural geopolitical successor. As Poland's domestic politics undergo intense polarisation in the 2010s, both explicitly and implicitly the Jagiellonians are again coming to the fore. The Polish Foreign Ministry-funded 'Jagiellonian Ideals' project (2017) frames toleration and peaceful co-existence with eastern partners as the dynasty's key legacy, in apparent echoes of Halecki. Meanwhile, President Andrzej Duda's 'Three Seas' diplomatic initiative (2017) advocates tighter cooperation among Central European states lying between the Baltic, Adriatic and Black Sea, in a move described by some commentators as a revival of Piłsudzki's vision of a Polish-led 'Jagiellonian' eastern federation.[68] In these strands of post-1918 political memory, the Jagiellonians have become a slogan for Polish debates over the role, nature and destiny of Central Europe itself in the modern world.

Alongside these official rhetorics, there exists a final category of Jagiellonian memory in post-1989 Poland, which we might term civic and commercial. Some memory theory suggests that fragmentation, pluralisation and growing heterogeneity of social memory is a characteristic of the digital age.[69] While not all historians agree, the growth of the internet and civil society in Poland since 1989 do enable us to observe local communities, and local consumers, in the act of remembering the Jagiellonians – in statues of the dynasty appearing across provincial Poland, in historical re-enactments and in heritage merchandise.[70] A wave of Jagiellonian statue-building, commissioned by local history societies or town councils, has swept Polish small towns since the 1990s. New monuments of Jogaila, for example, have sprung up in Leżajsk (1997), Jedlnia (2010), Niepołomice (2010), Legnica (commissioned 2012), with a further one planned in Nałęczów.[71] Statues of Casimir IV have been erected in Malbork (2010) and Chojnice (2012), and mooted in Gdańsk and Kuźnica (2009).[72] In 1993, a mounted bust of Sigismund I was erected in Kleszczele (population 1,300).[73] King Sigismund Augustus has been newly memorialised in Knyszyn (1997) and Augustów (2007), and his sister Anna in Kalisz (2014).[74] Most of these monuments seek to commemorate a specific link between the Jagiellonians and the town's own history: the bronze Jogaila in Jedlnia, for example, holds a reproduction of his 1387 founding charter for the town. Town websites present these statues as tourist attractions, and as a source of civic pride and identity – these royals thus acquiring a range of locality-specific meanings, in a devolution of national memory. The Polish historical re-enactments studied from an anthropological perspective by Małgorata Gałęziowska also reveal a sense of local ownership of the national past, with costumed participants even identifying with the Jagiellonians *against* politicians and elites. Jacek Szymański, who played King Jogaila at the 2010 Grunwald battle re-enactment, for example, complained to local media that the re-enactors suffered in the heat (in their commitment to the dignity of Polish history), while the Polish President and other officials in attendance ignored them, instead drinking coffee behind closed doors in the local museum.[75]

Since 1989, a certain commercialisation of Jagiellonian memory is detectable. Gałęziowska found that a large part of the Grunwald re-enactment site is given over to stalls selling medieval or Jogaila souvenirs, and this trend is reflected more broadly on the internet, where Jagiellonian-heritage merchandise abounds on Polish websites. One can purchase T-shirts emblazoned with Matejko's portrait of Jogaila, a 'Sigismund Augustus' strategy board game, or hand-decorated, costumed dolls of Jagiellonians, in porcelain, papier-mâché or plastic (e.g. as repurposed Mattel Barbie and Ken figures).[76] Since around 2000, there has been a boom in Jagiellonian-themed historical novels – while some are markedly experimental, such as Twardoch's fantasy time-travel novel *Eternal Grunwald*, most focus on royal love affairs and royal women as a form of relatively light entertainment.[77] Despite the apparent continuities of form with the nineteenth century (local monuments, ceremonies, historical fiction), the tenor of Jagiellonian memory in the twenty-first century is quite different. In tone, this civic-commercial memory might be said to cover a spectrum from outright trivialisation, through light entertainment, to relatively painless nostalgia. Gałęziowska, indeed, adds that even the Battle of Grunwald has become 'a rather neutral plane for remembering the past'.[78] Here the wider context of the current (and intensively studied) mnemonic landscape is crucial: the extreme traumas of World War II and Communist totalitarianism, and the unresolved memory wars raging around these, have displaced Jagiellonians well into the background of Polish cultural memory and identity discourse. Most local town statues erected since 1989, for example, commemorate twentieth-century atrocities or Pope John Paul II. The emotional and political power wielded by these royals in the Partition period has started to ebb away: the colours on Matejko's Jagiellonian canvases still glitter, but the sense of national tragedy they once conveyed so forcefully has dissipated, and migrated elsewhere.

Enduring motifs?

While the functions of Jagiellonian memory have shifted substantially over the centuries, it is also the case that many of the actual contents of this memory, its chief motifs, have stubbornly recurred. Erll has enjoined scholars to study 'travelling memory' as stories pass geographically through space, but segments of memory also travel persistently across time, vertically not horizontally.[79] We may touch on a few of those motifs here, the first of them being a Polish 'golden age' under these rulers. Golden Age rhetoric first emerged in the immediate aftermath of Sigismund Augustus's death (1572), as an early modern retrospective judgement on this ruling house. The late king's sister Sophie, dowager duchess of Brunswick-Lüneburg (d.1575), wrote to the Polish royal council in 1573 of the 'flowering age' seen 'over the past two hundred years, under the rule of the Jagiellonians'.[80] In 1585, a poem composed for the wedding of Princess Anna Jagiellon praised the royal line which had 'given Poland golden centuries'.[81] Jan Matejko's visual cycle of Polish history included the canvas *The Golden Age of Literature* (1888/9), with scholars disputing beneath portraits of Jagiellonian rulers.[82] Zygmunt and Maria Wojciechowski's 1946 history praised the Jagiellonians as 'a golden age of our past'.[83] The historian Aleksander Gieysztor introduced a 1987 Jagiellonian exhibition in Warsaw by invoking 'these golden centuries'.[84] This trope persists – in 2014, the *Economist* magazine featured on its cover Matejko's *Prussian Homage*, under the headline 'Poland's New Golden Age: The Second Jagiellonian Age'.[85] News stories in Poland have regularly claimed since 2013 that a major new costume drama on the Jagiellonians is soon to be filmed by HBO, entitled *Złoty Wiek*, 'The Golden Age'.[86] Here, we find one aspect of Jagiellonian rhetoric conspicuously recurring in Poland from the 1570s to the 2010s.

A second major motif in Jagiellonian memory which has likewise persisted since the early modern period is that of the *poczet królów polskich*, the portrait cycle of Polish kings. We have seen how this genre flourished in the early modern period: in printed *icones* from the 1560s, on the walls of Thorn town hall (1640s), in King Stanisław August's Marble Room (1769–71), and even outside major cities, for example in the *poczet* cycle commissioned by the Pauline monastery of Częstochowa in the eighteenth century.[87] Jan Matejko's own 1892 *Poczet Królów Polskich*, a series of forty-four drawings, has been hugely popular – painstakingly painted onto the walls of Mielec town hall in southeastern Poland in 1907–8, and the book itself reprinted at least twenty-six times in Poland, in the 1990s running to virtually a new edition every year.[88] This key mode of Jagiellonian memory also has appeal to contemporary artists: a set of wooden statues of Polish kings was carved in Szydłów castle in 2012, while a life-size waxwork figure of Jogaila has been made in Kraków, to initiate a *poczet* cycle on the Kościuszko mound outside the city (2010).[89] Indeed, the *poczet* is so well-established a trope in modern Polish culture, that in 1995 it inspired an album by the Polish rap group T-Raperzy z nad Wisłą, which included four comic-pedagogic tracks on the Jagiellonians.[90] This memory motif, connected to the legitimisation of monarchy, statehood and nationhood, has travelled effectively down the centuries as a powerful long-term transmitter, or container, of Jagiellonian memory.

To give a final example, the 1410 Battle of Grunwald is another major carrier of Jagiellonian memory. The basic narrative of the battle has for centuries derived primarily from the detailed Latin description given by the chronicler Jan Długosz (d.1480) in his *Annales Regni Poloniae*. The memory 'script' offered by Długosz's chronicle, written seventy years after the event, directly informed nineteenth-century historical novels and Matejko's paintings, and continues to underpin Grunwald re-enactments and children's story collections, which lavishly illustrate and re-tell Długosz's passages.[91] Grunwald, as the most celebrated battle in national history, has a complex mnemonic field of its own, but it overlaps directly with, and can serve to amplify, the memory of Jagiellonian kings. In Polish cultural memory, Jogaila himself has arguably become a signifier of Grunwald, rather than vice versa.

Historians are primed to examine change over time, contingency and context – how, then, are we to interpret the disconcertingly stubborn, long-term repetition of the same phrases, stories or iconography? Here, it can be useful to consider scholarship on fairy tales. Folklorists and literary theorists have stressed the one-dimensional, symbolic qualities of fairy-tale characters, as figures existing in some sense outside historic time. As Jo Eldridge Carney has pointed out, 'the fairy tale as a form consistently includes various motifs and discrete narrative units that are recycled and reassembled'. She points out that it is the repetition of known motifs which makes fairy tales predictable and legible to the reader/listener.[92] Max Lüthi's observation that 'the form of folk-tales does not derive from their content but has a life of its own' is one that scholars of memory might choose to ponder.[93] Long-term Jagiellonian memory in Poland might thus have acquired similarities with the narrative structure, or genre, of the fairy tale. Perhaps memory of the deep past, structurally, reconfigures itself over time as fairy tale – part morality tale, part fantasy. Indeed, the Polish children's book *A Treasury of Polish Fairy Tales and Legends* (2014) overtly does just that, presenting Jogaila at Grunwald as fairy story, alongside tales of mermaids, dragons and magical sub-aquatic cities.[94]

Conclusions

Like all memory, Polish cultural recollections of Jogaila-descended royalty over 500 years are built on certain persistent omissions: a glossing over of the problematic non-Polishness of these kings (the family being of Lithuanian-Ruthenian-Austrian-Italian descent), their status as regularly absentee rulers who spent extended periods in the Grand Duchy of Lithuania rather than the Polish polity, and their membership of a highly international network of royals which also ruled Bohemia and the enormous kingdom of Hungary, with kinship ties all over the Holy Roman Empire. A negation of and hostility towards extra-Polish dynasticism is, for example, a recurring feature of Polish national historiography of this royal line.[95] Polish traditions of Jagiellonian memory have thus been built, in the long term, on a denial of or deafness to the very different experiences and memories of this royal line in neighbouring societies in the ex-Jagiellonian region.

These gaps in memory merely point, however, to some more fundamental problems revealed by this story – dynasty as a very slippery container for memory (national or otherwise).[96] It is not just that the most successful Renaissance dynasties, with their composite states, cosmopolitanism and supra-national political frameworks, are awkward vehicles for national or single-monarchy memory.[97] Rather, the problem with investigating memory of 'the Jagiellonian dynasty' is that the idea of dynasty itself evolves, and is not a historic constant. In recent years, memory studies have become alert to the problems posed by 'nation' as a mnemonic category – because this word is itself a complex construct with its own dynamic history, accepting it as the 'natural' object or focus of collective memory is problematic.[98] Similar problems occur with 'dynasty'. The idea or phrase 'Jagiellonian dynasty' is not a historical given, or a historical constant, but a notion which evolved slowly over time. 'Dynasty' is not a word used in sixteenth-century Polish texts, for example. The actual nomenclature of 'Jagiellonians' itself only meaningfully entered Polish politics in the late sixteenth and seventeenth centuries, and it was only in the nineteenth century that 'Jagiellonian dynasty' became a dominant, self-evident phrase in Polish historical scholarship and wider cultural discourse.[99] There are thus risks in accepting 'Jagiellonian dynasty' as a natural subject/object of Polish memory and historical consciousness. We risk projecting the notion of a Jagiellonian dynasty backwards, looking for evocations and memories of it in periods when that idea per se might not yet have existed in the form in which we understand it, if at all. Some of what has been discussed in this essay, from the 1570s to the 2010s, was indeed conscious memory of a Jagiellonian royal house *per se*; but not all of it. The 'what' being remembered risks dissolving, the further back we look, if it is rooted in modern or at least retrospective concepts. What we call memory of the Jagiellonian dynasty in Poland is, from one point of view, a kaleidoscope of detachable fragments or narratives which might interact, join forces or split up at different moments: its constituent particles might include individual kings (e.g. Sigismund Augustus), the collective kings of Poland, a Jagiellonian family, the monarchy, the Polish nation, Wawel, the Battle of Grunwald, or the Polish Renaissance. So we have to take care that we do not falsely or anachronistically reify dynasty, any more than nation, in studying their long-term cultural representations. Benedict Anderson famously argued that nationalism is a work of the imagination; the same is true of dynasty, and its memory, in every century.[100]

Notes

1. M. Wojciechowska and Z. Wojciechowski, *Polska Piastów, Polska Jagiellonów*, Poznań, 1946, p. 467: 'Czasy zygmuntowskie są i pozostaną złotym okresem naszej przeszłości. Pierwsze kroki dziecka poznającego Polskę kierujemy do kaplicy Zygmuntowskiej i do arkad zamku wzniesionego na Wawelu przez Zygmunta. Przeżywamy niezapominane chwile radosnego zachwytu.'
2. By Poland in this essay, we will mean materials produced in the Polish language from the sixteenth century onwards, but also early modern Latin texts on the Jagiellonians composed within the lands of the Polish monarchy.

3 For the leading surveys of Polish Jagiellonian history, see A. Bues, *Die Jagiellonen: Herrscher zwischen Ostsee und Adriai*, Stuttgart, 2010; P. Jasienica, *Jagiellonian Poland*, trans. Alexander Jordan, Miami, 1978; and U. Borkowska, *Dynastia Jagiellonów w Polsce*, Warsaw, 2011.
4 The memory of Polish royal dynasties is little studied. For an exception, see M. Eiden, *Das Nachleben der schlesischen Piasten: dynastische Tradition und moderne Erinnerungskultur vom 17. bis 20. Jahrhundert*, Cologne, 2012.
5 For Polish memory of modern history, see for example U. Blacker, A. Etkind and J. Fedor, eds, *Memory and Theory in Central Europe*, New York, 2013; R. Traba and H. Henning Hahn, eds, *Polsko-niemieckie miejsca pamięci*, 5 vols, Warsaw, 2012–15; M. Pakier and J. Wawrzyniak, *Memory and Change in Europe: Eastern Perspectives*, New York, 2016.
6 J. Pollmann, plenary session lecture at 'Remembering the Reformation' conference, Cambridge, September 2017; see also J. Pollmann and E. Kuijpers, 'Introduction', in E. Kuijpers, J. Pollmann, J. Muller and J. Steen, eds, *Memory before Modernity: Practices of Memory in Early Modern Europe*, Leiden, 2013, p. 12.
7 G. Feindt, F. Krawatzek, D. Mehler, F. Pestel and R. Trimçev, 'Entangled Memory: Towards a Third Wave in Memory Studies', *History and Theory* 53, 2014, pp. 24–44; and Pestel et al., 'Promise and Challenge of European Memory', *European Review of History* 24, 4, 2017, pp. 495–506.
8 Pestel et al., 'Promise and Challenge of European Memory', p. 500.
9 For the satire, attributed to Bishop Stanisław Ciołek (d.1437), see A. Lewicki and A. Sokołowski, eds, *Codex epistolaris saeculi decimi quinti*, vol. I, Kraków, 1876, pp. 47–52; J. Długosz, *Annales seu cronicae incliti Regni Poloniae*, vols 10–12, Warsaw, 1985–2005; Maciej of Miechów, *Chronica Polonorum*, Kraków, 1519 and 1521.
10 Anonymous chronicle, published in A. Przeździecki, *Jagiellonki Polskie w XVI wieku*, Kraków, 1868, vol. III, appendix 12, pp. 361–92; M. Kosman, 'Zygmunt August w opinii współczesnych i potomnych', *Pamiętnik Biblioteki Kórnickiej* 19, 1982, pp. 19–76. On this king's reputation, see also Mickūnaitė in this volume, pp. 28–29.
11 For Jagiellonian rhetoric in sixteenth-century orations, see N. Nowakowska, I. Afanasyev, S. Kuzmová, G. Mickūnaitė, S. Niiranen and D. Zupka, *Dynasty in the Making: The Idea of the Jagiellonians, c.1385–1660* (forthcoming); J. Ludovicus Decius, *De Jagiellonum familia, De Sigismundi regis temporibus*, Kraków, 1521.
12 M. Gumowski, 'Trzy serie portretów Jagiellońskich', *Wiadomości Numizmatyczno-Archaeologiczne* XIX, 1937, pp. 41–66; J. Ruszczycówna, 'Nieznanie portrety ostatnich Jagiellonów', *Rocznik Muzeum Narodowego w Warszawe* 20, 1976, pp. 5–119.
13 On Vasa self-presentation, see J. Chrościcki, *Sztuka i polityka: funkcje propagandowe sztuki w epoce Wazów, 1587–1668*, Warsaw, 1983.
14 *Sigismundi III . . . Poloniae et Sueciae Regis . . . Cracoviam ingressus*, Kraków, 1587.
15 Ibid., fo. B.
16 Ibid., 'verum quod & dignae memoriae sint, & antiquitatis studiosis non iniucundum id futurum putemus, ipsas effigies ad vivum, quantum fieri potuit, expressas cum epigrammatibus suis subiicere visum fuit'.
17 For the principal study, see J. Lileyko, 'Władysławowski pokój marmurowy na zamku królewskim w Warszawie i jego twórcy', *Biuletyn Historii Sztuki* 37, 1, 1975, pp. 13–29.
18 Lileyko, 'Władysławowski pokój marmurowy', pp. 27–8.
19 M. Rożek, 'Źródła do fundacji i budowy królewskiej kaplicy Wazów przy katedrze na Wawelu', *Biuletyn Historii Sztuki* 25, 1, 1973, pp. 3–9.
20 Rożek, 'Źródła do fundacji', p. 7; and 'Uzupełnienie do fundacji królewskiej kaplicy Wazów', *Biuletyn Historii Sztuki* 36, 2, 1974, pp. 393–6.
21 See K. Janicki, *Vitae Regum Polonorum elegiaco carmine descriptae*, Kraków, 1565; T. Treter, *Regum Poloniae Icones*, Rome, 1591; J. Głuchowski, *Icones książąt y królów polskich*, Krakow, 1605; S. Neugebauer, *Icones et vitae principum ac regum Poloniae omnium*, Frankfurt, 1620; A. Obodziński, *Pandora starożytna monarchów polskich*, Kraków, 1640.

22 T. Chrzanowski, *Działalność artystyczna Tomasza Tretera*, Warsaw, 1984.
23 Głuchowski, *Icones*.
24 J. Flik, *Poczet królów polskich w zbiorach Muzeum Okręgowego w Toruniu*, Toruń, 2nd edn, 2000.
25 See A. Chyczewska, *Marcello Bacciarelli, 1731–1818*, Wrocław, 1973, pp. 63–6; J. Lileyko, *Zamek Królewski w Warszawie*, Warsaw, 3rd edn, 1986, pp. 204–5.
26 Chyczewska, *Marcello Bacciarelli*, p. 63.
27 Ibid., p. 64. King Stanisław August also had Bacciarelli's *icones* reproduced as medals: M. Męclewska, 'Prawda i legenda o medalierskiej serii królów Polskich z czasów Stanisława Augusta', 2004, conference paper published online, http://mazowsze.hist.pl/files/Kronika_Zamkowa/PDF_bez_tytulowych/Kronika_Zamkowar2005-t1_2_(49_50)/Kronika_Zamkowa-r2005-t1_2_(49_50)-s29-43/Kronika_Zamkowa-r2005t1_2_(49_50)-s29-43.pdf, accessed 12.10.14.
28 For a history of Polish nationalism in this period, see B. Porter, *When Nationalism Began to Hate: Imagining Modern Politics in Nineteenth Century Poland*, New York, 2000.
29 See M. Baár, *Historians and Nationalism: East Central Europe in the Nineteenth Century*, Oxford, 2010; and J. Maternicki, 'Miejsce i rola "Kwartalnika Historycznego" w dziejach historiografii polskiej', *Kwartalnik Historyczny* 95, 1, 1988, pp. 3–20.
30 For example, M. Bobrzyński, *O ustawodawstwie nieszawskim Kazimierza Jagiellończyka*, Kraków, 1873; Antoni Prochaska, *Król Władysław Jagiełło*, 2 vols (Kraków, 1908); *Acta Tomiciana*, Poznań, 1852–.
31 J. Lelewel, *Polska: dzieje i rzeczy jej*, 20 vols, Poznań, 1858–86. The publication history of this work is complicated, and its dates of printing are interpreted variously by scholars.
32 See Piotr Biliński and Paweł Plichta, eds, *Krakowska szkoła historyczna a Polskie Towarzystwo Historyczne*, Kraków, 2017.
33 M. Bobrzyński, *Dzieje Polski w zarysie*, Warsaw, 1879; X. Liske, *Studia z dziejów wieku XVI*, Poznań, 1867. For these debates in Polish nineteenth-century scholarship, see N. Nowakowska, 'Jagiellonians and Habsburgs: The Polish Historiography of Emperor Charles V', in S. C. Dixon and M. Fuchs, eds, *The Histories of Emperor Charles V*, Aschendorff, 2005, pp. 249–73.
34 J. Krawyczyk, *Matejko i historia*, Warsaw, 1990; for Matejko in the context of Polish nineteenth-century art and its world, see A. Ryszkiewicz, *Malarstwo Polskie: romantyzm, historyzm, realism*, Warsaw, 1989.
35 Ryszkiewicz, *Malarstwo*, p. 22.
36 After the 1856 debut, these works were: *Zygumunt I Conferring Nobility on the Professors of the Jagiellonian University* (1858); *The Poisoning of Queen Bona* (1859); *The Jester at a Ball at the Court of Queen Bona* (1862); *Sigismund Augustus and Barbara Radziwiłł at the Court of Vilnius* (1867); *The Union of Lublin* (1869); *The Raising of King Zygmunt's Bell* (1874); *The Battle of Grunwald* (1878); *The Battle of Varna* (1879); *The Prussian Homage* (1882); *The Death of Sigismund Augustus* (1886); *The Baptism of Lithuania* (1888); *The Founding of the Jagiellonian University* (1889); *Dmitr of Goraj and Queen Jadwiga* (date unclear).
37 For example, Józef Simmler, *The Death of Barbara Radziwiłł* (1860); Wojciech Gersson, *The Ghost of Barbara Radziwiłł* (1886) and *Sigismund Augustus as Widower* (1886). Henryk Rodakowski (d.1894) and Leon Wyczółkowski (d.1936) also painted one Jagiellonian subject each. For memories of Barbara in Lithuanian tradition, see Mickūnaitė in this volume.
38 Ryszkiewicz, *Malarstwo*, pp. 39, 51–2.
39 Józef Kraszewski, *Matka Królów* (Warsaw, 1883), *Dwie Królowe* (Warsaw, 1884) and *Infantka* (1884); Lucjan Rydel, *Zygmunt August* (Kraków, 1913); Stanisław Wyspiański, *Zygmunt August* (Warsaw, 1930); Henryk Sienkiewicz, *Krzyżacy* (Gdańsk, 1900).
40 H. Sienkiewicz, 'O Powieści Historycznej', *Słowo*, 1889, nr. 98–101, re-published at http://hamlet.edu.pl/sienkiewicz-opowiesci, accessed 20.9.17, 'objaśnienie i dopełnienie'.

41 Przeździecki, *Jagiellonki Polskie*.
42 For this period in Wawel's history, see the special edition of *Waweliana*, III, 1994.
43 See H. Górska, 'Restauracja katedry na Wawelu przez Sławomira Odrzywolskiego na przełomie XIX i XX wieku', *Waweliana* III, 1994, pp. 123–41; and A. Petrus, 'Fundusz centowy Aleksandry z Borkowskich Ulanowskiej na odnowienie Zamku Królewskiego na Wawelu (1894–1939)', *Waweliana* III, 1994, pp. 109–22.
44 Petrus, 'Fundusz centowy', pp. 109–22.
45 Although the tombs of earlier (Piast) kings were less numerous, it was the discovery of the tomb of Casimir the Great (d.1370) in 1869 which had arguably triggered the cathedral restoration movement; see P. Dabrowski, *Commemorations and the Shaping of Modern Poland*, Bloomington, IN, 2004, pp. 1–2.
46 A. Sołtys, 'Pomniki Antoniego Madeyskiego na tle problemu restauracji katedry krakowskiej', *Studia Waweliana* III, 1994, pp. 157–67.
47 See M. Piszczatowska, 'Pochód na Wawel', *Spotkania z Zabytkami* 8, 2008, pp. 38–9, 'Przyszłe pokolenia dzieci swoje uczyć będą historii naszej w mrokach Katedry, u stop *Pochodu*.'
48 W. Bałuś, 'Wawel dziewiętnastowieczny: poziomy interpretacji', *Waweliana* III, 1994, pp. 11–18.
49 Dabrowski, *Commemorations*, pp. 161–2.
50 For studies of the 1910 commemorations, see D. Radziwiłłowicz, *Tradycja grunwaldska w świadomości politycznej społeczeństwa polskiego w latach 1910–1945*, Olsztyn, 2003; Dabrowska, *Commemorations*, pp. 163–83; and M. Gałęziowska, 'Świętowanie wybranych rocznic bitwy pod Grunwaldem formą komunikacji rytualnej państwa i narodu', *Kultura i Społeczeństwo* 4, 2012, pp. 83–108.
51 Radziwiłłowicz, *Tradcyja grunwaldska*, p. 45.
52 For the monument, see Dabrowski, *Commemorations*, pp. 165–70
53 K. Bartoszewicz, *Księga pamiątkowa obchodu pięćsetnej rocznicy zwycięstwa pod Grunwaldem*, Kraków, 1911, plate 28.
54 Radziwiłłowicz, *Tradycja grunwaldska*, pp. 47–8. Some 130 objects were displayed.
55 Bartoszewicz, *Księga pamiątkowa*.
56 These are featured on civic websites: www.nowysacz.pl/pomniki-sdeckie; https://pl.wikipedia.org/wiki/Pomnik_kr%C3%B3la_W%C5%82adys%C5%82awa_Jagie%C5%82%C5%82y_w_Przeworsku; https://pl.wikipedia.org/wiki/Pomnik_W%C5%82adys%C5%82awa_Jagie%C5%82%C5%82y_w_Mrzyg%C5%82odzie; http://dynow.fotopolska.eu/Dynow/b4353,Pomnik_krola_Wladyslawa_II_Jagielly.html, accessed 15.11.16.
57 See local history accounts for Dynów and Mrzygłód, where the 'rescuers' are all carefully named: http://mariten.blog.onet.pl/2010/06/16/pomniki-grunwaldu-w-rzeszowie-i-okolicach-cz-5-dynow-blazowa-hermanowa-strazow-palikowka/, accessed 10.15; and http://pl.wikipedia.org/wiki/Pomnik_W%C5%82adys%C5%82awa_Jagie%C5%82%C5%82y_w_Mrzyg%C5%82odzie, accessed 27.9.17.
58 To cite just a very few examples: F. Papeé, *Jan Olbracht*, Kraków, 1936, and *Aleksander Jagiellończyk*, Kraków, 1949; W. Pociecha, *Geneza hołdu pruskiego, 1467–1525*, Gdynia, 1937; L. Kolankowski, *Polska Jagiellonów: dzieje polityczne*, Lwów, 1936; see also B. Stachoń, *Polityka polska wobec Turcji i akcji anty-tureckiej w wieku XV do utraty Kilii i Bialogrodu, 1484*, Lwów, 1930.
59 See P. Wandycz, 'Poland's Place in Europe in the Concepts of Piłsudski and Dmowski', *East European Politics and Societies* 4, 3, 1990, pp. 451–68.
60 O. Halecki, 'Idea Jagiellońska', *Kwartalnik Historyczny* 51, 1937, pp. 486–510, at p. 510: 'ogląda się za nową ideą przewodnią i intuicyjnie zwraca się w tym celu ku dawnej, lecz zawsze świeżej idei jagiellońskiej'.
61 For the 1960 monument and depicted faces of anonymous Slav soldiers, see I. Grzesiuk-Olszewska, *Polska rzeźba pomnikowa w latach 1945–1995*, Warsaw, 1995, pp. 219–21; for the ceremonies, Gałęziowska, 'Świętowanie wybranych rocznic', pp. 89–93.

62 See for example H. Zins, *Ród Ferberów i jego rola w dziejach Gdańska w XV i XVI wieku*, Lublin, 1951; G. Labuda, *Szkice z dziejów Pomorza*, vol. I, Warsaw, 1958.
63 www.polskaniezwykla.pl/web/place/30785,elblag-plac-kazimierza-jagiellonczyka. html, accessed 20.11.17.
64 See official article on Szczecin city webpages, www.szczecin.pl/chapter_59232.asp?soid=5074F05E915C46CCA57B66C998F77328 accessed 20.11.17.
65 R. Ślązak, 'Polityka piastowska, czy jagiellońska', *3obieg.pl*, November 2013, http://3obieg.pl/polityka-piastowska-czy-jagiellonska, accessed 23.11.16; see also A. Górski, 'Idea jagiellońska', *Niezależna* website, December 2013, http://niezalezna.pl/49037-idea-jagiellonska.
66 Discussed in M. Przydacz, 'Polityka zagraniczna wobec Białorusi', in Paweł Musiałka, ed., *Główne kierunki polityki zagranicznej rządu Donalda Tuska w latach 2007–11*, Kraków, 2012, pp. 279–94, at p. 282.
67 J. Wojas, 'Idea jagiellońska w XXI wieku', *Portal Spraw Zagranicznych*, June 2009, www.psz.pl/122-opinie/idea-jagiellonska-w-xxi-wieku, accessed 23.11.16: 'Jeżeli Polsce na stałe uda się tworzyć wschodni wymiar UE to być może w najbliższym czasie odzyskamy pozycję jaką miała na arenie międzynarodowej Polska Jagiellonów.'
68 For media discussion of 'Three Seas', see Marcin Kuśmierczyk, 'Trójmorze: czym jest koncepcja forsowana przez Prezydenta Andrzeja Dubę?', Onet news website, 4 July 2017, http://wiadomosci.onet.pl/kraj/trojmorze-czym-jest-koncepcja-forsowana-przez-prezydenta-andrzeja-dude/7mmjm4f, accessed 9.17; and Anon., 'Czesi popsują plany PiS na Trójmorze? Nie chcą być częścią anyniemieckiego paktu', *Newsweek Polska*, 19 June 2017, www.newsweek.pl/swiat/polityka/trojmorze-pomysl-polskiego-rzadu-na-antyniemiecka-koalicje-w-ue,artykuly,412012,1.html, accessed 9.17.
69 See Kuijpers et al., *Memory before Modernity*; and discussion of this point by Kuzmová in this volume, p. 72.
70 J. Pollmann, *Memory in Early Modern Europe, 1500–1800*, Oxford, 2017.
71 Niepołomice, www.metalodlew.pl/ogloszenia/aktualnosci/aktualnosc/pomnik_krola_wladyslawa_jagielly_na_600_lecie, accessed 21.11.16; Leżajsk, http://aordycz-lezajsk.blogspot.co.uk/2012/05/pomnik-wadysawa-jagiey.html, accessed 21.11.16; Legnica, http://fakty.lca.pl/legnica,news,53376,Na_Tarninowie_stoi_pomnik_krola_Jagielly_.html, accessed 21.11.16, Nałęczów, http://naleczow.net/galeria-sztuki/marian-pudelko/853-jagiello-popiersie-marian-pudelko.html, accessed 21.11.16.
72 Malbork, http://malbork.naszemiasto.pl/artykul/zdjecia/malbork-pomnik-krola-kazimierza-jagiellonczyka-juz-stoi,594122,gal,582698,t,id,tm,zid.html, accessed 27.9.17; Chojnice, http://czas.tygodnik.pl/a/rzezby-w-parku-tysiaclecia-juz-stoja, accessed 5.10.15, in the Park Tysiąclecia; Gdańsk proposal, www.mmtrojmiasto.pl/257305/o-jagiellonczyku-i-jego-pomniku, accessed 21.11.16; Kuznica statue design competition, www.kuznica.org.pl/index.php?option=com_content&view=article&id=79:jagiellonczyk&catid=1:latest-news&Itemid=50, accessed 1.10.14.
73 www.polskaniezwykla.pl/web/place/gallery,1,24172.html, accessed 22.11.16.
74 Knyszyn, www.ciekawepodlasie.pl/info.htm#52/pl/i/pomnik_krola_zygmunta_augusta; Augustów, http://augustow.fotopolska.eu/Augustow/b79379,Pomnik_krola_Zygmunta_II_Augusta.html; Kalisz, www.kopernik.kalisz.pl/index.php/wizualizacja-pomnika-anny-jagiellonki, all accessed 21.11.16.
75 Gałęziowska, 'Świętowanie wybranych rocznic', p. 98.
76 T-shirts, http://koszulki-historyczne.spreadshirt.pl/wladyslaw-jagiello-czern-D1I10837 933, accessed 22.11.16; boardgame, http://przystanekplanszowka.pl/2013/07/sigis mundus-augustus-wyrok.html, accessed 22.11.16; dolls, www.polartcenter.com/King_Zygmunt_II_August_1520_1572_p/9190007.htm; http://galeria-barbie.blogspot.co.uk/2011/07/kolekcja-historyczna.html, accessed 22.11.16. For heritage merchandise at Grunwald re-enactments, see Gałęziowska, 'Świętowanie wybranych rocznic', pp. 95–6.
77 A. Sapkowski, *Narrenturm*, Warsaw, 2002, *Boży bojownicy*, Warsaw, 2004, and *Lux Perpetua*, Warsaw, 2007; and S. Twardoch, *Wieczny Grunwald*, Warsaw, 2010; R. Czarnecka, *Signora Fiorella: kapeluszniczka królowej Bony*, Kraków, 2010, and

Barbara i król, Poznań, 2013; Z. Gołaszewski, *Aleksander i piękna Helena*, Warsaw, 2014; A. Zerling-Konopka, *Izabela Jagiellonka: Los tak chciał*, Warsaw, 2015.
78 Gałęziowska, 'Świętowanie wybranych rocznic', p. 105: 'Obchody grunwaldzkie są dość neutralną płaszczyzną świętowania przeszłości.'
79 A. Erll, 'Travelling Memory', *Parallax* 17, 4, 2011, pp. 4–18; Feindt et al., 'Entangled Memory'; Pestel et al., 'Promise and Challenge of European Memory'.
80 Przeździecki, *Jagiellonki Polskie*, vol. IV, p. 23: 'I któż nie doczyta się tego, co się działo przed dwiema sty lat, co przez ten czas wszystek rządu a sprawy Jagiełłów? Co za kwitnący wiek oni z sobą wnieśli . . .'
81 Anon., *Pieśni nowe o królu polskim Stefanie Pierwszym . . . wespółek y o Krolewnie Annie*, ?Kraków, 1576, fo. Aiv: 'Plemia Zygmunta onego świategoo . . . któregoś dał Polszcze złote wieki'.
82 Sigismund I, Sigismund Augustus and Anna Jagiellon are all depicted. See E. Suchodolska and M. Wredet, *Jana Matejki dzieje cywilizacji w Polsce*, Warsaw, 1998.
83 Wojciechowska and Wojciechowski, *Polska Piastów*, p. 467. Henryk Łowmiański's *Polityka Jagiellonów*, ed. Krzysztof Pietkiewicz, Poznań, 1999, composed between 1942 and 1948, also conveyed the sense of a cultural, political and economic Polish golden age: 'The name of the Jagiellonian dynasty invokes the former greatness of Poland'; 'Z nazwą dynastii jagiellońskiej kojarzy się pojęcie dawnej świetności Polski, potęgi politycznej i tężyzny narodowej, pomyślności gospodarczej i rozkwitu kulturalnego . . .' (p. 1).
84 A. Gieysztor, 'Przedmowa', in *Polska Jagiellonów, 1386–1572*, Warsaw, 1987, p. 9: 'tych złotych stuleci'.
85 V. von Bredow, 'Poland's New Golden Age: The Second Jagiellonian Age', *The Economist*, June 2014.
86 http://superseriale.se.pl/newsy/zloty-wiek-nowy-serial-o-jagiellonach-w-tvp-zastapi-klan_786752.html, accessed 1.12.16.
87 K. Szczekocka-Mysłek, *Jasnogórski poczet królów i książąt polskich*, Warsaw, 1990.
88 I. Sapetowa, *Malarski poczet królów i książąt polskich według rysunków Jana Matejki w sali obrad Rady Powietowej w Mielcu*, Warsaw, 1992; J. Matejko, *Poczet królów i książąt polskich*, with text by Stanisław Smolka and August Sokołowski, Vienna, 1893, and reprinted in at least twenty-six editions: e.g. Warsaw, Alfa (1957); Kraków, Wydawictwo Artystyczno-Graficzne (1958, 1960, 1961, 1967, 1969, 1971); Warsaw, Wspólna Sprawa (1960); Warsaw, Czytelnik (1978, 1980, 1987, 1991, 1993, 1996, 1998); Warsaw, Krajowa Agencja Wydawnicza (1980); Warsaw, Wydawnictwo Radio i Telewizji (1988); Kraków, Oficyna Parol (1993, 1994); Warsaw, Świat Książki (1996, 2011); Warsaw, Interpress (1996); Warsaw, Diogenes (2000); Warsaw, Świat Książki (2003); Katowice, Media Partner (2003).
89 www.polskaniezwykla.pl/web/place/28964,szydlow-poczet-krolow-polskich.html, accessed 20.9.17; and http://krakow.naszemiasto.pl/artykul/krakow-wladcy-z-silikonu-stana-na-kopcu-kosciuszki,468472,art,t,id,tm.html, accessed 2.12.16.
90 www.discogs.com/T-Raperzy-znad-Wis%C5%82y-Poczet-Kr%C3%B3l%C3%B3w-Polskich/release/1450898, accessed 2.12.16.
91 Długosz, *Annales*; Gałęziowska, 'Świętowanie wybranych rocznic'; Marta Berowska, 'Dwa krzyżackie miecze', in Marta Berowska and Magdalena Grądzka, *Skarbiec Baśni i Legend Polskich*, Warsaw, 2014, pp. 21–5.
92 J. Eldridge Carney, *Fairy Tale Queens: Representations of Early Modern Queenship*, New York, 2012, pp. 2, 5, drawing on the work of M. Lüthi, *The European Folk Tale: Form and Nature*, trans. John D. Miles, Bloomington, IN, 1986.
93 Lüthi, *The European Folk Tale*, p. 3.
94 Berowska and Grądzka, *Skarbiec*.
95 See for example K. Baczkowski, *Zjazd wiedeński 1515: geneze, przebieg i znaczenie*, Warsaw, 1975, pp. 5–6; Gieysztor, 'Przedmowa'; Łowmiański, *Polityka*, p. 460; A. Sucheni-Grabowska, 'Jagiellonowie i Habsburgowie w pierwszej połowie XVI w.', *Sobótka* 4, 1983, pp. 449–67, at pp. 449–50.

96 An issue addressed in this volume also in the essays on Bohemia and Hungary.
97 See also the Introduction, above, p. 20.
98 See Introduction, above, pp. 2–3.
99 See Nowakowska et al., *Dynasty in the Making*.
100 B. Anderson, *Imagined Communities: Reflections on the Origins and Spread of Nationalism*, London, 1983.

3

THE MEMORY OF THE JAGIELLONIANS IN THE KINGDOM OF HUNGARY, AND IN HUNGARIAN AND SLOVAK NATIONAL NARRATIVES

Stanislava Kuzmová

While rulers from the lineage of Jogaila, i.e. Jagiellonian dynasty, ruled Poland for almost 200 years, they were sovereigns of the neighbouring Kingdom of Hungary for a relatively short period of time. Several decades after the brief episode of Wladislaus III of Poland (and Wladislaus I of Hungary), a counter-king who died at the Battle of Varna fighting the Turks (1440–44), Wladislaus II gained the crown in 1490, succeeded by his son Louis II, who died in another battle against the Turks at Mohács in 1526. These thirty-six years in the history of the country came to be known in historiography as the 'Jagiellonian period'. As an epilogue to this era, women from the same family, Anna and Isabella, were married to the two competing rulers of the divided Hungary after the disaster of Mohács.

Ever since 1526, the defeat of Mohács has served as the prism through which the Jagiellonian rule has been perceived and judged. The lost battle and its aftermath changed the situation in Central Europe: it meant the beginning of the dominance of the Habsburgs, seen by some as the loss of Hungarian independence, and the constant presence of the Ottomans. From this perspective, those years could only be seen as decline and failure (and the rulers weak and incompetent). Contemporaries already transmitted this image of the Jagiellonian period, contrasting it with the 'golden age' of Matthias Corvinus, king of Hungary from 1458 to 1490. Historians often got caught in this trap. Over 500 years the Hungarian Jagiellonians occupied the 'in-between', a transitory space within the greater narrative, uncomfortably squeezed in between golden age and disaster. This study tries to investigate the place of the Jagiellonians – what is remembered about them – in the historical and cultural memory related to the Kingdom of Hungary and its successor states, especially as it developed and fed into Hungarian/Magyar and Slovak national (and linguistic) historical narratives and discourses of collective memory.[1]

Investigating regional memory of a phenomenon like the Jagiellonians through the questioning of individual sets of collective memories and traditions of polities and nations is not an easy task. Establishing a unit, i.e. a group bearing the collective memory and traditions, is itself a problematic issue. The changing borders and fluidity of political units in the given region, 'Central Europe', do not make the task easier. If we take as a basis the historical Kingdom of Hungary, which was ruled by the Jagiellonian rulers for some period in the fifteenth and sixteenth centuries, we need to deal with several fluid and intertwined sets of collective memories, most noticeably in the framework of national narratives.[2] We want to look at how the past – the Jagiellonian kings in the Kingdom of Hungary and their rule – was understood and interpreted, and also at how the past relates to the present (memory). Who were the bearers of the memory, or who 'owned' the history? In this region, history became a professional scientific discipline and an institutionalised craft in tandem with the rise of national awareness and in many cases the establishment of nation-states. The particular structure within which history was and has mostly been understood and interpreted was the framework of a particular nation, a structure which was then also projected onto the past.[3] In the case of our subject of study, the rulers of the kingdom, the national framework is dominant and almost omnipresent.[4] Historiography is only one of the means of remembering and re-constructing the past. Various other practices and media of memory, not limited to professionals of the craft, have been employed and have been in constant dialogue with historiography. This study aims to show their interplay.

'Macro-historical narratives of memory' usually present, in a somewhat simplified way, an evolution of memory and memory practices towards hegemonic nationalist memory cultures of the nineteenth and early twentieth centuries.[5] The state played an important role in the process of change in memory practices, the management of the past (memory politics), and new forms of historical consciousness. Studies of memory politics have dealt mostly with the thriving and dynamic period around 1800 – when national traditions were being invented – the time of huge historical paintings, monuments and museums, days of commemoration and state history curricula, new mass media (stamps, schoolbooks, street names, etc.). All these media, and also many non-state actors, groups demanding a place in the public domain, were involved in memory politics well before the advent of nationalism, at various levels of society (from princes and churches to village communities), because of their claims to rights, authority, and legitimacy.[6] Despite this, there are examples of '"national" memory cultures emerging, with or without central state intervention', from the early modern period onwards,[7] and the Hungarian, Hungarian/Magyar and Slovak are among them (and start to differentiate from each other).

The image of Jagiellonians over time is rather static overall. All in all, they are mostly presented as weak kings, without the authority or ability to decide upon crucial issues, but rather the subjects or victims of others, be it bad advisors, powerful lords, or circumstances. The roots of the main trends and schematic images associated with Jagiellonians in Hungary (on which the national narratives also draw) lie in the sixteenth century. The main set of ingredients, the reservoir of motifs and information, the content, were already assembled then; these were later reshaped, seasoned, and processed in various ways. These earliest works were also important in forming the tradition concerning the rulers and main events and became a source not only for historians, but also for writers and painters.

The emblematic image of King Wladislaus II (1490–1516) is that of a weak and poor king – *Dobzse László*, omnipresent in popular knowledge – nodding and saying yes, 'dobře' (in Bohemian), or 'dobzse' (in Hungarian),[8] to any question or request. The tradition is an old one, dating from the sixteenth-century Bohemian chronicler Jan Dubravius (1552), who also mentions how the king had to beg for wine for dinner as the royal cellars were empty.[9] Thanks to the episodes involving Wladislaus's appreciation for Hungarian cuisine and his need to beg for food, Hungarian popular culture sometimes associates the term 'lacikonyha', which means an open-air kitchen, or cheap street- or market-food from a stand, with Wladislaus, although it probably has nothing to do with him.[10] The sharp contrast between the reign of Matthias Corvinus and Jagiellonian rule is a commonplace among historians dating back to Wladislaus's contemporaries (the reports of ambassadors, speeches at the diets, and especially the sixteenth-century, post-Mohács popular tradition of the 'good king Matthias'). The Jagiellonian kings did not have their own historians to glorify their deeds and create a memory about them: Antonio Bonfini (d.1503), the court historian of Matthias Corvinus (d.1490), actually continued under Wladislaus II Jagiellon, but his writings present a nostalgia for the reign of Matthias and when he fell ill and later died, no royal historian succeeded the famous Italian humanist at the Jagiellonian court.[11]

Louis II (r.1516–26) is, meanwhile, remembered as a young, partially irresponsible king, controlled by his advisors and wife, but above all as dying at Mohács. The memories of the eyewitnesses and participants of the events leading to the Battle of Mohács and its aftermath are also inevitably biased, as their authors had their own subjective view of the events and their own agendas in mind. Of the most influential ones, the account of the Battle of Mohács by Stephen Brodarics, dedicated to the Polish king Sigismund I, is an apology for Louis (and the Hungarians) – here, he is a courageous, even virtuous, martyr and hero who dies for his country.[12] Another source, the memoirs of Georgius Sirmiensis/Szerémi (on the period 1456–1543), full of rumours and frustration, presents a rather negative picture of the period; he is not so impressed by Louis, an ignorant and frivolous young man.[13] Another piece of recurrent information, or rather a legend, mentioned by Szerémi among others, originated soon after the battle: allegedly, King Louis did not die while escaping from the battle, but was killed by Hungarian noblemen.[14]

Following the division of the Hungarian kingdom after Mohács, different traditions formed in two rival political centres, when Ferdinand I of Austria (1503–64) and John Szapolyai (c.1487–1540), both crowned as kings of Hungary, initially fought for the throne: the royal Hungary in the west (first supporters of Ferdinand and the House of Austria on the throne), and Transylvania, which formed a semi-independent Protestant principality in the east (first supporters of so-called national king, John Szapolyai). Their historiographical traditions, 'regional narratives' (related to their confessional, political and cultural expectations), as well as their perception of Mohács (and the figure of Louis), differed.[15] The positive memory of Louis as a hero, based on Brodarics, was cherished especially by the official circles of royal Hungary ruled by the Habsburgs with its centre in Vienna (this is the historiographical tradition of widely-disseminated royal historian Istvánffy),[16] and by proponents of the anti-Turkish campaign.[17] Compared to the conscious efforts of the Vasas to follow and use the preceding dynasty, the Habsburgs do not seem for the most part to have used similar imagery. This is no doubt due partially to the fact that the Jagiellonians had not ruled for such a long and continuous time in the kingdoms of Bohemia and Hungary, as they had in Poland and the Grand Duchy of Lithuania. The Habsburgs had their own traditions to follow. The succession was also officially due to election by the estates and not inheritance from relatives or on the basis of the succession agreements with the Jagiellonians.

The immensely popular chronicle of Gaspar Heltai (in Hungarian, based on Bonfini) contributed to the negative tradition, especially in the Transylvanian and Protestant context.[18] Both the defeat at Mohács and the gaining of the Hungarian crown by the Habsburgs, associated with the Jagiellonians through marriages and succession agreements, were seen by a part of the Hungarian 'nationalist' elites as the loss of independence (although the kingdom still maintained its internal sovereignty and its elites participated in central administration), and influenced perspectives on Jagiellonian rule to a great extent. The 'national' rhetoric was used in propaganda as early as the sixteenth century, for example at the Rákos diet in 1505 and in the camp of John Szapolyai after Mohács. This tradition, however, gained force when the past was viewed through the prism of feudal uprisings: movements of the seventeenth and early eighteenth centuries agitating for rearrangements between the kingdom and the monarchy, and between the Hungarian political elite and the Habsburg court.[19]

Beginnings of positivist historiography, the Enlightenment and public memory

In the second half of the eighteenth century, history-writing moved towards a more critical, source-based approach, which the new scholarship on the Jagiellonians reflected. Jesuit historians collected sources and wrote political histories of the kingdom.[20] With a rising awareness of national and linguistic identities, this new historiography contributed to the formation of historical consciousness and modern collective identities.[21] The 'encyclopaedic' historians, especially Stephanus Katona (1732–1811) and Georgius Pray (1723–1801), started to use names for dynasties as successions of rulers in order to periodise the history of the realm. The era of the so-called 'national' Arpadian dynasty was followed by 'the period of kings from foreign houses' or 'mixed', including the Angevins, the Jagiellonians, and others, before the Habsburgs acquired the throne.[22] Katona's detailed *Historia critica* lists Wladislaus II as the thirty-fifth king of Hungary: Lithuanian by origin, Polish by nationality, Bohemian by title.[23] The value of the *Historia* lay especially in the fact that all events were supplied with references and extensive quotations from sources, rather than in some further analysis or narrative. While the histories were largely written in Latin, the rising awareness of national identity, related also to language, played a role in the differing perceptions of some historical figures and events. Slovak/Slavic intellectuals within the Hungarian kingdom insisted on the Slavic share in the country's history.[24] The Jagiellonians Wladislaus I and Wladislaus II were counted among the 'Slavic kings', and the use of Slavic language by individual kings was also emphasised.[25]

When we look beyond historiography, whilst Jagiellonians were extolled in the dramas written and staged at Jesuit (and Piarist) schools in Poland and Lithuania, they did not have such an important place in Hungary: among the heroes of the moralising and didactic plays were St Ladislaus and Emeric, Matthias Corvinus, and his father John Hunyadi (with King Wladislaus I in a supporting role only). Some plays about the Battle of Mohács, in which Louis II could serve as a moral patriotic example, were performed (their printed programmes indicate that these were mostly based on Brodarics's account of the battle).[26]

Thanks to the reach and scale of new memory media, the historical narrative reached the broad public. State-controlled public education, including history, was introduced to schools at the end of the eighteenth century (*Ratio educationis*).[27] In a multi-ethnic and multilingual empire, its aim was to strengthen centralisation, but in some cases it could conflict with the efforts of national awakening movements. A multi-edition compendium of the history of the Reformed Church for Hungarian and Transylvanian village schools in the Hungarian language, *Hármas Kis Tükör* (*Small Triple Mirror*) by István Mányoki Losontzi, contains the basic information and strengthens the stereotypes about the Jagiellonians: Wladislaus II is king 'dobzse', and, as a pious man, his ascension to the throne is commented upon with the proverb 'King Matthias died, justice is gone'; the celebrated Tripartitum law collection (1514) after the peasant uprising is mentioned, and an account of fights against the Turks is given, with Louis II, 'premature' in everything, dying in Csele stream and buried in Székesfehérvár. Isabella and her son John Sigismund are mentioned in an overview of Transylvanian history.[28]

In another didactic piece, a fictive dialogue of Hungarian kings in the land of the dead, authored by Ladislaus Bartolomeides (a Protestant parish priest, born and active in present-day Slovakia) and published in 1799 in memory of the late Joseph II, Wladislaus II joins King Matthias and other Hungarian kings (St Stephen, Louis the Great), who welcome the emperor to the other world.[29] The following debate among the great kings playfully teaches pupils and includes numerous well-known motifs concerning Wladislaus: he was a crowned king and had his son Louis crowned as a child too; Wladislaus understands Slovaks (to whom the piece is addressed, in their language); Wladislaus nods with 'dobře, dobře'. One of the leading motifs of the work is that rulers were only appreciated posthumously. Joseph quotes the proverb 'King Matthias died, justice has died with him' and addresses Wladislaus, pointing out that the saying accuses him. Wladislaus, however, excuses himself with the well-known scheme of a kind but weak king present in historiography: the king did not hurt anybody, wanted to be good towards all estates, but his good will was abused by magnates; he was poor and often did not have enough to eat and drink. This is the recurrent picture which we know from a variety of sources across centuries. Wladislaus reminds Emperor Joseph that it was through him that the House of Austria received the Hungarian throne, and Joseph assures him of his respect for the Jagiellonian king as one of his ancestors. The piece is a good example of what standard, general, and expected knowledge about the Jagiellonian king was at the end of the eighteenth century, and also teaches a country-patriotic attitude.

Towards the end of the eighteenth century, the memory of Louis II was revived alongside the Battle of Mohács, which became the subject of several artistic works. The theme had appeared rarely in the previous century, for instance in an epic poem by László Liszti (Listius), in Hungarian (1653), relying heavily on the Latin text of Brodarics, filled with Hungarian patriotic and religious feelings (an unlikely heroic epic topic at the time, which was to find its way into the libraries and symbolic discourse of Hungarian aristocrats later).[30] Another epic poem, *Magyar gyász, vagyis második Lajos királynak a mohácsi mezőn történt veszedelme*, also based on the account of Brodarics, was written by Etédi Sós Márton (1792).[31]

The second battle of Mohács (or Nagyharsány) in 1687, which marked the end of the Turkish period in Hungary, was a spur to remembering the battle of 1526. On its centenary, Ladislaus Eszterházy, bishop of Pécs, commissioned Stephan Dorffmaister (1725–97) to paint scenes of the two battles (i.e. 1526 and 1687), representing the beginning and the end of the Turkish era, and a historicising portrait of Louis II in full armour (1787).[32] Dorffmaister also painted the scene of the death of Louis II on his horse for Szentgotthárd Cistercian Abbey (1795–96), in the same armour.[33] Another painter, József Borsos, painted copies of Dorffmaister's works, and his copy of Louis' portrait (1837) bears an inscription: 'Rex, Patriam Populosque suos, Regnique penates / Propugnaturus fortiter occubuit.'[34] Thus, the young king is identified as the one who fought and died for his people and *patria*, cohering with the earlier positive tradition about Louis II.

This representation of the young Louis II is interesting because of the silver armour, rendered in detail, after a piece which was believed to be the original armour of Louis II in Vienna. The interest in material memory as a method for depicting a historical object, and thus also the subject person in the painting in an authentic manner, was in keeping with contemporary fashion. The armour, a piece from the Seusenhofer workshop in Innsbruck, was to become one of the typical attributes of Louis in later memory as well, and can be seen in later depictions of the king, including the statue of Louis II on the façade of the Hungarian Parliament, dating from the turn of the twentieth century. The silver armour with its specific decoration has become an object, an artefact, which serves as a mnemonic marker. The earliest accounts of the battle already speak of Louis drowning in the stream because of his heavy armour; thus, this was an easily-intelligible sign connected with the young king. Later, in 1876, the Seusenhofer piece was exhibited at Ambras in Innsbruck.[35] Despite all this, Louis would not have been able to wear it at Mohács in any case – this armour had for a long time in fact been erroneously identified as a gift of Emperor Maximilian to the nine-year-old Louis on the occasion of his engagement to Mary in 1515. This was the reason why in 1933 it was given by the Kunsthistorisches Museum to the Hungarian National Museum. In fact, the silver child armour was a gift from Ferdinand to Sigismund Augustus in 1533, on the occasion of the marriage of his daughter.[36] The memory of Louis II was thus inextricably connected to the Battle of Mohács. At the time, though, Mohács, both as a theme and as a place, did not occupy a crucial position in the public or national discourse.[37] It was to play a more and more significant role in the Hungarian national movement in the coming century, inspiring the authors of visual arts and literature, with Louis at times becoming an unlikely national symbol, rather than a full-fledged historical person.

The nineteenth century and national history until 1849

The first half of the nineteenth century, especially the Reform period in the 1830s and 1840s, was both a period of professionalisation and institutionalisation of historiography, and of public demand for national history and its dissemination. In the Kingdom of Hungary, as a unit of the Habsburg Empire, various nations and ethnic groups based their rights for self-determination on historical-cultural and/or natural criteria. They related to and appropriated the history of the country, and its particular parts and rulers, in different ways and to varied extents.[38] In national Romantic constructions, where the nation was the main subject of history, the Jagiellonian rulers were not amongst the top heroes, with the kings appearing mostly as background figures, but some events associated with their reigns became reference points.

National histories were penned by historians who themselves wanted to make history, like Mihály Horváth (1809–78), the founder of the Hungarian national liberal historical school, cabinet minister in the revolutionary government in 1849, and an exile after its defeat.[39] His general evaluation of the rule of the two kings in *The History of Hungary* was uncompromising. Under the title 'The Age of National Decay Caused by the Unruly Oligarchs', he argued that the Jagiellonians had harmed the country, which had decayed from a flourishing power under Matthias to the edge of the grave; the nation and the country suffered due to mismanagement, and this diminishing further opened the door to Reformation. This decline was caused by the moral corruption of institutions and people in power.[40]

The peasant revolt of 1514, with the cruel punishment and tragic fate of the main actors, as one of the signs of decline, was popular among Reform period writers, who wanted to call attention to social problems of the nation on all levels of society. Perpetual servitude was introduced as a result of the suppressed revolt and remained in force until 1848, although its impact is not considered as extensive as understood by earlier historians. One of the leading politicians of the Reform era, József Eötvös, wrote an extensive historical novel, *Hungary in 1514* (1847). Although the theme is historical (Eötvös conducted extensive research and the novel features both historical and fictional characters), it is written in the fashion of realism and social criticism, with a topical message.[41] A similar focus on the people is seen in other aspects. In the spirit of national Romanticism, intellectuals promoting their national cause turned with renewed interest to folk traditions, and collected songs and other manifestations of folk culture. The Jagiellonians made occasional appearances here, especially thanks to songs about the Battle of Mohács, which had originated in sixteenth-century newsletters and epic songs. Among the Slovak and Czech songs, based on written sources, manuscripts and oral traditions collected by slavicist Ján Kollár and his collaborators in several volumes of *Národnie spievanky* (1834), was a song about the battle of Mohács, *O bitvě Moháčské čili o porážce krále Ludvíka II.*, which expresses empathy with the fate of the unlucky young king.[42] Similar songs about Louis and the battle are found in Croatian.[43] It is assumed that some historical songs and tales in the Hungarian language also originated shortly after the battle.[44]

A folk song about 'our good king Polish Ladislas' ('Lengyel László jó királyunk') also exists. It is actually a children's game, 'a bridge play', known in many variants in Central Europe: two groups oppose each other, and one has to run through to the other side, which is trying to catch them. One of the possible interpretations is that the king is Wladislaus I the Jagiellonian, and the game may possibly refer to his struggle for the crown against the party of Queen Elizabeth of Luxemburg (1409–42), the mother and regent of Ladislas Posthumous.[45] Ferenc Kölcsey, the renowned author of the future Hungarian national anthem, praised the fact that Hungarian children had been playing the game of 'Our Good King Polish Ladislas' for generations in his essay, *National Traditions* (1826).[46] In his essay, the poet explained the spirit of the historicism and Romanticism attached to national efforts, in which literature is aimed at cultivation of the national spirit, by looking back to the past deeds of the nation and erecting poetic and non-poetic monuments to it, including folk culture.[47] The 'Hunyadi era' (of the magnate John Hunyadi, d.1456, and his son King Matthias Corvinus) was considered the golden heroic age of Hungarian history by a number of Hungarian intellectuals. In this spirit, the poet János Arany, among numerous others, translated into Hungarian the poetic epitaph of Wladislaus I, who died at Varna, ascribed to the famed Renaissance poet from the court of Matthias Corvinus, Janus Pannonius, a text which was a frequent reference point for Hungarian writers for centuries.[48] Topics from national history were suitable for both epic poems and novels; glorification, tragedy and Romantic ideals were the ingredients. Great King Matthias was one of the most popular subjects, but the Battle of Mohács was also one of them.

After 1849: independence struggle and loss – Hungarian Mohács and Louis

Before the mid-nineteenth century, the Battle of Mohács, which lent itself to the Romantic fashion of heroic tragic themes, became an established symbol of a catastrophe falling upon the nation, although references to Louis II himself were generally made in passing.[49] The narratives of victimhood and martyrdom were part and parcel of Romantic national discourse. The Hungarian revolutionary struggle of 1848 against the centralising forces failed after the defeat at Világos in 1849 (already earlier, smaller non-Magyar, Slavic nations had joined the imperial side), and Hungarian-Magyar intellectuals turned back to Mohács and its aftermath as a parallel of their own defeat and the tragic destiny of the nation. In a poem by the famous poet János Arany, 'More was lost at Mohács' (1856), a rider speaks about all the things lost, one by one. The 'Mohács code' found a stable place in art, and in many cases there is no mention of King Louis at all. Around the same time, however, the figure of the king was used within the symbolic discourses of other media. Several paintings present the image of Louis II dying at Mohács, or more often, his body found at the scene of the battle, as an embodiment of the suffering Hungarian nation, but also as a victim of the fights between its divided representatives.

Paintings representing historical figures played a role in the formation of Hungarian nationhood and in the difficult years of the 1850s and 1860s became 'carriers of the nation's cultural memories', thanks to the 'secret codes' to which a suppressed community with some background knowledge could turn.[50] The power of these pictures lies in their dramatic themes, impressive characters, and spectacular expression. The paintings capture 'tragic stories, failed heroes, visions of devastation and decay', which symbolise the sad contemporary situation – historical victims such as King Louis II symbolised the subdued nation.[51] Rather than the image of the king in armour falling from his horse, Soma Orlai Petrics (1822–80) employed a novel iconographic theme, and painted *The Discovery of the Body of Louis II*, in Munich (1851). It depicts the moment when the body, which looks unharmed in white, clean cloth, is discovered lifted up from the marshy land, while the entourage, men of various ranks, and a woman (Dorottya Kanizsai, wife of Count Perényi) pay tribute to him and mourn, while one of them holds up the king's crown. The sky is cloudy and dark, representing the hopeless situation of the country, but the crown is a sign of hope. The integrity of the king's body and the presence of the crown in paintings has been a topic for art historical as well as broader debates due to the painting's lack of realistic representation. Petrics's aim, however, was to produce a historical allegory, with a composition resembling the *Pietà* around the body of Christ, representing the kingdom, complete and intact, even when dead and entombed.[52] Debate also surrounded the unusual subject-choice of King Louis. Clearly, it was not evident at the time that this incapable king should be perceived as a hero, let alone as the embodiment of the nation, which, as it were, suffered as a result of his actions. Toldy, a patron from the same circle of intellectuals as Petrics, wrote to the artist:

> Friend, what is the merit of Louis II? Well, and finding his body, which is in every respect an insignificant event! He was an insignificant ruler of foreign origin. He had nobody's sympathy. Shall we be sorry for him as a young man, as a king? Due to him the nation's illness got deadly, and Mohács was

just the day of his irreversible death! . . . The nation has not lost anything with him . . .[53]

Other heroes of the Hungarian nation were considered a better and more natural choice, and the place of the lost battle amongst the glorious moments of the nation's history was heavily debated.[54] In his defence, Petrics referred to historian Jászay's book (1846) as his source of inspiration for the positive representation of the king, coming from the Jeremiad-like *querela Hungariae* verses composed shortly after Mohács, especially by Protestant authors.[55] Sinkó points out that two traditions about Louis II had already existed before the nineteenth century: the positive concerning his heroic death, and the negative concerning his incapacity and the corruption of those around him. New iconography, the discovery of the body of Louis, represented national autonomous thinking, while the old one, Louis on his horse falling and drowning, was connected with patriotism related to the empire, wrote Sinkó.[56] The change of iconography contributed to Louis' positive image; at the same period new memorials to Louis appeared at Mohács.[57]

Another Romantic painter, Bertalan Székely (1835–1910), followed Petrics in depicting the same theme (1860), introducing a few differences (absence of the crown and the woman).[58] This was the first large painting by the artist, who had also studied in Munich, where he was one of the pupils of Karl von Piloty – interestingly,

FIGURE 3.1 Bertalan Székely, *The Discovery of the Corpse of King Louis II*, 1860, SzépművészetiMúzeum/Museum of Fine Arts, 2017

at the same time as the Polish painter Matejko, famous for his paintings of Polish Jagiellonian rulers (1859).[59] His piece was sent to Pest to be part of an exhibition, and in 1862 it was exhibited at the World Exhibition in London, before finding its way to the Hungarian National Gallery 'thanks to the pressure of the contemporary public'.[60]

The establishment of art exhibitions and national museums changed the function of artworks during national movements in this period, making them more accessible to a public whose national consciousness they could boost. The contribution made by media such as newspapers, besides books, and information technologies in the second half of the nineteenth century was also substantial.[61] The Battle of Mohács, and with it the unlucky and tragic Louis II, became the most prominent Jagiellonian memory in the Kingdom of Hungary (especially the Hungarian-Magyar national discourse) in this period, although Louis was still not a major figure remembered from the past.

After 1867: dualism period

In the second half of the nineteenth century, especially after the Austro-Hungarian Compromise of 1867 (which partly re-established the sovereignty of the Hungarian kingdom *vis-à-vis* Vienna), more varied platforms opened for historical scholarship, some of which were designed to conduct systematic research (source collections, etc.), whilst others aimed to help popularise history and respond to the public demands of national Romanticism. The dominance of Magyar nationalism in historical studies grew. The emphasis on the conflict of the Hungarian nobility with the Habsburgs, the *labanc* (pro-Habsburg) and *kuruc* (anti-Habsburg) interpretations of Hungarian history, and the idealisation of the role of the nobility in political leadership all influenced the interpretation of the Jagiellonian period and of the post-Mohács situation after 1526.[62]

One of the outstanding specialists writing on the early modern period, Vilmos Fraknói, praised it for its diets, as 'the age of estates', which were not signs of anarchy and crisis, but of modern parliamentarism – a feature which was to be appreciated by numerous later students of history.[63] In the *History of the Hungarian Nation*, published in 1896, he praised the Hungarian nation for being able to rise again after losses like Varna (1444) and later Mohács (1526), and go on in their mission of defending Christianity. After foreign dynasties, King Matthias Corvinus had restored the national kingdom.[64] The historian saw the origins of the crisis in the reign of King Matthias, another reason for the election of Wladislaus II. He claimed that, had John Corvinus (King Matthias's illegitimate son) been elected, Hungary would have had to face the ambitions of both the Habsburgs and the Jagiellonians, as well as the Turkish threat, and 'only the members of the Jagiellonian dynasty were ready to accept the principle of electing a king', as Sebők has summarised.[65] In the same spirit, the Hungarian Historical Society (Magyar Történelmi Társulat) commissioned (in 1899) the project of writing 'the history of aspirations and struggles of the Hungarian nation for independence, starting with the Rákos diet of 1505 to the Peace of Satu Mare/Szatmár', planned in ten to twelve volumes.[66] The first volume, written by Dezső Szabó under the title *Struggle for the National Kingdom, 1505–1526*, describes the period as a recurrent struggle for the Hungarian throne between the Habsburgs and the Jagiellonians (1440s, 1490s), interrupted by 'national kingship'. Wladislaus and Louis too were to blame for the growing influence of the Habsburgs in Hungary: Wladislaus II 'had the good habit of always promising what they asked from him', including the Vienna agreements of 1515, and even if Louis had not died at Mohács, the development would have been similar, and the subjects would have had to fight him.[67] The estates and diets were the leading topics, as they were anachronistically perceived as a development towards national independence. Szabó offered a more balanced view of the somewhat ambiguous 'national party', filled with fewer nationalist sentiments, in his study of the diets under Louis II, which provoked polemics by scholars such as G. Szekfű.[68] In this period, József Fógel wrote works on the courts of Wladislaus II and Louis II.[69] A series of biographies of figures from Hungarian history, aimed at both specialist and non-specialist audiences, appeared through the cooperation of the Hungarian Historical Society and the Academy of Sciences: the Jagiellonian kings were not discussed in the fifty-eight volumes, but Isabella,[70] the Polish Jagiellonian wife of John Szapolyai and later regent in Transylvania, and Mary, wife of Louis II,[71] made appearances alongside important Hungarian heroes like George Dózsa, Stephen Werbőczy, and John and Matthias Hunyadis.[72]

Towards the end of the dualist monarchy (1867–1918), despite both professionalisation and the use of critical methods, history was retold in the framework of a national awakening. The Hungarian-speaking Magyar elites dominated the political scene. In the 1870s, the moderate national-liberal policy of Ferenc Deák and József Eötvös gave way to a new generation of politicians who promoted the idea of a homogeneous Hungarian, meaning ethnically and linguistically Magyar, political nation, a process which led to Magyarisation. It was the golden age of national historicism, self-idealisation and pathetic national narratives, representing the official Hungarian (a term increasingly synonymous, ethnically and linguistically, with Magyar) current, which dominated public life, whilst the historical memory of minority groups was marginalised. The 1896 public celebrations marking the millennium of the arrival of the Hungarians in the Carpathian Basin was one of the peaks of this political-national historicism, and the demand for an idealised past increased. This made the tensions between the Hungarian-Magyar and other historical narratives more visible.[73]

Jagiellonian kings made only marginal appearances in the 1896 millennium celebrations and memorials, unlike the heroes from Hungarian history, starting with the conquest through St Stephen and Ladislaus, then the last Arpadians, the Hunyadis, later uprisings, and most recent history. Their reign is remembered for Mohács and Verbőczy's collection of law. The Hunyadis are remembered, and the Arpadians are celebrated as the national dynasty, while the Angevins divided the nation into classes and destroyed the nation unified by the Arpadians, until the Hunyadi heroes returned glory to the nation. Matthias Hunyadi is the last national king after St Stephen, the greatest king of Hungary. 'The codification of law' in the Jagiellonian period is praised, as is Wladislaus for signing it.[74] The representative ten-volume synthesis of Hungarian history, written by a group of historians and edited by S. Szilágyi on the occasion of the millennium (1896–98), focused on the development of the Hungarian nation.[75] A general history project (the twelve-volume *Great Illustrated History of the World*, edited by Henrik Marczali), also aimed particularly at the educated public, was also a big success. When treating Jagiellonian kings, the emphasis is typically on their weakness. The Jagiellonian chapter underlines the significance of royal authority for the wellbeing of the country and contrasts the state of the kingdom with the reign of Matthias, warning about the danger of inner discord. The election of Wladislaus, weak due to his character and conditions, is seen as 'the triumph of oligarchy'.[76] The *Pallas Nagy Lexikon*, a big popular encyclopaedia, had entries on the 'Jagiellonians', as 'a Polish royal dynasty' (and 'largely beneficial to Poland'), and the 'Jagiellonian period', which is a 'sad period of Hungarian history, because the wonderful victorious period under Matthias ended with the loss at Mohács', the decline of royal authority, marked by the struggle of lower nobility with oligarchs, and decay visible in all spheres – public order, the financial situation, mismanagement, and even constitutional life. Wladislaus is described as a prototype of powerlessness, who replied to everything with *dobzse*. Louis' rule is characterised by the constant Turkish threat and the loss at Mohács, and includes the usual basic information.[77] In these texts there is a tension between professional historiography and social demand: history in the streets, in reading rooms, in public spaces, in journals, historical novels, paintings, architecture, opera and music, required 'a simplified reading of the past', even a myth-making, which helped forge both national identities and Magyarisation.[78]

The tragic destiny of King Louis and the events around the Battle of Mohács were still the subject of Hungarian literary works in the second half of the nineteenth and early twentieth century, including historical novels[79] and dramas staged in theatres.[80] Like many other novels, Baksay's *Dáma*, which offers a dark picture of desolate emptiness and a paralysed nation, was first printed in a serialised collection of novels attached to the popular weekly *Vasárnapi Újság* in 1898. These novels were also illustrated, thus spreading the visual representation of historical figures and events. One of the images shows Louis falling from the horse in his armour (interestingly, with decoration well known from other representations of the armour).[81] Jagiellonian rulers featured not only in literature loaded with national symbolism and social criticism, but also in entertainment literature. After the fashion of Walter Scott, the historical novels of the prolific writer Mór Jókai (who enjoyed a large foreign readership) were meant as entertainment and an escape from political realities. Despite his critics, these works were popular with the public. The novel *Friar George* (first edition 1893)[82] maps the history of Hungary from the rule of Wladislaus II to 1551, when the main character, the Pauline monk and governor of Transylvania, George Martinuzzi (1482–1551), was murdered. King Wladislaus II, a tender-hearted 'Dobzse László', desolate after the queen's death, paying his debts with the volumes from the Corvina library;

Louis II, born too early, with the legend of his murder after the escape from Mohács; and Isabella with her son in Transylvania – they all appear as background characters, depicted colourfully in the by then popularised schematised and anecdotal fashion.[83] Jókai was also the author of a popular overview of Hungarian history, *A magyar nemzet története regényes rajzokban*. Wladislaus II is again 'Dobzse László', pious but poor, begging for food, while the rich magnates rule the country. Louis II is unlucky; when describing Mohács, Jókai says, 'Poor young king! . . . There was not a greater martyr in the nation than him . . .',[84] and adds that everything would have been different, had there been at least one true patriot beside the young king. They inherited a powerful country and left it weak when they died. Jókai himself refers the reader to his novel for a depiction of the period.

Paradoxically, small nations within the monarchy such as the Slovaks showed exactly the opposite tendency as a reaction to a homogeneously Magyar official national myth: a considerable resignation regarding their own history, a weakened role for historical memory and its fixation in folk culture and plebeian character, especially in the late monarchy. Still, some Slovak historians constructed arguments supporting the historical rights of the nation, building on the previous, especially Jesuit, apologetic writings. In his synthesis of the medieval history of the Kingdom of Hungary (1871), F. Sasinek emphasises the share of Slovaks in the original kingdom and their equal standing with other nations, arguing for the continuous autonomous political position of the territory of Slovakia within Hungary until the late Middle Ages. When discussing Jagiellonian kings, Sasinek draws on Palacký and Horváth, besides others; he puts emphasis on the Slavic origin of the Jagiellonian kings, their ability to understand the language and talk to their subjects in Bohemia,[85] and the Slavic name of Wladislaus.[86] Sasinek evaluates Wladislaus as a good man who was unable to discipline the oligarchs (whilst also lacking self-confidence and strength in his missed chances to 'create a strong dynasty' and unite his crowns with the Polish one), arguing further that 'Hungarian historians' only criticise him, without considering the lack of true patriotic characters on whom he could rely.[87] The same argument is used when evaluating Louis II. First, Louis II is depicted, drawing on Palacký, as a careless and frivolous young man under the influence of bad advisors.[88] Sasinek judges, however, that despite the traditional sayings about Louis' prematurity in everything, the king was able in both body and mind, and 'more than once showed wise and considerate behaviour, and in dangerous times gave proof of his vigour and courage; nevertheless, because of his reckless and tender heart he did not prove fit for the grave royal task, which makes kings responsible in front of God and the people'.[89] The Jagiellonians were not national heroes, and their rule was not the golden age in either Hungarian or other national narratives within the kingdom.

After World War I

The end of World War I was also the end of the Habsburg monarchy. After its dissolution, new states were established in Central Europe: Hungary, formally a monarchy with a regent, but significantly smaller after the Trianon Peace (1920), and Czechoslovakia, as the common state of Czechs and Slovaks. The changed situation required also new interpretations of history, and to some extent had an impact on the perception of memory of Jagiellonians in Hungary. Some stereotypes, however, persisted.

Compared to the overcrowded Hungarian historical memory, Slovak historiography and memory within Czechoslovakia oscillated between ahistoricism, a refusal of Hungarian history, and a story of gradual national emancipation, using the cliché of oppression. One of the first textbooks repeated the stereotype that the Jagiellonians had 'reigned badly', whilst their subjects suffered at the hands of a nobility who did not care to defend them against the Turks.[90] The refusal of Hungarian history was very strong in the synthesis of Slovak history written by František Hrušovský (1903–56), with several editions of his textbook appearing in Slovakia during World War II. Written with a nationalist perspective, it employed the leitmotif of the Slovak nation beginning its existence in a free, independent Slovak state after a long millennium in a foreign state under the rule of non-Slovak rulers. Thus its history is not a history of rulers' lineages. The special position of the upper Hungarian, 'i.e. Slovak', middle nobility is emphasised with respect to royal elections, including their support for Prince John Albert's bid for the Hungarian throne in the 1490s, against his brother Wladislaus, and also the contributions of numerous 'Slovak mercenaries' to his independent campaign against the Turks in 1497. Hrušovský then continues to repeat commonplaces about the weak rule of Wladislaus, when the lords seized all the power and the peasants suffered. There is certain sympathy for Louis II, who was able but corrupted by bad advisors and weakened by struggles between various parties.[91]

Public memory: new Hungarian Mohács

After the historical continuity of this central idea – the emergence of the nation-state – was undermined, the Hungarian national discourse, meanwhile, needed to be rephrased, which resulted in either 'nostalgic exaltation' of the lost past and the search for a scapegoat, or a new claim of 'homogeneous ethno-national statehood' in ethnic or populist terms.[92] These changes also impacted on the treatment of the 'national' monarchy under Matthias Corvinus, followed by decline under the Jagiellonians and the resulting loss of national independence, which gradually settled into a good arrangement with the composite monarchy of Austria-Hungary under the Habsburgs. The nation-state was the central question in Hóman and Szekfű's multiple-volume *A Hungarian History*, reprinted several times in the 1930s, a representative achievement of Hungarian historiography (in terms of general historical knowledge) at the time, and written in the spirit of the history of ideas (*Geistesgeschichte*). In the Jagiellonian period, when the estates ruled instead of weak sovereigns, the authors discovered some positive elements in non-political areas.[93] In their view, the rule of the estates was a negative sign – 'with the election of the Polish-born Czech king Wladislaus, Hungary moved away from the West', from the Renaissance and the modern absolutism (of Matthias), towards the Slavic states for centuries, with rule by the estates and the threat of disintegration.[94]

In the interwar period, the parallel between Mohács and Trianon, two 'national traumas', played a crucial role in perspectives on Jagiellonian rule (an 'age of decline leading to a catastrophe'), in public opinion as well as in historiography.[95] On the occasion of the 400th anniversary of the battle in 1926, several works incorporating new research were published, literary works were produced, and events and exhibitions were held and reported country-wide in newspapers.[96] The foundation stone of the votive church at Mohács was laid, wreaths were laid at the battlefield and at King Louis' memorial at Csele stream, with regent Horthy, the minister of culture, and several others delivering speeches at the ceremony.[97] A collected volume with a preface by the minister of culture, with revisionist phrases dreaming about a new renovation mirroring that which occurred after Mohács, offered historical and ethnographic studies on the topic.[98] New novels inspired by Mohács were published around 1926, meeting public demand: *Mohács*, from a trilogy by Gyula Krúdy (1878–1933),[99] and *Black Bridegrooms* by Irén Gulácsy (1927). Thanks to the published works of historians from recent years, they could disseminate historical knowledge to the public through their imaginative rendering of the events.

Krúdy's 'historical documentary novel', with the subtitle *The Struggle of Two Orphan Kids*, was a counter-reaction to heroic and pathetic representations of the Mohács disaster and historical characters.[100] Early after its publication, it was criticised for choosing 'pastel colours' instead of a grand 'historical painting of Piloty style', and a 'subjective Stendhal style' rather than that of Victor Hugo for a great national epic; it was argued that such great, fatal themes should not be presented to the public from a subjective, impressionistic viewpoint.[101] Another critic observed that the so-called historical novel supposedly depicting one of the greatest cataclysms of Hungarian history devoted more space to the love reveries of the decadent adolescent royal couple than to serious issues.[102] Rather than focusing on a national cataclysm, Krúdy's *Struggle* explores the stories of individuals, their everyday lives, which are exposed and suddenly changed by a great event like Mohács. It is a return to the nineteenth-century historical novel (possibly polemical given the existing tradition of the theme, as represented in Jókai's *György Fráter* and Eötvös's *Hungary in 1514*), but rather than drawing morals or explaining, he creates a 'kaleidoscope' held together by the protagonists.[103] Louis and other historical figures are livelier, full-fledged persons: Louis and Mary discuss practical things like money, and do everyday things like eating – Louis is 'a true Jagiellonian, who gave himself with body and soul to the delight of eating'; at the Danube bank he even recommends Mary try 'lacipecsenye', called so after his poor father; he talks about his parents and childhood, in which Wladislaus is still figured as the 'dobzse' king. Compared to Jókai's earlier novel, for example, Louis is a person with abilities and the will to reign, but is constrained by ancient Hungarian, foreign (to him) laws, rather than just being a puppet in counsellors' hands.

Unlike Krúdy, Iren Gulácsy (1894–1945) looked to history to provide a lesson for a present lacking national unity and heroic self-sacrifice, and tells a story of the failures and triumphs which make up the history of the Hungarian nation for over 1,000 years, according to a contemporary reviewer.[104] Her popular *Black Bridegrooms* takes the reader to the turbulent years of the early sixteenth century, between 1504 and 1534, and follows the life of Imre Czibak, bishop of Várad and Transylvanian dignitary, a historical figure (together with Pál Tomori), with Louis II present from birth to death in the background, alongside the stereotypically tender-hearted 'dobzse' Wladislaus, sitting in the glorious palace of Matthias, with the Polish ambassador Tomicki scheming with the king and the Szapolyais about marriages and agreements.

After World War II

For much of the historiography and memory of post-1948 Hungary, Jagiellonian rulers were irrelevant or merely background characters. Some themes, especially those related to the Battle of Mohács, its causes and consequences, and the peasant revolt of 1514 and thus the overall evaluation of the period, found new echoes in the 1960s and 1970s. There was a passionate debate in Hungarian historiography over the alternative policies the country could have pursued in the 1500s and over the causes and effects of the Battle of Mohács.[105] The debate was motivated by the situation of Hungarian politics after the suppression of the revolution in 1956, and during the Kádár regime (1956–88), as yet another parallel to the national disaster. It was opened in 1966 by the 'iconoclastic' work of István Nemeskürty, written in a readable, popular style, whose main thesis was that the defeat at Mohács itself was not such a decisive catastrophe as had been previously considered, but that the true disaster was in fact caused by the Hungarian 'ruling class', who fought among themselves and pursued their particular interests in the aftermath of Mohács, leaving the country easy prey for the Turks at a later date.[106] His thesis was criticised immediately by several writers, intellectuals, and historians in Hungarian journals and newspapers, whilst the ensuing public debate provoked more reactions from non-historians and historians (among them, Géza Perjés and Ferenc Szakály, who turned to study sources on the issue and later wrote entire books on Mohács).[107] In 1976 Tibor Klaniczay blamed neither the Jagiellonians nor the Hungarian leaders, but rather traced the crisis back to earlier times. He defended kings who found themselves in much weaker positions than their predecessors, whilst also relying on the same stereotypes when describing their behaviour. He asks what sort of man Louis II, the main character of the Mohács drama, in fact was. He was a young king who grew up quickly; he was neither a bad nor a stupid man, but still a child, who lived as if in 'carnival' at the palace with his wife and entourage. 'Both Wladislaus and Louis were good men', he writes; they could not refuse any request. Yet the wider context in Communist Hungary was a de-heroisation of the ruling class and the destruction of the illusions about 'the national nobility', which often went hand in hand with a renewed focus on the peasantry, the people, and the nation in the broader sense (often in a people-democratic, Communist vocabulary). An ideal topic was the peasant revolt of 1514 led by Georgius Dózsa (a crusade that went wrong), one of the top events associated with the rule of Wladislaus II, although its historiography did not pay much attention to the king itself, preferring to analyse the role of the 'people' or 'nation', and the signs of 'feudal anarchy' at the expense of the sovereign and the 'ruling class'.[108]

The deeply-rooted social memory of the Jagiellonian period is reflected in an unfinished, unusual, essay by the Hungarian intellectual István Bibó on the values of Christianity, modernity and the contemporary situation – and on whether events of the early sixteenth century slowed down the development of Hungary as compared to the West for some 500 years (a fear that had returned after 1945). In his contrafactual, virtual history he makes 'Count Dózsa' rescue Louis II from drowning in the Csele stream at Mohács; the young king then lives long enough to unite the three kingdoms after the Polish Jagiellonians die out in the 1570s, and his line happily continues for generations with 'a slightly drunk Dobzse VII. István'.[109]

The 450th anniversary of the Battle of Mohács in 1976 was another occasion to form a memory of the event and the figures involved. The Mohács Historical Memorial was opened at the battlefield. The finds of bones of the troops and subsequent archaeological research on the field and graves in the 1960s and 1970s shifted the focus from individual heroes to the people. The efforts to build a memorial and open it in time for the anniversary were imbued with national sentiment among the people.[110] In the opening speech at the unveiling of the memorial, where the statue of Louis was just one of many heroes remembered, G. Ortutay recalled those occasions in history such as in 1514–26 (mentioning Eötvös's novel *Hungary in 1514*), 1848 and 1919, when the people felt that they were part of history.[111] A collected volume of studies from the conference held there was published following the celebrations.[112]

Recent memory

In the last decades, starting with the fall of Communism, historians have re-evaluated many aspects of Jagiellonian rule in Hungary and corrected some long-living assumptions. Some of these had already been destabilised earlier, among them the circumstances of the decline when compared to the rule of Matthias Corvinus (1458–90), so often glorified by national history-writing and memory. The thesis of diminishing royal power and central authority stands, but the person-alities of Jagiellonian kings do not perhaps emerge quite so badly. Traditionally, the rulers and the high nobility, that is, the ruling elite, have been held responsible for the development and downfall of the kingdom. More recently, however, the predominant position has become that the marks of crisis were already visible during the rule of the Jagiellonians' predecessor King Matthias, and whilst arguments and struggles between various parties contributed to the negative developments and tragic consequences, external factors, especially Ottoman attacks and the reluctance of other countries apart from the papacy to offer assistance, catalysed by internal issues, were ultimately decisive for the destiny of the kingdom and its fall.[113] In many recent overviews of fifteenth-century Hungary, the narrative is centred on the relation between the crown and the estates and the shift of power from monarchic to aristocratic; many studies deal with estates, diets, laws, royal election.[114] Other important currents in present Hungarian historiography of Jagiellonian rule are the royal court,[115] foreign relations, humanist literature and Renaissance culture, in the studies of which continuities rather than ruptures are generally emphasised. The two kings, and especially Wladislaus, are still considered by historiography to have been incompetent and damaging to the kingdom. Instead of the commonplace and caricatured image, however, historians have recently argued that the Jagiellonian kings had considerable strengths, positive character traits and even peaceful authority and decisive power, features blurred by centuries of distortion.[116]

In line with this re-evaluation is a volume on the Jagiellonian era produced for a broader public, entitled *Towards Mohács*, by Tringli, which is part of the recently published *History of Hungary* series.[117] He summarises the above-mentioned corrections regarding the financial and military situation and other stereotypes about the period. He accentuates the division of the Jagiellonian dynasty into two branches: the Polish-Lithuanian and the Hungarian-Bohemian (especially after 1490), with two centres in Krakow and in Buda, which, despite cooperating, often pursued independent foreign policies. Popular overviews of history and popularising articles try to bridge the gap between the professional historiography and public knowledge, but the distorted image of the Jagiellonians, and particularly the 'dobzse' king, Wladislaus II, persists: in an online overview of the ten biggest mistakes in Hungarian history on a popular Hungarian website, the election of Wladislaus features as number 10.[118]

The memory of Mohács as the symbol of national tragedy – not necessarily concerned with Louis II – has been critically studied in a number of academic and popular volumes.[119] The National Memorial Park at the battlefield was renovated in 2011 and an exhibition building in the form of the Holy Crown was added.[120] Memorial gatherings, organised by local government but attended more widely, take place there on the day of the battle every year. Mohács resonated, although not substantially, also in literature, but, as in history, its heroes cannot compete with the popularity of Matthias Hunyadi – Corvinus – in fiction.[121] One author was inspired by his visit to the Mohács memorial park to write a work of historical fiction: *Four Kings, One Sultan* (2014), which creates a fictitious diary of Louis in which he discloses his personal feelings in the months preceding the battle. The author creates fictitious sources, well grounded in the circumstances, so that an uninformed reader can mistake the book for a collection of authentic sources in translation.[122] A multi-disciplinary conference focusing on the legends concerning the death of King Louis II in battle or shortly afterwards, inspired by a controversial attempted interpretation of sources by medical specialists, was held on the 490th anniversary of the battle. In the preface to this work, Pál Fodor summarised that nineteenth-century Hungarian historiography 'managed to draw a perfect caricature' (of Jagiellonians and Hungary under their rule), which scholarship has taken over, until Kubinyi and his followers 'started its rehabilitation and have shown that the Jagiellonian Hungarian state was not worse than others'.[123]

General Slovak histories do not typically devote much space to Jagiellonian rule, which is mostly presented as an age of weak rulers and feudal anarchy, when the aristocracy oppressed the peasants – the uprising of 1514 and its consequences are mentioned, as well as the Battle of Mohács as the turning point in Central Europe, with the beginnings of the Habsburg Empire and Ottoman occupation of large parts of the kingdom.[124] Another, different example of a less well rooted Jagiellonian public memory is the recent installation of a statue of Polish King Jogaila and his wife Hedwig of Anjou in Budapest as a representation of Polish-Hungarian cooperation within the EU, which shows that the Jagiellonians can also represent ties with Poland in the memory discourse.

The presence of Jagiellonian rulers in historical memory in the Kingdom of Hungary (and its successor states) is rather insignificant when compared to their predecessors and successors. The Jagiellonians were mostly evaluated in relation and comparison to a few important points – Matthias Corvinus, and the Battle of Mohács (which ultimately brought the Habsburgs to the Hungarian throne). The former represented one of the golden ages of Hungarian history, whereas the aftermath of the latter was perceived as utter chaos, the disintegration of power, and, in national-speak, the loss of independence. Although subject to some changes, in historiography and culture, the memory of these historical periods formed from the sixteenth century onwards remained within the same basic framework: the positive, golden age of Matthias Corvinus, opposed by the negative, chaotic post-1526 era. The gap between these two poles was filled by the reign of the Jagiellonians – the 'in-between' period. Viewed from either of these two vantage points, Jagiellonians appeared as epitomes of decline and weakness, and their personal failures in government were often presented as one of the causes of this downwards trajectory, even further deepened after the loss at Mohács, which logically followed their weak and incapable rule. Since the nineteenth century Mohács has gained an extra symbolic meaning in the Hungarian-Magyar national movement, and in this context the foreign Louis has been perceived as an unlikely embodiment of the nation. Nevertheless, the evaluation and related symbolic cultural capital of the Jagiellonians as kings of Hungary has oscillated from insignificance to the negative, as opposed to their important place in especially Polish memory. Recently, historians have tried to balance this evaluation, but in general terms it is hard to free them from the legacy of these long-lasting simplifications and look at them in their own right, without implicitly building them into the teleologies of Hungarian history formed over the centuries.

Notes

1. Hungarian (Magyar) and Slovak traditions, including the Latin-written, will be the focus, for practical reasons; other involved traditions – Croatian, partially Romanian, Serbian – will be referred to briefly where necessary and are discussed by other studies in the volume and in the Introduction, where a bigger picture of the 'regional' memory of the Jagiellonians in Central Europe is presented. Due to the limited space, this is going to be an overview, often sketchy, trying to present the main trends. Another problematic adjective is 'Jagiellonian': we use the dynastic name, but these persons were not always remembered particularly as 'Jagiellonian' (we try to point out some emphatic instances where they are). The relation and conflation between 'Jagiellonians' and the 'Jagiellonian' period needs also to be taken into consideration.
2. E.g. on the Habsburgs in the region – G. Heiss, Á. v. Klimó, P. Kolář and D. Kováč, 'Habsburgs' Difficult Legacy: Comparing and Relating Austrian, Czech, Magyar and Slovak National Master Narratives', in S. Berger and C. Lorenz, eds, *The Contested Nation: Ethnicity, Class, Religion and Gender in National Histories*, Basingstoke and New York, Palgrave Macmillan, 2008, pp. 367–404. See also Introduction, on entangled pasts, p. 3.
3. G. Gyáni, 'Changing Relationship between Collective Memory and History Writing', *Colloquia*, 19, 2012, pp. 138–41; S. Berger, L. Eriksonas and A. Mycock, eds, *Narrating the Nation: Representations in History, Media and the Arts*, Oxford and New York, 2008. There were various understandings of 'nation' in the given context, referring to the kingdom (or state or regional unit), or to an ethno-linguistic group, which were, especially in the nineteenth century, conflicting.
4. Other frameworks of memory, local, religious, dynastic, familial, and so on, could be present at the time, but the national one is dominant (in the investigated period). They are pointed out occasionally.
5. J. Pollmann and E. Kuijpers, 'Introduction. On the Early Modernity of Modern Memory', in *Memory before Modernity. Practices of Memory in Early Modern Europe*, E. Kuijpers, J. Pollmann, J. Müller and J. van der Steen, eds, Leiden and Boston, 2013, pp. 1–23.
6. Pollmann and Kuijpers, 'Introduction', pp. 5–6, relying on agendas set by Anderson, Hobsbawm, Gellner.
7. Pollmann and Kuijpers, 'Introduction', p. 10.
8. In the meaning *bene*. This orthography, neither the proper Czech, nor Polish, is typically used in Hungarian, thus somewhat illustrating the awkwardness and foreignness of the Slavic-speaking king in non-Slavic historiography.
9. *Jo. Dubravii Olomuzensis episcopi Historia Bohemica a Thoma Jordano...*, Francofurti, 1687, pp. 831–2.
10. The term is based on 'Laci', familiar for László. https://hu.wikipedia.org/wiki/Lacikonyha; *Magyar néprajzi lexikon III. (K–Né)*, ed. Gy. Ortutay, Budapest, Akadémiai, 1980, pp. 382–3. Online http://mek.oszk.hu/02100/02115/html/3-1117.html. J. Prohászka, 'A lacikonyha mivoltának és nevének kérdéséhez', *Magyar Nyelv*, 1965, vol. 61, no. 1, pp. 96–100.
11. A summary is available in I. Tringli, *Mohács felé 1490–1526*, Magyarország története 8, Budapest, 2009.
12. S. Brodericus, *De conflictu hungarorum cum Solymano Turcarum Imperatore ad Mohach historia verissima*, P. Kulcsár, ed., Budapest, 1985.
13. G. Sirmiensis, *Epistola de perditione regni Hungarorum*, Monumenta Hungariae Historica, Series 2, Scriptores, vol. 1, ed. Gustáv Wenzel, Pest, 1857.
14. F. Gábor Farkas, 'II. Lajos rejtélyes halála I.', *Magyar Könyvszemle*, 2000, vol. 116, no. 4, pp. 443–63, and part 2, 'II. Lajos rejtélyes halála II.', *Magyar Könyvszemle*, 2001, vol. 117, pp. 33–66. There is a conference volume devoted to this issue: F. G. Farkas, Zs. Szebelédi and B. Varga, eds, *"Nekünk mégis Mohács kell ..." II. Lajos király rejtélyes halála és különböző temetései*, Budapest, 2016.

15 Zs. Tóth, *The Making of Mohács . . . Occurrence, Regional Discourse and the Building of the "National Past" in Comparative History. A Case Study*. Available online: www.academia.edu/3847061/The_Making_of. . .Mohacs, accessed 21.3.14, pp. 1–17.
16 On the early memory of the battle, and Istvánffy, see M. Birnbaum, *Humanists in a Shattered World*, Columbus, OH, Slavica Publishers, 1986. More on the early memory is to be found in N. Nowakowska et al., *Dynasty in the Making*, ch. 4 (forthcoming).
17 I. Mihály, *"Magyarország panasza": a Querela Hungariae toposz a XVI–XVII. század irodalmában*, Debrecen, 1995. In this case, the Battle of Varna (and Wladislaus I) and other battles were often mentioned together.
18 G. Heltai, *Krónika az magyaroknak dolgairól*, ed. M. Kulcsár, introduction by P. Kulcsár, Budapest, 1981. The seventeenth-century Transylvanian historians often ignored the Battle of Mohács together with the previous history of the kingdom, or even confused it with the Battle of Varna; Tóth, *The Making of Mohács*, pp. 14–16.
19 Some light on the popular and national ideology at the diets is shed in M. Rady, 'Rethinking Jagiello Hungary (1490–1526)', *Central Europe*, 2005, vol. 3, no. 1, pp. 14–17. Through this optic, the Transylvanian principality was seen as a national Hungarian project, unlike the realm reigned by the Habsburg rulers. G. Pálffy, *The Kingdom of Hungary and the Habsburg Monarchy in the Sixteenth Century*, Boulder, CO, 2009, pp. 6–7, 159–61.
20 G. Szabados, 'The Annals as a Genre of Hungarian Jesuit Historiography in the 17th–18th Centuries. From the State History to the History of the State', in A. Steiner-Weber, ed., *Acta Conventus Neo-Latini Upsaliensis: Proceedings of the Fourteenth International Congress of Neo-Latin Studies*, Leiden, 2012, pp. 1067–75; G. Szabados, 'Jezsuita "sikertörténet" (1644–1811). A magyar történettudomány konzervatív megteremtőiről', in G. Tóth, ed., *Clio inter arma. Tanulmányok a 16–18. századi magyarországi történetírásról*, Budapest, 2014, pp. 203–26. More generally, see I. Deák, 'Historiography of the Countries of Eastern Europe: Hungary', *American Historical Review*, 1992, vol. 94, pp. 1041–63.
21 B. Trencsényi and M. Kopeček, eds, *Discourses of Collective Identity in Central and Southeast Europe (1770–1945)*, vol. 1: *Late Enlightenment. Emergence of the Modern 'National Idea'*, Budapest, 2006; R. J. W. Evans, 'The Politics of Language in Hungary', in H. Scott and B. Simms, eds, *Cultures of Power in Europe during the Long Eighteenth Century*, Cambridge, Cambridge University Press, 2007.
22 The designation 'House of Arpad' and 'Arpadian era', referring to the kings who ruled the Kingdom of Hungary between 1000 and 1301, was a construction (similar to the Jagiellonians), and was, alongside the story of pagan roots, one of the cornerstones of the Hungarian national myth. See A. Gerő, 'A National Fable: The Case of the House of Árpád', which provoked debate. Online: http://geroandras.hu/en/blog/2016/03/24/national-fable/, accessed 13.10.17. The history of these terms is discussed by G. Szabados, '907 emlékezete', *Tiszatáj*, 2007, vol. 61, no. 12, pp. 64–70, p. 67. The concept of national dynasty (we come across it almost everywhere, beyond historiography) and the periodisation of the Hungarian history in this 'Hegelian' spirit was used in the nineteenth century, and also in the interwar period (Bálint Hóman and Gyula Szekfű).
23 *Historia critica regum Hungariae. Ex fide domesticorum et exterorum scriptorum concinnata*, 42 vols, Pest, 1779–1817; *Historia pragmatica Hungariae concinnata a Stephano Katona . . .*, 2 vols, Buda, 1782–4.
24 The polemics and apologetics concerned especially the early history of the nation, the coming of the Hungarians to the Carpathian Basin and the beginnings of the Hungarian kingdom. Slavic writers focused on pre-Hungarian history (e.g. Samuel Timon, Ondrej Mesároš, Pavel Jozef Šafárik, Jan Kollár and Ján Hollý).
25 While accepting the idea of the ethnic origin of the kings, speaking of 'Hungarian blood' from St Stephen until Andrew III, that is, the Arpadian dynasty, they discuss Slavic kings both before and after the extinction of the kings of Hungarian blood. For example, J. Papánek, J. Fándly and J. Sklenár, eds, *Compendiata historia gentis Slavae*, Tyrnaviae, 1793, p. 232.

26 Plays on Mohács: Jesuit collegium in Cluj (1757 – *Ludovicus II.ad Mohatsium*, 1770 – *Ludovicus secundus*), Kőszeg (1776 – *Ludovicus ad Mohaczem cum nobilitatis flore caesus*), Piarist collegium in Nitra (1752 – *Luctuosus Ludovici II Hungarorum Regis ad Mohács occasus*) and in Szegen (1768 – colloquium *Res gestae Ludovici secundi*). I. Varga and M. Z. Pintér, *Történelem a színpadon. Magyar történelmi tárgyú iskoladrámák a 17.–18. században*, Budapest, Argumentum, 2000, pp. 41, 46–7, 56–7, 133–5. As an exception, there was also a play on Jagiello, *Jagello Magnus Dux Lithuaniae in Poloniae regem electus*, in 1738 in Sopron, and on Prince Casimir in Prešov in 1771; G. Staud, ed., *A magyarországi jezsuita iskolai színjátékok forrásai, II. 1561–1773, Kollégiumok*, Budapest, MTA, 1986.

27 For an overview, see M. É. Ducreux, 'Nation, état, education. L'enseignement de l'histoire en Europe centrale et orientale', *Histoire de l'education*, 2000, vol. 86 (Histoire et Nation en Europe centrale et orientale XIXe–XXe siècles), pp. 5–36.

28 I. Losontzi, *Hármas kis tükör, melly I. A' szent históriát, II. Magyar Országot, III. Erdély Országot, annak földével, polgári – állapatjával, és históriájával, gyenge elmékhez alkalmozott módon a' nemes tanulóknak summásan, de világosan elö-adja és ki mutatja*, Pozsony, 1777, pp. 124–30, 162–5. More than seventy editions exist between 1771 and 1854.

29 L. Bartolomeides, *Rozmlauwánj Jozefa Druhého s Matěgem Prwnjm Korwýnus řečeným, w Králowstwj Zemřelých Při Přjtomnosti některých giných Vherských Králů držané*, Praha, 1799, cf. A. Kalous, *Matyáš Korvín*, p. 397, n.155. Kalous is preparing an edition of the work; I would like to thank him for sharing with me the unpublished transcription.

30 *Magyar Márs avagy Moháchmezején történt veszedelemnek emlékezete*, Vienna, Cozmerovius, 1653. K. Péter, 'Mohács nemzeti tragédiává válik a magyar történetben', in András Kiss and Veronka Dáné, eds, '"... éltünk mi sokáig 'két hazában' ..."', Tanulmányok a 90 éves Kiss András tiszteletére', *Speculum Historiae Debreceniense* 9, Debrecen, 2012, pp. 17–27; P. Illik, *A Mohács-kód. A csatavesztés a magyar köztudatban*, Budapest, Unicus Műhely, 2015, pp. 14–15.

31 E. S. Márton, *Magyar gyász; vagy-is Második Lajos magyar királynak a mohátsi mezőn történt veszedelme*, Pesten, 1792. A few years after, in 1795, the epic was reworked into a drama in five acts, *Mohácsi veszedelem*, by Imre Ihászi, and shown also in Pest.

32 G. Galavics, 'Dorffmaister István történeti képei', in L. Kostyál and M. Zsámbéky, eds, *"Stephan Dorffmaister pinxit"*. *Dorffmaister István emlékkiállítása*, Szombathely, 1997, pp. 85–6; the scene of the battle of 1526 – cat. no. 42; the portrait (Kanizsai Dorottya Múzeum in Mohács) – cat. no. 44, and A. Mikó and K. Sinkó, eds, *Történelem – Kép. Szemelvények múlt és művészet kapcsolatáról Magyarországon*, A Magyar Nemzeti Galéria kiadványai 2000/3, cat. no. VI-31. On the paintings see also D. Csorba, 'II. Lajos király halála historiográfiai nézőpontból', in Farkas et al., *"Nekünk mégis Mohács kell ..."*, pp. 160–1. Recently, Csorba presented an overview of Hungarian memory of Louis II.

33 Kostyál and Zsámbéky, *"Stephan Dorffmaister pinxit"*, cat. no. 64; Mikó and Sinkó, *Történelem – Kép*, no. VI-30, p. 396 (Hungarian National Gallery).

34 Galavics, 'Dorffmaister István történeti képei', p. 85; cat. nos. 82–4.

35 G. Klösz, 'Műtárgyfotó – II. Lajos páncélja és egyéb magyar vonatkozású tárgyak az 1876. évi műipari kiállításon az ambrasi Kunstkammerből' [online photograph]: http://gyujtemeny.imm.hu/gyujtemeny/mutargyfoto-ii-lajos-pancelja-es-egyeb-magyar-vonatkozasu-targyak-az-1876-evi-muipari-kiallitason-az-ambrasi-kunstkammerbol/6857, accessed 14.10.17.

36 On the identification of the armour, see B. Thomas, 'Der Knabenharnisch Jorg Seusenhofers fur Sigmund II. August von Polen', *Zeitschrift des deutschen Vereins für Kunstwissenschaft*, 1939, 6, pp. 221–34; Z. Zygulski, *Broń w dawnej Polsce na tle uzbrojenia Europy i bliskiego wschodu*, Warsaw, 1975, pp. 195–6.

37 The memory of the event, rather weak before the nineteenth century, was reinforced when the bishop of Pécs, József Király, took the initiative in 1817 to build a memorial

chapel at the location of the battle at Mohács, where the paintings of Dorffmaister were also made available to the public, and funded a mass to be sung annually on its anniversary. 'Király József pécsi püspök alapítványa a mohácsi csata kultuszának ápolására – 1817 (Részlet)', in J. B. Szabó, ed., *Mohács*, Budapest, Osiris, 2006, pp. 478–9 (after *Tudományos Gyűjtemény*, 1829, no. 4, pp. 56–8).

38 For an English language overview, see for example S. B. Vardy, *Modern Hungarian Historiography*, Boulder, CO, 1976; B. Trencsényi, 'Writing the Nation and Reframing Early Modern Intellectual History in Hungary', *Studies in Eastern European Thought*, 2010, vol. 62, pp. 135–54; M. Baár, *Historians and Nationalism: East-Central Europe in the Nineteenth Century*, Oxford, 2010.

39 On Horváth, see Baár, *Historians and Nationalism*, pp. 35–9.

40 M. Horváth, *Magyarország történelme*, vol. 3, Pest, 3rd edn, 1871, p. 423. Horváth himself was not a medievalist and his work is based on the source collections of the eighteenth-century historians (not archival research), but he turned to the history of society as a whole instead of the history of the nobility and rulers. See F. Sebők, 'Hungarian Priest Historians on the Jagiellonian Era', in L. Löb, I. Petrovics and Gy. Szőnyi, eds, *Forms of Identity: Definitions and Changes*, Szeged, József Attila Tudományegyetem, 1994, pp. 89–95, 90–2.

41 J. Eötvös, *Magyarország 1514-ben. Regény*, Pest, 1847, available online: http://mek.oszk.hu/04700/04774/, accessed 14.10.17. On the theme of the Peasants' Revolt among Reform period Hungarian writers, see F. Kulin, *Hódíthatatlan szellem. Dózsa György és a parasztháború reformkori értékeléséről*, Budapest, 1982. The topic appears in Slovak literature of critical realism as well, e.g. a drama, *Dóža* (1866), by a Slovak intellectual, priest and historian, Jonáš Záborský.

42 http://zlatyfond.sme.sk/dielo/1078/Kollar_Narodnie-spievanky-1-Spevy-historicky-pamatne/25 Source: Czech print *O nešťastné bitvie a porážce Uhrú od národu tureckého učiněné a o smrti velmi smutné a žalostivé paměti Ludvika jeho milosti*, 1526. See Z. Kákošová, 'Podoby zobrazenia Turka a tureckých reálií v slovenskej literatúre 16. a 17. storočia', *Bohemica Litteraria*, 2010, vol. 13, no. 1–2, pp. 31–45, p. 38. Czech sources mention two to three songs about Mohács: see Č. Zíbrt and Z. Nejedlý, eds, 'Dvě písně o bitvě u Moháče 1526', in *Časopis Musea Království českého*, Mikuláš Konáč z Hodiškova, 1905, vol. 79, pp. 370–4; F. Dvorský, ed., 'Truchlivá píseň o zahynutí Ludvíka, krále Českého', in *Časopis Musea Království českého*, 1864, vol. 38, pp. 389–92.

43 On Croatian songs see F. Fancev, 'Mohacka tragedija od god. 1526. suvremenoj hrvatskoj pjesmi', *Nastavni Vjesnik*, 1934/5, vol. 43, pp. 18–28.

44 There is a folk song about Mohács from Baranya county mentioned by writer Sándor Baksay at the turn of the twentieth century: a stanza about the king drowning in the stream used in his work *Dáma*; L. Kéky, *Baksay Sándor*, Budapest, Franklin-Társulat, 1917, p. 70.

45 The folk song is briefly discussed, including English translation and literature, by J. M. Bak, 'Good King Polish Ladislas: History and Memory of the Short Reign of Władysław Warneńczyk in Hungary', in J. M. Bak, *Studying Medieval Rulers and Their Subjects: Central Europe and Beyond*, Balázs Nagy and Gábor Klaniczay, eds, Variorum Collected Studies Series, 956, Farnham, Ashgate, 2010, pp. 182–3. It is included in the great corpus of Hungarian folk music edited by Béla Bartók and Zoltán Kodály. There are numerous Slavic versions of the piece too.

46 F. Kölcsey, 'Nemzeti hagyományok', in *Kölcsei Kölcsey Ferencz minden munkái*, vol. 3, ed. F. Toldy, Pesten, 1860, pp. 28–9. The importance of preserving national traditions is also the topic of another of Kölcsey's essays, *Mohács* (1826).

47 J. Neubauer, 'General Introduction', in *History of the Literary Cultures of East-Central Europe: Junctures and Disjunctures in the 19th and 20th Centuries*, vol. 3, *The Making and Remaking of Literary Institutions*, ed. M. Cornis-Pope and J. Neubauer, Amsterdam and Philadelphia, John Benjamins, 2007, pp. 17–18.

48 The epitaph was actually of a later date, written and printed by Christophorus Manlius a century later, in 1573; see the convincing argument of G. Szentmártoni Szabó, '"Romulidae Cannas", avagy egy ál-Janus Pannonius-vers utóélete, eredeti szövege és válodi szerzője', in *Convivium Pajorin Klára 70.születésnapjára*, Debrecen and Budapest, 2012, pp. 183–94, who also traces the afterlife and reception of the epitaph in Hungarian literature; it was used by Mór Jókai in his description of the Battle of Varna in *A magyar nemzet története regényes rajzokban*, discussed below.

49 The popularity of the theme of Mohács in the nineteenth century is well documented with the table of literary, polemic, religious and other works published between 1820 and 1894 produced by Illik, *A Mohács-kód*, pp. 15–17.

50 Z. Tóth, 'The Hungarian Peculiarities of National Remembrance: Historical Figures with Symbolic Importance in Nineteenth-Century Hungarian History Paintings', *AHEA: E-Journal of the American Hungarian Educators Association*, 2012, vol. 5, pp. 1–16. Other significant historical paintings with this function represent heroes of anti-Turkish wars, or St Stephen.

51 Tóth, 'The Hungarian Peculiarities', p. 5. In the same period and same spirit, Isabella became a subject of a painting by Sándor Wagner, *Queen Isabella Taking Leave of Transylvania* (1863).

52 Oil on canvas, 200 x 290 cm, Debrecen Calvinist Collegium. On the painting and its context, as well as the new iconography of Louis II and his cult, see the study by K. Sinkó, 'Historizmus-Antihistorizmus', in Mikó and Sinkó, *Történelem – Kép*, pp. 109–10; catalogue volume entry no. XI-2 by K. Sinkó, 'A Mohácsnál elesett II. Lajos testének feltalása', in Mikó and Sinkó, *Történelem – Kép*, pp. 600–2.

53 Toldy to Orlai, 16 September 1851 (MNG Adattár 2126/1927), quote after Sinkó, translation mine; K. Sinkó, 'Kontinuitás vagy hagyomány újrateremtése? Történeti képek a 19. században', in Szabó, *Mohács*, p. 473 (also quoted in Mikó and Sinkó, *Történelem – Kép*, p. 601). The debate pieces in newspapers in 1851 and the correspondence with Toldy and Eötvös concerning the painting are listed in the catalogue from the 2011 Munkácsy museum exhibition by students on *Orlai Petrics Soma*, Z. Galamb and K. Keserű, available online: www.munkacsy.hu/dokumentumok/dir6/2211_491_Orlai_ Petics_Soma_kiallitasi_kalogus.pdf, accessed 14.10.17, pp. 154–5, 164–5, 167–8.

54 Another debate in newspapers was provoked by a lithograph of the Battle of Mohács, this time not with Louis emphasised, by Mór Than (1856) in the journal *Hölgyfutár*; for more see Sinkó, 'Kontinuitás vagy hagyomány újrateremtése?', in Szabó, *Mohács*, pp. 474–5; E. Révész, 'Történeti kép mint sajtóillusztráció 1850–1870', in Mikó and Sinkó, *Történelem – Kép*, pp. 580–97; and catalogue no. XI-5, pp. 604–6. See a selection of extracts from the debate: 'A Napkelet és a Hölgyfutár című lap polemiája Than Mór mohácsi vész című képéről, 1857', in Szabó, *Mohács*, pp. 500–4.

55 P. Jászay, *A magyar nemzet napjai a Mohácsi vész után*, Pest, 1846, pp. 104–7, 530–3. The book, which among others dealt with the reports of finding the body of Louis and the rumours about his death, or murder, stirred interest and had an impact beyond historiography. For the tradition of *querela Hungariae* etc., see Mihály, *"Magyarország panasza"*.

56 Sinkó, 'Kontinuitás vagy hagyomány újrateremtése?', p. 474.

57 The Dorffmaister paintings were moved to the memorial chapel (1856–9), and a relief image of the falling Louis was installed at his memorial built at the Csele stream (1864). Cf. also the empire-patriotic description of Mohács as the king's tomb in F. Körner, ed., *Vaterländische Bilder aus Ungarn und Siebenbürgen, der Woiwodina und dem Banat, Kroatien, Slawonien, der Militärgrenze sowie Dalmatien: in Schilderungen aus Natur, Geschichte, Industrie und Volksleben*, Leipzig, 1858, vol. 3, pp. 109–13.

58 Oil on canvas, 140 x 181.5 cm, Budapest, Hungarian National Gallery. Other historical paintings by him include *Battle of Mohács* (1866) and *Ladislas V and Ulrich Cillei* (1870). For more on the painting and the context in the catalogue of an exhibition of Bertalan Székely's paintings, see Zs. Bakó, 'Adatok a Székely Bertalan életmű kutatásához', in *Székely Bertalan (1835–1910), kiállítása: Magyar Nemzeti Galéria*

1999. szeptember 30-2000. január 30. Ungarische Nationalgalerie 30. September 1999– 30. Januar 2000, Zs. Bakó, A. Kiséry, H. Schmőr-Weichenhain and S. Vadasi, eds, Budapest, 1999, pp. 13–16, catalogue entry no. 27 and various sketches in preparation, nos. 21–6, pp. 102–8, online: http://library.arcanum.hu/en/view/ORSZ_NEMG_kv_53_ Szekely/?pg=0&zoom=h&layout=l. Catalogue entry no. II. 1. 17. K. Sinkó, 'Székely Bertalan', in I. Nagy, ed., *Aranyérmek, ezüstkoszorúk. Művészkultusz és műpártolás magyarországon a 19. században*, A Magyar Nemzeti Galéria kiadványai 1995/1, Budapest, 1995, p. 234.

59 For Matejko, see Nowakowska on Poland, in this volume, p. 55.

60 K. Sinkó, 'A művészi siker anatómiája 1840–1900', in Nagy, *Aranyérmek*, p. 28. A Hungarian newspaper published a black-and-white reproduction of Székely's painting accompanied by a short text in 1900. The article retrospectively commented on the first big work of the by then famous artist, and praised it for combining foreign influences with national spirit, the grief and awe, and both realistic representation and dramatic expression. Based on the information in *Vasárnapi Ujság*, 1900. márczius 18. The image is in the digital database of the Hungarian National Library online: http://dka.oszk.hu/html/kepoldal/index.phtml?id=41294, accessed 14.10.17.

61 On the importance of these influences, see also Tóth, 'The Hungarian Peculiarities', pp. 10–11; E. Révész, 'Történeti kép mint sajtóillusztráció 1850–1870', in Á. Mikó and K. Sinkó, eds, *Történelem – Kép, Múlt és művészet kapcsolata Magyarországon. Kiállítási katalógus*, Budapest, Magyar Nemzeti Galéria, 2000, pp. 580–97.

62 S. B. Vardy, 'The Social and Ideological Make-up of Hungarian Historiography in the Age of Dualism (1867–1918)', *Jahrbücher Für Geschichte Osteuropas*, Neue Folge, 1976, vol. 24, no. 2, pp. 208–17.

63 Sebők, 'Hungarian Priest Historians'. Fraknói also wrote a biography of Werbőczy, the author of the collection of custom law and representative of the lesser nobility at the diets, *Werbőczy István élete*, Budapest, 1899; and Fraknói, 'Werbőczy István a mohácsi vész előtt', *Századok*, 1896, vol. 10, pp. 437–69, 597–639. He did a lot of indispensable research, especially on the relations with the papacy; V. Fraknói, *Magyarország a mohácsi vész előtt*, Budapest, 1884; *Monumenta Vaticana Historiam regni Hungariae illustrantia*, Budapest, 1884.

64 V. Fraknói, 'A Hunyadiak és a Jagellók kora (1440–1526)', in Sándor Szilágyi, ed., *A magyar nemzet története*, Budapest, Athenaeum, 1896, vol. 4.

65 Sebők, 'Hungarian Priest Historians', pp. 93–4. He also published on the election of Wladislaus, and other royal elections: V. Fraknói, 'II. Ulászló királlyá választása', *Századok*, 1885, vol. 19, pp. 1–20, 97–115, 193–211; V. Fraknói, *A magyar királyválasztások története*, Budapest, Athenaeum, 1921.

66 D. Szabó, *Küzdelmeink a nemzeti királyságért 1505–1526 (A magyar nemzet önállóságáért és függetlenségéért vívott küzdelmek története az 1505-iki rákosi országgyűléstől a Rákoczi-emigratio kihaltáig*, vol. 1, Budapest, 1917, introduction.

67 Szabó, *Küzdelmeink a nemzeti királyságért 1505–1526*, pp. 127, 226. Szabó supports this with a quotation from a letter in AT 8, 157: Hungarians did not care whether Louis died, 'they hated him, because he lived according to German customs, he loved Germans, scorned Hungarians and felt good only among Germans'. The nineteenth-century anti-German sentiments conveniently mirror the rhetoric of some sixteenth-century sources.

68 D. Szabó, *A magyar országgyűlések II. Lajos korában*, Budapest, 1909. For the debate and the historiography of this period, see also F. Sebők, 'Új törekvések a Jagelló-kori rendiség kutatásában a XX. század elején', *Acta historica*, 1992, vol. 96, pp. 47–53.

69 J. Fógel, *II. Ulászló udvartartása (1490–1516)*, Budapest, MTA, 1913; J. Fógel, *II. Lajos udvartartása*, Budapest, 1917.

70 E. Veress, *Izabella királyné*, Magyar Történeti Életrajzok, Budapest, 1901.

71 T. Ortvay, *Mária, II. Lajos magyar király neje 1505–1558*, Magyar Történeti Életrajzok, Budapest, 1914.

72 S. Márki, *Dósa György*, Magyar Történeti Életrajzok, Budapest, Athenaeum, 1914.
73 On the millennium celebrations in general, e.g. K. Varga, ed., *1896: A Millenniumi Országos Kiállítás és az ünnepségek krónikája*, Budapest, 1996.
74 This is a summary provided by László Kőváry in a book devoted to the millennium celebrations and memorials in 1897, *A millennium lefolyásának története s a millennáris emlékalkotások*, Budapest, 1897, ch. 2, pp. 36–43.
75 *A magyar nemzet története*, ed. Sándor Szilágyi, Budapest, 1896, with the part on the Jagiellonians in volume 4 written by V. Fraknói, 'A Hunyadiak és a Jagellók kora (1440–1526)'. See above.
76 H. Marczali, ed., *Nagy képes világtörténet*, vol. 6, ed. J. Csuday and Gyula Schonherr, Budapest, Révai Testvérek, electronic edition online: www.elib.hu/01200/01267/html/06kotet/06r05f31.htm, accessed 23.10.17.
77 *Pallas Nagy Lexikona*, Budapest, Pallas Irodalmi, 1893–97, online edition: http://mek.oszk.hu/00000/00060/, accessed 14.10.17. The lexicon also has entries on Wladislaus I, Louis II, Isabella, Anna Jagiellon.
78 Ducreux, 'Nation, état, education', paras 27, 34, 35.
79 For example, K. P. Szathmáry, *Sirály*, 3 vols, Pest, 1855; S. Baksay, *Dáma. Történeti körkép Kimnach László rajzaival*, Budapest, 1899. Szathmáry also wrote a novel *Izabela* in 1859.
80 Lajos Bartók, *Mohács után* (1898), and later Géza Voinovich, *Mohács* (1922); Dezső Szomory, *II. Lajos*, one of the *Királydrámák*/Royal dramas (1922).
81 S. Baksay, *Dáma*. Journal edition in *Vasárnapi újság regénytára*, 1898, vol. 14–40, with illustrations by László Kimnach, including Louis falling from the horse in the armour (p. 101), and also the reproduction of Bertalan Székely's famous painting (p. 102), available online: http://epa.oszk.hu/00000/00030/02342/pdf/02342.pdf, accessed 14.10.17.
82 M. Jókai, *Fráter György*, Budapest, 1972.
83 He used the synthetical works of Szalay and Horváth. P. Kasza, 'Brodarics István tevékenysége irodalomtörténeti megközelítésben', PhD dissertation, Szeged, 2007, p. 160. Online: http://doktori.bibl.u-szeged.hu/919/1/Kasza_doktori.pdf, accessed 13.10.17.
84 Jókai, *Fráter György*, chapter 'A mohácsi vésznap', available online: http://mek.oszk.hu/00800/00840/html/jokai102.htm, accessed 23.10.17.
85 F. V. Sasinek, *Dejiny kráľovstva uhorského*, vol. 2, Turčiansky Sv. Martin, 1871, p. 133.
86 He insists that the names Ladislaus and Wladislaus, László and Ulászló, are identical, although differentiated in histories of the kingdom written in Latin, Hungarian and German, which he considers uncritical and even laughable in the Slavic world. See Sasinek, *Dejiny kráľovstva uhorského*, vol. 2, p. 138, n. 2. See also p. 307, n. 1, on the same topic, where he explains why he calls Wladislaus II 'Wladislaus VII'.
87 Sasinek, *Dejiny kráľovstva uhorského*, vol. 2, p. 353, on elections in Poland, pp. 316, 329.
88 Sasinek, *Dejiny kráľovstva uhorského*, pp. 370–371.
89 Sasinek, *Dejiny kráľovstva uhorského*, pp. 389–90.
90 J. Koreň, *Dejiny československého národa. Dejepis pre slovenské ľudové školy (a pre opakovacie školy)*, Prešov, 1921, pp. 23–7.
91 F. Hrušovský, *Slovenské dejiny*, Turčiansky Sv. Martin, Matica slovenská, 3rd edn, 1939, pp. 12–13; chapter 'Slovakia during the Rule of the Jagiellonians', pp. 146–9.
92 Trencsényi, 'Writing the Nation', p. 138.
93 In intellectual and cultural areas, there is even flourishment; B. Hóman and G. Szekfű, *Magyar történet*, 5 vols, Budapest, 1936, vol. 2 (1939), pp. 564–611. F. Sebők, 'A Jagelló-kori rendiség kutatása a két világháború között', *Aetas*, 1993, vol. 4, pp. 35–6.
94 B. Hóman and G. Szekfű, *Magyar történet*, Budapest, 1928, chapter 'A rendek uralma Mohácsig', available online: www.elib.hu/00900/00940/html/
95 On the topic of 'new Mohács' in poetry, see Illik, *A Mohács-kód*, pp. 47–51.
96 For a summary of the events and works related to the anniversary, see Illik, *A Mohács-kód*, pp. 51–3. On newspaper reports see also Szabó, *Mohács*, pp. 527–36.

97 In Szabó, *Mohács*, pp. 531–5. R. Kerepeszki, 'Horthy Miklós mohácsi beszéde, 1926. Emlékezethely a politikai gondolkodásban és a nemzetközi kapcsolatok történetében', in M. Takács, ed., *A magyar emlékezethelyek kutatásának elméleti és módszertani alapjai*, Loci Memoriae Hungaricae 2, P. S. Varga, O. Száraz, Debrecen, Debreceni Egyetemi Kiadó, 2013, pp. 309–20.
98 Preface, by K. Klebelsberg, to I. Lukinich, ed., *Mohács emlékkönyv 1526*, Budapest, 1926.
99 G. Krúdy, *Királyregények: Mohács, Festett király, Az első Habsburg*, Budapest, Szépirodalmi kiadó, 1979.
100 Positive review by P. Kürti, 'Mohács. Krúdy Gyula regénye Pantheon-kiadás', *Nyugat*, 1927, vol. 8, online: http://epa.oszk.hu/00000/00022/00417/13025.htm, accessed 13.10.17. See also Z. Kelemen, *Történelmi emlékezet és mitikus történet Krúdy Gyula műveiben*, Budapest, Argumentum Kiadó, 2005.
101 A review of the 'centenary novels' about Mohács in B. Marcell, 'A Mohács centenárium regényei', *Korunk*, May 1927, http://korunk.org/?q=node/4314, accessed 13.10.17.
102 The words of the novelist László Németh as recalled by Z. A. Bán, *The Knight of Mist. Gyula Krúdy (1878–1933): A Portrait*, available online: www.hlo.hu/news/the_knight_of_fogginess, accessed 13.10.17.
103 This is Anna Horváth's interpretation: A. Horváth, 'Krúdy Gyula Mohács-trilogiája. Egy történelmi tényregény születése', PhD dissertation, Budapest, 2010, available online: http://doktori.btk.elte.hu/lit/horvathanna/diss.pdf, accessed 13.10.17.
104 Marcell, 'A Mohács centenárium regényei'.
105 For a recent summary of the debate see V. Erős, 'A Mohács-vita', *Magyar Szemle*, 2014, vol. 23, no. 5–6, pp. 55–76. An earlier summary by S. B. Vardy is 'The Changing Image of the Turks in Twentieth Century Hungarian Historiography', in *Clio's Art in Hungary and Hungarian America*, New York, Columbia University Press, 1985, pp. 147–70. A selection of contributions to the debate is reprinted in Szabó, *Mohács*, pp. 558–612.
106 I. Nemeskürty, *Ez történt Mohács után: Tudosítás a magyar történelem tizenöt esztendejéről 1526–1541*, Budapest, 1966.
107 G. Perjés, *Az országút szélére vetett ország*, Budapest, Magvető, 1975; F. Szakály, *A mohácsi csata*, Budapest, 1975. An analysis of both works and their use of sources appears in G. Gyáni, 'Elbeszélhető-e egy csata hiteles története? Metatörténeti megfontolások', *Hadtörténelmi közlemények*, 2006, vol. 119, no. 1, pp. 121–33; Illik, *A Mohács-kód*, pp. 19–30. One of the most important contributions to the debate is T. Klaniczay, 'Mi és miért veszett Mohácsnál?', in *Hagyományok ébresztése*, Budapest, 1976, pp. 200–6. Domonkos Kosáry dealt with the pre-Mohács period 1500–26 and Hungarian foreign policy: D. Kosáry, *Magyar külpolitika Mohács előtt*, Budapest, 1978; a shortened version appears in the Mohács collected volume published in 1986 – see note 115, below. Analysis by I. Tringli, 'Kosáry Domonkos és a Mohács-vita', *Magyar Tudomány*, 2013, vol. 12, pp. 1437–41. As in the earlier periods, the theme of Mohács was reflected in literature as well, with a collection of drama pieces by Gyula Háy (1900–75), a Hungarian Communist intellectual imprisoned after 1956 and then exiled, published as *Királydrámák* (6 pieces) in 1964 (some written earlier), but not staged.
108 I. Nemeskürty, *Krónika Dózsa György teteiról*, Budapest, Kossuth, 1972. J. Szűcs, *Nemzet és történelem*, Budapest, 1973. Among the studies written in the 1970s: G. Barta and A. Fekete Nagy, *Parasztháború 1514-ben*, Budapest, 1973; and a collection of sources: A. Fekete Nagy, V. Kenéz, L. Solymosi and G. Érszegi, eds, *Monumenta rusticorum in Hungaria rebellium anno MDXIV*, Budapest, Akadémiai Kiadó, 1979. For a different and more recent perspective, a 'bottom-up' narrative, and individual memories of participants, see G. Erdélyi, 'Tales of a Peasant Revolt: Taboos and Memories of 1514 in Hungary', in Kuijpers et al., *Memory before Modernity*, pp. 93–109.

109 I. Bibó, 'Ha a zsinati mozgalom a 15.században győzött volna... Bibó István címzetes váci kanonok beszélgetései apósával, Ravasz László bíboros érsekkel a római katolikus egyház újkori történetéről, különös tekintettel a lutheránus és kálvinista kongregációkra. Egyház-, kultúr-és politikatörténeti uchrónia', in I. Bibó, *Válogatott tanulmányok*, vol. 4, Budapest, 1990, pp. 265–82. In similar vein, he debated with contemporary historians like István Szabó over the interpretation of the post-1945 events. Szabó, a historian of the peasantry, essentially claimed that development in Hungary was slowed down compared to the West for 500 years, from the early sixteenth century and the suppression of the 1514 uprising under the rule of Wladislaus II, followed by the loss at Mohács and subsequent events. I. Bibó, 'A magyar társadalomfejlodés és az 1945. évi változás értelme', in I. Bibó, *Válogatott tanulmányok*, vol. 3, Budapest, Magvető, 1986, pp. 5–124. This is also discussed in G. Kovács, 'Változatok a történelemre. Bibó István Uchróniája', *2000*, 1997/július, pp. 51–2.
110 G. Kovács, 'A mohácsi történelmi emlékhely. Szimbolikus harc a történelmi emlékezetért', in T. Hofer, ed., *Magyarok Kelet és Nyugat közt. A nemzettudat változó jelképei*, Budapest, 1996, pp. 283–303. A website exists for the memorial: www.mohacsiemlekhely.hu/, accessed 23.10.17.
111 Gy. Ortutay, 'Mohács emlékezete. Elhangzott a Mohácsi Történelmi Emlékhely felavatásán', in Szabó, *Mohács*, pp. 537–42.
112 F. Szakály, ed., *Mohács Tanulmányok a mohácsi csata 450. évfordulója alkalmából*, Budapest, 1986, especially the study of Ferenc Szakály.
113 A. Kubinyi, 'Historische Skizze Ungarns in der Jagiellonenzeit', in A. Kubinyi, *König und Volk im spätmittelalterlichen Ungarn*, Herne, 1998, pp. 323–66. See A. Kubinyi, 'A Jagelló-kori Magyar állam', *Történelmi szemle*, 2006, vol. 48, no. 3–4, pp. 287–307; A. Kubinyi, 'The Road to Defeat: Hungarian Politics and Defense in the Jagiellonian Period', in J. M. Bak and B. Király, eds, *From Hunyadi to Rákóczi: War and Society in Later Medieval and Early Modern Hungary*, New York, 1982, pp. 159–78; for military development, J. B. Szabó, 'A mohácsi csata és a "hadügyi forradalom"', *Hadtörténelmi közlemények*, 2004, vol. 117, pp. 443–78, and 'A mohácsi csata és a "hadügyi forradalom". II. rész. A magyar hadsereg a mohácsi csatában, *Hadtörténelmi közlemények*', 2005, vol. 118, pp. 573–627; and for the financial and military situation, Rady, 'Rethinking Jagiello Hungary'.
114 For example, the chapter on Hungary in the fifteenth century (ch. 27): J. Bak, 'Hungary: Crown and Estates', in C. Allmand, ed., *New Cambridge Medieval History*, vol. 7, c.1415–c.1500, Cambridge, 1998, pp. 707–26.
115 Among others, A. Kubinyi, 'Alltag und Fest am ungarischen Königshof der Jagellonen 1490–1526', in Kubinyi, *König und Volk im spätmittelalterlichen Ungarn*, pp. 184–206; O. Réthelyi et al., eds, *Mary of Hungary: The Queen and Her Court 1521–1531*, Budapest, Budapest History Museum, 2005. Catalogue and collected volume of the exhibition organised by Budapest History Museum, 30 September 2005–9 January 2006, Slovenská národná galéria, 2 February–30 April 2006.
116 The best summary in English is T. Neumann, 'King Wladislaus II: Weak Ruler or Victim of Circumstances?', unpublished lecture, Prague, 2011, available online: www.academia.edu/5627572/King_Wladislaus_II_Weak_Ruler_or_Victim_of_Circumstances_Unpublished_the_written_version_of_a_lecture_held_in_Prague_2011_, accessed 5.8.16. On Wladislaus's authority see, for example, T. Neumann, 'Királyi aláírás és pecséthasználat a Jagelló-kor elején', *Turul*, 2010, vol. 83, no. 2, pp. 34, 47–9; T. Oborni and Sz. Varga, 'A béke mint a hatalmi propaganda eszköze Jagelló (II.) Ulászló és Szapolyai (I.) János uralkodása idején', in *A történettudomány szolgálatában. Tanulmányok a 70 éves Gecsényi Lajos tiszteletére*, Budapest, 2012, pp. 251–65. Neumann offered a corrected view of Wladislaus also in a popular article on the occasion of the 500th anniversary of Wladislaus's death in 2016 for the magazine of early modern history 'A "Dobzsekirályról" egy kicsit másképp – Ötszáz éve halt meg II. Ulászló', http://ujkor.hu/content/dobzsekiralyrol-egy-kicsit-maskepp-otszaz-eve-halt-meg-ii-

ulaszlo, accessed 5.8.16. The rather traditional, simplified view of an incapable and uninterested Wladislaus is also found in the overview by P. Engel, *The Realm of Saint Stephen. A History of Medieval Hungary, 895–1526*, London and New York, I. B. Tauris, 2001, p. 347.
117 Tringli, *Mohács felé 1490–1526*, pp. 109–11.
118 In the Hungarian piece written on the 500th anniversary of Wladislaus's death (quoted by Neumann, 'A "Dobzsekirályról"'), archived at: http://nol.hu/pagenotfound/top-10-a-magyar-tortenelem-legnagyobb-tevedesei-1600631, accessed 2.4.17.
119 János Szabó's book on Mohács, aimed at the general public, refutes the 'legends' and 'myths' about the battle; the reception and memory of Mohács over time is treated in a collection of sources in the series *Nation and Memory*, devoted to important events and topics from Hungarian history. Szabó, *Mohács*. Studies on the myths include 'Mohács legendáink nyomában', *Korunk*, 2012, no. 3, pp. 27–33; 'Mohács', *Rubicon*, 2013, no. 8, pp. 4–19. See Illik, *A Mohács-kód*, on the public memory of the battle, its reception, working with political speeches, publicists, studies and textbooks, novels, poems and internet discussions.
120 More on the website of the memorial: www.mohacsiemlekhely.hu/. On the architecture of the exhibition building, see: http://epiteszforum.hu/felejtes-helyett-feltamadas-mohacs-uj-koronaja.
121 For example, time-travelling superheroes were transported from the Mohács battlefield to 2014 Budapest in a Hungarian comic fantasy novel, *Mohács Kommandó* – the joint effort of historical fantasy writer Bán Mór (the author of a novel cycle on the Hunyadis) and Attila Fazekas.
122 T. Várkonyi, *Négy király, egy szultán*, Budapest, 2014. See also the review by Attila Bárány, in *Turul*, 2015, vol. 88, pp. 33–5. The work is praised by a specialist of the period as well.
123 P. Fodor, 'Hollók évadja. Gondolatok a mohácsi csatáról és következményeiről', in Farkas et al., *"Nekünk mégis Mohács kell . . . "*, p. 8.
124 D. Kováč, *Dejiny Slovenska*, Praha, Nakladatelství Lidové noviny, 1998, pp. 46–9. See also a university textbook aimed at broader audiences, which offers a more balanced picture: P. Kónya et al., *Dejiny Uhorska*, Bratislava, Trio Publishing, 2014, especially pp. 156–69. Another overview by M. Kučera, *Slovenské dejiny I. Od príchodu Slovanov do roku 1526*, Literárne informačné centrum, 2011, pp. 306–12, emphasises 'feudal anarchy' and 'crisis of feudal society'.

4

DID BOHEMIAN JAGIELLONIANS EXIST?

Ilya Afanasyev

It would be self-evidently nonsensical to ask whether Bohemian Jagiellonians existed. Or would it? When Immanuel Wallerstein asked, as he himself emphasised, an 'absurd question', whether India existed, he wanted to make the following point, formulated, again, somewhat provocatively: 'What happened in the distant past is always a function of what happened in the near past' (for example, 'India' is not an objective entity, geographical, cultural or political, but an idea that, for all the ancient origins of the word, came to be shaped and reified in its current political and geographical form over the course of colonial and postcolonial history).[1] This of course means that what 'we' discern in the infinite complexity of past reality is predicated on the conceptual lenses that also have their own histories, rooted in material, social, political and ideological processes and transformations in each given period. These histories may not necessarily be located in a past that is 'near' to us; on the contrary, they can be 'long' and transgress the boundaries of different periods, more or *less* 'recent'. Often, 'we', both professional historians and 'lay' persons, forget about those histories and, instead, take our conceptual apparatuses for granted and treat them as reliable tools in our attempts to represent the past or, even worse, perceive them as integral elements of that past. Asking absurd questions may help us to destabilise this false sense of comfort and (re)discover the histories of how we have come to think of a given past in a particular way.

When I ask whether Bohemian Jagiellonians existed, the goal is not to cause the reader to doubt my (or her) sanity by denying that Kings Ladislaus II and Louis II reigned in the Kingdom of Bohemia in 1471–1526.[2] Rather, the point is to question two major historical categories that underpin the notion of 'Bohemian Jagiellonians'. The first one is explicit in the phrase itself: 'the Jagiellonians', a form of identification. The second is implicit: 'dynasty', a meta-concept that supposedly defines the institutional and ideological framework in which such identifications functioned across pre-modern history.

It must be made clear from the very beginning that a critical approach to these concepts is not at all my individual insight: it is a (preliminary) outcome of the collective work of the 'Jagiellonians Project', conceived and led by Natalia Nowakowska at the University of Oxford. From the early stages of our project it has become evident that, contrary to the predominant view in historiography that treats 'dynasty' as a given, as an unproblematic term denoting a 'really existing' institution of pre-modern politics, 'dynasty' does not map straightforwardly onto source evidence. There is no space here to develop either a complex critique of 'dynasty' or any version of a new positive interpretation of the medieval and early modern evidence that does exist.[3] It suffices to say that the historiographical notion of 'dynasty' (not necessarily articulated through the formal definitions of the term, but, instead, transpiring from historians' rhetoric and argumentation), as a bounded and named family group acting as a self-conscious political agent on the basis of 'dynastic' (self)-identification and in pursuit of 'dynastic' interests, is problematic. The same applies to the standard 'dynastic' chronologies – a tradition of splitting national master narratives into 'dynastic' blocs, named after distinguishable ruling families that can also be dated precisely ('dynasty X' began in year Y and ended in year Z). A theoretical departure point of this essay is the claim that this institutional-conceptual complex of 'dynasty' is not so much a part of medieval reality but is rather a set of retrospective projections, a history of which may be traced by looking at the 'memory' of a particular 'dynasty' from the early modern period to our current moment.

My empirical starting point is the following observation: if we zoom in on the year 1526, when King Louis II died at the Battle of Mohács, the event that today marks the end of the 'Jagiellonian period' in Czech history, we notice that neither the concept of 'dynasty' nor the collective name 'Jagiellonians' was in use in the Kingdom of Bohemia at the time. Thus, rather than being an empirical foundation for the future historical memory of Ladislaus and Louis, both the 'dynasty' and 'the Bohemian Jagiellonians' were invented retrospectively.[4] But before I try to map the development of this conceptual process, a theoretical clarification is due. Adopting a constructivist stance and talking about 'invention' does not always mean claiming that something was invented *ex nihilo*. Rather, concepts, institutions, productive forces, social relations and all other objects and actors of history, are continuously assembled and re-assembled. This implies that, when I state that 'dynasty' and 'the Bohemian Jagiellonians' were invented retrospectively after 1526, I do not claim that these inventions are completely separated and isolated from what was going on in the lifetimes of Ladislaus and Louis. On the contrary, genealogical notions, political vocabularies and ideas, and political practices of the historic period are among necessary elements of the later process of forging 'the Jagiellonians' and coining the concept of 'dynasty'. These developing notions – 'dynasty' and 'the Jagiellonians' – are, in their own right, not singular things once invented and then stable in meaning and identity, but rather 'moving targets', reinvented in different periods and contexts.

The initial framework in which this essay has been written is the task of tracing the 'memory' of 'the Jagiellonians' in 'Czech' tradition, understood as the sum of historiographical and fictional (literary), visual and official representations produced in 'Czech' lands from 1526 until the present day. There are inevitable conceptual problems with this frame. It is difficult to escape from the methodological nationalism of this approach, which projects the existence of 'Czechness' as a singular phenomenon with a continuous history, even if one explicitly states that there is no ethnic, linguistic, cultural, or any other essence to it. While 'Bohemian'/'Czech' identifications were constructed and deployed in each given moment over the long period considered here (and, moreover, these moments are indeed connected with each other, rather than totally isolated episodes), there is still a leap from this observation to an assumption that this identification constitutes a meaningful and singular container within which the history of another phenomenon, representations of 'the Jagiellonians', for example, can be located and made sense of.

This difficulty is augmented by the problematic aspects of the concept of 'memory' – the theme of this essay and the volume as a whole. 'Collective memory' has been theorised extensively over the last decades and this essay cannot aspire to make a contribution to this wide and rich field.[5] But it is important to point out at least one fundamental problem with the concept of (collective) memory: the subject that it projects but does not quite name openly. Who is actually doing the 'remembering'? When an ethnic/geographic/national qualifier is introduced in this conversation, it is difficult to avoid constituting (purposefully or unwittingly) 'the nation' as the subject and agent which is remembering something, which, of course, returns us to the issue of methodological nationalism, personification of an abstract ideological concept and its reification. A possible solution might be to stop talking about 'memory', with all its problematic leaps from individual psychology to alleged collective remembering by a 'group',[6] and instead, discuss historical representations, which are obviously created by particular actors, reproduced through particular apparatuses and received (and then potentially memorised) by particular audiences.[7] Thus this essay becomes an investigation, not of 'memory', but of how Ladislaus II and Louis II came to be represented through 'dynastic' identification in the space of, first, the Kingdom of Bohemia, incorporated into the lands controlled by the 'House of Austria' ('the Habsburgs'), and, second, the consecutive nation-states formed after the disintegration of Austro-Hungary in 1918.

In addition to these theoretical problems, there is a straightforward technical difficulty with the project of tracing the historical representations of 'the Jagiellonians' within various versions of the 'Bohemian/Czech' past over the last five centuries: the material is simply too large for any kind of systematic interpretation (not to mention, proper contextualisation). Instead, I shall rely on an approach vaguely inspired by what David Armitage calls 'serial contextualism'.[8] Thinking about the invention of 'dynasty' and of 'the Jagiellonians' as a named family seen as a bounded group and a historical agent, I shall focus on two broad chronological periods. I shall start with the period from 1526 to the early seventeenth century, within which, as it will be argued, two significant transformations in the frameworks defining the representations of Ladislaus and Louis occurred. First, the notion of 'the Jagiellonians' was introduced to the Bohemian political and cultural space for the first time. Second, an observable transition occurred in historical writing, which moved from continuous regnal/national narratives split into the reigns of individual monarchs, to national narratives split into periods of rulership by discrete named lineages. At the same time, this was still before 'dynasty' became the term and concept of choice, both to make sense of the nature of the ruling lineages and to mark the chronology of history.

After considering this early modern period, I shall leap forward to an even more cursory investigation of the representations of 'the Jagiellonians' in the age of academic historical writing: the long period from the mid-nineteenth to the early twenty-first century (which, obviously, can itself be split into various epochs characterised by different conjunctures). At this stage of modern nationalism and professional historiography, the concept of 'dynasty' became significant. Far from a superficial change in terminology, this concept brought about a fundamental shift in the perception of medieval ruling families as, above and beyond passive identifications, actual historical agents, alongside social groups and nations. What seems to characterise this period is the increasing omnipresence of 'dynasty' as the key concept applied to 'the Bohemian Jagiellonians' in all possible variations of historical representations, ranging from professional historical writing through museums to visual imagery in popular culture. Curiously, this growing hegemony of 'dynasty' is accompanied by a lack of reflection on the meaning and historicity of the concept. This essay is a very preliminary and provisional reflection on, or, to borrow a genre from our colleagues in social sciences, an 'exploratory study' of, how 'dynastic' representation has come to dominate our understanding of both 'the Jagiellonians' in Bohemia in particular, and medieval political culture in general.

An early modern moment: inventing 'dynastic' time

When Louis II died in the aftermath of the Battle of Mohács on 29 August 1526, nobody in Bohemia thought of this event as the end of 'the Jagiellonians' in the kingdom. At least, this is what can be claimed on the basis of the surviving evidence. For the period immediately after Mohács, we have sources of various genres, none of which, however, refer to 'the Jagiellonians'. A few songs on the death of the king were composed and disseminated as political pamphlets at the time, for example, but they treat Louis as an individual ruler, not as a member of any named lineage, not to mention 'dynasty'.[9] The same can be said about historical narratives. Bartoš Pisař, the author of a historical text focusing on the events of the political struggle in Prague in 1524–26 and finished in the early 1530s, treated Louis II in the same manner. Although Bartoš was not uninterested in the familial aspect of royal politics (and, for instance, singled out kinship ties between

Sigismund of Poland and the Zapolyas as a factor in power struggles and noted a familial connection between Louis and Ferdinand I), he did not describe Louis as a 'Jagiellonian' or a member of any 'House', and, it seems, was not thinking in the categories of a shift between two ruling 'dynasties' in 1526.[10]

We can observe the same absence of the 'Jagiellonians' as a named family and ruling house in other sources, including those of more consequence in terms of political practice. The correspondence of Louis II's sister Anna (1503–47), who came to play a key role in the succession contest after the death of her brother and was instrumental to the establishment of her husband Ferdinand's regime in the Kingdom of Bohemia, is one such source. In a letter to the city of Breslau/Wrocław in Silesia, likely one of many similar letters sent by her to different political actors in the Kingdom of Bohemia, Anna complained of the attacks of 'tyrannical Turks' on her kingdom and laid the groundwork for her succession claim in both Hungary and Bohemia. It is interesting to observe how she presents herself in this letter. Anna writes of herself as a *'geboren koenigin* – born queen – of Hungary and Bohemia', and also mentions her membership in the royal lineage and stem, *'Geblut'* (*Gepluet*) and *'Stamm'* in the German original of the letter, of the kings of Hungary and Bohemia.[11] So, in this letter, Anna's succession rights are framed within the notion of regnal lineage, rather than in an isolated and internally coherent 'dynasty'. At the same time, it is undeniable that we are here dealing with an amalgamation of familial and royal identities and idioms.[12] But, perhaps, this is exactly where one can locate a crucial gap between the concept of 'dynasty', that separates a ruling family into a distinct institution in its own right, and much more interconnected early modern ideas of the intersections between 'the familial' and 'the political'.

The impressive proliferation of historical writing in the Czech lands over the course of the middle of the sixteenth century provides us with rich material to discuss the development of the memory of Ladislaus and Louis in the decades following 1526. Two significant and influential, if in many ways quite different, chronicles composed by Václav Hájek z Libočan in Czech (1541) and Jan Dubravius in Latin (1552) structure their representation of Ladislaus and Louis in very similar ways, predicated on the shared model of a national master narrative. Both historical texts construct the story of 'the Bohemians' as a people, coming in the initial moment of 'ethnogenesis' to the land where the current kingdom is located. This national narrative is inseparable from the story of the people's rulers, initially dukes and then kings, who provide a direct line of succession from the founder of the nation, named Čech. This paradigm of regnal and ethnic continuity does not emphasise any 'dynastic' breaks, each king simply follows the previous one, and Ladislaus and Louis are straightforwardly included in this list without any attempt to treat them as the representatives of a particular 'family', 'house' or 'dynasty'.[13] Curiously, Jan Dubravius at least used the concept of the house, 'domus' in Latin, quite systematically in relation to the House of Austria.[14] Perhaps we should contrast this with the later retrospective construction of 'dynasty' in historiography where the 'dynastic' model is assumed to be universally applicable to all medieval ruling families.

The same principle of memorialising Ladislaus and Louis within the paradigm of regnal continuity is reflected in other sources, most visibly in Martin Kuthen. Kuthen's print, titled *Icones ducum regumque Bohemiae* (1540), literally represents the entirety of Czech history through a continuous series of portraits of its rulers from Čech to Ferdinand I.[15] An identical frame was used in what is arguably a more official form of memory: a gallery with the portraits of Bohemian dukes and kings, ending with Ladislaus, Louis and Ferdinand, displayed at the royal palace in the castle in Prague. While the original images did not survive the fire in the castle in 1541, a visual representation is preserved in what is now MS 8043 in the collection of the Austrian National Library.[16] Initially, this was a copy of the destroyed gallery made by a Bohemian high official for Ferdinand I.

This way of commemorating Ladislaus and Louis – as two individual kings in a continuous line of national rulers – dominated not only historical representations, but also other forms of official memory, used by Ferdinand I in his policy of establishing and consolidating his rule in Bohemia (and Hungary). This tendency is prominent in all sources related to Anna, Ferdinand's wife and Ladislaus II's daughter. Both in various documents produced in the attempts to secure the succession of Ferdinand's children to the Bohemian throne on the basis of Anna's inheritance rights, and in the funeral speeches after her death in 1547, her familial identity plays a significant role, but it is used to establish her connection to the line of the Bohemian and Hungarian kings, not to any separate lineage as such. Her male relatives – the father and the brother – are referred to, but as individuals, not as the members of a named lineage, *familia*, house or 'dynasty'.[17] The same combination of the individualisation of Ladislaus and Louis' memory and its appropriation in the interests of the House of Austria's legitimacy may be traced in the famous backgammon board with depictions of Charles V and Ferdinand I at the centre, surrounded by significant relatives from other polities. In this rich object produced in the 1530s, Ladislaus and Louis are positioned alongside the Burgundian and Spanish relatives of the two brothers, literally incorporated to augment their prestige and their association with various polities across Europe.[18]

A clear moment of change, when Jagiellonian identification finally became visible in sources directly related to Bohemia, came with the Polish interregna and elections in the 1570s.[19] At this moment, the Habsburgs 'discovered' their Jagiellonian identity. I will use just two examples to illustrate this (re)creation of the Jagiellonian identification. The first case is a speech delivered by Vilem of Rožmberk in 1572 to support the candidature of Ernest to the Polish throne.[20] In this speech Maximilian II is presented as originating through his maternal lineage (*genus*) from 'the House of the Jagiellonians (ex Jagellonum Domo)'.[21] In 1575, one of the speeches addressed by the representatives of Ferdinand 'Habsburg' to the Polish electors included a significant and explicit reference to 'the Jagiellonians': the envoys noted that it was not necessary to praise Ferdinand's *maternum genus* to their audience. 'Nota est vobis sancta Jagellonis propago.'[22]

This discussion of the 'discovery' of their Jagiellonian origins by 'the Habsburgs' can also be related to a well-known and important monument – the Royal Mausoleum in the cathedral in Prague. It was built in Innsbruck by Alexander Colyn, who worked for Ferdinand of Tyrol (d.1595) and the Emperor Maximilian II (d.1576). The mausoleum was commissioned by Ferdinand and Maximilian after the death of Ferdinand I in 1564, with its first version finished in 1573 and moved to Prague in 1577. By this time Maximilian II had died, and the Emperor Rudolf (r.1576–1612) ordered the mausoleum to be enlarged to include the figure of Maximilian and to create a new crypt in which all the Bohemian kings buried in the cathedral were to be re-interred. Rudolf also commissioned some additional decorations of the mausoleum, including the bas-reliefs of Czech kings and queens on its walls. There are three large bas-reliefs with the coats of arms on the eastern side of the mausoleum: those of Maximilian, Ferdinand and Anna. Anna's coat of arms in this case is a combination of Hungarian strips and Bohemian lions, thus emphasising her royal status and crown rights, but not presenting any 'dynastic' identification in its own right. The angels positioned on top of the mausoleum also hold coats of arms, and two of them are rather interesting. The angel on Anna's side has two coats of arms: he holds the same Hungarian-Bohemian one (strips and lions) in his left hand, but the heraldry in his right is curious: it has Hungarian strips in the first and third sectors, but two other fields look like the Polish Royal Eagle and the Lithuanian knight with a double cross. One may assume that this was supposed to emphasise Anna's connection to the Polish-Lithuanian polity and its royal family, at the time of another Polish interregnum and another cycle of the Habsburgs' attempts to become kings of Poland.

Perhaps even more important than that discovery of the 'Jagiellonian' identification in 'Habsburg' diplomatic rhetoric was a more fundamental restructuring of historical narratives, which now became explicitly split into different lineages that ruled one after another, whereas the earlier chronicles simply show regnal and national continuity. The best way to illustrate this massive shift is to look at the two editions of the *Historical Calendar*, published by the most important printer in late sixteenth-century Bohemia, Daniel Adam z Veleslavína (1546–99). His first *Kalendář hystorycký* (a major historical compendium, a popular and influential work) was published in 1578, and then reprinted in 1590. In this second edition, at the very beginning of the calendar, the author inserted a section called 'The Lineages of Dukes and Kings [Rodové Knižat a Králův] that ruled in Bohemia from the first duke Czech and up to Rudolf II'.[23] The first 'rod' is the lineage of Krok, with a genealogical table; then follows the 'rod' of Bohemian dukes from Přemysl. Of course, most interesting for us is *Rod Králův Polskýchih kteříž posslí z kmene Knížat Litewských* (The Lineage of the Polish kings, who originated from the stem of the Lithuanian dukes). Daniel Adam noted that 'two of them' ruled in Hungary and Bohemia: Ladislaus II and his son Louis. The genealogical table is also interesting: it starts from Gedemin, goes through Anna to Maximilian II, but also includes Sigismund III; Sigismund II Augustus, however, is described as *Král Polský, toho rodu poslední* – the last Polish king from that lineage. Basically, here we can already see the standard pattern of structuring national narratives by 'dynasties' which is so familiar to us today. It is important, however, to emphasise

108 Ilya Afanasyev

that we find this pattern in a clear form only in the late sixteenth century, while medieval texts, both historical and genealogical, prioritised regnal continuity as the main narrative structuring device. This former model found its fully developed realisation in one of the most influential early modern histories of Bohemia: the Jesuit Bohuslav Balbín's *Miscellanea historica Regni Bohemiae* (1680s). The 'dynastic' organisation of a regnal (national) narrative is clearly conveyed in the genealogical tables inserted in the text, each representing not a singular ducal/royal line, but a separate 'genealogia' of each 'stirps' (lineage) from which the given kings of Bohemia originated.[24] Among others, there is 'genealogia Jagellonica, ex qua stirpe duos Reges in Bohemia habuimus: Wladislaum II & Ludovicum II' (we may note in brackets that Balbín also starts his Jagiellonian genealogy from Gedemin). In this genealogical table (see Figure 4.1), the chronology organised around the principle of singling out different ruling lineages meets an explicit identification with a familial name. At least on the surface the only aspect of the 'modern' vision of 'dynasty' that is still missing is the clear notion of

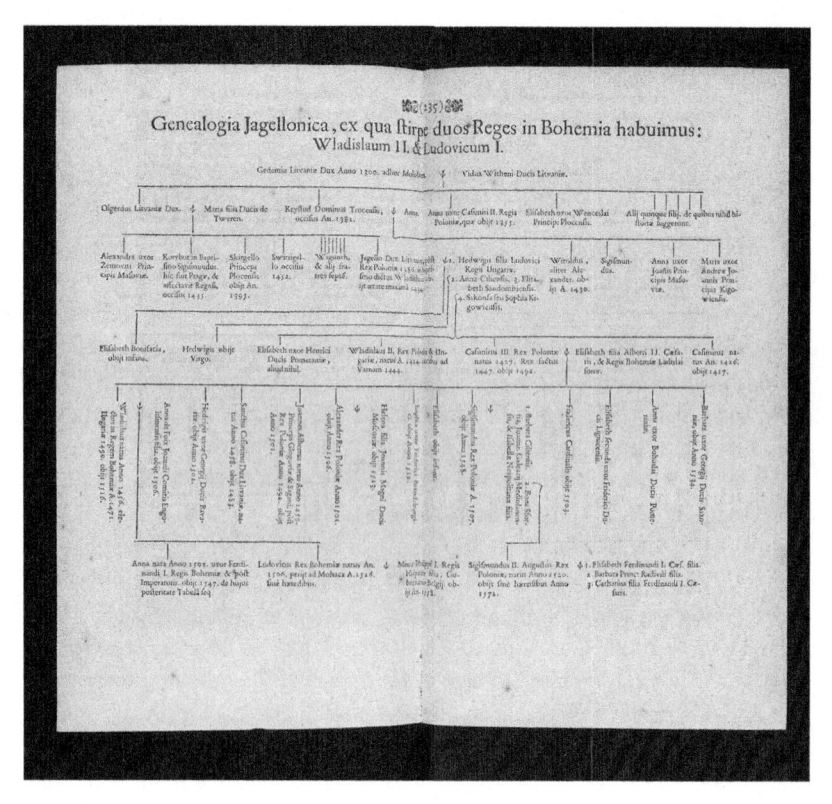

FIGURE 4.1   Jagiellonian genealogical table; Bohuslav Balbín, *Miscellanea historica Regni Bohemiae; Liber Regalis VII* (Prague, 1687); Sectio V. Duo Reges Bohemiae; Pater & Filius ex Familia Jagellonica, pp. 223–39, at p. 235: 'Genealogia Jagellonica'

agency, the representation of it as a conscious actor. Also, Balbín does not use the word 'dynasty' here.

'The Jagiellonians' between professional historiography and cultural representations

'When I began my historical studies in 1823, I quickly became convinced of the importance of the Vladislav age', wrote František Palacký in the 1860s in the introduction to the fifth and last volume of his monumental *Dějiny národu českeho v Čechách a v Moravě* (*The History of the Czech Nation in Bohemia and Moravia*).[25] It is impossible to analyse Palacký's comprehensive account of the 'Jagiellonian period', which amounts to hundreds of pages, here.[26] I will restrict myself to noting two isolated but, in the context of this essay, significant aspects. First, although Palacký was still using '*rod*' ('lineage') as the most common term to denote royal and princely families, 'dynasty' also appeared in his works, both historical, such as the *History of the Czech Nation*, and explicitly political, for example, the *Idea of the Austrian State* (first published in German). Pending further investigation, we may speculate that the history of 'dynasty' as a word in the Czech language is somewhat similar to other European languages: appearing first as a multi-semantic antiquarian term to refer to power, not necessarily directly connected to any genealogical notions, a form of territorial unit, or perhaps a lordship, and, second, by the early to mid-nineteenth century, becoming a common, even if not precisely defined, term for a line of rulers passing an office down through familial succession.

A second noteworthy aspect of Palacký's treatment of 'the Jagiellonians' is the direct relevance of the period to some of the crucial political issues in the historian's own time. Most obviously, the history of the treatises and the intermarriage between 'the Jagiellonians' and 'the Habsburgs' was closely related to the question of the inheritance rights of the latter dynasty in Bohemia, central to the official historical narrative legitimising the House of Austria's control of the Czech lands. Palacký's approach to this (one may assume) sensitive theme was quite careful, not to say circumspect. Still, he clearly emphasised the significance of both Ladislaus II's attempts to guarantee the succession rights of his daughter Anna and, especially, the agreements accompanying the double marriage between Ladislaus's children Louis and Anna and Emperor Maximilian I's grandchildren concluded in Vienna in 1515. These arrangements influenced both 'the might and standing of the Habsburg dynasty [*moc a postawení dynastie Habsburské*] and the future of the Czech nation'.[27] Perhaps tellingly, Palacký ended his history quite abruptly with the death of Louis in 1526, omitting the discussion of Ferdinand's election as the king of Bohemia and the contested issue of his wife's inheritance rights in this process.

History textbooks constitute a useful source that can be used to further explore this theme. Textbooks were published in the Bohemian lands from the mid-nineteenth century onwards in multiple editions (as well as two languages) and addressing the needs of different types of schools. I cannot even begin to scratch the surface of this potentially fruitful topic here. Even a cursory study of several dozens of those textbooks, however, reveals an interesting discrepancy between those authors who simply reproduced the in part fabricated story of Ferdinand I's hereditary rights to the Bohemian kingdom and those who mention the 1526 rejection of his claims by the Bohemian estates.[28] To cite just one telling case of 'Habsburg' loyalism, a history textbook published in 1879 stated, outright falsely, that

> in accordance with old inheritance treatises and as the husband of Louis's sister Anna, Ferdinand had a claim to the Bohemian and Hungarian crowns. The Bohemian estates unanimously elected him to their throne and acknowledged that from that time onwards the Habsburg lineage [*rod habsburský*] would have the same inheritance rights as were earlier held by the Luxembourg lineage.[29]

What is noteworthy here is not only a direct manipulation of historical facts (the Bohemian estates did not acknowledge any such rights in 1526), but also the projection of clearly demarcated, named and legally defined 'dynasties' onto both the medieval and early modern past. A proper examination of this topic would naturally require systematic analysis of all textbooks, as well as their contextualisation in each given political moment and the history of school education in nineteenth-century Bohemia. At this point, I would only like to emphasise that, while it might retrospectively seem as if the history of the 'Jagiellonian period' lacks political and ideological significance, especially in contrast to such ideologically loaded phenomena as the Hussite movement or figures like Charles IV, it was not always the case. Whilst 'the Jagiellonians' did not play a role in the ideological battles over the 'meaning of Czech history' raging from the late nineteenth century onwards (and there is a possible exception to even this rule in Masaryk's claim that 1487, when peasants were supposedly transformed into serfs, was the most tragic year in Czech history),[30] before 1918 and the disintegration of Austro-Hungary, the question of inheritance rights of Anna and the passage from 'the Jagiellonians' to 'the Habsburgs' remained a pertinent and contested issue.

If we enlarge the scope of our investigation and ask what place the Jagiellonian period (1471–1526) in general, and 'the Jagiellonians' in particular, occupy in the national master narrative of Czech history in the long and continuing period of professional historical writing, we will be obliged to say that, in spite of Palacký's insistence on the significance of the late fifteenth and early sixteenth centuries, they remain marginal in both academic historiography and various popular representations.[31] There are of course exceptions to this rule; first and foremost amongst these is Josef Macek's monumental four-volume *The Jagiellonian Age in the Bohemian Lands, 1471–1526*.[32] Tellingly, though, the volume '*In memoriam Josefa Macka*', published by Miloslav Polívka and František Šmahel in 1996, whilst dedicated to the memory of Macek, for whom 'the Jagiellonians' were evidently one of the central themes of his whole scholarly career, did not include a single article on the 'Jagiellonian' kings of Bohemia.[33] Usually, when 'the Jagiellonians' receive any kind of systematic attention, it is within the genre of the continuous representation of national history, reminiscent of the structure and genre of Palacký's paradigmatic oeuvre. We can think here of both the terse outlines of Czechoslovak history published during the 'Socialist' period and especially the new narrative histories of the 'Bohemian lands' that have appeared in the last couple of decades.[34] Amongst the latter, the volume on Czech history 1437–1526 authored by Petr Čornej (with the 'culture' section covered by Milena Bartlová for the series *Velké dějiny zemí Koruny české* (*The Great History of the Lands of the Bohemian Crown*)) is the most significant, devoting around half of its length to a meticulous presentation of the history of 'the Jagiellonians' and the 'Jagiellonian' period.[35] Also, more recently, yet another general textbook-type volume on the Jagiellonian period, by Jaroslav Čechura, has appeared.[36]

It is very curious, however, that even this framework of continuous national master narrative, in which 'the Jagiellonians' might seem to have an undeniable claim to at least some space, does not always work out in their favour. Instructively, a recent series of books on the history of particular 'dynasties' in Czech history, which had already covered the Přemyslids and the Luxembourgs, was continued with a volume titled 'The Hussite Century'.[37] This volume extends to the year 1485 (when the religious peace of Kutná Hora was achieved) and thus includes the early 'Jagiellonian period'. It, however, leaves a gap before the beginning of the 'Habsburg' era, the subject of some future volume(s). Allowing anecdotal evidence, I have been told by a Czech historian involved in the production of the series that the editorial team had decided to omit, at least for the time being, the missing volume on 'the Jagiellonians', not least because there are not enough potential contributors with interests in the period. This seems to be a perfect illustration of the ambiguous half-neglected place of 'the Jagiellonians' in the current construction of Czech national history.

But this is only one side of the story. For one thing, one must not forget the very important, critical and insightful work currently being produced by several Czech historians, working on different themes, chronologically related to the 'Jagiellonian period'. Without aspiring to come up with an exhaustive list, one should definitely mention the work of Antonín Kalous and Petr Kozák, as well as numerous art historians, above all, Milena Bartlová.[38] It may be helpful to note that some of the best work on 'the Jagiellonians' in the context of Czech historiography has been done in the framework of region-specific studies, such as Kozák's research and source editions related to Silesia,[39] and Hlobil and Petrů's publications on humanism and renaissance in Moravia.[40] It would be unjust towards colleagues and simply preposterous to claim that this short essay can offer a serious historiographical analysis of Czech publications on 'the Jagiellonians' specifically, not to mention the Jagiellonian period in general.[41]

Instead, one may single out some broad explanatory paradigms which are shared, at least to an extent, between professional historiography and various other forms of cultural representation. One seemingly deeply influential paradigm is predicated on the dichotomy between 'internal' regnal politics dominated by local elites and 'international' dynastic politics pursued by the kings. This view, which remains an influential vision of the Jagiellonian period in contemporary Czech historiography, has been reproduced by scholars over the last few decades, and can already be found in Josef Petráň's introduction to the paradigmatic volume on late Gothic art in Bohemia published in 1978 (as is often the case with 'the Jagiellonians' in Czech-language literature, art historians played a key role in developing their image).[42] Pondering the concept of 'dynasty' and its problematic uses in modern historiography, one may argue that this picture is based on the potentially misleading notion of 'dynastic politics', which takes 'dynasty' for granted and automatically projecting the notion of 'dynastic interests' as a historical explanation. Furthermore, this concept also seems to offer a rather simplistic understanding of the role of kings or, more precisely, princely/royal office in late medieval and early modern political culture and practice. In fact, it misses the high level of investment that local elites put into creating, reasserting and negotiating the identity of their kings, even in polities where royal power looks, in hindsight, almost nominal. This role of elites in projecting images of kings is, however, acknowledged by some of those historians and art historians who focus on the growing influence of the estates in the late Middle Ages and early modern period. Among the latter, Milena Bartlová's critical work should be especially emphasised, which is in part a reaction to the exaggerated focus on royal courts as the centres of power and art patronage.[43] This court-centred interpretation of the period, which takes the agency of kings for granted, was already strongly present in art historical debates on the Jagiellonian period in the 1970s, and is still quite influential, as the recent publications of Jiří Kuthan, above all his grand volume *Royal Art under George of Poděbrady and the Jagiellonians*, attest.[44]

The importance of this paradigm of 'dual power' (of elites controlling 'internal' politics and kings engaging in 'international' 'dynastic' politics) lies also in its strong presence in more 'popular' representations of 'the Jagiellonians'. Perhaps the best example is the collection of cartoons *Obrázky z českých dějin a pověstí* (*The Images from Czech History and Legends*), first published in Prague in 1979.[45] This book, displaying the national meta-narrative of Czech history as a series of humorous illustrations with short textual commentaries, has been reprinted (with purely cosmetic changes following the political transformations in the late 1980s and early 1990s) multiple times up to the present day and is probably one of the most influential sources of historical knowledge in the Czech Republic, outside of formal school curricula. The representation of 'the Jagiellonians' in this comic book is instructive. First, we see all the stereotypical references to the weak and somewhat ridiculous kings, focusing especially on Ladislaus II. The topos of 'Kral Dobre' (the king agreeing to every request) is of course there, as well as another anecdotal phrase ascribed to the Bohemian nobility of the period, punning on the alleged meekness and powerlessness of Ladislaus: 'Je to náš král a my jsme jeho páni' ('This is our king and we are his lords').[46] An image of the king playing with his toys reinforces the mocking effect. Secondly, we find a more curious claim: 'In any case King Ladislaus cared more about the affairs of his lineage ['rod'] than of the Czech state' (see Figure 4.2).[47] In a less serious but ultimately similar form,

FIGURE 4.2 Cartoon depicting Jagiellonian rulers, from the Czech history book for children *Obrázky z českých dějin a pověstí* (Prague, 1979) © Zdeněk Adla – heirs, 1979; Illustrations © Jiří Kalousek – heirs, 1979; Illustrations © Jakub Kalousek, 1996

the same logic of private, 'dynastic' interests is ascribed to Ladislaus, while the business of 'the state' is controlled by local elites.

This representation taps into the generic paradigm of 'weak kings' that dominates both early modern, modern and contemporary representations of 'the Jagiellonians' in Czech history. This tradition was clearly articulated as early as the sixteenth century by such authors as Vaclav Hajek and Jan Dubravius, was picked up in the nineteenth century by the classic authors of Czech national history, and remains omnipresent in both popular and professional representations. In addition to 'The Images from Czech History and Legends' discussed above, one can quote another somewhat similar medium – 'The History of the Brave Czech Nation', originally published by Lucie Seifertová as a comic book in 2003, and then turned into a popular cartoon in 2010–12.[48] Here 'the Jagiellonians' play the same role in the national narrative: that of weak kings, to be laughed at rather than praised for their heroic achievements. Curiously, this weakness can be reinterpreted as a positive trait in slightly different historiographical and ideological contexts, a process evident in, for example, the works of Josef Macek.[49] Macek takes the image of the weak – both personally and politically – King Ladislaus but rewrites it into a largely positive characteristic, as enabling the existence of the 'Monarchy of the Estates', which amounts to a positive reinterpretation of the period not as a time of 'feudal anarchy' and/or a 'weak state', but as laying the foundations for a 'liberal' democratic-oriented vision of the region's history.

As I noted previously, art history and art monuments tend to play an especially significant role in the representation of 'the Jagiellonians' in modern and contemporary Czech contexts.[50] A perfect illustration of this is the exhibition 'Jagiellonian Europe', that opened in Kutná Hora in 2012 as the first stage of an international tour with follow-up exhibitions in Poland and Germany.[51] The exhibition was curated by the art historian Jiří Fajt, one of the principal co-investigators of a Leipzig-based project on the Jagiellonians, their history and, in particular, the art associated with them and their period. The story of the exhibition also shows the ambiguous place of the Jagiellonians in the dominant version of Czech history: originally planned for Prague Castle, it was then moved to a less prominent venue in Kutná Hora (the instalment of a new presidential administration in Prague Castle might have had something to do with the relocation). Still, the exhibition itself, as well as the other media representations it triggered – most prominently, a series of thirteen radio programmes on 'the Jagiellonians' and the art from their period hosted by one of the channels of the Czech public radio company[52] – must have been the most prominent recent public and cultural event commemorating the 'dynasty' for audiences in the Czech Republic.

There is no space here to analyse all the various (albeit often random) cultural productions related to 'the Jagiellonians' in the Czech Republic. There exist a couple of recent historical novels of dubious quality, a staged docudrama movie (airing on Czech TV from time to time), as well as multiple local commemorative paraphernalia. The state-focused popular children's books about the rulers of 'the

Czech lands' that, not unlike early modern regnal lists, represent national history as a continuous line from early dukes to contemporary presidents are undoubtedly very important. 'The Jagiellonians', of course, have their place in this projection of political and national continuity. An example meriting specific mention is the 2012 issue of the popular historical magazine *Dějiny a současnost* (History and the Present) devoted to 'the Jagiellonians'. The issue in question featured a special section of articles on 'the Jagiellonians' written by leading Czech historians and art historians (alongside one historian from Hungary), and also placed them on the front cover: 'The Jagiellonians: A Ruling Dynasty at the End of the Middle Ages'.[53] It would be appropriate to draw this discussion to an end by emphasising an illustration related to 'the Jagiellonians', which the editors of the journal chose for the cover of their issue. It is a reproduction of Bertalan Székely's *The Discovery of the Body of Louis II*. Originally painted in Munich in 1860 by a 'Hungarian' Vienna-educated artist, and reproduced on the cover of a Czech-language history magazine 150 years later, this image perfectly exemplifies the reductive nature of 'national memory' as an analytical concept. Beyond the straitjacket of 'national' traditions, we should think of memory or, as I have been trying to insist in this essay, historical representations, as a transtemporal and transregional process.

Beyond 'memory' and 'oblivion': a conclusion

It seems fair to say that the field of memory studies is, to a great extent, structured by the dichotomy of 'memory' and 'oblivion'. Its main research agenda is the investigation of what is getting 'remembered' and 'forgotten', and the mechanisms and causes by which this material is selected, predicated on some explicitly political agenda. Historical representations of 'the Jagiellonians' in today's Czech Republic do not really fit into this paradigm. 'The Jagiellonians' are not used in any emphatic attempts to construct national narratives and ideologies. But they are not 'forgotten' either. It is a speculative claim, but one can be sure that everyone who went to school in the Czech Republic or earlier Czechoslovakia knows at least the name of this 'dynasty'. People with some knowledge of history are likely to have at least a few associations with 'the Jagiellonians': most commonly, the Battle of Mohács and, even more frequently, the famous historical monuments and art objects, such as the Vladislav Hall in Prague Castle. How to make sense of this form of historical knowledge that is not actively instrumentalised, but is also neither suppressed nor constitutive of a latent archive?

One way to answer this question is to suggest that, while memory studies often focuses on specific events, figures or phenomena (their explicit promotions or contestations), conceptual structures, reproduced and reified through various ideological apparatuses (educational institutions or museums, which are either directly governed by the state or at least regulated by it), are actually constitutive of both historical representations and their memorialisation. Perhaps it makes sense to focus on the most intense moments of ideological production, which may reveal the particular political stakes in the organisation and contestation of historical representations. But there may also be a danger of not seeing the wood for the trees.

Specific attempts to weaponise the past for the political process may be interesting, and, for all the overshadowing of 'the Jagiellonians' in the Czech Republic by other historical figures such as Charles IV or Jan Hus (whose spectacular memorialisations were very visible in 2015 and 2016, which happened to be important anniversaries), not to mention the characters and phenomena of more recent history, they still occasionally appear in political discourses. In the context of the so-called 'refugee crisis' in Europe, for example, the Czech far right has, somewhat surprisingly, rediscovered 'the Jagiellonians': references to the Battle of Mohács and to Louis II as the king who died protecting 'Europe', 'the West' and the Czech lands from 'Islam' have begun to appear in the speeches and publications of some racist Czech politicians. Curiously, these 'Christian kings' were deployed as the positive 'other' to be contrasted with allegedly 'Islamophilic' EU bureaucrats and the 'liberal/left' politicians who are failing to protect 'Christian Europe' from the 'Muslim threat'.[54] Even mentioning this rhetoric may be giving it too much relevance and significance, but this is a good illustration of how fairly neutral figures can suddenly acquire political meaning in changing circumstances.

Still, I would argue that such explicit politicisation matters less than the deeper ideological structures that define what is represented, and how, in both professional and public historical discourses and imageries. The dynastic-national complex, assembled in the long period of conceptual transformations from the early modern period to the twenty-first century, has become and remains, in spite of various critical challenges, the hegemonic vision of history in 'the West'. As any idea that has acquired material force through its inclusion in the institutional frameworks of the state apparatuses and 'civil society' – the whole web of schools, universities, museums, various forms of art and literature and, simply, everyday logics 'inhaled' by individuals through above-mentioned mechanisms – this conceptual complex determines what we see in the past. One minor, but, I believe, very instructive example of how this conceptual structure is materialised in everyday life is the existence of three parallel streets in the Prague district of Žižkov named after 'the Přemyslids', 'the Luxembourgs' and 'the Jagiellonians' ('Přemyslovská', 'Lucemburská' and 'Jagellonská'). Here we see the idea of national history split into 'dynastic' sections represented via and even literally transformed into urban topography. More generally, we can understand such historical representations as a form of ideology – a thought-institutional complex that closes the gap between a particular vision of the past and the past's real totality, of inevitably and infinitely complex and contradictory nature. While 'dynasty', coupled with 'the nation', remains the hegemonic paradigm of history, the 'Bohemian Jagiellonians' will continue to exist in our imagination. But if (or when) this ideological complex is deconstructed, a different historical representation of the period from 1471 to 1526 in the Kingdom of Bohemia in particular, and 'pre-modern' history in general, is likely to arise.

Notes

1 I. Wallerstein, 'Does India Exist?', in Wallerstein, *The Essential Wallerstein*, New York, 2000, p. 310.
2 It may be useful to provide a very short narrative of the 'Jagiellonian' rule of Bohemia. Ladislaus, the eldest son of King Casimir IV of Poland, was elected king of Bohemia in 1471, after the death of King George of Poděbrady. Initially, Ladislaus II's Bohemian title was contested by King Matthias Corvinus of Hungary, but in 1479 the Peace of Olomouc ended the war for the Bohemian Crown. Both kings kept their Bohemian titles, Ladislaus II retained control over Bohemia, but Moravia, Silesia and Lusatia were ceded to Matthias. After the death of Matthias Corvinus in 1490, Ladislaus II was elected king of Hungary and moved his court from Buda to Prague. Following two contested marriages, Ladislaus II married Anne de Foix-Candale in 1502, who gave birth to their daughter Anna in 1503 and son Louis in 1506. In 1509 Louis, still a toddler, was crowned king of Bohemia in Prague. In 1515 a double betrothal agreement was concluded between the children of Ladislaus and the grandchildren of Emperor Maximilian I (from the 'House of Austria'): Louis was to wed Mary (d.1558) and Anna Ferdinand, the future Charles V's younger brother. Ladislaus II died in 1516 and was succeeded in both Bohemia and Hungary by Louis II. Louis II died in the Battle of Mohács against the Ottoman army on 29 August 1526. This date marks the end of the 'Jagiellonian dynasty' in the traditional chronology of Czech national narrative. For a detailed political history of the 'Jagiellonian period' in the Kingdom of Bohemia, see P. Čornej and M. Bartlová, *Velké dějiny zemí Koruny české*, Prague, 2007, vol. 6, pp. 403–704 (the chapter written by Bartlová offers a very helpful overview of the period's culture). For an even more detailed classic nineteenth-century account of Bohemian political history in 1471–1526, see F. Palacký, *Dějiny národu českého v Čechách a v Moravě*, 5 vols, Prague, 1937 [1836–67], vol. 5. Josef Macek's four-volume investigation of the 'Jagiellonian age' covers not only political, but also social, economic, religious and cultural histories of the period: J. Macek, *Jagellonský věk v českých zemích: 1471–1526*, 4 vols, Prague, 1992–99, I. Hospodářská základna a královská moc; II. Šlechta; III. Města; IV. Venkovský lid, Národnostní otázka.
3 One such interpretation will be offered in the collective monograph co-authored by the members of the ERC Jagiellonians Project: N. Nowakowska et al., *Dynasty in the Making* (forthcoming).
4 The research of other members of the 'Jagiellonians Project' at Oxford suggests that 'the Jagiellonians' as a collective name and identification was forged in Poland and the Grand Duchy of Lithuania only in the early sixteenth century. See Introduction in this volume, and Nowakowska et al., *Dynasty in the Making*.
5 Among the foundational works in memory studies, see M. Halbwaschs, *Les cadres sociaux de la mémoire*, Paris, 1925, or a version in English: Halbwachs, *On Collective Memory*, trans. L. Coser, Chicago, 1992; P. Nora et al., *Les Lieux de mémoire*, 3 vols, Paris, 1984–92; J. Assmann, *Kollektives Gedächtnis und kulturelle Identität*, Frankfurt am Main, 1988, or a version in English: Assmann, *Cultural Memory and Early Civilisation: Writing, Remembrance and Political Imagination*, Cambridge, 2011; A. Assmann, *Cultural Memory and Western Civilisation: Functions, Media, Archive*, Cambridge, 2011. For a recent overview and an introduction to theoretical debates, major approaches and empirical studies, see A. L. Tota and T. Hagen, *Routledge International Handbook of Memory Studies*, London, 2015.
6 A helpful critique along these lines is offered in W. Kansteiner, 'Finding Meaning in Memory: A Methodological Critique of Collective Memory Studies', *History and Theory*, 41, 2002, pp. 179–97.
7 I am grateful to Matthew Rampley who suggested that 'historical representation' could be a better concept than 'memory' to explore this material, when a version of this essay was discussed at the research forum on East Central Europe at the University of Birmingham.

8 D. Armitage, 'What's the Big Idea? Intellectual History and the Longue Durée', *History of European Ideas*, 38, 2012, pp. 493–507.
9 See Fr. Dvorský, ed., 'Truchlivá pisen o zahynuti Ludvika krále Českého', *Časopis českého musea*, 38, 1864, pp. 389–92.
10 K. J. Erben, ed., *Bartošova Kronika pražská od léta páně 1524 až do konce léta 1530*, Prague, 1851.
11 *Národní archiv Archiv České koruny (1158–1935) 1962, monasterium.net*: http://monasterium.net/mom/CZ-NA/ACK/1962/charter, accessed 19.9.17.
12 Sylva Dobalová has been doing important work on the art historical side of such uses of Anna's claims for the legitimisation of Ferdinand's rule (with which I am familiar due to her papers presented in Prague and Oxford). Especially interesting is Dobalová's reinterpretation of the bas-reliefs of the Summer Palace in Prague Castle's complex (built under Ferdinand) as a visual reflection of the transmission of Anna's rights to Bohemia to Ferdinand.
13 J. Dubravius, *Historiae Regni Boiemiae, de rebus memoria dignis, in illa gestis, ab initio Boiemorum, qui ex Illyria venientes, eandem Boiemiam, in medio propemodum superioris Germanie sitam, occupauerunt*, Prostannae, 1552; V. H. Libočan, *Kronika česká*, J. Linka and P. Voit, eds, Prague, 2013, pp. 1026–92.
14 It should be noted that, while Jan Dubravius did not represent 'the Jagiellonians' as a House in his *History*, in an earlier speech addressed to Sigismund I of Poland he did refer to Sigismund and his kin, including the kings of Hungary and Bohemia Ladislaus and Louis, as a *domus*. See Jan Dubravius, *Historia Bohemica, ab origine gentis . . .*, Hanau, 1602, pp. 273–7, at p. 274.
15 M. Kuthen, *Catalogus ducum Regumque Bohaemorum in quo summatim gesta singulorum singulis Distichis continentur. In super additae sunt eorum facies Iconicae & ad viuum deliniatae*, Prague, 1540.
16 ÖNB, Vienna Codex MS 8043.
17 See especially J. L. Brassicanus, *Phoenix sive luctus Austriae ob mortem incomparabilis heroinae D. Annae Quiritium, Pannonum ac Bohemorum Reginae, etc.*, Vienna, 1547. The text is rich in genealogical details but does not operate according to a clear 'dynastic' logic and does not refer to 'the Jagiellonians'. As a short digression, we may note a curious moment related to the memory of Anna in the Bohemian context. Her (extremely positive) image was reflected, among other places, in Balbín's late seventeenth-century genealogy of the House of Austria, where she is included as the wife of Ferdinand I, with a note that she was 'the most beloved by the Bohemian nation' (see note 24 below). This positive representation seems to have a long history and was forged around her death (if not already in her lifetime). A very instructive case in this sense is a vernacular description of the revolt of the estates against Ferdinand in Bohemia in 1547–48, written shortly after the events by Sixt of Ottersdorf. This source, critical of Ferdinand and his regime, contains a rather detailed description of Anna's death and funerals. In spite of his opposition to Ferdinand, Sixt was very positive towards Anna and mourned her death. In his detailed (even if topical) account of her death, Anna is represented as the Czech nation's mother and protector. See K. J. Erben, ed., *Výbor z literatury české*, 2 vols, Prague, 1868, II, col. 1378–94, at 1380–2.
18 The backgammon board is displayed in the Kunsthistorisches Museum in Vienna.
19 On the Habsburgs' involvement in the Polish royal elections in the 1570s, see a detailed study: C. Augustynowicz, *Die Kandidaten und Interessen des Hauses Habsburg in Polen-Litauen während des Zweiten Interregnums, 1574–1576*, Vienna, 2001.
20 Státní oblastní archiv v Třeboni, Histroica Třeboň 4834.
21 Státní oblastní archiv v Třeboni, Histroica Třeboň 4834., fol. 3. 'Dominus noster clementissimus, Caesar Maximilianus . . . iunctus fuerit maternum genus ex Ser . . . ma Jagellonum Domo, atque acteo a fratre praestantissimi quondam Regis Sigismundis primi ducens, ac proavum maternum inclytum et celeberrimi nominis Regem quondam Casimirum tertium [sic], qui et ipse Coniugem ex Domo Austriaca habuit. Regis Vri

Sigismundi Augusti nuper defuncti aviam, utpote Alberti Caesaris Hungariae et Bohemiae Regis Filiam.'
22 F. Veržbovskij, *Dve kandidatury na pol'skij prestol Vil'gel'ma iz Rozenberga i èrcgercoga Ferdinanda, 1574–1575. Po neizdannym istočnikam*, Saint Petersburg, 1889, p. 199.
23 D. A. z Veleslavína, *Kalendař hystorycký, krátké poznamenánj wssechněch dnůw gednohokaždého měsýce přes celý rokI*, Prague, 1590.
24 B. Balbín, *Miscellaneorum Historicorum Regni Bohemiae Decadis I. Liver VII. Regalis; seu De Ducibus, ac Regibus Bohemiae. In quo gesta Regum praecipua, tum Genealogiae omnium Familiarum apud nos imperitantium (Czechi; Gentis Ducis ac Patris, Croci, Przemysli, deinde Regum Lucemburgicorum, Austriacorum, Habspurgensium, Cunstadaeorum, Jagellonidarum, ac tandem iterato Austriacorum) diligenti semper ad Chronologiam respectu, proponuntur & Notis Historicis, aut ethicis illustrantur*, Prague, 1687. Sectio V. Duo Reges Bohemiae; Pater & Filius ex Familia Jagellonica, pp. 223–39, at p. 235: 'Genealogia Jagellonica'.
25 Palacký, *Dějiny národu českeho v Čechách a v Moravě*, V, p. 6.
26 On Palacký see, among many others: M. Baár, *Historians and Nationalism: East Central Europe in the Nineteenth Century*, Oxford, 2010, pp. 29–35, *passim*; K. Činátl, 'Palackého dějiny a historická paměť národa', *Dějiny - teorie - kritika*, 6, 2009, pp. 7–35.
27 Palacký, *Dějiny národu českeho v Čechách a v Moravě*, V, p. 437.
28 I am very grateful to Magdaléna Šustová from the National Pedagogical Museum of J. A. Comenius in Prague who provided me with those numerous nineteenth- and twentieth-century history textbooks, even if (so far) I have failed to use these interesting sources to their full potential.
29 J. Vávra, *Gindelyho učebnice dějepisu pro školy měštanské*, Prague, 1895, vol. 2, p. 46.
30 T. G. Masaryk, *The Meaning of Czech History*, Chapel Hill, NC, 1974, p. 143.
31 K. Činátl, *Naše české minulosti, aneb, jak vzpomínáme*, Prague, 2014 – an interesting study of Czech historical memory, unsurprisingly, does not cover the representations of 'The Jagiellonians'.
32 Macek, *Jagellonský věk v českých zemích: 1471–1526*.
33 See M. Polívka and F. Šmahel, eds, *In Memoriam Josefa Macka (1922–1991)*, Prague, 1996.
34 Fr. Graus et al., eds, *Přehled československých dějin. Díl. I. Do roku 1848*, Prague, 1958, pp. 287–99; and J. Purš and M. Kropilák, eds, *Přehled dějin Československa. Díl I/1. Do roku 1526*, Prague, 1980, pp. 521–60.
35 P. Čornej and M. Bartlová, *Velké dějiny zemí Koruny české*, vol. 6, pp. 403–704.
36 J. Čechura, *České země v letech 1437–1526. II. Díl. Jagellonské Čechy (1471–1526)*, Prague, 2012.
37 P. Cermanová, R. Novotný and P. Soukup, eds, *Husitské Století*, Prague, 2014.
38 A. Kalous, *Matyáš Korvín, 1443–1490: uherský a český král*, České Budějovice, 2009.
39 P. Kozák, 'Zikmund Jagellonský: králův bratr na knížecím stolci', *Vlastivědné listy Slezska a severní Moravy*, 37, 2011, pp. 6–10; P. Kozák, 'Zástavní pán nebo 'freyer Fürst'? Několik poznámek k opvské vládě Zikmunda Jagellonského', *Acta historica Universitatis Silesianae Opaviensis*, 1, 2008, pp. 87–97.
40 I. Hlobil and E. Petrů, *Humanism and the Early Renaissance in Moravia*, trans. Jana and Michael Stoddart, ed. Marek Perůtka, Olomouc, Votobia, 1999.
41 For an analysis of the historiography of the period see J. Fajt, 'Das Zeitalter der Jagiellonen in den Ländern der Böhmischen Krone und die tschechische Historiographie', in E. Wetter, ed., *Die Länder der Böhmischen Krone und ihre Nachbarn zur Zeit der Jagiellonenkönige (1471–1526): Kunst, Kultur, Geschichte*, Ostfildern, 2004, pp. 15–30.
42 J. Petráň, 'Stavovské království a jeho kultura v Čechách (1471–1526)', in J. Homolka, J. Krása, V. Mencl, J. Pešina and J. Petráň, eds, *Pozdně gotické umění v Čechách (1471–1526)*, Prague, 1978, pp. 14–24.

43 The case is presented in a short form in M. Bartlová, 'Světec, král a skutečný vládce: Nástěnné malby v kapli sv. Václava za vlády Jagellonců' [A Saint, a King and the Real Rulers: Wall Paintings in the St Wenceslas' Chapel under the Reign of the Jagiellonians], *Dějiny a současnost*, 4, 2012, pp. 32–5.
44 J. Kuthan, *Královské dílo za Jiřího z Poděbrad a dynastie Jagellonců. Díl první. Král a šlechta*, Prague, 2010.
45 Z. Adla, J. Černý and J. Kalousek, *Obrázky z českých dějin a pověstí*, Prague, 1979.
46 Adla et al., *Obrázky z českých dějin a pověstí*, p. 96.
47 Adla et al., *Obrázky z českých dějin a pověstí*.
48 L. Seifertová, *Dějiny udatného českého národa*, Prague, 2003.
49 An analysis of Macek's work on the Jagiellonian age is offered in P. Čornej, *Historici, historiografie a dějepis*, Prague, 2016, pp. 370–80. See also B. Jiroušek, *Josef Macek: mezi historií a politikou*, Prague, 2004.
50 Instructively, a rare recent volume directly dedicated to the 'Jagiellonian period' in the Czech lands was produced by art historians: V. Kubík, ed., *Doba jagellonská v zemích české koruny (1471–1526): konference k založení Ústavu dějin křesťanského umění KTF UK v Praye*, České Budějovice, 2005.
51 For this project and exhibition, see Zupka and also Introduction in this volume.
52 www.rozhlas.cz/leonardo/historie/_zprava/jagellonci-a-kutna-hora-1-cast--1080908, accessed 20.9.17.
53 *Dějiny a současnost*, 4, 2012.
54 For narratives of this type, see for example Petr Hampl, 'Pevnost Česká republika nebo kavárna Česká republika?', http://petrhampl.com/pevnost-nebo-kavarna, accessed 10.11.17.

5
REMEMBERING JAGIELLONIANS IN GERMAN-SPEAKING LANDS

Dušan Zupka

Introduction: from hero to zero

The perception and memory of the Jagiellonian dynasty in German-speaking lands underwent several phases from the sixteenth to the twenty-first century. Their place in historical consciousness gradually shifted from centrality to a genuinely marginal, if not completely neglected, position. In 1548, at the peak of the dynasty's international importance and glory and on the occasion of the funeral of King Sigismund I (1506–48), the bishop and historiographer Marcin Kromer proudly announced the rhetorical question 'Who has not heard of the Jagiellonians?'[1] Their status among the princely houses of the Holy Roman Empire was so prominent that Bishop Stanislaw Orzechowski could add that 'there are few among the German princely houses who are not related to the Poles (i.e., Jagiellonians) by blood'.[2] Reading these lines, one might get the impression that nothing could endanger the prominent position of the late medieval/early modern Polish royal dynasty, both in contemporary politics and in the historical traditions of the German-speaking lands; as was the case, for instance, with their counterparts, the Habsburgs and the Medici. But, almost five centuries later in 2013, when the German national radio broadcaster aired a detailed reportage of the *Europa Jagellonica* exhibition in Potsdam, it could not find a better title than '*Das unbekannte Herrschergeschlecht Mitteleuropas*' (The unknown ruling house of Central Europe) to introduce the Jagiellonians to a German audience.[3] The report states that the Polish-Lithuanian ruling house of the Jagiellonians ruled considerable parts of Central Europe for almost 200 years. Nonetheless, in German countries, it remains virtually unknown.[4]

The Jagiellonians entered the political geography of the German-speaking lands in great number in the last quarter of the fifteenth century.[5] The number of royal daughters of kings Casimir IV, Sigismund I of Poland, and Ladislas II of Hungary and Bohemia who married into the realms of the Holy Roman Empire meant a

TABLE 5.1 The Jagiellonian princesses and their marriages into the Holy Roman Empire

Year	Bride	Groom	Region	Family	Wedding place	Children
1475	Hedwig (1457–1502) Duchess of Bavaria	George	Bavaria	Wittelsbach	Landshut	4
1479	Sophie (1464–1512) Margravine of Brandenburg-Ansbach	Frederick	Brandenburg-Ansbach	Hohenzollern	Frankfurt an der Oder	18
1491	Anna (1476–1503) Duchess of Pomerania	Bogislaw X	Pomerania	Greif	Stettin	8
1496	Barbara (1478–1534) Duchess of Saxony	George the Bearded	Saxony	Wettin	Leipzig	10
1515	Elisabeth (1482–1517) Duchess of Legnica/Liegnitz	Frederick II	Liegnitz/Legnica	Piast	Liegnitz	1
1521	Anna (1503–47) Queen of the Romans, Hungary and Bohemia	Ferdinand I	Austria	Habsburg	Linz	15
1535	Hedwig (1513–73) Electress of Brandenburg	Joachim II	Brandenburg	Hohenzollern	Krakow	6
1556	Sophie (1522–75) Duchess of Brunswick-Wolfenbüttel	Henry the Younger	Brunswick-Lüneburg	Welf	Wolfenbüttel	0

considerable internationalisation of the dynasty and their promotion and acceptance into the highest spheres of Central European politics.[6]

Connections with the Jagiellonians brought significant advantages for many principalities and princely houses in the Holy Roman Empire. The Hohenzollerns in Brandenburg, the Wettins in Saxony, and the Wittelsbachs in Bavaria – all these princely houses promoted their status and prestige by marrying their sons to Polish princesses and consequently adding royal blood to their lineages. For the Austrian Habsburgs, a marital connection with the Jagiellonians through the pairing of Ferdinand and Anna and Mary and Louis (1515) opened the door to royal thrones in Hungary and Bohemia, and so significantly extended their Central European power.[7] The memory of Jagiellonian princesses also remained present in most of these lands for practical reasons. In the seventeenth and eighteenth centuries these memories became a potent weapon in the succession crises and inheritance disputes of several German princely houses. This essay attempts to sketch the essential paths and crucial moments of the long journey of the Jagiellonians, from high estimation to neglect and disappearance in the memory of the German-speaking lands.

Ein gedechtnis machen: material vestiges of the Jagiellonians

The daughter of Polish King Sigismund I and his wife Bona Sforza, Sophie (1522–75), married into the Duchy of Brunswick-Wolfenbüttel in 1556. After the death of her husband, Duke Henry the Young, in 1568, she moved to her dowager castle in Schöningen, where she led a quasi-independent ducal life.[8] Among other Renaissance-styled efforts, such as the construction of a great library and an art collection, she also began to rebuild the castle and the adjacent gardens, turning it into a modern Renaissance residence. All of these efforts, together with acts of charity and piety like the construction of a hospital for the poor in Schöningen, were meant to inscribe the memory of the Jagiellonian princess in local history. This is evidenced explicitly in a funerary oration written by her confessor, Lazarus Arnoldi, who in 1575 wrote that Sophie aimed to 'preserve the memory that a born Queen of Poland and Ducal widow of Brunswick lived and held her court in these places'.[9] She also left a mark on the portal leading to her other residence at Jerxheim. To this day an inscription reminds all passers-by and visitors that it was constructed by the Duchess Sophie.[10] These attempts at memorialisation through vestiges of art, architecture and other visual media were characteristic for all Jagiellonian princesses, as well as for all the ruling houses they married into.

Towns, churches, palaces and monasteries scattered over the territory of the former Holy Roman Empire (for this essay, predominately modern-day Germany, Bohemia, Poland and Austria) preserve a number of artefacts related to the Jagiellonians. Many towns hold the tombs of princesses married into local princely houses. Categorically the most impressive and luxurious is the imperial necropolis built for Anna, Queen of Bohemia and Hungary (1503–47) and her husband, the later Roman Emperor, Ferdinand I (1503–64) in St Vitus Cathedral in Prague.

This impressive work of art was more than adequate for a couple who, as is witnessed by numerous contemporary sources, shared an unusually affectionate and loving marriage.[11] The tomb, known as the Colyn Mausoleum, was built by Alexander Colyn between 1566 and 1590 and also houses their son Emperor Maximilian II (r.1564–76). Adam Lecuir is generally considered the sculptor of another significant tomb, dated to the last quarter of the sixteenth century. This tomb is found in St Mary's Church in Wolfenbüttel, preserving the remains of Duke Henry the Young together with his second wife, Duchess Sophie Jagiellon (see Figure 5.1). The statue representing the Jagiellonian princess bears her monograph 'HS' (*Herzogin Sophie*) and an inscription referring to her regnal origin.[12] The third daughter of King Casimir the Great (1427–92) and Elisabeth Habsburg (1436–1505), Barbara (1478–1534), found her resting place meanwhile in the beautiful Dome in Meissen, where she is buried next to her husband, George the Bearded (1471–1539). Barbara is depicted dressed in a noble coat, holding a rosary in her hand. A carved Polish eagle and an inscription remind us of the Polish royal daughter and the Saxonian duchess buried here.[13] Barbara's older sister, Sophie, Margravine of Brandenburg-Ansbach (1464–1512), was buried in the Cistercian monastery in Heilsbronn. This foundation was programmatically built to commemorate the members of the Hohenzollern dynasty. The reverse of the famous Heilsbronn altarpiece of the Three Magi preserves a remarkable depiction of the margravial family of Sophie and her husband Frederick. One side depicts Frederick with the couple's sons, whilst the other shows Sophie with their daughters. Seventeen of their eighteen children are represented, which allows historians to date the construction of the altarpiece to between 1501 and 1503. Sophie is represented kneeling, dressed in a luxurious dress, but without the usual crown which symbolised her royal origin. Reference to her Polish descent is made by a simplified coat of arms in the form of the Polish eagle.[14] Other Jagiellonian princesses who married into German-speaking lands did not have the same luck, as their respective tombs have been either destroyed or lost in the course of time. This is the case for the tombs of Anna, Duchess of Pomerania, in Edelna,[15] of Hedwig, Duchess of Brandenburg, in Cölln,[16] and of Hedwig, Duchess of Bavaria, in the Cistercian monastery in Raitenhaslach, which was destroyed during the secularisation.[17]

Another way to keep the memory of the Jagiellonians alive was to commission artefacts, commemorative objects and architectural representations. In 1558 an anonymous painter depicted Queen Anna of Bohemia and Hungary (d.1547) posthumously, together with her husband Ferdinand I and all their fifteen children.[18] After the death of Anna, Duchess of Pomerania (1476–1503), her son Barmin XI (1501–73) left an epitaph to be constructed for her and her husband Duke Bogislaw X (1454–1523) in the Stettin castle chapel. This exceptional monument represented Duke Bogislaw kneeling with their sons to the left, while Anna knelt with their daughters on the right side of the crucifix. Unfortunately this masterpiece was destroyed during the heavy bombing of Stettin in the Second World War.[19]

Likewise, a posthumous portrait created by Lucas Cranach the Elder was supposed to keep the memory of Duchess Barbara of Saxony alive.[20]

The representation of the 1515 double wedding agreement and ceremonies that took place in Bratislava and Vienna is a special case in early modern memory. This was a unique event in the history of Austria, as well as of Hungary, Bohemia, and indeed all of the 'Jagiellonian-ruled' lands. During the famous 'First Congress of Vienna', the marital union between the Jagiellonians and the Habsburgs was sealed with a double betrothal. The children of the Hungarian and Bohemian king Ladislaus II Jagiello (1471/90–1516), Anna and Louis, were betrothed to the Habsburgs Mary and Ferdinand. This significant event, which proved to be pivotal for the growth of the Central European power of the Habsburgs, was a matter for historical memory. Most famously, the double marriage became the object of a grandiose plan for the so-called Triumphal Arch of Emperor Maximilian I (1459–1519), dating to 1515, that was intended to decorate the Imperial Palace in Innsbruck. This astonishing piece of art was created by none other than Albrecht Dürer himself. Requiring over 190 woodcuts composed into 36 paper sheets, and of considerable size (3 metres by 3.5 metres), it is one of the largest prints ever produced. The artist represented the grandiosity of Maximilian and the House of Austria in Goliath-like proportions. One of the most interesting woodcuts is dedicated to the moment of the betrothal of the future spouses at the 1515 congress. The main protagonist for the Habsburg side was Emperor Maximilian, whilst for the Jagiellonians King Ladislaus II of Bohemia and Hungary (d.1516) and King of Poland Sigismund I (d.1548) feature. In front of them one finds young Anna, Louis and Mary. Ferdinand was not included in the scene, as at the time of the 1515 wedding it was unclear whether Ferdinand or his brother, the later Emperor Charles V, would be the groom of Princess Anna Jagiellon.[21] This scene was repeatedly represented in art and historiography. In the late nineteenth century it was also the topic of a monumental photogravure commissioned by the Emperor Franz Joseph I and created by Vaclav Brosik in 1897.[22]

Geborene Königin von Polen: Jagiellonians in historical memory

The Jagiellonians' rule in the Holy Roman Empire was short-lasting and episodic. Between 1471 and 1526 Ladislaus II and Louis II were kings of Bohemia, and Ladislaus's daughter Anna was the queen of the Romans, i.e. of Germany, and eventually of Bohemia, from 1526 to 1547. Evidently these reigns were not enough to leave an indelible mark, and too scarce to be incorporated into the pantheon of the most venerable and glorious princely houses of the empire. Concentrating on the German-speaking lands (excluding Bohemia, treated in a separate chapter of this volume) the Jagiellonians remained a secondary topic of regional memory in all its variations (historic, visual, cultural, literary, etc.). They never reached the popularity of 'home' lineages and houses such as the Habsburgs, Hohenzollerns or Wittelsbachs.[23] In fact, the more time that elapsed after their real presence within the Holy Roman Empire's politics, the more they became at best a blurred and distant memory. From the extinction of the male line of the dynasty with Sigismund August's death in 1572, to the twenty-first century, memories of the Jagiellonians in German-speaking lands were first and foremost related to their royal status and the office of the Polish kings, and respectively to the fact that several German and Austrian princely houses were united with them through marital ties. This fact was an essential component in the motivations of local historians, chroniclers, court historians, architects and artists. Through their works, they tried to anchor the Jagiellonian princesses and their regnal relatives in Poland as members of a prestigious lineage of Polish kings, and reflected the memories of dynastic characters in their local contexts.

One type of source employs the Jagiellonians as a source of legitimacy during succession crises. The fierce struggle for the Polish throne began in 1586, after the death of Stephan Bathory, the husband of the 'last living Jagiellonian', Anna, queen of Poland (d.1596). Among the main contenders were the Habsburgs, represented by the Austrian Archduke Maximilian III (1558–1618), son of Emperor Maximilian II, the grandson of Anna Jagiellon (d.1547) and Emperor Ferdinand I. The other contender was Sigismund Vasa, son of Catharina Jagellonica (d.1583) and John III Vasa, king of Sweden and Finland. Thus, the competitors' grandmother and mother were cousins. Sigismund III Vasa emerged victorious, and was crowned in 1587.[24] The following year, a text in the form of a '*Zeitung*' (journal) was published as the '*Polnische Zeitung*', describing all the relevant events of the conflict.[25] The important part for our purposes comes at the end of the text where the author presents his intention:

> So that the reader can see with his own eyes, and so that he acknowledges rightly, how close both elected kings, the one from Sweden and the other from the House of Austria, are related to the Crown of the Jagiellonian lineage, we would like to present the reader to see with his own eyes the Jagiellonian kinship line in the following table.[26]

The *Zeitung* then follows this with a schematic genealogical table tracing the 'genealogy of the Jagiellonian lineage' from Gediminus to the children of Ladislaus II and Sigismund the Old. The goal of this work was to introduce local German-speaking readers to the complicated political issues in Poland and to explain the Habsburgs' legitimate right to succession. According to this picture, the Habsburgs had the same right as the Vasas as they were both closely related to the Jagiellonians.

The arguments given nicely illustrate the importance of the Jagiellonians after their extinction. Sigismund of Sweden, who relied on his blood ties (*Blutsverwandniss*) to Anna, is repeatedly introduced as 'Sigismund … from the Jagiellonian lineage of the Polish Kings, born son of Catharine'.[27] Further, the decision of the majority of Sejm to elect Sigismund was made on the basis of his proximity to Jagiellonian blood, according to the *Zeitung*.[28] Evidently, genealogical connections to the extinct Polish royal house became a pivotal argument in political struggles from the late sixteenth century and remained important for the dynasties of the Holy Roman Empire.

Another type of early modern source which preserves information on the Jagiellonians is the festive works published on the occasion of princely weddings. One such example was occasioned by the wedding of Anna Catharina Constantia (1619–51), daughter of the Polish king Sigismund III Vasa, to Philippe Wilhelm, Count Palatine of Neuburg, in 1642. The *Genii Serenissimorum Principum* was published in Frankfurt am Main, and dedicated to the spouses as a work providing a full description of their venerable descent.[29] One of the many branches of the lineage of the bride Anna Catharina Constantia is located under the heading 'Oliva Iagellonia'. Here, as has become traditional, the genealogical connection of the bride with the Jagiellonian lineage is drawn. Starting from Iagello (Iagello Magnus Lithuaniae ac Russie Dux ... atauus),[30] a direct line is drawn all the way to King Sigismund III, father of Anna Catharina Constantia. Interestingly, even though the author correctly marks the beginning of the 'Jagiellonians' with Jogaila's baptism and coronation in 1386, he doesn't perceive the death of Sigismund August in 1572 as a break in the continuity of the 'lineage'. What matters is that the line of Polish kings continues in Sigismund III, who was perceived as the legitimate heir of his 'Jagiellonian' predecessors. Sigismund III and his daughter Anna Catharina Constantia were considered members of the 'Oliva Iagellonia'.

Similarly, in the interregnum of 1668–69, the main rivals for the Polish throne were respectively perceived as representatives of the Piast lineage (Michael Koribut, 1640–73, King of Poland-Lithuania from 1669) and of the Jagiellonians (Frederick Wilhelm, Count Palatine of Rhine Neuburg). In the same year, a genealogical work was published in the German town of Nuremberg. The *Polnischer Königs-Stammen oder Beschreibung des Gross-Hertzoglichen Littauischen Geschlechts* was a propagandistic work produced with the intention of supporting the legitimacy of Michael Koribut's claim to the throne in Warsaw. Even the title claimed that Koribut was a descendant of an ancient lineage which had ruled Poland and Lithuania for almost 300 years, producing twelve grand dukes and kings.[31] The book opens with a simplified family tree, showing the 'Polish royal lineage' (*Polnischer Königs-Stammen*) starting from the Duke of Lithuania Vitenesius, his son Gediminus and grandson Olgerdus. From Oldgerdus the family tree splits into two main sections. One follows the progeny of Ladislaus Iagello (Jogaila), with all the following kings of Poland streaming from his branch. The other starts with the Lithuanian Duke Koributus, and leads to the current king of Poland Michael Koribut. Thus Michael is presented as the twelfth king of Poland, descended from the ancient lineage of dukes of Lithuania (i.e. Jagiellonians). Despite this, the work presents a somewhat disorganised and chaotic perception of Koribut as the descendant of Jagiellonians. The book's preface informs the reader that the abdicated Polish king Johan Casimir Vasa (r.1648–68) was the last king of the Jagiellonian lineage (*der letzte König in Pohlen Jagellonischer Linie*), and was succeeded by the current monarch Michael, whose ancestor was the brother of

Ladislaus Iagiello. The author also refers to the eleven Jagiellonian kings of Poland (*die elf Könige in Pohlen Jagellonischer Linie einander succediret*) and describes the two kings of Hungary and Bohemia (Ladislaus and Louis II) as of the same lineage (*zwey Könige in Hungarn und Boheim dieses Geschlechts*).[32] The work then continues with an outline of the rule of all the Jagiellonian kings starting with Ladislaus Jagiello, Ladislaus II, Casimir, John Albert, Alexander, Sigismund I, Sigismund Augustus, etc.[33] Interestingly enough, in this section the book declares that Sigismund Augustus was the last of the Jagiellonian male lineage.[34] Further, Sigismund Augustus's sister and successor Anna is later labelled as the last of the Jagiellonians (*die letzte des Jagellonischen Geschlechts*). The list then continues with Sigismund III, his son Ladislaus IV, and Johann Casimir. The latter left the Sejm the freedom to choose their new ruler by resigning from office. It seems that this genealogical work developed a system that would enable it to present Michael Koribut as the most suitable candidate for the Polish and Lithuanian throne based on a genealogical argument. All of the previous twelve kings had been 'Jagiellonian related'. From Ladislaus Iogailla (Jogaila) to Sigismund August (d.1572) and Anna (d.1596) respectively, the Jagiellonian *lineage* ruled both realms. Sigismund August was the last of the male line and Anna of the female. The next kings ruled as members of the Jagiellonian line (*Jagellonische Linie*) up to Johann Casimir. The new king Michael Koribut had traced his origin to Koribut, the brother of Jogailla (*Koributische Linie*), and so could invoke a legitimate claim on the Jagiellonian legacy, i.e. the royal and grand ducal thrones of Poland and Lithuania. As the pamphlet was published in Germany and was surely meant to serve readers in the Holy Roman Empire and other non-Polish countries, a detailed description of the genealogical ties of Michael to all the ruling lineages in Europe follows this family tree.[35]

The Jagiellonians also appear occasionally in later historiographical treatises published in German-speaking lands. Sporadic references to them are to be found in genealogical literature.[36] These appearances are sometimes a mere mention of the Jagiellonian princesses as members of the local ruling dynasties, as for instance in the genealogies of the Bavarian Wittelsbachs, *Genealogie des königlichen Hauses Baiern* (1834), where Hedwig is described as the daughter of the king of Poland Casimir, and *Genealogie der erlauchten Stammhauses Wittelsbach* (1870) which also mentions Hedwig as of the lineage of Jagello.[37] Other examples, in which the Jagiellonians are represented as a real ruling dynasty, can also be found, and here they are treated as a reference point for dynastic history on a European scale. This is the case in the famous *Bibliotheca Genealogica* of Johann Hübner published in 1729.[38] This bulky *opus* presented the early eighteenth-century German reader with a *summa* of all known published genealogies of real and imagined ruling houses, princely lineages, and divine rulers. Section I of Chapter 12 is devoted to the genealogies of Poland and Lithuania. The author divides his outline of the work into periods: from 'Noah onwards', then from 'Piasto to Casimir III', and finally the period of the 'Jagiellonian kings' derived from the old

Lithuanian dukes.[39] The work also introduces the readers to the most important genealogies of the Polish kings, published either in German territories or in Poland (*Decius' De Iagellonum Familia*; *Pistorius' Genealogia Regum Poloniae*, etc.). Overall, the insertion of Jagiellonian descent into local German princely lineages, from the sixteenth century to the eighteenth, was purely pragmatic, as such associations were intended to provide an advantage to one side of a conflict or to legitimise the claims of a ruling house on a certain territory or office. This tool was used by the Habsburgs in the eighteenth century when they turned to their derivation from Anna Jagiellon of Bohemia-Hungary (d.1547), married at the beginning of the sixteenth century to Ferdinand I Habsburg,[40] or by the Wettins in Saxony in 1716 when Augustus III argued for his genealogical descent from Barbara Jagiellon (d.1534) whilst making his case for the Polish throne.[41]

The image of the Jagiellonians in eighteenth- and nineteenth-century German-language historiography and historical literature was quite controversial. A symptomatic example is the treatment of Hedwig, Margravine of Brandenburg (1513–73). In a 1798 book concerning Hedwig's husband, Elector Joachim II, the author struggles to find a positive word for the Jagiellonian princess. She is depicted as an unlovable and weird person, responsible for her unfortunate fate (an accident which paralysed her) and for her poor treatment at the hands of Joachim II.[42] Hedwig appears in a much better light in a publication on the Hohenzollern Elector princesses (*Kurfürstinnen*) and queens written in the 1860s.[43] In this work, her life is assessed on the basis of primary sources and set correctly within the context of her historical epoch. It is probably the best piece of German-language historical scholarship on the Jagiellonians written in the nineteenth century. The other, earlier Hedwig (d.1502), the Duchess of Bavaria, also became the object of historical literature. A book called *Hedwig, die schöne Königstochter aus Polen* (Hedwig, the beautiful royal daughter from Poland), published in 1860 by an unknown author, deals with her life at the Burghausen castle.[44] Unfortunately, the book heavily distorts historical reality and supports a negative representation of the duchess as a poor and unlucky victim of her negligent husband and, finally, her own sad fate. This is suggested by the subtitle of the book, which describes it as a 'mourning-picture from the 15th century' (*Trauergemälde aus d. 15. Jahrhundert*).

This picture of Hedwig was deeply rooted in the consciousness of Bavarian historiography and literature. Previous scholarship has proven that this was a result of the systematic defamation of Hedwig's husband George carried out by the Munich branch of the Wittelsbachs and their loyal authors. One of their chief narrative strategies was to depict him as a cruel and merciless tyrant who mistreated his beautiful wife. Unfortunately, this picture triumphed for a long time, thriving well after the end of the early sixteenth-century Bavarian succession crisis in which the Munich branch had prevailed.[45] An illustrative example of this approach to remembering Hedwig can be found in the commemorative poem on Hedwig printed on the 400th anniversary of her death in the *Burghauser Anzeiger* in 1902.

Here we again encounter the traditional genre of the *Trauerlied* (mourning song). The author clearly works to maximise the grieving atmosphere:

Hedwig, Hedwig, much-beloved!
As great in suffering as in beauty.
Who does not grieve
About your dark lot?
Oh, you did not find here peace,
Nor a faithful heart's reward.
Broken and early departed,
You blessed the Ducal throne.[46]

The poem then continues, stating that although all Landshut once praised her as Europe's most beautiful bride (*Landshut sah dich hochgefeiert, als Europa's schönste Braut*), the Polish king's daughter was then moved and stayed behind the Burghausen walls.

This picture of Hedwig Jagiellon persevered throughout the twentieth century and became her standard memorialisation in Germany (or at least in Bavaria). The climax of this distorted and historically incorrect vision of the Bavarian duchess was reached in a popular historical fiction book written by local author Manfred Böckl called *Die Braut von Landshut* (The Bride from Landshut) with the subtitle 'Das tragische Leben von Herzogin Hedwig' (The tragic life of the Duchess Hedwig). The story presents the Jagiellonian princess as a traditional victim of a contemporary dynastic policy that sent her to a foreign and unknown land. At first, she hoped to have a happy marriage with her '*Traumprinz*' George, but this soon transformed into a nightmare. The novel repeats all the customary clichés; the fiction, for instance, that she was 'deported' to the Burghausen castle, where her husband only rarely visited her. Thanks to its success, the book, originally published in 2001, was reprinted in a second edition in 2016.[47]

The Jagiellonian princesses were also remembered in historically-neutral or even positive ways. In 1986 Wolfgang Hopfgartner determined that the red marble block situated on the floor of the Raitenhaslach monastery church was the only remaining part of the Wittelsbach family tomb (of the Landshut branch). The last person to be buried there was the Jagiellonian Duchess Hedwig in 1502. The tomb had been destroyed during the secularisation, but was preserved in depictions from the eighteenth century. In 1987 a commemorative inscription was added to the church:

To the memory of Hedwig of Bavaria/
Born Queen of Poland/
Bride of the Landshut/ Wedding/1457–1502[48]

The inscription is accompanied by the Bavarian and Polish coats of arms. Another instance of commemoration can be found in Stettin (Sczeczin) in today's Poland.

Having had a considerable German population in the past, this town was for a long time the capital of the Pomeranian dukes. Bogislaw X, one of the most important members of this dynasty, married Anna Jagiellon in 1491. Today, they are both memorialised in one of the main squares of the town, which leads to the beautiful Pomerian ducal castle, in a monumental larger-than-life statue made in 1974 by Leonia Chmielnik and Anna Paszkiewicz. The inscription on the statue refers to the famous wedding in 1491 which united Bogislaw and 'Anna Jagiellonka'.[49]

The Jagiellonians in German-speaking lands: recent assessments

Currently, the Jagiellonians seem to be enjoying renewed interest in twenty-first-century German-speaking lands. The essential change has come from the sphere of German-language scholarship. A new picture of the Polish-Lithuanian dynasty is being formed, based on serious historical and art historical research. Thanks to these efforts, the image of the Jagiellonians is achieving a more realistic, and more trustworthy, shape. The major steps in the introduction of the Jagiellonians to the map of the German-speaking historical consciousness were performed by the publication of a series of monographs and collective volumes. An introductory outline of the 'Jagiellonian subject' was produced by Almut Bues in her publication *Die Jagiellonen. Herrscher zwischen Ostsee und Adria* (Jagiellonians. Rulers between the Baltic and the Adriatic), published in the popular series Urban-Taschenbücher by Kohlhammer in 2010.[50] The Jagiellonian princesses have also become the subject of qualified historical research. A trio of monographs have shone detailed light on their lives and memories in their local (Franconian/Brandenburg, Brunswick, Bavarian) contexts. Jan Pirożyński has researched Sophie, Duchess of Brunswick-Wolfenbüttel,[51] Johann Dorner, Hedwig, Duchess of Bavaria,[52] and Agnieszka Gąsior has focused on Sophie, Margravine of Brandenburg-Ansbach.[53]

The first research project in Germany to be fully devoted to the Jagiellonians and their age was the Leipzig-based 'Die Bedeutung der Jagiellonen in der Kunst und Kultur Mitteleuropas 1454–1572' (The Role of the Jagiellonians in Art and Culture 1454–1572). The project was hosted by the Geisteswissenschaftliches Zentrum Geschichte und Kultur Ostmitteleuropas e.V. an der Universität Leipzig (GWZO) between 2000 and 2005. The emphasis of the research project was on the art historical representations of the dynasty, and the artistic developments of fifteenth- and sixteenth-century Central and Eastern European countries. One of the outcomes was the publication of a series of monographs and collective volumes as part of the *Studia Jagellonica Lipsiensia*. The volumes traced several historical and art historical developments of the 'Jagiellonian age' in Central Europe (for instance art history, cultural transfers, court culture, international relations, literacy, German-Polish relations, etc.).[54] Another result of the Leipzig project was the organisation of an international art historical exhibition, *Europa Jagellonica. Kunst und Kultur Mitteleuropas unter der Herrschaft der Jagiellonen*

1386–1572. The exhibition took place in three countries: Kutná Hora (Czech Republic), Warsaw (Poland), and Potsdam (Germany), in 2012 and 2013. In 2013 a German version of the exhibition guide was published, displaying artefacts of great historical importance connected to the Jagiellonians, many of which are being kept in German and Austrian galleries, museums, churches and towns.[55] The most recent exhibition to take part in the remembering of the Jagiellonians was organised to coincide with the 500th anniversary of the famous First Congress of Vienna of 1515, in 2015. The exhibition, called *Wiener Kongress 1515 Wendellpunkt Mitteleuropas: Jagiellonen und Habsburger* (The Congress of Vienna 1515. Turning point of Central Europe: Jagiellonians and Habsburgs), was hosted by the Kunsthistorisches Museum in Vienna.

Die Landshuter Hochzeit 1475 – to experience the Middle Ages

The perception of the great royal marriage between Hedwig Jagiellon (1457–1502) and the Bavarian Duke George the Rich (1455–1503) in 1475 is the best German-language example of wider Jagiellonian commemoration. This celebration, held in Landshut, became a model example of a lavish and extravagant wedding feast for all the later Middle Ages. The ceremony also became proverbial and served as a point of reference for many princely and royal weddings taking place in the region and beyond, and it makes for a useful case study.

The Landshut wedding was virtually forgotten and banished from local collective memory during the early modern period, and remained so until the last quarter of the nineteenth century. Despite this, the first step of the revival can be traced to the publication of historical sources relating to the wedding by Lorenz Westenrieder in 1789.[56] The Jagiellonians suddenly emerge out of the darkness in 1828, in – rather surprisingly – a masquerade ball. The first part of the tripartite Munich ball programme introduces dancers as guests at the ducal wedding taking place in fifteenth-century Landshut. This was the first, and remained for a long time the only, attempt to retrieve the 1475 Landshut wedding before the advent of the twentieth century.[57] A new wave of interest in the Landshut wedding theme came in the late 1880s. When the town council of Landshut weighed the possibilities for a thematic representation of the new town hall's main room (*Prunksaal*), the 1475 events were recalled. From amongst several suggestions, a theme focusing on the wedding between George and Hedwig won ultimate support. This was the beginning of the great cycle of paintings that emerged between 1882 and 1883 (with financial support from King Ludwig II of Bavaria). When, on 18 September 1883, the new town hall room opened to the public for the first time, it immediately astonished onlookers. Seven scenes from the most festive event in Landshut's history had been painted on the entire length of three walls. More than a hundred people were represented in the paintings.[58] The central scene depicted the arrival of the marital carriage with the bride. Hedwig, princess of Poland, was seated in the carriage, peeking out to catch a sight of her husband-to-be, George. The duke rode on a horse next to the carriage, with his gaze fixed on his new bride as he

FIGURE 5.1 Painting of the 'Jagiellonian' Landshut wedding of 1475, *Prunksaal* of Landshut town hall, Bavaria (completed 1883)

greeted her. Although Hedwig's arrival was depicted at the centre of the piece, the main aim was to celebrate the splendour and uniqueness of the event. All of the important members of the wedding are depicted, including the Emperor Frederick III, his son Maximilian, Prince Elector Albrecht Achilles, and all the other German and Austrian princes. Each contributed to the overall pageantry and lavishness of this event, which represented the self-consciousness and pride of the citizens of Landshut. Hedwig was important too, but she was not the central character of the whole story. And, as usual, her importance was derived from her status as a royal daughter of Poland, not from her Jagiellonian lineage.

The echo of the Landshut town hall decoration resonated in various places, both locally and nationwide, and gave rise to several reviews.[59] The end of the century also saw a publication devoted entirely to the Landshut wedding. Together, these factors gradually helped to make historical-regional consciousness more aware of a famous and unique, if distant, event in local history. This gave rise to the idea of a 'realistic rapprochement' to the wedding by a means never employed before in this region – a re-enactment of the wedding itself. The idea was promoted by two locals, Georg Tippel and Josef Linnbrunner, who came up with a plan of how to re-create and re-represent their city's most famous historical event. In 1902 they founded a society called '*Die Förderer*' (English: patrons, conveyors or sponsors) and ceaselessly followed their dream. Despite being the object of mockery and humour, they managed to prepare and host the first modern 'Landshut Wedding' performance within a year of founding *Die Förderer*.[60] On 15 August 1903, a festive parade comprising around 250 characters marched through the streets of Landshut. Among them was a local woman, Rosa Lindner (believed to be the most beautiful woman in town), representing the Polish royal daughter Hedwig Jagiellon.[61] The retinue then left the city walls and continued the programme on the fields outside, where the re-enactors mixed with onlookers and visitors, creating a festive, special day. The success of the modern Landshut Wedding, or the *Landshuter Hochzeit 2* as it came to be known, was immense. The organisers decided to turn it into an annual historical feast to articulate their town's pride and importance. They emphasised from the very beginning the need for as much accuracy and verisimilitude as possible in respect to the historical facts and context. On the occasion of the 500th anniversary of the wedding in 1975, the organisers attempted to re-enact the festivities with as much 'authenticity' as possible.[62] This attention to accuracy is reflected in the feast's programme, the clothes worn by the re-enactors, the objects used during the show, and by the continual addition of new components and spectacles.[63] By 1905 a festive play performed in the historic town hall had already been introduced. The piece, written by the famous Munich playwright Georg Schaumberg, was performed in the *coulisse* of the beautiful Landshut Wedding paintings. A jousting tournament was introduced in the 1920s, followed by festive dance, artistic performances, shows, and musical presentations. The feast scheduled for 2017 offered a rich programme comprised of the main parade, dance performances, a theatrical play, a masquerade, a fencing school, a sacral *Laudate Dominum*, a bridal pageant, etc.[64]

By the 1920s the modern Landshut Wedding was already being labelled as 'one of the most important historical festivals in Germany', whilst at the time of writing it is perceived as 'the most important and biggest historical festival in Europe'.[65] Its unique attraction is understood to lie in its mixing of history, theatre, and local patriotism. By 2013, the original 250 participants had become more than 2,000. The annual frequency of the festival has also changed over time. It became biannual in 1938, triannual in 1952, and in 1981 the organisers settled on a four-year cycle.[66] Today the '*1475 Landshuter Hochzeit*' is one of the most popular summer festivals in Germany. It attracts thousands of visitors from among both locals and tourists over four consecutive summer weekends. Its goals are twofold. On the one hand, it tries to sustain the local memory of the most important event in Landshut's history and tries to pass its reputation and importance down the generations. On the other hand, it serves as a unique attempt to retrieve the 'real' Middle Ages for contemporary people. The programme focuses everywhere on the local memory of Landshut – Bavaria – Wittelsbach. Princess Hedwig is an important figure in the festival, but she only provides a frame and adds prestige to the whole wedding, just like she did in the fifteenth century. The role and importance of the Jagiellonians is minimised as much as possible. But the personality of Hedwig, albeit in its distorted local and modernised manner, is still attractive. In this respect, Hedwig has entered the contemporary field of consumer-sensationalist society. The Jagiellonian duchess is omnipresent in the paraphernalia accompanying the Landshut Wedding commemorations. She is the main character of a popular children's book called *Jadwiga*, written by Marlene Reidel in 1978, which interprets her role within the wedding and later fate for young readers in an accessible manner. A puppet show called *Die geraubte Prinzessin* (The stolen princess) is also based on the theme of the Landshut wedding.[67] At the same time, however, Hedwig can be found on objects of art, or on the most traditional souvenirs that visitors purchase during their stay in Landshut. In this way, the memory of the Jagiellonian princess lives on through alternative media – beer glasses, cards, postcards, pins, plates, bowls, commemorative coins, stamps, or even beer bottle labels (*Hochzietsbier*), etc. Her role in the Landshut Wedding is also re-presented by media including DVD documentaries or music compilations on CDs.[68] It should however be added that Hedwig also appears in historical publications, especially in source editions related to the Landshut wedding. Recent decades have witnessed the publication of numerous works on this topic.[69]

The post-modern commemoration of the Landshut Wedding reached a new level by entering the world of popular comic books. *Die Landshuter Hochzeit von 1475* was published in 2008 as the third volume of a series of graphic novels dedicated to the exploration of local urban history called the 'Landshuter Stadtgeschichte'.[70] The marriage is presented as occurring during the golden age of Landshut (the era of the rich dukes) and as something fondly remembered by the local population to the present day. The focus is on the wedding of Hedwig, presented as the daughter of the king of Poland, and George, the young duke of Bavaria-Landshut. The comic book form enables the authors to present the well-known historical facts in a new light and to add elements of irony and humour. Although the story traces the conventional major events in the preparation and execution of the wedding, it follows historical fact strictly and makes no substantial errors. Hedwig is presented as a clever, self-conscious duchess who made her life in Bavaria suit her regnal origin. Again, her Jagiellonian provenance and kinship are not an issue, but the story of the Landshut spouses is at least presented with historical fidelity and accuracy.

Conclusions

All of the material assembled above should provide enough clear evidence to support the conclusion that memories of the Jagiellonians in German-speaking lands (especially in Germany and Austria) are anything but the memory of the Jagiellonian dynasty. In other words, the Jagiellonians have been, and are being, remembered in the German-language field without their dynastic context. They are first and foremost conceived of as Polish and Lithuanian rulers. The attraction of those princesses married into the Holy Roman Empire lies in their regnal origin and the royal aura they brought to their new ruling houses. By contrast, Jagiellonian dynastic kinship was important in only very specific cases (dynastic disputes, succession claims and legitimisation of rule).

Notes

1 S. Maciejowski and M. Kromer, *De Sigismundo Primo Rege Poloniae etc Duo Panegyrici funebres, dicti Cracoviae in eius funere, Nempe Sermo Samuelis Episcopi Cracoviensis & Regni Poloniae Cancellarij. Oratio Martini Cromeri, Canonici Cracoviensis & Oratoris Regij*, Mainz, 1550, fol. 101.
2 '... ut pauci sint ex omnibus Germanis principibus, qui consaguinei non sint Polonis ...' S. Orzechowski, *Ornata et copiosa oratio*, Venezia, 1548, fol. Av, Bv.
3 C. Altmann, 'Das unbekannte Herrschergeschlecht Mitteleuropas', Deutschlandfunk, 7.3.2013, www.deutschlandfunk.de/das-unbekannte-herrschergeschlecht mitteleuro pas.1148.de.html?dram:article_id=239699.
4 Altmann, 'Das unbekannte Herrschergeschlecht Mitteleuropas', 'Die polnisch-litauischen Jagiellonen haben fast 200 Jahre in weiten Teilen Mitteleuropas regiert. Trotzdem sind sie weitgehend unbekannt.'
5 Although dynastic connections had also been present in previous times. For instance, Frederick II, Elector of Brandenburg (1413–71), had been betrothed to the daughter of Ladislaus Iogaila, Hedwig (1408–31), in the 1420s and had spent several years at the Krakow court. After the death of his fiancée he returned to Brandenburg. Cf. G. Seifridus, *Genealogia Illustrissimorum Principum Marchionum Brandenburgensium exprobatissimis historiographis collecta per Georgium Seifridum medicinae doctorem*, Viteberge, 1555, p. 13.
6 M. Biskup, 'Die dynastische Politik der Jagiellonen um das Jahr 1475 und ihre Ergebnisse', *Österreichische Osthefte* 18, 3, 1976, pp. 203–17; U. Tresp, 'Eine "famose und grenzenlos mächtige Generation." Dynastie und Heiratspolitik der Jagiellonen im 15. und zu Beginn des 16. Jahrhundert', *Jahrbuch für Europäische Geschichte* 8, 2007, pp. 3–28; A. Gąsior, 'Dynastische Verbindungen der Jagiellonen mit den deutschen Fürstenhäusern', in M. Omilanowska and T. Torbus, eds, *Tür an Tür. Polen – Deutschland 1000. Jahre Kunst und Geschichte. Katalog der Ausstellung im Martin-Gropius-Bau Berlin, 23. September 2011–9. Januar 2012*, Köln, 2011.
7 J. Rogge, 'Nur verkaufte Töchter? Überlegungen zu Aufgaben, Quellen, Methoden und Perspektiven einer Sozial- und Kulturgeschichte hochadeligen Frauen und Fürstinnen im deutschen Reich während späten Mittelalters und Beginn der Neuzeit', in *Principes. Dynastien und Höfe im späten Mittelalter*, Stuttgart, 2002, pp. 235–76; K. Keller, 'Frauen und dynastische Herrschaft. Eine Einführung', in B. Braun, K. Keller and M. Schnettger, eds, *Nur die Frau des Kaisers? Kaiserinnen in den Frühen Neuzeit*, Wien, 2016, pp. 13–26; C. Nolte, *Familie, Hof und Herrchaft. Das verwandtschaftliche Beziehungs- und Kommunikationsnetz der Reichsfürsten am Beispiel der Markgrafen von Brandenburg-Ansbach (1440–1530)*, Stuttgart, 2005; K. F. Krieger, *Die Habsburger im Mittelater*, Stuttgart/Berlin/Köln, 1994.
8 A. Lilienthal, *Die Fürstin und die Macht. Welfische Herzoginnen im 16. Jahrhundert. Elisabeth, Sidonia, Sophia*, Quellen und Darstellungen zur Geschichte Niedersachsens 127, Hannover, 2007, pp. 241–84.
9 '*Sie wollte da ein gedechtnis machen, das eine geborne Königin aus Polen, und ein fürstliche wittwe von Braunschweig alda gelebet und hoffgehalten hette.*' J. Pirożyński, *Die Herzogin Sophie von Braunschweig-Wolfenbüttel aus dem Hause der Jagiellonen (1522–1575) und ihre Bibliothek. Ein Beitrag zur Geschichte der deutsch-polnischen Kulturbeziehungen in der Renaissancezeit*, trans. Kordula Zubrzycka, Wolfenbütteler Schriften für Geschichte des Buchwesens 18, Wiesbaden, 1992, p. 255.
10 'Hanc Sophia Henrici Iunioris regia coniux struxit ...' Pirożyński, *Die Herzogin Sophie von Braunschweig-Wolfenbüttel*, p. 102. Interestingly, on German territory, Sophie only fostered her local ducal identity together with her original regnal Polish identity. On the other hand when she was thinking about leaving a legacy back home in Krakow, her language was becoming straightforwardly dynastic. This is supported by her wish to create a marble genealogy of Jagiellonians which was supposed to be carved within the St Cross Chapel at Wawel Castle as a commemoration of this ruling lineage.

11 A. Kohler, *Ferdinand I. 1503–1564. Fürts, König und Kaiser*, München, 2003, pp. 98–9; P. S. Fichtner, *Ferdinand I. Wider Türken und Glaubensspaltung*, Wien, 1986, p. 28. For the Colyn monument, see also Afanasyev in this volume, p. 107.
12 'Von Gottes Gnaden Sophia geborne aus Königlichen Stam Pohlen Hertzogin zu Braunschwig und Luneburg.'
13 '... Durchlauchte Hochgeborne erliche togentliche Frowe Furstin und Frawe Fraw Barbara gebornne aus kunniglichem stam polen Hertzogin zu Sachssen...' M. Donath, ed., *Die Grabmonumente im Dom zu Meissen*, Leipzig, 2004, pp. 399–401.
14 A. Gąsior, 'Stufungen bildlicher Repräsentation. Die Darstellungen des Markgrafen Friedrich d. Ä. von Brandenburg-Ansbach und seiner Gemahlin Sophie von Polen', in U. Borkowska and M. Hörsch, eds, *Hofkultur der Jagiellonendynastie und verwandter Fürstenhäuser / The Culture of the Jagellonian and Related Courts*, Studia Jagellonica Lipsiensia 6, Ostfildern, 2010, pp. 314–17.
15 M. Wehrmann, 'Der Tod der Herzogin Anna (1503)', *Monatsblätter der Gesellschaft für Pommersche Geschichte und Alterthumskunde* 15, 1901, pp. 171–3; M. Wehrmann, *Genealogie des pommerschen Herzogshauses*, Stettin, 1937, p. 107.
16 Cf. E. Kirchner, *Die Churfürstinnen und Königinnen auf dem Throne der Hohenzollern*, Theil I und II, Berlin, 1866–67, p. 304.
17 E. Krausen, ed., *Germania Sacra*, Neue Folge 11. Die Bistümer der Kirchenprovinz Salzburg. Das Erzbistum Salzburg I. Die Zistersienserabtei Raitenhaslach. Berlin and New York, 1977, pp. 19, 103, 289.
18 B. Hamann, ed., *Die Habsburger. Ein biographisches Lexikon*, Vienna, 1988, p. 54.
19 A picture of the epitaph has been preserved. It is reproduced, for instance, in I. Jeschke, *Eine bemerkenswerte Frau: Anna von Polen, Gemahlin Herzog Bogislaws X*, in *Stettiner Hefte* 9, 2003, p. 17.
20 Gąsior, 'Dynastische Verbindungen', p. 215.
21 J. Fajt, ed., 'Ein Bandt von freuntschaft und lieb'. Eheverbindungen der Jagiellonen: Die jagiellonischen Prinzessinnen Hedwig d.Ä., Sophia, Barbara, Anna, Hedwig d.J., in *Europa Jagellonica. Kunst und Kultur Mitteleuropas unter der Herrschaft der Jagiellonen 1386–1572. Ausstellungskatalog / Exhibition Guide*, Potsdam, 2013, pp. 137–8.
22 Stored in the depositary of the Austrian National Gallery in the Belvedere in Vienna.
23 R. Stauber, 'Herrschaftsrepräsentation und dynastische Propaganda bei den Wittelsbachern und Habsburgern um 1500', in *Principes. Dynastien und Höfe im späten Mittelalter*, Stuttgart, 2002, pp. 371–402; J. M. Moeglin, 'Dynastisches Bewusstsein und Geschichtsschreibung. Zum Verständnis der Wittelsbacher, Habsburger und Hohenzollern im Spätmittelalter', *Historische Zeitschrift* 256, 1993, pp. 593–635.
24 For Sigismund III and Jagiellonian memory in Poland, see Nowakowska in this volume, p. 51.
25 *Polnische Zeitung. Von der Wahl und Krönunge dess Königs in Polen Sigmunds III. Printzen auss Schweden. Desgleichen. Wie Ertzhertzog Maximilian auss Osterreich auch erwehlter König in Polen ... Neben einer richtigen Geburts Liny des Jagelonischen Stammes... etc.*, s.l., n.l., 1588.
26 'Damit man aber bey dem augenscheine sehen / vnnd richtig erkennen moege / wie nahe die beyd erwehlte Könige / der aus Schweden vnd der aus dem Osterreichischen Hause / der Krone des Jagellonischen Stammes halben verwannt / wollen wir die Jagellonische Geburts Liny in folgender Tabul dem Leser richtig für augen gestellt haben.' *Polnische Zeitung*, p. 30.
27 'Sigismundus ... aus dem Jagellonischen der Polnischen Könige Stamme gebornen Königinne Catharinen Sohn.' *Polnische Zeitung*, p. 6.
28 '... weil er dem Jagellonischen Stamme...mit so naher Bluttfreundschaft verwannt.' *Polnische Zeitung*, p. 9.
29 *Genii Serenissimorum Principum Philippi Wilhelmi Comitis Palatini Rheni ... sponsi, et Annae Catharinae Constantiae, augustissimorum regum Sigismundi III filiae ...* Collegium Societas Iesu, Coliniae Agrippinae, Ex typographia Henrici Krafft, anno 1642.

30 'Iagello Magnus Lithuaniae ac Russie Dux, Serenissimae Principis Annae Catharinae Constantiae Atauus, serenissimi principis Philippi Vvilhelmi Tritauus Magnus, ad Poloniae Regnum & Hedvvigis Reginae thalamum eam lege admissus est, vt cum eam religionem Christianam amplecteretur. Quod cum non inuitus faceret, Ladislai in fonte Baptismi nomen, in regno Coronam accepit. Quam accessione, non modo haereditarias sibi ditiones Poloniae, sed & et Ecclesiae amplissimam gentem, Ducis exemplo, ad fidei signa, traductam, adiecit.' *Genii Serenissimorum*, p. 69.
31 *Polnischer Königs-Stammen oder Beschreibung des Gross-Hertzoglichen Littauischen Geschlechts, Aus welchem bey fast dreyhundert Jahren her, Zwölf daraus geborene oder demselben anverwandte Fürsten, Zu Königen in Polen erwehlet worden . . . Mit Einführung Des Neu-erwehlten Königs Michael Thomas Koribut geboren Hertzogs von Wissnowetz, Etc. Littauischer . . .* Nuremberg, 1669.
32 *Polnischer Königs-Stammen, Vorrede* fol. 1.
33 Interestingly, the work follows the traditional account of the most important events in the Jagiellonian rulers' reigns, although it gives astonishingly incorrect dates. For example, the wedding and baptism of Ladislaus Jagello was supposed to happen in 1486 and Louis II was supposed to die in 1562 (fol. 2); the coronation of Sigismund Augustus is dated to 1630 (fol. 3).
34 'der letzte dieses Jagellonischen Manns-Stammens', *Polnischer Königs-Stammen, Vorrede* fol. 3.
35 *Polnischer Königs-Stammen*.
36 I deal with the image of the Jagiellonians in genealogical literature from the Holy Roman Empire from 1572 to the 1650s elsewhere, so I will not consider these works here. See N. Nowakowska et al., *Dynasty in the Making* (forthcoming).
37 F. X. Zottmayr, *Genealogie des königlichen Hauses Baiern*, Füssen, 1834, p. 21; C. Häutle, *Genealogie der erlauchten Stammhauses Wittelsbach*, München, 1870, p. 116. The latter connects Hedwig to the Jagiellonian lineage, but gives incorrect information about her fifth son, not ascertained by any other source.
38 J. Hübner, *Bibliotheca Genealogica, Das ist: Ein Verzeichniß aller Alten und Neuen Genealogischen Bücher von allen Nationen in der Welt: den Liebhabern der Politischen Wissenschafften zur Bequemlichkeit gesammlet, und In eine richtige Ordnung gebracht*, Hamburg, 1729.
39 'Den Ursprung der Polnischen Könige von Noah an' . . . 'Die Könige in Polen von Piasto an bis auf Casimirum III' . . . 'Die alten Herzoge in Lithauen, und die daraus enstandenen Jagellonischen Könige', Hübner, *Bibliotheca Genealogica*, p. 572.
40 *Vorläuffig Historich-Politische Einleitung Zu der Hauptfrage, ob Die von König Ferdinand I. mit Seiner Gemahlin Anna Jagelonica, Königin zu Böheim, etc. etc. Durch L. s.l. 1745*, n.p.
41 A. S. Knöfel, *Dynastie und Prestige: Die Heiratspolitik der Wettiner*, Dresdner Historische Studien, vol. 9, Köln, 2009, p. 94.
42 A. Hartung, *Joachim II und sein Sohn Johann George. Ein Historisches Gemählde aus der brandenburgischen Geschichte*, Berlin, 1798, pp. 19–21.
43 Kirchner, *Die Churfürstinnen und Königinnen*.
44 *Hedwig, die schöne Königstochter aus Polen, Gemahlin Herzogs Georg des Reichen von Bayern-Landshut, und die Schatzkammern auf dem Schlosse zu Burghausen historisches Trauergemälde aus d. 15. Jahrhundert*; für theilnehmende Herzen geschrieben, Burghausen, 1860.
45 J. Dorner, *Herzogin Hedwig und ihr Hofstaat. Das Alltagsleben auf der Burg Burghausen nach Originalquellen des 15. Jahrhunderts*, Burghausen, Stadt Burghausen, 2004, pp. 178–183; U. Füetrer, *Bayerische Chronik*, München, 1909, p. 219.
46 The poem signed M.F. was published in the *Burghauser Anzeiger*, no. 19, on 18 February 1902. Burghausen Stadtarchiv. Reproduced in Dorner, *Herzogin Hedwig*, p. 188.
47 M. Böckl, *Die Braut von Landshut. Das tragische Leben von Herzogin Hedwig*, Bayerland, 2001.

48 'ZUR ERINNERUNG AN HEDWIG VON BAYERN/ GEBORENE KÖNIGIN VON POLEN/ BRAUT DER LANDSHUTER/ HOCHZEIT/ 1457–1502/.' H. Czerny, *Der Tod der bayerischen Herzöge im Spätmittelalter und in der frühen Neuzeit (1347–1579). Vorbereitungen – Sterben – Trauerfeierlichkeiten – Grablegen – Memoria*, München, 2005, p. 637.
49 Jeschke, *Eine bemerkenswerte Frau*, p. 6. For the Szczecin/Stettin statue of Anna, see also Nowakowska in this volume, pp. 59–60.
50 A. Bues, *Die Jagiellonen. Herrscher zwischen Ostsee und Adria*, Urban-Taschenbücher 646, Stuttgart, 2010.
51 Pirożyński, *Die Herzogin Sophie*.
52 Dorner, *Herzogin Hedwig*.
53 A. Gąsior, *Eine Jagiellonin als Reichsfürstin in Franken. Zu den Stiftungen des Markgrafen Friedrich d. Ä. von Brandenburg-Ansbach und der Sophie von Polen*, Studia Jagellonica Lipsiensia 10, Ostfildern, 2012.
54 For the list of the volumes see: http://research.uni-leipzig.de/gwzo/index.php?Itemid=506, accessed 4.9.17.
55 J. Fajt, ed., *Europa Jagellonica. Kunst und Kultur Mitteleuropas unter der Herrschaft der Jagiellonen 1386–1572. Ausstellungskatalog / Exhibition Guide*, Potsdam, 2013. Significantly, the long review of the exhibition published in the nationwide daily *Die Zeit* on 7 March 2013, by Mathias Messenhöler, opens with a rhetorical question: 'Die Jagiellonen – nie gehört?' (The Jagiellonians – never heard of them?). See: www.zeit.de/2013/11/Jagiellonen-Ausstellung-Potsdam, accessed 4.9.17. See also the essay by Afanasyev in this volume, p. 114, and the Introduction, p. 18.
56 L. Westenrieder, *Beiträge zur vaterländischen Historie, Geographie, Statistik und Landwirtschaft*, München 1789, pp. 105–221. Cf. M. Tewes, 'Die Landshuter Fürstenhochzeit 1475', in F. Niehoff, ed., *In eren liebt sie . . . Die Landshuter Hochzeit 1903–2005. Annäherungen an das Jahr 1475*, Landshut, 2005, p. 25.
57 T. Stangier, 'Hochzeitsgeschichte(n) – Eine Annäherung auf Umwegen', in Niehoff, *In eren liebt sie*, pp. 29–31.
58 F. Niehoff, 'Von Zauber, den der Rost des Alten auf das Gemüt des Menschen ausübt . . . Der Landshuter Rathaussaal als Erinnerungsort', in Niehoff, *In eren liebt sie*, pp. 32ff.
59 Niehoff, 'Von Zauber', p. 38.
60 M. Tewes, 'Die Landshuter Hochzeit 1903–2005. Annäharungen an ein mittelalterliches Fest', In Niehoff, *In eren liebt sie*, p. 40.
61 Niehoff, 'Von Zauber', p. 39.
62 F. Niehoff, '"Landshuter Hochzeit" als "experimentelles Mittelalter"', in F. Niehoff, ed., *Das Goldene Jahrhundert der Reichen Herzöge*, Landshut, 2014, p. 292.
63 Tewes, 'Die Landshuter Hochzeit', pp. 41–2.
64 www.landshuter-hochzeit.de/files/pdf/auffuehrung2017/programme_2017_en.pdf, accessed 4.9.17. Symptomatically enough, the official webpage of the event does mention Hedwig and gives the visitor the basic biographic information on her life. Her Jagiellonian origin is never mentioned.
65 'Grösste historische Festveranstalltung Deutschlands' and 'Grösstes historisches Fest Europas', in F. Niehoff, ed., *Landshuter Hochzeit seit 1475*, Landshut, 2013, p. 26.
66 Tewes, 'Die Landshuter Hochzeit', p. 43.
67 B. Niehoff, 'Es war Einmal . . . Die Landshuter Hochzeit für Kinder', in *In eren liebt sie*, p. 47.
68 *Landshuter Hochzeit*, produced by Jürgen Binder, Landshut, Studio SRI and studio 5, 2013 [CD].
69 The most important ones are T. A. Bauer, *Feiern unter den Augen der Chronisten. Die Quellentexte zur Landshuter Fürstenhochzeit von 1475*, Munich, 2008; S. Hiereth, 'Zeitgenössische Quellen zur Landshuter Furstenhochzeit 1475', *Verhandlungen des Historischen Vereins für Niederbayern* 85, 1959, pp. 1–64; S. Hiereth, 'Die Landshuter Hochzeit als Organisationsproblem. Landshuter Hochzeit 1475–1975', *Österreichische*

Osthefte 18, 1976; S. Hiereth, *Herzog Georgs Hochzeit zu Landshut im Jahre 1475. Eine Darstellung aus zeitgenossischen Quellen*, Landshut, 1988; E. Stahleder, 'Die Landshuter Hochzeit von 1475 nach dem widerentdeckten Bericht des "Markgrafschriebers"', in H. Bleibrunner, ed., *Beitrage zur Heimatkunde von Niederbayern*, Passau, 1976; E. Stahleder, *Landshuter Hochzeit 1475. Ein bayerische-europäisches Hoffest aus der Zeit der Gotik*, Landshut, 1984; S. M. Bleichner, *Die landshuter Füsternhochzeit 1475. Immaterielles Kulturerbe und Re-Inszenierung – ein axiologisches Phänomen*, Lehmanns Media, 2015 [e-book].

70 E. Werner, ed., *Landshuter Stadtgeschichte, Band III. Die Landshuter Hochzeit von 1475*, Landshut, 2008.

6

REMEMBERING A PAST PRINCESS

Catherine Jagiellon and the construction of national narratives in Sweden and Finland

Susanna Niiranen

Historical culture (the building up of archives, the classification of data, the writing of history, cultural representations and the organisation of events and celebrations) holds a major position as both a repository of transformable memory and a terrain where collective identity can be shaped and negotiated. This essay tackles the role a Jagiellonian princess, Catherine Jagiellon (1526–83), has been given in Swedish and Finnish history culture. It attempts to illustrate how her figure has entered the historical-cultural memory of both countries, forging and re-forging their national self-image from the end of the sixteenth century through the Cold War, and into contemporary school history teaching. This comparative case study highlights the differences as well as the similarities of collective memory and history culture associated with Catherine Jagiellon in two Nordic countries with a shared history.[1]

As a daughter (of Sigismund 'the Old', king of Poland and Grand Duke of Lithuania, r.1506–48), a sister (of King Sigismund Augustus, d.1572, and Queen Anna Jagiellon, d.1596, of Poland-Lithuania), a wife (of King John III of Sweden, r.1568–92) and a mother of a king (of Sigismund, king of Sweden, 1592–99, and of Poland-Lithuania, 1587–1632), and a queen consort in her own right, Catherine Jagiellon is a woman without many parallels in Swedish history. She came from abroad, bringing with her not only a magnificent dowry, but people and new ideas from the courts of Cracow and Vilnius. Respectively, she had to adapt herself to a new (Swedish court) culture and balance between two different royal houses, the Jagiellonians and the Vasas. The Jagiellonians had been Grand Dukes of Lithuania and kings of Poland, Hungary and Bohemia, whilst the Vasas were regarded as provincial Swedish nobles and newcomers among European monarchs.[2] For many Scandinavians, Catherine Jagiellon is the *Jagellonica*, the Polish-Italian princess, who introduced the fork and other novelties of Renaissance culture to the remote North.[3] The Latin name form *Cat(h)arina Jagellonica*, used in many early modern Latin documents, persevered over the centuries and is still the form by which Catherine Jagiellon is known in Scandinavia – as *Katarina Jagellonica* in Sweden and other Nordic countries, and as *Katariina Jagellonica* in Finland. She is the only Nordic royal consort to bear a Latinised name, a fact which associates her immediately with her European, Roman Catholic origin. In many early modern European regions, it was traditional for married women to keep their patrilineal family name as an indication that they were not fully assimilated into their husband's kin.[4] The name derives from Jogaila (c.1362–1434, Jagiełło in Polish), the first Grand Duke of Lithuania to become king of Poland. The name form *Catharina Jagellonica* was not a standard usage in her lifetime, but appeared when it was necessary to emphasise her birth, for instance in her testament in 1583: 'Ideo nos Catharina Jagellonica D.G. Infans Poloniae etc.'[5]

The documents concerning her life are relatively scarce, and are scattered across Polish and Swedish libraries and archives. The sixteenth-century collection of Swedish queens' documents designated K73 in the Swedish National Archives is a microfilmed gathering of letters and other documents, including a section dedicated to Catherine Jagiellon.[6] There is very little information available to suggest the mode by, and location at, which disparate elements of the collection were gathered together. At best, there may be a brief statement such as 'från ett polskt arkiv' (from a Polish archive) without any further information. These shortcomings are the result of the traditional characteristics of historical studies and archival methods in nineteenth- and early twentieth-century Sweden and Finland. At the time, archivists and historians concentrated on those documents that seemed best to illustrate the emerging Swedish state or the Finnish nation, as well as the development of the official administration and political decision-making. Letters and documents concerning women, even queen consorts, were often consigned to loosely organised files with labels such as 'Miscellanea'.[7] Despite this, research on two preserved inventories (one in Poland, the other in Sweden) has yielded almost-complete information on the splendid objects and the names of the courtiers Catherine brought from Vilnius to Turku (1562),[8] and from Finland to Sweden (1563),[9] as well as her plausible contribution to Nordic Renaissance art and architecture.[10] Similarly, her devout Roman Catholicism and support for the Catholic Reformation in Sweden have been documented.[11] Moreover, romantic minds tend to emphasise her loyalty towards her husband during the torments they faced: *nemo nisi mors*, i.e. 'nobody but death' (will part us), is an often cited quotation attributed to her in research, and can even be seen as her motto on the nineteenth-century stained-glass window of her funeral chapel in Uppsala.[12] Why have these characteristics (material culture, religion and family) been selected as vital parts of her memory in research and elsewhere? Apart from her name, is she remembered as a member of the Jagiellonian dynasty in Scandinavia? In this essay, the memory of Catherine Jagiellon in Sweden and Finland is investigated over a lengthy time-span, lasting from her death in 1583 to the present day.

When Catherine Jagiellon came to Turku as the newly-wed wife of the Duke of Finland, John (Vasa), in December 1562, Finland was an integrated part of the kingdom of Sweden: the Duchy of Finland. However, memories of the queen in

Sweden and Finland are treated separately for several reasons. First, her position in these two territories changes during her life: initially, she was the Duchess of Finland and, after a four-year period of imprisonment (1563–67) in Sweden and the Vasa brothers' battle for power, ending with Eric XIV's dethronement and John's coronation, she became the queen consort in Sweden. Secondly, her stays in Finland and Sweden are not commensurate; she stayed at the court of Turku, the capital of the then Duchy of Finland, for only eight months, whereas her sojourn in the territory of Sweden lasted for twenty years, from 1563 until her death in 1583. Thirdly, due to differences between the later historical and national development in Sweden and Finland, her memory is composed of radically distinctive elements in these countries, providing an interesting point of reference for historico-political comparison.

In this discussion, 'memory' – or, more specifically, 'collective memory' – is generally understood as a sort of living heritage, meant to be used to construct identity even if the borderline between memory and history is often difficult to pinpoint.[13] A useful concept in the attempt to analyse the memory of an early modern person without reference to personal, immediate memory is 'historical culture', briefly defined as a social and communicative system of interpretation, objectification and public use of the past.[14] It resembles the concept of living heritage, since a community's relationship with its past is often both effective and affective. This approach does not limit itself to academic historical literature, but also extends to advocate the investigation of broader layers and processes of historical consciousness, taking notice of the agents who create it and carry it out through a range of different media, the representations that it popularises and creative reception on the part of the audience, where possible. It is important to bear in mind that historical culture is not a stable system of historical representation, but a dynamic process through which different narratives, interpretations and debates relate a human group to its past.[15] In this case, Catherine Jagiellon can be seen as the nexus through which Finns and Swedes deal with their past(s) in varying time periods.

This essay focuses largely on physical sites of memory such as archives, museums, cathedrals, chapels, castles, and material objects such as inherited property, commemorative monuments, emblems, basic texts, and symbols, but it simultaneously attempts to take into consideration concepts and practices such as commemorations, exhibitions, generations, mottos, and rituals such as *loci memoriae*. Furthermore, a short overview of memory (re)-construction through education (national curricula and school textbooks) and entertainment ('popular culture') is provided.[16]

Sweden

The struggle for Catherine Jagiellon's memory began immediately after her death in the Royal Castle of Stockholm on 16 September 1583. Two Roman Catholic chaplains, Stanislaus Warszewicki and Johannes Ardulphus, asked King John III, the spouse of the late queen, for permission to place the coffin in the chapel of the castle and celebrate Mass for her soul before the official funeral. John, relying on his advisors, feared that riots would break out among the Lutheran burghers, and refused. Since the Jesuits were the most active participants in the implementation of the Catholic Reformation (also known as Counter-Reformation) in Sweden, all Catholics and especially Jesuits were considered extremely suspicious, representing the menace of a Roman Catholic takeover. Only on All Souls' Day were the chaplains allowed to celebrate a special Mass in commemoration of the late queen. However, her Lutheran husband, King John, was not present and Princess Anna (b.1568), whose inclinations towards Lutheranism were known, was probably also absent. Instead, Prince Sigismund (b.1566), an adherent to the faith of his mother, attended the Mass and received Communion, as did many of the members of the Roman Catholic community in Stockholm. No outbursts of violence were reported.[17]

Five months later, on 16 February 1584, Queen Catherine's funeral was held in Uppsala. Catherine's own wish had been to be buried in a Roman Catholic site such as Vadstena Abbey,[18] but due to increasing tensions between the 'old' and 'new' faith, as well as conflicts between different ethnic groups in Stockholm, John could not afford to take such a strong stance. Besides, the cathedral of Uppsala was not just another church: it is the tallest church building in the Nordic countries, the seat of the Swedish primate, and the last resting place of dignitaries since the Middle Ages, such as Eric the Holy (d.1160), the patron saint of Sweden, and King Gustav Vasa (r.1523–60), Catherine's father-in-law, labelled as the founder of both modern Sweden and the hereditary monarchy under the House of Vasa with his consorts. Later, the illustrious eighteenth-century botanist Carl von Linné and philosopher and mystic Emanuel Swedenborg would be buried there. Uppsala Cathedral was the coronation place of John and Catherine as well as that of John's predecessor, his half-brother Eric XIV. An old sacristy was converted into a chapel dedicated to Catherine, and a funeral monument was commissioned from the Flemish sculptor and architect Willem Boy, who was responsible for several important tombs in the Vasa family, including Gustav Vasa's funeral monument. The chapel dedicated to Catherine Jagiellon is known as the Jagiellonian chapel (*Jagellonska koret* in Swedish) and it is considered one of the most beautiful and expensive tombs, as well as one of the best-preserved Renaissance interiors, in Sweden.[19] Amazingly, it survived the cathedral fire of 1702. The stained-glass window, with its retrospectively-chosen motto 'nemo nisi mors', and a painting representing the city of Cracow are additions from the nineteenth century.[20] When Sigismund was crowned in Sweden in 1594, he planned to bring his mother's body from Uppsala for burial in the royal family tomb in Cracow together with the dead body of his little daughter, named Catherine, who had died soon after her baptism in the same year. The body of little Catherine travelled with Sigismund to Poland, but the mother and grandmother Catherine Jagiellon remained in her resting place in Sweden.[21]

The earliest known written evidence of the funerary chapel dates from 1591, and is recorded by the German traveller and diplomat Erich Lassota von Steblau (d.1616). In his diary, Lassota von Steblau shows a predominantly antiquarian and art historical interest in the chapel. He copies the long epitaph from the wall of the chapel. The epitaph describes Catherine's extraction, parents and grandparents, as well as her experiences in Finland and Sweden after she had left Vilnius.[22] Catherine Jagiellon's funeral and funeral chapel were described by the early seventeenth-century Swedish historian Johannes Messenius (1579–1636) in his *Scondia Illustrata*, a history of the Nordic countries in fourteen volumes, which treated Sweden's history from the Deluge to Messenius's own time.[23] Messenius was an alumnus of the Braunsberg Jesuit Collegium in Polish-ruled Prussia, and married to Lucia Grothusen, daughter of Arnold Grothusen, who was an instructor of the young Prince Sigismund. First, Messenius expressed his loyalty towards Catherine and Sigismund by constructing their familial memory through extensive genealogies, which illustrated how the Jagiellonian family was one of the oldest and most established dynasties in Europe.[24] When Sigismund did not show the expected gratitude, Messenius tried to gain the favour of Sigismund's rival, his uncle Charles IX, but instead, he was accused of conspiring with King Sigismund (III of Poland) and the Jesuits, and was removed to the remote prison of Kajaani in Northern Finland, where he wrote the *Scondia Illustrata* and *Rimkrönika om Finland* (Rime-chronicle of Finland). The latter, which is identical to volume 10 of the *Scondia Illustrata*, relates John and Catherine's story from their wedding and the Vasa brothers' power struggle to Sigismund and Charles' conflict over the Swedish throne. The most striking passage, however, is Messenius's account of Eric XIV's collusion with Ivan IV in order to 'murder his brother [John] in prison and send the woman [Catherine] to the Russian [Ivan] as his whore'.[25] Despite Messenius's apparent personal and opportunistic aims and his Gothicist tendency, his history writing is considered to possess some critical value by modern scholars, at least when compared with other Swedish historians of the time.[26]

Alongside these textual witnesses, the Jagiellonian chapel is also recorded in a few early modern visual sources, which likely contributed to both art historical interest in the funeral monument and historical interest in the person within the coffin. Erik Dahlbergh's collection of engravings *Suecia Antiqua et Hodierna* (1660–1716) has been described as a grand vision of Sweden during its period as a great power. Dahlbergh began his career in the military and spent time in Poland during his service.[27] One of the 353 plates of *Suecia Antiqua et Hodierna*, titled *Sacellum Templi cathedralis Upsaliensis, in quo sepulchrum Catharinae Jagellonicae, Reginae Sveciae*, represents the Jagiellonian chapel.[28] It is the only extant seventeenth-century visual source of the entire chapel we have, including both the lost epitaph and the altar with its painting. The lost epitaph is interesting since it likely depicts Catherine herself kneeling before the altar and the altar cross, the latter of which is identical with the sixteenth-century cross, which can now be found on display in the cathedral treasury.[29] The treasury also houses Catherine's funerary regalia (crown and sceptre) and the so-called C-pendant, probably given to Catherine in 1546, alongside two necklaces for her sisters, Princess Sofia and Anna, all commissioned by their father, Sigismund 'the Old'. The pendant, which

FIGURE 6.1 Engraving of Catherine Jagiellon's tomb in Uppsala cathedral, Johan Litheim (1663–1725), for Erik Dahlbergh's (1625–1703) *Suecia Antiqua et Hodierna*. Reproduction: National Library of Sweden

is made of gold, diamonds, rubies and enamel, and is engraved with the letter 'C', is depicted in the famous miniature painting of Lucas Cranach the Younger's workshop, dated c.1553–56.[30] The necklace was placed in her coffin in 1583, but removed in 1833, and has been kept in the cathedral treasury of Uppsala ever since.

Dahlbergh's Swedish contemporary Johan Peringskiöld (1654–1720), secretary of the college of antiquities and ardent documentarist of national antiquities, included Catherine Jagiellon's funerary monument in his *Monumenta Ullerakerensia cum Upsalia nova* (1719). The title of the copper engraving is *Monum: Sereniss: Reginae Catharinae Jagellonicae in templo Cathedrali Upsalensi.* Peringskiöld's detailed drawing focuses on the funeral monument and is a valuable primary source, in particular for the smaller coats of arms of the monument, which have now been lost or otherwise damaged. Unlike Dahlberg, Peringskiöld provides additional textual material, including accurate descriptions of the inscriptions of the monument, a short biography, and a very detailed description of the funerals, as well as a genealogical table, which records four generations of Catherine's ancestry on both sides, thus including Jogaila's parents' generation as the starting point of the Jagiellonian 'dynasty'.[31]

The Romanticism of the nineteenth century rediscovered the thrilling episodes of Catherine Jagiellon's life, particularly the imprisonment of the ducal couple by John's half-brother, the then King Eric XIV, who captured John and Catherine for political reasons, but had never approved of their marriage and also suffered from mental problems. The scenes of imprisonment in Gripsholm Castle were immortalised by the Polish painter Józef Simmler in 1859 as well as by the Swedish artists Carl Johan Billmark, in his series of watercolour-lithographs from Gripsholm in the 1850s, and Hugo Salmson in 1865. Simmler's painting is called 'Catherine Jagiellon in the Gripsholm prison',[32] while Salmson concentrates on the dramatic moment when 'Catherine Jagiellon shows her wedding ring to Jöran Persson'.[33] Carl Johan Billmark's 'John III's prison at Gripsholm: Duke Charles's chamber' shows the inhabitants and the interior of the room, which was first John's prison, but later became Duke Charles's chamber.[34] All of them depict Catherine as a Renaissance princess of sumptuous appearance. Both Simmler and Salmson show her holding a cross, a rosary or a necklace. Salmson's painting focuses on a scene in which the couple's captors offer Catherine an opportunity to live in a manor house during her husband's imprisonment. In response Catherine points out the inscription on her wedding ring, 'nemo nisi mors', to Jöran Persson, Eric XIV's notorious favourite and one of her captors, and chooses to follow her husband into prison. While Salmson depicts Catherine as a loyal wife, Simmler sees her primarily as a caring, Madonna-like mother holding little Sigismund, who was born during her captivity. In both paintings Catherine is clearly the main character, charged with emotive power and authority in contrast to the dark figures of John and the prison guards, who are placed more in the background of the image.

In contrast to Simmler and Salmson, Billmark's interpretation emphasises the more traditional roles of an early modern married couple: while a little girl (Isabella, who was born in 1564 and died before her second birthday in Gripsholm) tries to get Catherine's attention by crying and trying to climb on her knee, Catherine leans on her husband, whose figure is steady and calm. The onlooker observes the melancholic, but idle and even luxurious ambience in the room: splendid decoration and garments as well as books, wine and fruits. The image corresponds to what Eric had ordered, but the contemporary reports of guards tell us that the room was in bad condition before Eric ordered the renovation. Furthermore, a letter from Catherine Jagiellon herself complains that her weak health demands more Rhine wine and other necessities. She also expresses a wish to be treated according to her status, which suggests that they may have suffered from occasional shortcomings or a felt a lack of respect from the guards or other people staying in the castle.[35] In the first phase of their imprisonment, John's space and contacts were limited to one room; Catherine was allowed to walk in the garden under supervision, but not to talk to John's sisters when they visited Gripsholm.[36]

Gripsholm Castle is located less than forty miles west from Stockholm and is nowadays one of the most popular tourist attractions in Sweden. Catherine Jagiellon stayed there for four years, imprisoned with her husband, and gave birth to two children, but her memory is hardly visible and goes unused, even for publicity purposes. She is mentioned in a single phrase in the Gripsholm Castle guidebook under the entry 'Duke Karl's chamber': 'Tradition has it that Sigismund (I of Sweden, III of Poland) was born in this room in 1566, while Erik XIV was keeping Sigismund's parents – Erik's half-brother Johan (III) and his Polish-born consort Katarina – imprisoned at Gripsholm.'[37] After their release in 1568, the room was fitted out in the 1570s as a bedchamber for Duke Charles (1550–1611, later Charles IX of Sweden) and has remained virtually intact ever since. Interestingly, according to a nineteenth-century Swedish history book, the room was called 'Sigismund's chamber' or 'Duke John's prison'.[38] It is more than probable that the room was 'attributed' to Duke Charles by art historians, antiquarians and other scholars because of its contemporary interior decoration, including the ducal arms and the initials C.D. (*Carolus Dux*) as well as the initials of his motto in German: G.I.M.T. (*Gott Ist Mein Trost*). Only immaterial (historical facts and stories) memories of John, Catherine and Sigismund's stay in the room remain. As Pierre Nora has stated, modern memory is above all archival, and relies primarily on the materiality of the trace.[39]

Furthermore, since national hero Gustav Vasa had the castle built, and since it also contains attractions such as Gustav III's magnificent eighteenth-century theatre, it may feel unnecessary to find a 'memory niche' for a foreign consort, especially since few material objects of hers remain. The castle has been the home of the Swedish National Portrait Gallery, in the custody of the National Museum of Fine Arts, since 1822. The collection does not possess any portrait of Catherine Jagiellon. However, local folklore has maintained some remnants of Catherine Jagiellon's stay at Gripsholm: according to the local legend, Drottningkälla (the Queen's spring) in Nykvarn got its name when Catherine Jagiellon brought water to her husband, incarcerated in the castle.[40]

Although John III was famous for building and rebuilding castles in which he occasionally stayed with his consort and children, few of these castles or their related museums hold traces or actively maintain memories of Queen Catherine. Many of the buildings have suffered from great fires. Fires broke out at the Old Royal Castle, called *Tre Kronor* (Three Crowns), in Stockholm in 1697, Svartsjö Castle in Uppland in 1687 and Uppsala Castle in 1702, all practically destroying the buildings themselves, along with many documents and tangible memories. The first, Renaissance version of the Drottningholm palace (literally meaning 'Queen's islet'), built by John III and designed by Willem Boy in 1580 for Queen Catherine Jagiellon, burnt down in 1661. Because of Catherine Jagiellon's religion, Vadstena Castle and the Abbey on its lands held a special resonance for her, and Vadstena was the place where she remained safe during the upheaval of 1568, when the dukes and the nobles rebelled and Eric XIV was dethroned.

Eva Mattson, a Vadstena local, culture producer and art historian, has been an active memory carrier of Catherine Jagiellon in Sweden. She has prepared two fictional monologue presentations based on Catherine's life: 'As the stone carries life' (2012), on Catherine's stay at Vadstena Castle in 1568, and 'No one but death' (2014), on the year 1577, when Queen Catherine resided at Stockholm Castle and looked back on her life. The latter was related to an exhibition of historical dress at the Royal Armoury in Stockholm, and a replica of a sixteenth-century dress, hand-embroidered with 2,100 pearls, which was manufactured for the 'Catherine' of the production.[41]

The national Swedish history curriculum for basic education (*grundskolor*) puts special emphasis on the history of the Baltic Sea from the sixteenth to the eighteenth century.[42] Under this curriculum, history teaching should on the one hand focus on the 'global exchange' in which the region was involved during the two centuries, but on the other, on the 'growth and organisation of the Swedish state'. 'The Swedish Realm in the Baltic' as well as 'its causes and consequences for different individuals and human groups around the Baltic Sea', such as 'immigration and emigration', are mentioned in the curriculum as central themes. Whilst Catherine Jagiellon would fit perfectly into all these topics, recent available history textbooks suggest that a national master narrative based on state building by the early (male) Vasa monarchs is still the dominant theme. Unlike Gustav Vasa's and Eric XIV's spouses, who are introduced by their names, John III's wife (and likewise Sigismund's) is not mentioned at all.[43] The typical way to characterise her, if at all, is the following: 'John is remembered as a "builder-king" . . . He married a Polish Catholic princess and their son Sigismund became the King of both Poland and Sweden.' A drawing representing John and a picture of Gripsholm Castle as a specimen of the castles John rebuilt serve as the illustration.[44] Naturally, school textbooks do not paint a complete picture of school teaching, but they reflect the implementation of the national curriculum on a more practical level.

The current situation is at least partly due to the fact that recent research, especially that happening in Sweden, shows that interest in Catherine Jagiellon is waning.[45] Without research, interesting new interpretations cannot emerge to in turn feed the memory culture (and vice versa). This situation derives from the fact that the sources are scarce and dispersed. Moreover, it is a commonplace that archives are arranged according to the principles of political history and thus do not respond to the needs, for example, of gender or cultural historians. Many sources are neither studied nor even catalogued.[46] There are certainly several reasons for this, but for some Swedish historians – even for the most prominent ones – the Eastern Central European part of their history is 'only of peripheral interest', a perspective for which Lena Rangström was criticised when she chose to analyse 'the dethroned King' Sigismund and Constance of Austria's wedding (1605) in her book on Swedish royal weddings.[47] Sigismund's dethronement as king of Sweden in 1599, together with Catherine and her son's difficult minority position as representatives of Roman Catholicism in the era of emerging Lutheran orthodoxy in Sweden, may yield the conclusion that they were not among the victors, by whom history is usually written.[48] Furthermore, even as the queen consort of Sweden, Catherine was regarded as a Polish princess (and she voluntarily often identified herself as such), i.e. a foreigner, which may produce some kind of marginality or 'otherness' despite her seemingly sufficient adaptation to Swedish court culture. In contrast, her memory has not experienced such noticeable 'waning' in Finland.

Finland

Turku Castle, founded in the 1280s, is one of the oldest buildings still in use and the largest surviving medieval building in Finland. Therefore, the castle is a significant historical monument and a popular tourist destination, representing the centre of the former capital city of the country. Over the centuries, it has transformed from a medieval fortress into a Renaissance palace, and, in the late nineteenth century, from a derelict jailhouse into a museum. Today, it is primarily deployed as a monument to the medieval and Renaissance heyday of the castle. This is visible in the architectural forms that have been carefully restored and reconstructed. It also becomes apparent in various narratives or deployments, both visual (like the set of miniatures representing the different stages of the construction of the castle) and discursive (as during the guided tours).[49] Catherine Jagiellon's presence in the castle forms an essential part of these narratives. The history policy of Turku Castle responds to the needs of the audience, since it is one of the most popular tourist attractions and most visited museums in Finland.

Besides Gustav Vasa, John and Catherine were the only princely persons to reside in the Finnish part of the Swedish realm for any length of time, despite their stay being relatively short-term, lasting from Christmas 1562 to August 1563. When the bride came to Turku from Vilnius with her Polish-Italian court and splendid dowry, the ducal couple 'presided over a brilliant court-life which has no parallel in Finnish history'.[50] When he took up his residence in Turku Castle as the Duke of Finland, John spared no time in starting the renovations. The castle was renovated into a princely Renaissance-style dwelling in 1556–63 and extended to its current size. The renovation involved, for instance, the installation of water pipes made of lead and copper, a project which took 4,000 man-hours to complete over the years 1561–63.[51] The gloomy rooms of the old castle were replaced with light and airy halls in the Renaissance style. The so-called Renaissance Floor with the 'King's Hall', a chamber in the tower for Duke John and Catherine Jagiellon's suite, and the 'Queen's Hall' and chamber were constructed in the 1550s. Even a wooden latrine was built outside the wall. All of these rooms were destroyed in the fire of 1614. The decorations, including the wooden ceiling and open fireplace, were reconstructed in the renovations of 1946–61 after contemporary models in Sweden. The tapestries hanging on the walls are reproductions, but the walls are original. The Queen's chamber, in which Duchess Catherine lived, is situated beyond the Queen's Hall. A copy of the Lucas Cranach workshop portrait hangs on the wall. It is a gift to the castle, presented by the Polish government in 1933. A large, woven textile on the wall towards the tower is also connected to Catherine Jagiellon. The modern tapestry, designed by the Finnish textile artist Dora Jung, represents Catherine and John, in addition to a priest on Catherine's side and a lay advisor next to John. The text on the textile, 'Nemo nisi mors', commemorates Catherine's famous and perhaps slightly fabricated (who knows) fidelity toward her husband at the moment of their capture in 1563. The textile was made for the re-opening of the castle in 1961.[52]

Renovation work had been going on for some years when, in 1941, the castle was badly damaged by a fire caused by bombing during the Second World War. After the war, restoration work restarted and was completed in 1961. An important

FIGURE 6.2   Tapestry depicting Catherine Jagiellon and Duke John, Turku Castle, Finland, designed by Dora Jung (1961). Permission courtesy of Ulrika-Kristina Teir

source of knowledge and inspiration was the doctoral thesis by Carl J. Gardberg (1959), historian and archaeologist and future head of the Finnish National Board of Antiquities, on the construction history of Turku Castle during the period of the early Vasas. Gardberg's investigations and findings have been invaluable in plotting the medieval and Renaissance narratives of Turku Castle, particularly that of Catherine Jagiellon's journey from Vilnius to Turku and her brief stay in the Duchy of Finland's capital. Gardberg's popular history book *Three Catherines at Turku Castle* enjoyed both academic and commercial success. Three editions of the original Swedish version (1985) have appeared, whereas the Finnish translation (1988) has appeared in up to seven editions.

Since there are no material remnants of Catherine and John in Finland, the exhibition 'Catherine Jagiellon, Princess of Poland, Duchess of Finland, Queen of Sweden 1526–1583', in the newly renovated Turku Castle, set out to temporarily fill this gap in 11 June–6 July 1965.[53] The initiative came from Poland and the exhibition was thought to be a part of the state visit of Edward Ochab, the chairman of the Council of State of Poland. The exhibition was organised by the Polish Ministry of Culture and Art and introduced 125 items, mainly from the museums of Cracow, to a Finnish audience. It included medals, manuscripts, the miniature portraits of Catherine's family attributed to Lucas Cranach the Younger's workshop, and Catherine's seal stamp from the year 1562. One of the most impressive objects was a wooden gilded eagle, the symbol of the Polish kingdom, with the Vasa coat of arms on its chest. A scale model of Wawel Castle, alongside maps illustrating Catherine's and John's journeys between Poland, Sweden and Finland, was also displayed in the duchess's rooms of the castle. In his inauguration speech, the mayor of Turku, Väinö J. Leino, emphasised the international character of the city of Turku and reminded listeners that the 'noble chatelaine always has a place in our hearts', while the Polish ambassador Edward Pietkiewicz treated cultural cooperation between Poland and Finland as a historical and continuous phenomenon, unbroken since the time of Catherine. The speeches were meticulously summarised in the Finnish press and many of the main newspapers additionally published articles on Catherine Jagiellon written by Polish experts. The reporting of the event also had affective tones: Finnish newspaper titles described Catherine Jagiellon as having 'returned to', 'come back to' or 'revisited' the castle, Turku, or Finland once more. The rhetoric has been seen as a nostalgic desire for the golden period of the castle, with the extraordinary international pomp and dramatic flavour that Catherine Jagiellon introduced, but also as a laudable prelude to good relations between Poland and Finland before Edward Ochab's visit. The Polish head of state, together with the President of Finland, Urho Kekkonen, honoured the exhibition with his presence. In retrospect, the event can be analysed as a perfect example of successful cultural diplomacy during the Cold War. A Finnish museologist, Solveig Sjöberg-Pietarinen, wrote in her editorial for the 2005 international museum day that, through the 1965 Turku Castle exhibition, Catherine Jagiellon was able to bring down the iron curtain.[54]

Jean Sibelius (1865–1957), a Finnish composer of the late Romantic and early modern period, is often credited with having contributed to the development of a

Finnish national identity during the struggle for independence from the Russian Empire, through his music. Sibelius found inspiration in nature, Nordic mythology and history. The first set of his *Scènes historiques* presents a suite taken from music for a patriotic pageant, staged in 1899 and originally including a tone poem *Finlandia*, a covert protest against increasing censorship from Russia, which was published separately. The splendour of the court of Duke John and Duchess Catherine at Turku is portrayed in the third tableau of *Scènes historiques*, called 'Festivo'. According to an established Sibelius scholar, Erik Tawastjerna, the piece finds Sibelius 'in cosmopolitan mood and is among his best character-pieces in a non-Finnish style'.[55]

Like Sibelius, his contemporary the poet Eino Leino (1878–1926) exploited Finnish nature, mythology, folklore and history extensively in his works. In 1919, two years after Finland's independence, Leino published a collection of poems called 'Songs of Duke John and Catherine of Jagiellon', inspired by his own, difficult love story with the Estonian Aino Kallas.[56] The poems are written in dialogue form between the two lovers Duke John and Catherine Jagiellon. The story begins on a ship en route from Vilnius to Turku, continues at the Renaissance court of Turku Castle and thereafter in captivity at Gripsholm. One of the Gripsholm poems, called 'Nil nisi mors', retells the story of Catherine's determination to stand alongside her husband in every situation. They are depicted as inseparable. A powerful graphic illustration of the poem by the Finnish painter and artist Tapio Tapiovaara (1908–82) included in later editions portrays a merger between the couple with John's chains and Catherine's wedding ring as vital symbols.[57] The last poems of the collection, called '*Rime*' in Italian, depict Catherine comforting John in his difficult situation. The collection ends with a strongly symbolic image of Catherine's initials 'CI' within a heart, surrounded by a crown of thorns and crowned with a modernised Nordic bridal crown. Thus, Tapiovaara encapsulated her life and memory in romantic symbols of passion (including suffering), love and marriage. At the core, however, is her name, marking both her personal identity and her membership of the Jagiellonian family. Catherine is frequently called a 'child' or 'maiden' of the Jagiellonians in the poems. In one passage, the family are briefly characterised as 'cruel' rulers. In the same stanza, the Sforzas are said to be known for their crimes, whereas the Vasas are depicted as 'noble', but 'great both in virtues and vices'.[58] Metrically, Leino's poems on the Renaissance ducal couple mostly follow the Italian stanza form (*ottava rima*), which originated in the late thirteenth and early fourteenth centuries. Leino is much loved and widely read in Finland today, but the strict formalism of this collection means that it is not among his most popular poetry. The book was translated into Polish in 1981.[59] Leino's poems can be read not only as a dialogue between two lovers but also as a dialogue between a young nation (Finland, represented by John and his Duchy) and the 'old' Europe (represented by Catherine Jagiellon) in a historico-political situation in which Finland was searching for its place as 'a nation among nations'. The Finnish nationalists, or fennomans, wanted to build future unity around the Finnish language, since culture and science had mostly been in the hands of the country's Swedish-speaking elite. Historical traditions and links with Sweden were to be rejected, as was the continuing dependence on Swedish culture.[60] As a non-Swedish (and non-Russian) person, Catherine Jagiellon perfectly matched this requirement, bringing a taste of the desired opulence and Europeanness to the Finnish past.

Another Finnish author who used Catherine Jagiellon's figure in his fiction was Mika Waltari (1908–79), internationally best known for his best-selling novel *The Egyptian* (1945). Waltari wrote his first historical novel, *Catherine Månsdotter*,[61] on Eric XIV's wife, in 1942, during the Second World War hostilities between Finland and the Soviet Union, referred to as the Continuation War. In this context, the book has been interpreted as an allegory of Finland's position between the great powers. Although Waltari's first historical novel has been criticised as an overly schematic novel lacking nuanced characters apart from the protagonist Catherine Månsdotter (d.1612) herself, it enjoyed wide popularity in Finland.[62] It was soon published in seven editions and translated into thirteen languages.[63] As Catherine Månsdotter's sister-in-law, Catherine Jagiellon has a role in the story as one of those supporting characters criticised as predictable. However, her literary depiction differs substantially from Leino's romantic figure. Waltari's Catherine Jagiellon is filled with pride, arrogance and determination. She is a hard, power-seeking woman, 'sinewy as a steel bow'. Interestingly, in light of the circumstances under which the book was written, one of Catherine Jagiellon's dominant personality traits is a deep affection for Finland. Waltari's Catherine does not shed a tear at the moment of her imprisonment, but cries and demonstrates a deep affection when considering the loyalty Finnish people have shown to her during and after the siege of Turku Castle by Eric XIV's troops.[64] In effect, John hates his older, vainglorious wife, but the couple are unified by their shared fondness for Finland and by their vested interests in power.[65] More so than her husband, Catherine is 'in love with this strange, hard country' whose inhabitants, first imagined as 'harsh and reserved', turn out to be most loyal until the end. Alongside her husband, she nevertheless learned the 'difficult, strange language' of the poor, but fabulous country she appreciates so much.[66] Duke John and Duchess Catherine's alleged fondness for the territory they ruled over inspired Finnish nationalists, but the belief that they spoke the local language has also been persistent among Finnish scholars.[67] Apparently, John had some talent for and interest in foreign languages.[68] In his epitaph it is said that Finnish was among the languages he mastered, but we have scarce evidence of his real language skills beyond this kind of panegyric.

In Scandinavian collective memory (if there is one), Catherine Jagiellon is primarily the figure who brought the fork to the North and, with the fork, the whole European, Polish-Italian Renaissance civilisation, with its material splendour and distinguished manners. It is seldom mentioned that she brought one of the first known apothecaries to Finland. It was, however, probably John who introduced the fork to Swedes before his wife. John had stayed in England in 1559–60 when he was involved in the marriage negotiations between his brother Eric and Elizabeth I of England. In England, two forks were acquired for his residence.[69] The marriage negotiations foundered and John returned to Sweden, with or without the forks. Nevertheless, the forks (bigger and smaller, silver and gilded) of Catherine's dowry are the first known in Finland. The material culture of 'first forks, carpets and curtains' and the dazzling court life at Turku Castle still predominate in her memory in Finnish school history books, although visual representations of her are often based on inaccurate sixteenth-century pictures,[70] or alternatively imaginative eighteenth-century lithographs.[71] In Finnish school history books, Catherine Jagiellon is not swept aside, but has a relatively vibrant legacy – at least when compared with other women. In the present-day upper secondary school, the history of the Swedish era is a voluntary course and is not among the most popular history courses for students. Therefore, for the majority (around 90 per cent) of the younger age groups, elementary school history classes provide the only knowledge of that period. A recent textbook for 12-year-old pupils[72] introduces only two women in the period from Antiquity to Absolutism: they are the sisters-in-law Catherine Jagiellon and Catherine Månsdotter. In another equivalent textbook the only two are Saint Birgitta of Sweden and Catherine Jagiellon.[73] Both entries are illustrated with the portrait attributed to Lucas Cranach the Younger's atelier. The worksheets in each book contain tasks on Catherine, both based on the Turku Castle playing cards, which would be completely appropriate if either book indicated that the image does not represent Catherine Jagiellon, but is rather associated with a long-standing tradition of her memory in Finland.

The resulting picture is depressing particularly from the point of view of gender history, since the texts ignore not only many women of importance, but also gender aspects in general. Under these conditions, introducing a whole page on Catherine Jagiellon is a significant achievement. Because of the emphasis on political history, from which women were usually excluded, their role in schoolbooks is to fill gaps in family and religious history. Catherine is portrayed not only through her family (the Jagiellonians and the Vasas) and religion, but particularly through material culture. In the newest national curriculum, the core objective is to learn the nature of history and so-called history skills (e.g. interpretation) rather than specific contents of history. For sixteenth-century history, for instance, teaching concentrates on changes in science, art, and human beliefs.[74] Therefore, the role of Catherine Jagiellon in Finnish history may be investigated from these points of view in future school history teaching.

In Turku, there are some slight remnants of folklore, which may however be of later creation. In the Katariinanlaakso (Catherine's Valley) nature reserve, there is a large, table-like stone, which is called 'Katariinan kivi' (Catherine's Stone) by locals. According to tradition, it was the place where the court picnicked and danced around the stone in springtime. In the same area, there is a whole neighbourhood called 'Katariina', with street names such as 'Jagellonicankatu' (Jagellonica's street), 'Katariinantie' (Catherine's road), 'Juhanankatu' (John's street) and 'Hannuntyttärentie' (Hansdotter's[75] road). In Turku, and especially at Turku Castle, the remembrance culture continues to exist, for example in seminars and exhibitions.[76]

Conclusion

The Latin epitaph on the wall of the Jagiellonian chapel in Uppsala Cathedral over Catherine Jagiellon's tomb begins with these words: 'You, stranger, might wonder who I am and who I was . . .', just as if she or the court writer(s) were afraid of her sinking into oblivion. Although the underlying fear of being forgotten seems to be a fundamental human characteristic, emphasised in monumental inscriptions,[77] the fear of Catherine or her inner circle was not completely unjustified.

Creating a narrative in history is about making choices, inclusions and exclusions in order to communicate meanings. In history writing, family, religion and material culture are generally easily associated with women, a trend discernible in previous research on Catherine Jagiellon. However, nuances can be seen. In Finland, the textual and visual narrative created for Catherine Jagiellon, which can be called 'memory', is steadfastly associated with Turku Castle and its Renaissance court in 1562–63. It has inspired both Finnish nationalists and artists during the period of national Romanticism as well as politicians and journalists during the Cold War. Her memory continues to play a role, albeit not a major one, in Finnish history culture, including school history and popular culture. As one of the only members of royalty ever to have resided in Finland, she has brought an international, even exotic, flavour to a young nation's identity. On the other hand, as source material is scarce, the use of her memory remains flexible and can be easily adapted for different purposes.[78] An essential part of her memory is based on her birth family, best visible in her name, Jagellonica.

By contrast, in Sweden, which has a long history of various ruling families and interesting royal personalities, as well as a strong national identity with the master narrative of state building from the sixteenth century towards its development as a great power, there has not been much of a need to maintain her memory. The figure of Queen Christina of Sweden (r.1632–54), who stunned her contemporaries by refusing to marry, abdicating her throne and converting to Roman Catholicism, has dominated the memory of early modern Swedish queens. In the 'Jagiellonian context', there is a further connection here: after her abdication in Sweden in 1654, Christina launched an attempt to set herself up as the future queen of Naples. Catherine Jagiellon's maternal grandmother had been Isabella of Aragon (1470–1524), also known as Isabella of Naples. Bona Sforza's fabulous heritage was situated in the Kingdom of Naples, which was not in the end a particularly plausible reason for Christina's desire to rule in Naples.[79] In another failed scheme, Christina attempted to have herself made queen of Poland following the last Vasa of the Polish branch and the last descendant of Catherine Jagiellon, John Casimir of Poland (1609–72). She would have had the opportunity to become queen of Poland earlier, in 1644, when John Casimir's elder brother and Christina's second cousin, Ladislaus IV, proposed to her, but she turned him down. Nevertheless, in both countries – even if less so in Finland than in Sweden – the memory of Catherine Jagiellon, and even more that of her son Sigismund, seems to suffer from ethnic, cultural, religious and political exteriority. However, especially in Finnish national Romanticism, their 'otherness' has also been exploited to affirm cultural and political identity.

Notes

1 Finland was part of the Swedish kingdom from around 1150 until the year 1809, when Finland became an autonomous part of the Russian Empire as the Grand Duchy of Finland. Finland gained its full independence from Russia in 1917.
2 R. I. Frost, 'Obsequious Disrespect: The Problem of Royal Power in the Polish-Lithuanian Commonwealth under the Vasas, 1587–1668', in R. Butterwick, ed., *The Polish-Lithuanian Monarchy in European Context*, Basingstoke, 2001, pp. 150–71, p. 160.
3 See, ex. A. Hahr, *Drottning Katarina Jagellonica och Vasarenässansen: studier i vasatidens konst och svensk-polsk-italienska förbindelser*, Uppsala, 1940; C. J. Gardberg, *Turun linnan kolme Katariinaa*, trans. Irma Savolainen, 1993, pp. 48–116.
4 On women's names in the Middle Ages and early modern era, see M. Bourin and P. Chareille, eds, *Genèse médiévale de l'anthroponomie moderne*, 2, 2: Persistances du nom unique. Désignation et anthroponomie des femmes. Méthodes statistiques pour l'anthroponymie. Etudes d'anthroponymie médiévale, IIIe et IVe Rencontres, Azay-le-Ferron, 1989–1990, Tours, 1992; C. Peters, *Women in Early Modern Britain 1450–1640*, Basingstoke, 2003; G. Signori and C. Rolker, *Konkurrierende Zugehörigkeit(en): Praktiken der Namengebung im europäischen Vergleich*, Konstanz, 2011; C. Rolker, *Das Spiel der Namen: Familie, Verwandschaft und Geschlecht im spätmittelalterlichen Konstanz*, Konstanzer Geschichts- und Rechtsquellen 45, Ostfildern, 2014.
5 'Therefore, we Catharina Jagellonica, D[ei] G[ratia], Princess of Poland etc.' (trans. SN): J. H. Schröder, *Testamentum Catharinae Jagellonicae, Reginae Sveciae. Præside mag. Joh. Henr. Schröder . . . p. p. Carolus Wilhelmus Pålman. Reg*, Uppsala, 1831, p. 1.
6 Swedish National Archives (Riksarkivet), Stockholm, Royal Archives, Swedish Queens, sixteenth century, SE/RA/710003/02/001/K 73, 'Katarina Jagellonica' (microfilm).
7 A. Lahtinen, '"There's No Friend Like a Sister": Sisterly Relations and the Rhetoric of Sisterhood in the Correspondence of the Aristocratic Stenbock Sisters', in A. Korhonen and K. Lowe, eds, *The Trouble with Ribs: Women, Men and Gender in Early Modern Europe*, Helsinki, 2007, pp. 180–200, p. 184.
8 Cracow, B. Książąt Czartoryskich, 2743/II, l. 1–227 (A. Przeździecki, ed., *Jagiellonki polskie 3, w XVI. wieku: obrazy rodziny i dworu Zygmunta I i Zygmunta Augusta Królów polskich*, Kraków, 1868, appendix, pp. 311–26); E. G. Palmén, 'Puolan kirjallisuudesta poimittuja tietoja Suomen historiaan', *Historiallinen Arkisto* XVIII, Helsinki, 1903, pp. 336–61.
9 'Hertig Johans och hertiginan Katarinas egendom på Stockholms slott 1563–64', *Kungliga och furstliga personers enskilde egendom*, vol. 3, 1556–94, Stockholm, Royal Palace Archives; R. Hausen, *Förteckning öfver Hertig Johans af Finland och hans gemål Katarina Jagellonicas lösegendom 1563*, Helsinki, 1909.
10 A. Hahr, *Drottning Katarina Jagellonica och Vasarenässansen: studier i vasatidens konst och svensk-polsk-italienska förbindelser*, Uppsala, Almqvist & Wiksell, 1940; P. Gillgren, *Vasarenässansen: konst och identitet i 1500-talets Sverige*, Stockholm, 2009, e.g. pp. 39, 75–6, 89–92, 128–38.
11 H. Biaudet, *Le Saint-Siège et la Suède durant la seconde moitié du XVIe siècle: études politiques. 1, 1*, Paris, 1907; H. Biaudet, *Documents concernant les relations entre le Saint-Siège et la Suède durant la seconde moitié du XVIe siècle*, Paris, 1907; O. Garstein, *Rome and the Counter-Reformation in Scandinavia until the Establishment of the S. Congregatio De Propaganda Fide in 1622*, Oslo, 1963.
12 The story is based on Jöran Persson's reports to Eric XIV on the royal prisoners. Anders Fryxell, the nineteenth-century editor of the reports, which he describes as 'drafts most difficult to read', added asterisk-marked explanations such as the account of Catherine pointing at her ring and choosing captivity with her husband and two servants instead of a manor house with a full staff of servants, A. Fryxell, *Handlingar rörande Skandinaviens historia* 3, Stockholm, 1817, p. 16.
13 See Pierre Nora's pioneering work: P. Nora, 'Between Memory and History: Les Lieux de Mémoire', *Representations* 26, Special Issue: Memory and Counter-Memory,

Spring, 1989, pp. 7–24, p. 8; memory studies in history have been strongly associated with the world wars and the Holocaust. On the 'memory boom' of the twentieth century – the efflorescence of interest in the subject of memory inside the academy and beyond it as well as various means of remembrance – see, for instance, J. Winter, *Remembering War: The Great War between History and Memory in the 20th Century*, New Haven, CT, 2006.

14 J. Rüsen, 'Was ist Geschichtskultur? Überlegungen zu einer neuen Art, über Geschichte nachzudenken', in K. Füssmann, H. T. Grütter and J. Rüsen, eds, *Historische Faszination. Geschichtskultur heute*, Köln, Weimar and Wien, 1994, pp. 3–26; B. Guenée, *Histoire et culture historique dans l'Occident médiéval*, Paris, 1980; J. Assmann, *Das kulturelle Gedächtnis. Schrift. Erinnerung und politische Identität in frühen Hochkulturen*, Munich, 1992; a valuable web resource on historical culture, theory of history and historiography is maintained by Fernando Sánchez Marcos, Professor Emeritus of Early Modern History at the University of Barcelona. The web portal has served as a source of knowledge and inspiration also for this essay; see F. Sánchez Marcos, *Historical Culture*, www.culturahistorica.es/historical_culture.html, trans. Philip Banks, accessed 7.2.16.

15 On methodological critique of the use of collective memory, see W. Kansteiner, 'Finding Meaning in Memory: A Methodological Critique of Collective Memory Studies', *History and Theory*, May 2002, pp. 179–97.

16 Pierre Nora defines sites of memory in the following way: 'Where [cultural] memory crystallizes and secretes itself': Nora, 'Between Memory and History', p. 7; on spaces of memory or of remembrance, see also A. Assmann, *Erinnerungsräume: Formen und Wandlungen des kulturellen Gedächtnisses*. Munich, 1999.

17 Garstein, *Rome and the Counter-Reformation in Scandinavia*, pp. 255–6.

18 *Testamentum Catharinæ Jagellonicæ, reginæ Sveciæ*, ex schedis bibliothecæ acad. Upsal. editum. Venia ampl. fac. philos. Upsal: præside mag. Joh. Henr. Schröder . . . p. p. Carolus Wilhelmus Pålman Stip. Grönvall. Vestmanno-Dalekarlus. In Audit. Gustav. die XI Jun. MDCCCXXXI. H. A. M. S. Diss., Uppsala, 1831.

19 A. Hahr, *Katarina Jagellonicas gravvård i Uppsala domkyrka. Särtryck ur Uppländsk bygd*, Uppsala, 1940, pp. 143–53, p. 143; Gillgren, *Vasarenässansen*, p. 130.

20 On the other window of the chapel there is the motto of John III, 'Deus protector noster', and on the opposite wall above John's monument a painting representing the city of Stockholm; see H. Bengtsson, *Uppsala domkyrka 6. Gravminnen*, Uppsala, 2010, p. 65.

21 J. A. Pärnänen, *Le premier séjour de Sigismond Vasa en Suède 1593–1594*, Annales academiae scientiarum Fennicae B XXVIII, 1933, p. 169; Garstein, *Rome and the Counter-Reformation in Scandinavia*, vol. II, Oslo, 1980, pp. 157–8.

22 *Tagebuch des Erich Lassota von Steblau: Nach einer Handschrift der von Gersdorff-Weicha'schen Bibliothek zu Bautzen herausgegeben und mit Einleitung und Bemerkungen begleitet von Reinhold Schottin*, Halle, 1866, pp. 162–4.

23 J. Messenius, *Scondia Illustrata*, vol. 7, Stockhomliae, 1702, 68.

24 J. Messenius, *Genealogia Sigismundi*, Dantisci Ex molybdographia Viduae Guillemothanae, 1608.

25 J. Messenius, *Suomen riimikronikka*, trans. and ed. Harry Lönnroth and Martti Linna, Helsinki, 2004, p. 259.

26 The cultural movement of Gothicism identified ancient Goths with Swedes. The belief was based on Jordanes's account of the original Gothic homeland in Scandinavia. The Gothicists took pride in the Gothic tradition that the Ostrogoths and their king Theodoric the Great, who assumed power in the Roman Empire, had Scandinavian ancestry. The idea was expressed in the medieval chronicles and permeated the sixteenth-century Swedish histories of Johannes Magnus (*Historia de omnibus gothorum sueonumque regibus*) and his brother Olaus Magnus (*Historia de gentibus septentrionalibus*). In the seventeenth century, Messenius and his colleague at the University of Uppsala, Olof Rudbeck, continued the tradition in their writings. Gothicism contributed to claims

of political legitimacy based on assertions that Sweden was the cradle of the Goths or that the conquest of the Roman Empire was proof of Swedes' military valour and power through history. K. Neville, 'The Land of the Goths and Vandals: The Visual Presentation of Gothicism at the Swedish Court, 1550–1700', *Renaissance Studies* 27, 2013, pp. 435–59; cf. B. Lindberg, 'Introduktion: nationalism och nationell identitet i 1700-talets Sverige', in A. Karlsson and B. Lindberg, eds, *Nationalism och nationell identitet i 1700-talets Sverige*, Uppsala, 2002, pp. 7–15, pp. 9–10.
27 On Erik Dahlberg's life and works, see I. Corswant-Naumburg, *Greve Erik Dahlbergh: kungligt råd, fältmarskalk och generalguvernör: "hiärtan alldra kiäreste herr far"*, Visby, 2008.
28 E. Dahlbergh, '59', *Suecia Antiqua et Hodierna* I, Stockholm, 1667–1705.
29 This drawing was completed in the last quarter of the seventeenth century; see Gillgren, *Vasarenässansen*, pp. 128–31.
30 Portraits of members of the Jagiellon family, workshop of Lucas Cranach the Younger, 1553–56, in the Princes' Czartoryski Museum in Cracow, Fundacja XX Czartoryskich przy Muzeum Narodowym, XII-536 XII-545.
31 J. Peringskiöld, *Monumenta Ullerakerensia cum Upsalia nova*, Stockholm, 1719, p. 74.
32 J. Simmler, *Katarzyna Jagiellonka w więzieniu w Gripsholmie*, Warsaw, 1859. See E. Micke-Broniarek, *Gallery of Polish Painting: Guide*, Warsaw, 2006.
33 H. Salmson, *Katarina Jagellonica uppvisar sin vigselring för Jöran Persson*, Stockholm, 1865; E. Hultmark, *Kungliga Akademiens för de fria konsterna utställningar 1794–1887 – Förteckning över konstnärer och konstverk*, Stockholm, 1935, p. 239.
34 C. J. Billmark, *Johan III:s fängelse på Gripsholm. Hertig Karls kammare*, Stockholm, National Museum, NMH A 450/1982; see also I. Andersson, *Gripsholm, slottet och dess samlingar*, Stockholm, Nordisk Rotogravyr, 1937, p. 102.
35 C. Jagiellon, 'Letter to the stadtholder (*ståthållare*) of Stockholm Castle', Gripsholm, 17 May 1567, *Handlingar rörande Skandinaviens historia*, vol. 4, Stockholm, 1817, pp. 52–3.
36 On Catherine Jagiellon and Duke John's captivity, see I. Andersson, 'Erik XIV, Johan III och Gripsholm', in *Gripsholm, slottet och dess samlingar*, Stockholm, Nordisk Rotogravyr, 1937, pp. 93–102, esp. pp. 96–9.
37 U. G. Johnson, *Gripsholm Castle*, Stockholm, 1989, p. 6.
38 O. Carlén, *Gripsholm slott, dess historia, tafvelsamling, m.m.*, Stockholm, 1877, p. 10.
39 Nora, 'Between Memory and History'.
40 Nykvarn city council, www.nykvarn.se/upplevaochgora/kultur/drottningkallan.4.3652 860f14ade737119898c.html, accessed 24.11.15.
41 'No one but death' was made in cooperation with the Royal Armoury, the Polish Institute and the Polish Embassy in Stockholm: www.bringtolife.se/jagellonica.html, accessed 17.2.16.
42 Skolverket, *Läroplan för grundskolan, förskoleklassen och fritidshemmet 2011 (reviderad 2016)*, historia, Stockholm, 2016, pp. 196–205, 198–9.
43 P. Ljunggren, *Upptäck historia*, Stockholm, 2015, pp. 110, 138–40.
44 G. Körner and P. Lindberg, *PULS Historia*, Grundbok, 2012, p. 128; see also H. Almgren and H. Albin Larsson, *Alla tiders historia*, Malmö, Bas. Interaktiv. Gleerups Utbildning AB, 2013–16: https://gleerupsportal.se/gbook/v3/?refresh=1454599772&id=161, accessed 10.2.16.
45 R. Ragauskienė, 'The Marriage of Catherine Jagiellon and John III Vasa in Vilnius (1562)', in E. Saviščevas and M. Uzorka, eds, *Lithuania-Poland-Sweden. European Dynastic Unions and Historical-Cultural Ties. Studies of the Palace of the Grand Dukes of Lithuania*, vol. XXI, Vilnius, 2014, pp. 102–19, p. 106.
46 A revealing example is the microfilmed collection of the sixteenth-century Swedish Queens' documents in the National Archives in Stockholm. In Catherine Jagiellon's case, original sources can only be traced with difficulty, if at all, since the only information available is 'from a Polish archive'. Stockholm, National Archive, Swedish Queens, sixteenth century, Catherine Jagiellon, K73.

47 See Professor Dick Harrison's review of Lena Rangström's book *En brud för kung och fosterland: kungliga svenska bröllop från Gustav Vasa till Carl XVI Gustaf*, Stockholm, 2010: D. Harrison, 'Kungliga svenska bröllop från Gustav Vasa till Carl XVI Gustaf. Ett stycke kunglig populärhistoria', *Svenska Dagbladet*, 19 June 2010, www.svd.se/kultur/litteratur/ett-stycke-kunglig-popularhistoria_4886905.svd, accessed 16.5.16.
48 M. Nyman, *Förlorarnas historia: Katolskt liv i Sverige från Gustav Vasa till drottning Kristina*, Uppsala, 1997.
49 For Turku Castle as a case study of a mnemonic 'practised place' and 'narrative space', see Petja Aarnipuu's doctoral thesis: P. Aarnipuu, *Turun linna kerrottuna ja kertovana tilana*, Helsinki, 2008.
50 C. J. Gardberg, *Turku Castle. A Tour of the Stronghold*, Turku, 1980, p. 5.
51 C. J. Gardberg, *Åbo slott under den äldre vasatiden. En byggnadshistorisk undersökning*, Helsinki, 1959, pp. 309–10; M. Stenroos et al., *Turkulaisen veden pitkä matka Halistenkoskelta Turun keskuspuhdistamolle*, Turku, 1989, p. 60.
52 Gardberg, *Turku Castle*, pp. 23–6.
53 See the exhibition catalogue, *Katariina Jagellonica. Puolan prinsessa, Suomen herttuatar, Ruotsin kuningatar. 1526–1583: puolalaisten museoiden järjestämä näyttely Turun linnassa, 11.6.–6.7.1965*, Turku, 1965.
54 The information on the reception of the exhibition in Finnish newspapers is based on S. Sjöberg-Pietarinen, 'Kun Katariina Jagellonica rautaesiripun puhkaisi', 18 May 2005, *Turun Sanomat*, www.ts.fi/mielipiteet/paakirjoitukset/1074044966/Solveig+SjobergPietarisen+aliokirjoitus+Kun+Katarina+Jagellonica+rautaesiripun+puhkaisi, accessed 22.2.16.
55 E. Tawaststjerna, *Sibelius: 1865–1905*, vol. 1, trans. R. Layton, Berkeley and Los Angeles, 1976, p. 221.
56 Leino describes the collection as 'the last romantic's gift to his beloved'. H. Sihvo, 'Eino Leino: runo ja elämä', in H. Mäkelä, ed., *Elämän kirja. Valikoima Leinon tuotannosta*, Helsinki, 1980, pp. 15–35, p. 30.
57 The illustration of the poem 'Nil nisi mors' by Tapio Tapiovaara aka 'Tapsa', in E. Leino, *Juhana Herttuan ja Catharina Jagellonican lauluja*, 1919; 6th edn, Helsinki, 2001, p. 41.
58 The poem 'Chorus mysticus', in Leino, *Juhana Herttuan ja Catharina Jagellonican lauluja*, p. 42.
59 E. Leino, *Pieśni księcia Jana i Katarzyny Jagiellonki*, trans. J. Litwiniuk, Helsinki, 1981; Warszawa, 1981.
60 J. Paasivirta, *Finland and Europe. The Period of Autonomy and the International Crises, 1808–1914*, Minneapolis, 1962, p. 66.
61 M. Waltari, *Kaarina Maununtytär*, Helsinki, 1942.
62 P. Rajala, *Unio mystica. Mika Waltarin elämä ja teokset*, Helsinki, 2011.
63 The number of translations is taken from *The Finnish Literature in Translation* database, Finnish Literature Society, http://dbgw.finlit.fi/kaannokset/index.php?lang=ENG, accessed 23.2.16.
64 M. Waltari, *Kaarina Maununtytär*, 6th edn, Porvoo and Helsinki, 1947, pp. 126–8.
65 Waltari, *Kaarina Maununtytär*, pp. 281–3.
66 Waltari, *Kaarina Maununtytär*, pp. 127–8.
67 See Miia Ijäs, 'Katariina Jagellonica – vaimo, kuningatar, diplomaatti', *Genos. Journal of the Genealogical Society of Finland* 2, 2009, pp. 52–9, p. 56; Hockman, Tuula, Kuninkaan valvonnan alle. In A. Lahtinen and M. Ijäs, eds, *Risti ja lounatuuli. Rauman seurakunnan historia keskiajalta vuoteen 1640*, Helsinki, Finnish Literature Society, 2015, pp. 89–123, p. 113; cf. Gardberg, *Turun linnan kolme Katariinaa*, pp. 70–1.
68 See, for instance, William Cecil's (the secretary of state to Elizabeth I of England) and the French Hubertus Langetus's description of John's good spoken Latin during his visit to England for marriage negotiations between Elizabeth and his brother Eric in 1559–60: L. Ericson, *Johan III. En biografi*, Lund, 2004, pp. 63, 70.

69 Ericson, *Johan III*, p. 67.
70 The image was reproduced in the famous Turku Castle playing cards, and from there it was disseminated to school history books.
71 Carl Müller's 1820s lithograph of Catherine Jagiellon (based on C. J. [sic; Carl Theodor] Löwstädt's (1789–1829) original picture) is an oft-used image in history textbooks: *The Picture Collections of the National Board of Antiquities of Finland*, 2008, www.kuvakokoelmat.fi/pictures/view/HK10000_2008, accessed 25.11.16.
72 J. Bruun et al., *Ritari*, Helsinki, 2015, p. 122.
73 R. Eskelinen and M. Troberg, *Matkalippu historiaan*, Helsinki, 2008, p. 153.
74 The national core curriculum for basic education was renewed in 2014. New local curricula that are based on this core curriculum were implemented in schools from August 2016. Finnish National Board of Education, *National Core Curriculum for Basic Education 2014*, Helsinki, 2016.
75 Catherine Hansdotter (1539–96) was John's illegitimate wife and mother of four children before his marriage to Catherine Jagiellon.
76 For example, a seminar on the theme 'Baltic castles and Catherine Jagiellon' was held at Turku Castle on 19 May 2016. The organiser was the Polish Embassy in Finland, since Poland held the Presidency of the Baltic Sea States Council in 2016; Catherine Jagiellon also appeared in the exhibition 'Game of Power – Reformation in Finland', which ran from 17 February 2017 to 4 March 2018, produced by the Museum Centre of Turku.
77 C. Lévi-Strauss, *Anthropologie structurale*, Paris, 1985, 1st edn 1958, t. 1 (Commemoration, p. 264); M. Augé, *Les formes d'oubli*, Paris, 1998.
78 On this point, see also Mickūnaitė in this volume, pp. 28–43.
79 Catherine Jagiellon's mother, Bona Sforza, queen of Poland, also Duchess of Bari and Princess of Rossano, returned to her native Bari before her death. Her huge inheritance was situated in the Kingdom of Naples, then belonging to Spain. The king of Spain owed her 430,000 Neapolitan ducats, whereas the king of Naples had assigned her 44,400 ducats annually as interest, payable out of the customs of Foggia. Bona and her children being dead, part of this capital devolved to her grandson Sigismund III, who had assigned it to the republic; yet both he and his sons, Ladislaus IV and John II Casimir, took care to receive the interest. On the background of the inheritance, see Biaudet, *Le Saint-Siège et la Suède*, pp. 337–64 ; on Christina of Sweden, see P. Englund, *Silvermasken: En kort biografi över drottning Kristina*, Stockholm, 2006; on her plans regarding the Naples throne, see S. Åkerman, 'Queen Christina and Messianic Thought', in D. S. Katz and J. I. Israel, eds, *Sceptics, Millenarians, and Jews*, Leiden, 1999, pp. 142–60, esp. pp. 159–60.

7

THE JAGIELLONIANS IN BELARUS

A gradual release of memory

Simon M. Lewis

Belarus is intimately connected with the history of the Jagiellonian dynasty. The marriage between Jogaila (c.1362?–1434), Grand Duke of Lithuania, and Jadwiga (Hedwig) (c.1374–99), Queen of Poland, which led to a dynastic union between the two states, was formally agreed at Kreva Castle, now in Belarus, in 1385. Jogaila's fourth wife Sophia (c.1405–61), who bore him the heirs who went on to form a ruling dynasty, was a princess of Halshany from a noble family of Drutsk; both places are in Belarus. They were married in 1422 in the castle at Navahrudak, the Belarusian town believed by some historians to have been the first capital of the Grand Duchy of Lithuania. The Jagiellonian rulers presided over Poland and Lithuania for nearly two centuries (1386–1572 in Poland; 1377–92 and 1440–1572 in Lithuania), with their dominion as Grand Dukes of Lithuania extending over all the land that we today identify as Belarus.

But of course, in those days it was not *Belarus*, and herein lies the obstacle for modern Belarusian historiography and memory. Belarusian writers, activists and scholars who have sought to interpret the legacy of the Jagiellonian dynasty have necessarily faced choices on how to render the symbolic 'Lithuanianness' and/or 'Polishness' of the pre-modern rulers. For many Belarusian accounts, as we will see, the Grand Duchy of Lithuania carries an inherent value as the country that 'preceded' Belarus. It has been an unchallenged dogma in a major branch of Belarusian history-writing that, as a recent popular animated film about the country's past succinctly put it, 'Belarus was called Lithuania then.'[1]

However, even when a direct continuity between the Grand Duchy and today's Belarus is assumed, the Jagiellonians are difficult to categorise in binary terms of self and other. The two major events that bookend Jagiellonian rule in Lithuania, the Kreva Union of 1385–86 and the Lublin Union of 1569 (which established a formal political union between the two states), both have the dismantling of boundaries and binaries as defining features. The first union was followed by a civil war in Lithuania (1390–92), as a result of which Jogaila's cousin Vytautas ('the Great', c.1350–1430) prised away *de facto* sovereignty from the dynasty's founder until his own death four decades later. At the same time, Jogaila remained Supreme Duke, nominally retaining sovereignty in Lithuania whilst ruling Poland as king. Jogaila's heirs regained Lithuania ten years later, but here as well, there are overlaps that confound their categorisation as unequivocally Lithuanian or Polish, or even simultaneously both: Casimir Jagiellon (1427–92) was Grand Duke of Lithuania for seven years (1440–47) before also being elected to the Polish throne (1447–92), and his son Alexander Jagiellon (1461–1506) was Grand Duke of Lithuania between 1492 and 1501, when he acceded to the Polish throne, and he then reigned in both lands until 1506. Only Sigismund I 'the Old' (1467–1548; r.1506–48) and Sigismund Augustus (1520–72; r.1548–72) held both thrones simultaneously for the duration of their careers, the latter presiding over the formal unification of the two states. Thus, writers wishing to discuss the Jagiellonians as part of Belarusian history through the prism of Lithuania have variously demonised or downplayed the Polish influence of all members of the dynasty, singled out or emphasised the 'Lithuanian periods' of Casimir and Alexander, or glossed over all the complexities to brazenly imply that all of this history simply 'belongs' to Belarus.

There is a distinct chronology to the emergence of Belarusian memory of the Jagiellonians. The first nationally-conscious Belarusian histories of the early twentieth century sought to inscribe an ethnolinguistic concept of Belarusianness into the distant past. Some demonised the dynasty's representatives and others found aspects that were worth incorporating into the nationalist narrative; yet overall, their treatment of the Jagiellonians was limited in scope. Soviet-era Belarusian historiography almost completely eschewed the Jagiellonians for two principal reasons: first, a dominant Russo-centrism, which meant that the legacy of monarchs who brought the Belarusian territories under Polish cultural influence was treated as negative; and second, the ideology of Marxism-Leninism, which dictated that the focus should be on socioeconomic trends rather than rulers (see also Chapters 8 and 9 on Ukraine and Russia). The collapse of the Soviet Union introduced greater pluralism into the study of history in the country, and the early 1990s saw the 'revival' of Belarusian nationalist thought. The new histories sought to 'recover' interpretations of the past that had been previously suppressed, and as a result, they largely resembled the works of the early pioneers. Only in the second post-Soviet decade has a willingness to study Jogaila and his descendants emerged as a significant phenomenon in Belarus.

Between demonisation and tentative nationalisation: early Belarusian nationalist historiography on the Jagiellonians

In the course of the nineteenth and early twentieth centuries in the former territory of the Polish-Lithuanian Commonwealth, where there had previously been one political nation – the imagined community of Polish-speaking aristocrats – there gradually emerged a series of separate ethnolinguistic communities which demanded political representation. The codification of vernacular languages, combined with their increasingly extensive use in multiple spheres of writing, contributed to the gradual development of separate national movements.[2]

Belarus, however, was a notable latecomer to this trend. One important reason for this was that printing in Belarusian was banned in the Russian Empire until 1905, and Belarus since the Partitions of the Commonwealth had been fully incorporated into Russia (unlike for example the majority-Ukrainian lands, half of which had been annexed by the Habsburg Empire, where Ukrainian writing could flourish).[3] Once the Tsarist ban was lifted, the first Belarusian history was published in 1910, and the first standardised grammar appeared in 1918.[4]

Early Belarusian historiography is tinged with rebellion against the hegemony of polonophone culture and Russian imperial domination. Vatslau Lastouski (1883–1938), the author of the first Belarusian history, argued in a popular pamphlet published in 1918 that 'the history of Belarus is [. . .] the struggle of the Belarusians against foreign Russian and Polish invaders'.[5] This pugilistic rhetoric can explain why the Jagiellonians are treated with disfavour by Lastouski and many of his contemporaries: the dynasty is associated with the cultural polonisation of Belarus (i.e. the Grand Duchy of Lithuania). Following Jogaila's accession to the Polish throne and pledge to Catholicise his subjects in 1386, the reign of the Jagiellonian dynasty is treated as the beginning of the decline of Ruthenian culture and as a catastrophic rupture in the linear narrative of Belarusian historical development.

In his 'Short History of Belarus' (*Karotkaia historyia Belarusi*) of 1910, Lastouski's overt aim was to provide a 'fundament on which the life of the nation is built'.[6] He sought, therefore, to Belarusianise the past: to show that the Belarusian nation-state that he hoped to establish in the near future[7] was endowed with a rich history of sovereignty and independence. Not surprisingly considering the explicitly political purpose of the book, Lastouski's account is purely narrative and does not cite any sources. He calls the Grand Duchy of Lithuania a 'Lithuano-Ruthenian state', a term he employs to signify that the medieval polity incorporated two 'nationalities', Lithuanians and Belarusians – although the former are distinctly marginalised in his account. The 'Belarusian boyars' of the Grand Duchy are presented as a united force who acted with the interests of the 'nation' in mind. Moreover, it is implied that Orthodox Christianity is the 'true' Belarusian religion: those who converted to Catholicism after Jogaila's coronation are castigated as 'supporters of Poland and everything that is Polish', whereas the Orthodox faithful 'remained on the side of the country's interests, on the side of the national'.[8] Thus, Lastouski projects anachronistic and essentialist categories of modern-day nationality into the past in order to foster Belarusian patriotism in the present.

Although Lastouski does not go so far as to explicitly criticise Jogaila (*Iahailo* in his spelling), it is clear that he considers Vytautas (*Vitout* in his Belarusianised spelling)[9] more worthy of Belarusian admiration. Having rebelled against Jogaila and gained power over Lithuania, Vytautas represents a rupture in the dominion of the Jagiellonians over the Grand Duchy. Whereas Jogaila is characterised by

Lastouski as a 'weak, coarse, short-sighted individual'[10] and is described chiefly in terms of his acquiescence to Polish demands, Vytautas is credited with, for instance, 'founding a separate metropolitanate for Belarus, [and] establishing a national church'.[11] Overall, Lastouski declares: 'Belarus breathed more easily under Vytautas. The princes and boyars had it tough, but the people lived better.'[12]

In Lastouski's account, later Jagiellonian rulers fare no better than Jogaila. Casimir's (*Kazimir Iahailovich*) reign (Grand Duke, 1440–92) is introduced as a time when 'the separate history of Belarus ends'.[13] Lastouski maintains a populistic division between the effectively 'foreign' rulers and 'authentically' Belarusian-Lithuanian society: 'During *Kazimir*'s reign [. . .] questions about an inseparable union between the two states [Poland and Lithuania] are raised, but Lithuania and Belarus continue to fight for their independence and reject unity with Poland, which would threaten to destroy the national consciousness of Belarusians [. . .]'[14] However, Casimir is credited with issuing a major legal Statute 'in the Belarusian language'[15] (in 1468; Lastouski incorrectly gives 1492), and with presiding over a prosperous period of history. Nonetheless, the overall picture is that of the suppression of Belarusian national culture. Casimir's heirs are given fairly short shrift, with commentary on the rulers focusing on the official relationship between Lithuania and Poland and their pernicious effects on Belarusian interests. Alexander (*Aleksandr Iahailovich*, Grand Duke 1492–1506) is said to have favoured a full union between the states in order to 'make it easier' for him to 'balance the interests of Lithuania and Poland, which were fully divergent' – a turn of phrase that makes him seem both weak and indecisive, as well as antipathetic to Belarusian demands. Sigismund I 'the Old' (*Zhyhimont Stary*, Grand Duke 1506–48) is described very fleetingly indeed. And Sigismund Augustus's (*Zhyhimont Auhust*, d.1572) most prominent deed is the signing of the Union of Lublin in 1569, after which 'the Lithuano-Ruthenian state [. . .] lost its ability to continue fighting [for its independence]'.[16] Thus, Lastouski is consistent in his marginalisation of the Jagiellonian dynasty: Belarusian sovereignty thrived *despite* Jogaila and his descendants, but was eventually defeated by the Union of Lublin.

A somewhat different approach is employed by Usevalad Ihnatouski (1881–1931), the author of the second Belarusian historical monograph, 'A Short Sketch of the History of Belarus' (*Karotki narys historyi Belarusi*, 1919).[17] Ihnatouski declares an overall aim that is similar to that of Lastouski: national cultural and political rebirth through the spread of previously suppressed historical knowledge. He also follows Lastouski in not providing a scholarly apparatus as his book is intended as a pedagogic aid for primary school teachers. Yet his nationalisation of the medieval Grand Duchy of Lithuania – which he calls a 'Lithuano-Belarusian state' – places less emphasis on the detrimental effects of Polish-Lithuanian rapprochement, instead accenting the continued flourishing of Belarusian culture throughout the period of Jagiellonian rule. Thus, after Jogaila's accession to the Polish throne:

> there is no fundamental change in life. Lithuania and Belarus will continue to live their own separate life for a long time, up to the second half of the

sixteenth century, defending themselves from the [Polish] influence that has started to emerge.[18]

Ihnatouski's generally more positive assessment of the Jagiellonian era envisions a gradual decline of Belarusian autonomy, culminating in the nadir of the Union of Lublin. As such, it allows for a positive appraisal of the earlier members of the dynasty as defenders of Belarusian national interests.

Ihnatouski demonstrates, for example, that 'Lithuania and Belarus frequently had their own Grand Dukes, which went against the conditions of the Union of 1386'.[19] In other words, rulers of the Grand Duchy who did not, for part or all of their reign, have a dual role as kings of Poland are ascribed a 'Lithuano-Belarusian' belonging. These include Grand Dukes who were not direct descendants of Jogaila, i.e. Vytautas (*Vitaut* in Ihnatouski's spelling), Švitrigaila (*S'vidryhaila*, 1430–32) and Sigismund Kęstutaitis (*Sihizmund I*, 1432–40), as well as members of the Jagiellonian dynasty: Casimir ('*Kazimer I* in Lithuania and Belarus', '*Kazimer IV* in Poland') and Alexander (*Aleksander*). The fact that these two Jagiellonians ruled in Lithuania alone before they also gained the Polish crown is offered as (the only) evidence that 'individuals who were both Lithuano-Belarusian rulers and Polish kings considered themselves to be more Lithuano-Belarusian rulers than Polish kings in the first period after the 1386 Union'.[20] Sigismund Augustus, on the other hand, is said to have 'placed the interests of Poland above those of Lithuania and Belarus'.[21]

Therefore, Ihnatouski does not go so far as to claim outright that Casimir and Alexander were Belarusian, and whilst he writes very little of any substance about their reigns, he does identify them as positive influences in the development of Belarusian cultural autonomy. He dedicates a section of his monograph to Belarusian 'cultural work' (*kul'turnaia pratsa*) in the period in question, arguing:

> Although the country was gradually ruined year upon year, and both the material and spiritual culture on which our forefathers had worked were destroyed, we nonetheless see a development of Belarusian culture, and even a widespread development [. . .] The culture of the period of the Lithuano-Belarusian state has an overt and clear Belarusian direction and is conducted in the Belarusian language.[22]

This emphasis on language as the kernel of national identity is bolstered by assertions that Casimir's Statutes of 1454 and 1468 were written 'in Belarusian', as were the comprehensive legal codes issued in 1529, 1566 and 1588 (the Statutes of the Grand Duchy of Lithuania).[23] Overall, Ihnatouski focuses on demonstrating that Belarusian national life thrived during the 'period of the Lithuano-Belarusian state', despite the incremental onset of polonisation. The Jagiellonians are by no means central to his argument, but they are not, as in Lastouski's account, obstacles to the evolution of Belarusian culture. For Ihnatouski, the reigns of Casimir and Alexander Jagiellon were periods of relatively unconstrained national development.

By the time of Sigismund Augustus, however, the Polish influence had gained the upper hand over Belarus's striving for sovereignty.

Other examples of early Belarusian nationalist historiography tend towards either of these two ideological poles, i.e. Lastouski's patriotic indignation at a perceived marginalisation of Belarusian interests under the Jagiellonians, and Ihnatouski's passive acceptance of (some of) the Jagiellonians into the master narrative of Belarusian national development.

For instance, Lastouski's comparison of Jogaila and Vytautas is extended by Adam Stankevich (1882–1949), a Roman Catholic priest and nationalist intellectual who, after the division of the territory of Belarus between Poland and the Soviet Union in 1921–22, was active in Polish-controlled Wilno (Vilnius). Among other historiographical works, Stankevich published a pamphlet in 1930 to mark the 500th anniversary of the death of Grand Duke Vytautas (*Vitaut* in his spelling). Here, he gives a politically charged account of Vytautas as a defender of Belarusian interests against the polonising endeavour of Jogaila: '*Vitaut*'s idea was an idea about the independence of Lithuania and Belarus at its own expense. *Iahaila*'s idea was an idea about the independence of Poland at the expense of Lithuania and Belarus.'[24] Thus, whereas Lastouski had clearly favoured Vytautas, but refrained from overtly pitting them against each other and demonising Jogaila, Stankevich takes this further step. In another, broader work intended for young readers written in the 1940s under German occupation, Stankevich strengthens his opprobrium against Jogaila: '*Iahaila* was liked neither by the Belarusians nor the Lithuanians. That was because he did not commune with the people and had a very unpleasant personality. He was simple-minded, lazy, very suspicious of others, untrustworthy and harsh.'[25] However, Stankevich's antagonism does not stretch to all of the Jagiellonians. Like Ihnatouski, he approves of Casimir and Alexander Jagiellon: 'And after [*Vitaut*], Belarus and Lithuania frequently have other princes of their own, which contravened *Iahaila*'s pledge to the Poles. Thus, for example, *Kazimer I* (1440–47) and *Aliaksandar* (1492–1501) were lords of Belarus and Lithuania who ruled separately from Poland.'[26] Here, Stankevich gives the dates during which both Grand Dukes ruled in Lithuania only, eliding the fact that both went on to be Polish kings as well. His highly selective use of history serves an essentialising nationalist agenda that draws crisp, non-porous divisions between the categories of 'us' Belarusians and 'them' Poles.

Stankevich's position is disputed by Iazep Naidziuk (1909–84), another nationalist historian who was active in interwar Poland and in Nazi-occupied Eastern Europe. In the 1943 monograph 'Belarus Yesterday and Today: A Popular Sketch of the History of Belarus' (*Belarus' uchora i sian'nia. Papuliarny narys z historyi Belarusi*),[27] Naidziuk's version of events is similar to that of Ihnatouski in that it emphasises the successful resistance of Belarusian culture against the 'imperialistic'[28] onset of Polish cultural influence. However, whereas Ihnatouski had hardly mentioned Jogaila in his monograph, Naidziuk attempts to incorporate the first Jagiellonian into the Belarusian historical canon. He does this by re-evaluating the historical comparison of Vytautas and Jogaila. On the one hand, 'during *Vitaut*'s time the Grand Duchy was at the height of its powers' and '*Vitaut* was one of the best, most intelligent and most powerful Belarusian rulers'.[29] On the other hand, Jogaila's influence was also beneficial, and his 'role in Belarusian history' has not yet been 'sufficiently studied' by other Belarusian historians.[30] Naidziuk makes the bold claim that:

> By marrying the Polish Queen Jadwiga (Hedwig), *Iahaila* did not in fact join the Grand Duchy to Poland, but Poland to the Grand Duchy. The Grand Duchy was larger than Poland in both territory and power. Culture was developing no more slowly in Belarus than in Poland. Many people in Belarus were of higher culture than those in Poland [...] When *Iahaila* was in Krakow, he did not repudiate the Belarusian culture in which he had been brought up. On the contrary, he brought outstanding artists from Belarus to Krakow, and they decorated his palaces and various places of worship in Poland. *Iahaila* did not cease to speak in the Belarusian language. He spoke Belarusian up to his death.[31]

This avowedly revisionist stance emerges as a defence of Jogaila against the attempts by Lastouski and especially Stankevich to vilify the ruler. In addition, Naidziuk calls for more historiographical attention to be paid to the figure of Sophia of Halshany, Jogaila's fourth wife: 'the activity of Princess *Son'ka Hal'shanskaia*, like that of *Iahaila*, is still waiting for its Belarusian historian'.[32] As we shall see, many decades would pass before this call would be heeded.

Overall, despite tangible differences in the portrayal of individual rulers and minor variations in terminology,[33] the early Belarusian nationalist historians adopt a near-uniform approach to the history of Jagiellonian rule. This historiography is a normative endeavour that applies pre-conceived criteria to the evaluation of individual reigns: the Jagiellonians are judged solely on their perceived contribution to the 'development' of Belarusian national culture, whether or not they 'spoke Belarusian', and the extent to which they resisted or failed to resist the onset of political and cultural polonisation.[34] Jogaila proves to be divisive: opinions on his rule fall into two polarised camps. Casimir and Alexander tend to receive more favourable reviews, though not universally. The two Sigismunds are hardly mentioned, other than references to their acquiescence to polonisation.

The Jagiellonians in Belarus between Russian imperial history and early Soviet ideology

Whilst the first Belarusian nationalist ideologues wrote exclusively in the Belarusian language and propounded an unambiguous political message, other contemporaneous historians published in both Russian and Belarusian, and their work was not explicitly conceived in terms of opposition to the prevailing regime. Both Mitrafan Dounar-Zapol'ski (1867–1934) and Uladzimir Picheta (1878–1947) were successful academics under the Tsarist and then, for a time, the Soviet regimes (both encountered political difficulties during the Stalinist terror, but Picheta was rehabilitated after the Second World War). Both authors produced detailed scholarly histories of the medieval Grand Duchy of Lithuania that are less polemical in nature and include references to other works of scholarship. Whilst neither historian focuses explicitly on the Jagiellonian dynasty, writing instead about the history of the Lithuanian state and broader socioeconomic processes, their works can be seen as early and rare examples of a more measured exposition of the history of Jagiellonian rule.

Dounar-Zapol'ski was a native of the Minsk region who was educated as a historian at the Imperial University in Kiev at the turn of the century. The Russian-language monograph published in 1901 and based on his Masters dissertation, 'The State Economy of the Grand Duchy of Lithuania under the Jagiellonians' (*Gosudarstvennoe khoziaistvo Velikogo Kniazhestva Litovskogo pri Iagellonakh*),[35] is an in-depth historical study of the entire Jagiellonian period. On the one hand, the study provides almost no information about the rulers themselves;[36] rather, it is a detailed economic history that examines social relations, legal reforms and modes of state revenue in the medieval Grand Duchy. Jogaila and his heirs are frequently mentioned, but are generally incidental to the macrocosmic scope of the work. On the other hand, the chronological framing and the title of the work suggest that Dounar-Zapol'ski considered the period from Jogaila's accession to the death of Sigismund Augustus to be a self-contained historical epoch. Unlike the Belarusian nationalist historians examined above, Dounar-Zapol'ski employs a pluralised collective noun, 'the Jagiellonians' (*Iagellony*). Thus, this is the first book by a Belarusian historian to conceive of the reigns of Jogaila and his heirs as a dynastic era.

Picheta was a decade younger than Dounar-Zapol'ski, and he emerged as a young scholar at the end of the Tsarist era: he studied in Moscow under the pre-eminent Russian historian Matvei Liubavskii, and his doctoral monograph, on agrarian reform under Sigismund Augustus, was published in 1917.[37] Four years later he published a short Russian-language book on the 'History of the Lithuanian State until the Union of Lublin' (*Istoriia litovskogo gosudarstva do Liublinskoi unii*),[38] a narrative history of the Grand Duchy. Like Dounar-Zapol'ski's earlier study, both of Picheta's books make little reference to 'Belarus'; instead, they examine the 'Lithuanian' or 'Lithuano-Russian state' and 'Lithuanians' (*litovtsy*), terms which denote a geographical and political belonging rather than ethnolinguistic identity. The influence of Ruthenian/Slavic culture (in the form of for example the Chancery Slavonic language, which Belarusian nationalist historians usually refer to as 'Belarusian') is described as 'Russian' (*russkii*). These terminological choices reflect both authors' conformity with the dominant imperial notion of Belarus as a 'primordially Russian' land.

Thus, whilst Picheta's accounts of the Jagiellonian era are grounded in facts, archival documents and statistics and employ scholarly apparatuses, they do contain traces of the author's submission to the prevalent political ideas of the time. Russian imperial policy in Belarus was above all directed against the 'pernicious' effects of Polish-language and Roman Catholic culture, and Picheta's books, which both culminate in the 1569 Union of Lublin, implicitly evaluate the Jagiellonians' acceptance of Polish influence in the Grand Duchy in negative terms. The earlier work, for example, concludes that Sigismund Augustus's agrarian reforms were a failure: they led to a 'weakening of the authority' of the Grand Duke and an increase in the economic and political influence of the landed nobility, which 'prepared the way for the dictatorship of [the nobility] in the united Polish-Lithuanian state [after 1569]'.[39] The 1921 history of the Lithuanian state bears important structural similarities to the histories by Lastouski and Ihnatouski: the reigns of the Jagiellonian rulers are conceptualised exclusively in terms of their balancing of Polish and Lithuanian interests within the two states, and the overall thrust of the narrative is a story of political and cultural decline by means of polonisation. Yet whereas the Belarusian nationalists lamented the loss of a proto-Belarusian state, Picheta suggests that it was Russian influence that was lost: 'by concluding the 1569 union, the Polish diplomats achieved their aims, having gained the best Russian lands from Lithuania'.[40]

The ascent to power of the communist regime in Belarus in 1921 resulted in major political and social changes. In the early to mid-1920s, the Soviet Belarusian regime encouraged a form of nation-building under the policy of *korenizatsiia* ('nativisation');[41] this was a period in which a historical consciousness was actively cultivated by the state, in order to 'appropriate the Belarusian "national" history for Soviet Belarus, as the legitimate heir and representative of the Belarusian national tradition'.[42] In line with the new cultural atmosphere, Picheta published a Belarusian-language monograph on the pre-1569 history of Belarus in 1924.[43] This work, however, is nothing more than a slight re-working (and translation into Belarusian) of his earlier history, with the major difference that the Grand Duchy of Lithuania was now referred to as a 'Lithuano-Belarusian state'. As such, no qualitative change in the appraisal of the Jagiellonians was forthcoming. As Lindner has shown in detail with a particular focus on Picheta (subsequent volumes of his history of Belarus were never published due to disagreements with the censors), the Soviet authorities wavered until the outbreak of the Second World War on what would be the 'correct' representation of Belarusian history.[44] The fact that, other than this minimally revised pre-Soviet work, no treatments of the Jagiellonians appeared suggests that the dynasty had fallen foul of the Soviet grand narrative for Belarus.

The consolidated Soviet worldview: the Jagiellonians erased

After the Second World War, the representation of the past in the USSR became a 'mechanism of the state-political system', whereby 'books by historians did not contain any mysteries and were as similar to each other as twin brothers, only rarely differing in the set of concrete facts they discussed, and in some of the finer points'.[45] In particular, a cult of memory was created around the myth of the Great Victory in the Great Patriotic War. This was especially significant for Belarus, as the war was construed as the very *raison d'être* of the republic. The partisan myth – that the entire republic had united under the banner of Soviet statehood to fight the German occupation – became the dominant basis of collective identity. The sheer volume of essentially similar material about the war made the cult of victory a cultural monolith. During the 1960s, no fewer than 60 per cent of academics employed at the Institute of History of the republic's Academy of Sciences worked in the department of the history of the war.[46] Pre-Soviet history, such as that of the early modern period in the Grand Duchy of Lithuania, was downplayed and distorted. As a result, the Jagiellonians were definitively marginalised.

The few treatments of the 'epoch of feudalism', as Marxist-Leninist teleology would have it, that exist from this period depict the Jagiellonian era as a dark age in which latent forces of anti-feudal and anti-Polish rebellion began to thrust themselves towards the enlightenment and emancipation of Soviet rule. This conception of history has both a class-based and a national dimension. For example, the introduction to a major collection of archival documents (which are translated into Russian) speaks of the 'struggle of the people's masses', which can be divided into two stages. In the early stage, which corresponds roughly with the Jagiellonian era (although it is not conceptualised as such): 'the predominant mode of action of the anti-feudal movement was to escape from the feudal lord'.[47] Meanwhile, 'the actions and movements of the peasant masses and urban lower classes were directly aimed at uniting the Belarusian people with the Russian'.[48] Both the action and inaction of the 'popular masses' are conceived in distinctly normative and politicised terms, as precursors to proletarian revolution and the 'unification' of Belarus and Russia.

This twofold ideological emphasis on the lower classes in Belarus and their supposed striving to be assimilated into Russia was inherently antithetical to the existence of any kind of historiography that explores the Jagiellonian dynasty. Not only were the Jagiellonians representatives of the ruling class, but their actions clearly hindered the inevitable and righteous progression of the Belarusian people to their Russia-led civilisational home. In the authoritative two-volume 'History of the Belorussian SSR' (*Istoriia belorusskoi SSR*),[49] Jogaila and his heirs are occasionally mentioned, but only in relation to the main actors of the historical process: the Belarusian popular masses. For example, Jogaila is said to have:

> issued a set of privileges in 1413 in Horodło [Russian: *Gorodlo*] on the Western Bug River after a congress of Lithuanian and Belarusian feudal lords. The Horodło privileges strengthened the dominant position of the Catholic Lithuanian feudals in the Lithuanian state, and therefore in Belarus [. . .] Conflicts between the Belarusian and Lithuanian feudals were further heightened.[50]

This passage shows the crisp contours that were drawn between Orthodox Belarusian and Catholic Lithuanian ethnic interests in the fourteenth century, and illustrates the extent to which the key category of Belarusian nationality was detached from the actions of the Polish-Lithuanian rulers: Jogaila's deeds work against the development of Belarusian nationhood by favouring the Lithuanians and Poles.

The one form of text in which the Jagiellonians are represented is the encyclopaedia. The 'Belarusian Soviet Encyclopaedia' (*Belaruskaia Savetskaia Entsyklapedyia*, 1969–75) contains a short and factual entry for 'The Jagiellonians' (*Iahelony*), who are understood as a 'dynasty of Dukes of the Grand Duchy of Lithuania (1377–92, 1440–1572), kings of Poland (1386–1572), Hungary (1440–44, 1490–1526), the Czech lands (1471–1526)'.[51] This entry also lists the 'most significant representatives': after *Iahaila* himself, '*Kazimir IV Iahelonchyk* [. . .] *Aliaksandr* [. . .] *Zhyhimont I the Old* [. . .] *Zhyhimont II Auhust* [. . .] *Ian Ol'brakht* [. . .] *Uladzislau III Varnenchyk* [. . .] *Uladzislau II Iahelonchyk* [. . .] *Liudovik II* [. . .]'. Thus, the Lithuanian dukes are listed first in chronological order, then the Jagiellonians who ruled in Poland only, and then the Jagiellonian kings of the Czech and Hungarian lands. Moreover, the Lithuanian dukes are all given their own entries, whereas Jan Olbracht, Ladislaus II and Louis Jagiellon are not. This suggests that the limited and localised historiographical focus on the dynasty in the encyclopaedia was Belarus-centric. Meanwhile, it is also noteworthy that only male members of the dynasty are considered to have been 'significant': the only Jagiellonian queen to merit an entry is Bona Sforza, whose role in introducing land reforms was considered important for the later development of the mass resistance movement.[52]

The post-Soviet years: the Jagiellonians Belarusianised

During the Perestroika period and in the aftermath of the collapse of the USSR, censorship was lifted and it became possible to publish very different interpretations of the history of Belarus. New, revisionist histories emerged that challenged the stereotypes of Soviet mythmaking, whilst many previously banned or obscured works were reprinted or published for the first time (e.g. Lastouski, Ihnatouski, Dounar-Zapol'ski, Naidziuk).[53] The early 1990s are commonly referred to as a period of 'national revival' (*natsyianal'nae adradzhenne*) in Belarus, and it was indeed the case that a re-discovery of pre-Soviet nationalist interpretations was a dominant phenomenon in historiography. Thus, regarding the Jagiellonians, the overall patterns of scholarship remained initially similar to those of the early twentieth century: the Jagiellonians were not a primary concern, although some tentative nationalisation of individual deeds or language use was possible.

Kastus' Tarasau's (1940–2010) book 'Memory about Legends' (*Pamiats' pra lehendy*, 1990), a collection of popular history essays, sets the trend for the mythologisation of Belarusian history with an explicit aim of reclaiming 'lost' memories.[54] Two of the three essays that approximately cover the Jagiellonian period of the Grand Duchy of Lithuania are devoted to sentimental ideas about the military glory of the Belarusian nation at battles, including Kulikovo (1380) and Grunwald (1410), in which Lithuanian forces led by Jogaila were involved. Tarasau provides narrative histories in broad brushstrokes, emphasising the Belarusian character of Jogaila's army by stating that 'with the exception of three or four fully Lithuanian *chorągwie*[55] (units), his army was composed of residents of eastern Belarus'.[56] Jogaila's role as a military leader is also downplayed at the expense of the collective will of the Belarusian soldiers: the decision not to join the Tatar forces at Kulikovo is attributed to 'the people whom [*Iahaila*] led, his *chorągwie*, his army. The only factor that forced him not to join the battle was the mood of the Belarusian units, that is, the majority of the army.'[57] A third chapter details events from the reigns of Casimir, Alexander and Sigismund I, but again the focus is on celebrating Belarus's military achievements and literary flourishing rather than examining the history of Jagiellonian rule.

Whilst Tarasau's book is an avowedly non-historical and even pseudo-literary work, its overall traits are also shared by state-sponsored academic publications of the early post-Soviet period, such as the collectively authored 'Sketches of the History of Belarus' (*Narysy history Belarusi*, 1994).[58] The introduction declares that the study's aim is a better understanding of the 'ethnogenesis (origins) of the Belarusians' and the 'development of the Belarusian ethnos, the formation of the Belarusian people and nation'.[59] This narrow ethno-national methodology conditions the study's almost total lack of attention to the rulers of the Grand Duchy of Lithuania, whilst the conception of the state itself renders Belarus a centre of all Eastern Slavdom: 'the strength of the Slavic origins of the Grand Duchy (9/10 of its territory and 8/10 of the population) pre-determined its Belarusian character and its "proto-Ruthenian" trajectory'.[60] Meanwhile, the 'Belarusian nation' is described as the 'hero' of historical events such as the Battle of Grunwald.[61] In contrast, a rare mention of a Jagiellonian renders Jogaila an unambiguous villain: '1387, when *Iahaila* became *Uladzislau* by converting to Catholicism, can be considered the year in which the social and legal status of the Belarusian lands changed within the Grand Duchy [. . .] [The privileges of the Union of Kreva] did not extend to the Orthodox feudals who drew their genealogies from the Belarusian, Ukrainian and Russian lands.'[62]

After 1994, the year in which the russophone, eastward-leaning populist Aliaksandr Lukashenka came to power as the first (and to this day only) president of Belarus, Belarusian nationhood became a contested and politicised field. Several scholars have argued that Belarus is unique among post-Soviet states in that a neo-Soviet narrative of nationhood remains a potent political force alongside a revisionist Belarusian nationalism. According to this view, contemporary Belarusian nationhood is split between eastward- and westward-facing, or Eurasian and European, discourses.[63] The Russo-centric narrative propounded by the Lukashenka regime holds that Belarusians were oppressed by the Poles and Lithuanians (conceived in ethnolinguistic terms) throughout pre-modern history, until the Russian Empire intervened by annexing a portion of the Commonwealth. In this account, the process of Belarusian self-realisation began in harmonious union with Russia, and truly flourished in the Soviet period, during which Belarus developed its own political and cultural institutions. Meanwhile, a broad swathe of opposition activists and cultural figures conceive of Belarus as part of pan-European civilisation; they claim that Belarus is an heir of the Grand Duchy of Lithuania and Polish-Lithuanian Commonwealth. Insisting on a civilisational border that separates Belarus from Russia, this narrative advances the argument that liberal values such as democracy and tolerance have always come naturally to Belarusians.

Following the theory of split Belarusian nationhood, we may expect that a clear division exists between the state's neo-Soviet downplaying of the significance of the Jagiellonian era and the nationalist opposition's heralding of the Lithuanian heritage, including that of the Jagiellonians. Indeed, in a number of cases, this polarisation seems to hold. A 1998 history approved by the Ministry of Education as a school textbook engages in a selective and one-sided polemic against the nationalist conception of history, while also reinforcing Soviet-style ideological notions of East Slavic unity: 'the Grand Duchy of Lithuania was a polyethnic state of four main nations – Belarusian, Ukrainian, Russian and Lithuanian'.[64] In this work, the period of Jagiellonian rule is considered a time in which 'the situation gradually began to change in a way that did not favour the Belarusian and other Western Russian principalities'.[65] An authoritative 2009 book on the 'Foundations of Belarusian State Ideology', which features a chapter on figures of historical importance for modern Belarus, does not mention a single member of the Jagiellonian dynasty.[66] In contrast, a collection of essays with an explicit aim of celebrating Belarus's role in the Polish-Lithuanian Commonwealth claims that the rule of Casimir Jagiellon (*Kazimir Iahailavich*) was the originator of a 'tradition of Belarusian parliamentarism' – clearly a statement with politically loaded implications of opposition to dictatorial rule.[67]

More generally, however, interpreting Belarusian memory discourse through the prism of the Jagiellonians complicates the picture. A notable trend, especially in the second post-Soviet decade and beyond, is an increasing willingness to explore the (Belarusian) history of Jagiellonian rule. In this common endeavour, which seems to occupy an ideological middle ground, boundaries between 'state' and 'opposition' are hard to draw; moreover, in a number of cases, the state appears to be explicitly posing as a promoter of Belarusian memory of the Jagiellonians.

The emergence of a specific interest in the Jagiellonians can be established from as early as 1992; the first post-Soviet treatment of Jagiellonian history is also the most bizarre. Leu Kazlou's (1938–) 'With the Permission of the King and Grand Duke' (*Z dazvolu karalia i vialikaha kniazia*, 1992) is a collection of stories about early modern rulers including Jogaila and his heirs.[68] It employs a literary and almost colloquial narrative style and contains comic-like sketched illustrations. Kazlou's anecdotes quote from historical sources, although citations are absent so it is difficult to establish the extent to which his translation into modern Belarusian is faithful to the original. The blurb on the book's inside cover promises 'improbable events', and the narrative tends to focus on corporeal aspects of the lives of the Jagiellonians. For example, Jogaila and Jadwiga's (Hedwig's) marriage is said to have been marred by the wife's suspicion that the Lithuanian Grand Duke lacked a key body part, and Sigismund Augustus's lack of children is attributed to his 'bad luck with wives'.[69] The author's preoccupation with the rulers' fertility does, however, result in a clear appreciation of the dynastic quality of the Jagiellonian era. For instance, Jogaila's marriage to Sophia of Halshany, a 'young and beautiful princess from our Belarusian lands', is said to have 'finally endowed [*Iahaila*] with dynastic infants'.[70]

Vitaut Charopka (1961–) is another author of popular historical biographies, whose book 'Destinies in History' (*Liosy u historyi*, 2005) features, amongst accounts of historical figures from the eleventh to the nineteenth century, several chapter-long portraits of Jagiellonians.[71] Charopka's style is literary, with liberal usage of figurative imagery and rhetorical flourish. The chapter on Jogaila, for example, begins: 'He was destiny's favourite son.' Likewise, his death is described as having been 'romantic'.[72] Moreover, whilst Charopka does not overtly appeal to the significance of his plotlines for present-day Belarusian identity, he is nonetheless prone to narrative nationalisation: for example, he explains Jogaila's superstitious habits with reference to 'Belarusian national superstition from pagan times' and calls Sophia of Halshany a 'patriot of the Fatherland' and a 'Belarusian princess'.[73] Charopka's mildly sensationalist focus is on the 'destinies' of individuals, although he does also describe the dynastic reach of the 'house of *Iahaila* [*rod Iahailavichau*]', which 'became famous. The sons of *Kazimir* occupied the Polish, Czech and Hungarian thrones, the Grand Ducal throne of Lithuania and Ruthenia, and his daughters intermarried with European rulers.'[74]

The Jagiellonian dynasty, and especially Sophia of Halshany, have also been the subject of a nationalising gaze from 'official' scholars and state bureaucrats, especially in 2005 and 2006 around the 600th anniversary of Sophia's birth (c.1405). In March 2006, the monthly journal published by the Belarusian presidential administration, *Belaruskaia Dumka* ('Belarusian Thought'), featured an article that celebrated the memory of historically important women, with a special focus on Jogaila's fourth wife. The authors place Jogaila and Sophia on an equal footing as the joint 'founders of the famous European grand-ducal and royal dynasty of the Jagiellonians', and briefly describe Sophia's continued influence on matters of state after Jogaila's death and the coronation of her son Casimir: 'for her son the queen-mother remained an advisor in important questions of domestic and international policy'.[75] Sophia is also said to have been 'a great patriot for her small motherland – Belarus'. Moreover, she 'brought up her grandchildren to love their motherland, Belarus'.[76] The incorporation of Sophia of Halshany into the canon of official memory is affirmed by the president himself: Lukashenka is quoted as saying 'the name of the Belarusian princess *Sof'ia*, who became the queen of Poland, entered the chronicle of Slavdom for all time. We have no right to forget the heritage of those who laid the foundations for the high spirituality and culture of our people.'[77] In line with this sentiment, the article reports that monuments to Sophia were unveiled in Drutsk and Halshany in 2005 to mark her sixth centenary. The one in Halshany bears the inscription 'To Sophia of Halshany, a daughter of the Belarusian land, the primogenitor of the Jagiellonian dynasty' – eliding Jogaila himself from the origins of the dynasty that bears his name. Furthermore, the National Bank of Belarus issued a commemorative coin in 2006 to celebrate Sophia, symbolically merging the image of Sophia and the crests of the historical houses of Halshany and Drutsk with the official iconography of the Republic of Belarus.

FIGURE 7.1 Monument to Sophia of Halshany. Photo by Radio Free Europe/Radio Liberty

In September 2006, a conference devoted to the Jagiellonians was held in Halshany and Navahrudak, the results of which are presented in an edited volume.[78] The conference began with a series of addresses by politicians and civil servants, who each propounded the official narrative about Sophia of Halshany being the 'founder of the mighty dynasty of the Jagiellonians'[79] and 'a daughter of the Belarusian people'.[80] Academic papers were presented by Belarusian, Polish, Russian and Ukrainian historians. The Belarusian contributions vary significantly in topic, from local history (e.g. the implementation of Magdeburg Law in the town of Baruny) to economic history (e.g. the agrarian reforms of Bona Sforza and Sigismund Augustus) to more politicised matters such as the language in use in the Grand Duchy of Lithuania ('the Belarusian language continued to preserve its dominant position in society')[81] and the 'myths and facts' surrounding Sophia of Halshany.

Overall, amidst the grandiloquent phrases that elevate (some of) the Jagiellonians to the status of national heroes, it is possible to glean the (re-)emergence of a scholarly historiographical literature that examines their dynastic history. A paper by A. A. Skep'ian (1974–), for example, offers a nuanced analysis of the cultural policies pursued by subsequent Jagiellonians, surveying the change of cultural orientation from Sophia of Halshany's preference for an Eastern (Orthodox) aesthetic to the increasing dominance of Hungarian and Italian influences under Bona Sforza.[82] Skep'ian avoids the revisionist striving to 'Belarusianise' Sophia of Halshany by instead referring to her 'Ruthenian spirit' ('*ruski dukh*', in inverted commas in the original),[83] and discusses various social and political factors that affected the interaction of the royal court and the artisanal guild. M. P. Kastsiuk (1940–) analyses the Jagiellonians as a dynasty within a comparative framework, noting that 'a distinct characteristic of the Jagiellonian dynasty was the fact that it had two dynastic origins – as the Grand Duke of Lithuania and as the King of Poland'.[84] He also questions the notion that Sophia of Halshany was *the* founder of the dynasty whilst also implicitly rejecting the presentist terminology of a 'Belarusian princess'.[85] Moreover, Kastsiuk's intervention rejects methodological nationalism in the study of the Jagiellonians by emphasising the transnational reach of the dynasty:

> A range of [Belarusian] publications[86] have asserted that the Jagiellonians, as the descendants of the Grand Duke of Lithuania and the King of Poland, ruled in the Grand Duchy of Lithuania from 1440. It is characteristic that in making this claim, it is not noted that the Jagiellonians also reigned in Hungary from 1440. The synchronicity of the beginnings of Jagiellonian rule in another country and our own is given insufficient weight because it must after all be the case that the dynasty established itself in the Grand Duchy of Lithuania and the Kingdom of Poland, and then began to exert its influence on other countries.[87]

Thus, a critical historiography about the Jagiellonians has appeared almost contemporaneously to the state's efforts to discursively nationalise them.

This increased attention to the dynasty is also beginning to be reflected in general histories, including those promoted by the state. Piotr Brigadin's (1949–) 'A History of Belarus in the Context of European History' (*Istoriia Belarusi v kontekste evropeiskoi istorii*, 2007), a Russian-language textbook based on a series of university lectures, contains a chapter on Belarus within the Grand Duchy of Lithuania that features reproductions of portraits of Jogaila and Sigismund Augustus, a brief analysis of the agrarian reforms of Sigismund Augustus, and translated extracts of Casimir's Statute of 1447.[88] There is also an explanatory note in one of the page margins which reads:

> The Jagiellonian dynasty ruled for two centuries in the Polish and Lithuanian states [. . .] In 1440–1444 and 1490–1526 the Jagiellonians occupied the Hungarian throne, and in 1471–1526 the Czech throne. Having intermarried with many European royal families, the Jagiellonians became one of the most influential dynasties in Europe.[89]

Whilst the basic facts that are set out here may not appear to differ greatly from the Soviet-era encyclopaedia entry cited above, the fact that such a summary is present in a widely used educational resource is a departure from previous practices.[90]

Meanwhile, Belarusian encyclopaedias have also embraced a more inclusive conception of the dynasty since the Soviet-influenced period. The entry for 'The Jagiellonians' (*Iahelony*) in the 'Encyclopaedia of the Grand Duchy of Lithuania' (*VKL: Vialikae Kniastva Litouskae. Entsklapedyia*, 2005–10) contains the names and short descriptions of not only Jagiellonian rulers, but also several spouses and children, including those who were more closely connected with Hungary or the Czech lands than with the Grand Duchy, including Anna Jagiellon (*Hanna*, 1503–47): 'the daughter of *Uladzislau II*, the last representative of the Czech-Hungarian branch'.[91] Whilst not all female members of the dynasty receive their own entries, non-ruling representatives such as Jan of Lithuania (*Ian*, 1499–1538), 'the illegitimate son of *Zhyhimont I* the Old, Bishop of Vilnius 1519–36 and of Poznań from 1536', do.[92] The very existence of a three-volume encyclopaedia dedicated to the history of the Grand Duchy of Lithuania is indicative of a turn towards a scholarly interest in this period of history. Its wide coverage of the Jagiellonians appears to confirm the increasing prominence of the dynasty in the Belarusian historical imagination.

The recent flourishing of Belarusian memory of the Jagiellonians has also extended beyond historical and pseudo-historical literature to the realm of belles-lettres and fiction. A book by Anatol' Butevich (1948–) that celebrates the history and heritage of Kreva Castle features lengthy narrative descriptions of the lives of the Jagiellonians as they unfolded within the castle walls, and devotes its entire second half to a detailed list of members of the dynasty as well as a timeline of events.[93] Butevich has also written a novel that dramatises the marriage of Jogaila and Sophia, and a 'documentary sequel' that presents the lives of their descendants through a hybrid mixture of narration and reproduction of archival materials.[94]

In addition, historical novels by Vol'ha Ipatava and Aleh Rukal' feature members of the dynasty as protagonists: the former recounts the conflict between Vytautas and Jogaila, while the latter depicts the Livonian Wars that affected the reign of Sigismund Augustus.[95] Fictional works by Raisa Baravikova and Ales' Pashkevich intertwine narratives in the Jagiellonian past and the post-Soviet present.[96] Finally, the prominence of Sophia of Halshany in Belarusian narratives is once again confirmed by a Russian-language musical entitled *Sof'ia Gol'shanskaia* ('Sophia of Halshany'), which was premiered in Minsk in June 2013.[97]

Thus, the growth in interest in the Jagiellonians crosses political divides and has begun to filter into a range of genres. This can be attributed to an unabating post-Soviet striving for Belarus to have its 'own' history, or read as a 'natural' process of recognition that the Jagiellonians were an important force in the history of the land. In either case, it appears reasonable to predict that the attention paid to the dynasty will continue to increase.

Conclusion

The Jagiellonians have had at best a chequered relationship with Belarusian national memory. Their legacy has often fallen foul of the grand narratives of Belarusian identity (e.g. in the writings of Lastouski and Stankevich, in the Soviet era and the early post-Soviet years), and in cases where they were looked upon more favourably by historians and intellectuals (e.g. Ihnatouski, Naidziuk), they have usually been appraised for acts that are scarcely elucidated by writers and that supposedly demonstrated the rulers' adherence to 'Belarusian' culture. Indeed, the dynasty has rarely been an object of actual historical analysis, with Picheta in the 1920s being until very recently the main example of a historian who chose to study the Jagiellonians on their own terms rather than incorporate them into the writer's own ideological outlook. On the whole, the Belarusian historiography of the Jagiellonians tells us more about Belarusian memory politics than it does about the medieval dynasty: it demonstrates that memory has been and is hotly contested in this country, and that the representation of the past depends greatly on the intellectual climate of the present.

Notes

1 The film is available with an English translation at: http://budzma.org/uncategorized/budzma-belarusans.html, accessed 19.1.17.
2 T. Kamusella, *The Politics of Language and Nationalism in Modern Central Europe*, Basingstoke, 2009, pp. 346–430; see also T. Snyder, *The Reconstruction of Nations. Poland, Ukraine, Lithuania, Belarus, 1569–1999*, New Haven and London, 2003.
3 Snyder, *The Reconstruction of Nations*, p. 47.
4 V. Lastouski, *Karotkaia historyia Belarusi*, Vil'nia, 1910; repr. Minsk, 1992; B. Tarashkevich, *Belaruskaia hramatyka dlia shkol*, Vil'nia, 1918.
5 V. Lastouski, *Shto treba vedats' kazhnamu belarusu?*, Mensk, 1918; repr. Berlin, 1944, p. 12.
6 Lastouski, *Karotkaia*, p. 5.

7 Lastouski was active as a member of the Council of the Belarusian People's Republic (*Belaruskaia Narodnaia Respublika*) that declared Belarusian independence in March 1918. However, the new state failed to gain international recognition, and the council was forced into exile in 1919. In 1921, as a result of the Treaty of Riga, the territory of Belarus was divided between the Polish Republic and the pro-Moscow Socialist Soviet Republic of Belarus. For a detailed history, see P. A. Rudling, *The Rise and Fall of Belarusian Nationalism, 1906–1931*, Pittsburgh, 2015.
8 Lastouski, *Karotkaia*, p. 31.
9 Belarusianised spellings of names vary significantly between authors, especially in this early period. Therefore, quotations give transliterations of the spelling used by the specific author under discussion, in italics.
10 Lastouski, *Karotkaia*, p. 25.
11 Lastouski, *Karotkaia*, p. 27.
12 Lastouski, *Karotkaia*, p. 30.
13 Lastouski, *Karotkaia*, p. 30.
14 Lastouski, *Karotkaia*, p. 33.
15 Lastouski, *Karotkaia*, p. 34.
16 Lastouski, *Karotkaia*, p. 46.
17 U. Ihnatouski, *Karotki narys historyi Belarusi. Lektsyi, chytanyia nastaunikam pachatkovykh shkol Menshchyny*, Mensk, 1919.
18 Ihnatouski, *Karotki*, p. 60.
19 Ihnatouski, *Karotki*, p. 61.
20 Ihnatouski, *Karotki*, p. 62.
21 Ihnatouski, *Karotki*, p. 62.
22 Ihnatouski, *Karotki*, p. 66.
23 Ihnatouski, *Karotki*, p. 69.
24 A. Stankevich, *Vitaut Vialiki i Belarusy (referat, chytany na urachystai akademii u Vil'ni u sali 'Apollo' 27.X. 1930h., u dzen' 500-lets'tsia s'mertsi Vitauta, Vialik. Kniazia Litouska-Belaruskaha*, Vil'nia, 1930, p. 15.
25 A. Stankevich, 'Raskazy z historyi Belarusi dlia shkolau i narodu', reprinted in A. Stankevich, *Z boham da Belarusi*, Vil'nia, 2008, pp. 63–72 (p. 63).
26 Stankevich, 'Raskazy z historyi Belarusi dlia shkolau i narodu', p. 70.
27 I. Naidziuk (and I. Kasiak), *Belarus' uchora i sian'nia. Papuliarny narys z historyi Belarusi*, original publication details unknown, 1943; repr. Mensk, 1993. N.B. the first edition of the work was authored by Naidziuk alone, and the reprinted edition was edited and revised by Ivan Kasiak.
28 Naidziuk, *Belarus' uchora i sian'nia*, p. 60
29 Naidziuk, *Belarus' uchora i sian'nia*, pp. 44, 46.
30 Naidziuk, *Belarus' uchora i sian'nia*, p. 47.
31 Naidziuk, *Belarus' uchora i sian'nia*, p. 47.
32 Naidziuk, *Belarus' uchora i sian'nia*, p. 48.
33 Another nationalist historian who treats the Grand Duchy of Lithuania in the Jagiellonian period as 'Belarusian' is Mikola Shkialionak, who was also active in the 1930s in Wilno. See his *Belarus' i susedzi. Histarychnyia narysy*, Belastok, 2003.
34 For parallel debates in Lithuanian tradition, see Mickūnaitė, above, pp. 30–32.
35 M. Dovnar-Zapol'skii, *Gosudarstvennoe khoziaistvo Velikogo Kniazhestva Litovskogo pri Iagellonakh, T. 1*, Kiev, 1901.
36 His 'History of Belarus', completed in 1924 but never published in the USSR, similarly contains no treatment of the Jagiellonians. M. Dounar-Zapol'ski, *Historyia Belarusi*, Minsk, 1994.
37 The more widely available second, Soviet edition is cited here: V. I. Picheta, *Agrarnaia reforma Sigizmunda Avgusta v Litovsko-Russkom gosudarstve*, 2nd edn, Moskva, 1958.
38 V. I. Picheta, *Istoriia litovskogo gosudarstva do Liublinskoi unii*, Vil'no, 1921.
39 Picheta, *Agrarnaia*, pp. 542–3.
40 Picheta, *Istoriia*, p. 73.

41 On *korenizatsia* as nation-building in Belarus, see N. Bekus, 'Nationalism and Socialism: "Phase D" in the Belarusian Nation-Building', *Nationalities Papers* 38, 2010, pp. 829–46; Rudling, *The Rise and Fall of Belarusian Nationalism*, pp. 123–63.
42 Rudling, *The Rise and Fall of Belarusian Nationalism*, p. 132.
43 U. Picheta, *Historyia Belarusi, chastka pershaia*, Moskva and Leningrad, 1924. He also continued to publish articles that expanded on his previous work concerning agrarian reform under Zygmunt Augustus. These originally appeared in Minsk-based journals between 1921 and 1927, especially *Trudy Belorusskogo gosudarstvennogo universiteta* ('Works of the Belarusian State University'), and are collected in U. Picheta, *Belorussiia i Litva XV – XVI vv. (issledovaniia po istorii sotsial'no ekonomicheskogo, politicheskogo i kul'turnogo razvitiia)*, Moskva, 1961.
44 R. Lindner, *Historiker und Herrschaft. Nationsbildung und Geschichtspolitik in Weißrußland*, München, 1999, pp. 147–300.
45 Iu. N. Afanas'ev, 'Fenomen sovetskoi istoriografii', in Iu. N. Afanas'ev, ed., *Sovetskaia istoriografiia*, Moskva, 1996, pp. 7–41 (pp. 21, 35).
46 Lindner, *Historiker und Herrschaft*, pp. 377–9.
47 Z. Iu. Kopysskii and M. F. Zaloga, eds, *Belorussiia v epokhu feodalizma. Sbornik dokumentov i materialov*, 4 vols, Minsk, 1959–79, I, *Tom pervyi: S drevneishikh vremen do serediny XVII veka*, 1959, p. 15.
48 Kopysskii and Zaloga, *Belorussiia v epokhu feodalizma*, p. 16.
49 L. S. Abetsedarskii, ed., *Istoriia belorusskoi SSR v dvukh tomakh*, 2 vols, 2nd edn, Minsk, 1961. A larger (five-volume) Belarusian-language history was published the following decade, with many of the same editors. It contains minimal conceptual alterations. On the centuries of Jagiellonian rule, see I. M. Ihnatsenka et al., eds, *Historyia Belaruskai SSR u piatsi tamakh*, 5 vols, Minsk, 1972–75, I, *Tom I: Pershabytnaabshchynny lad na terytoryi Belarusi. Epokha feadalizmu*, 1972, pp. 143–292.
50 Abetsedarskii, *Istoriia*, I, 70.
51 P. Brouka et al., eds, *Belaruskaia Savetskaia Entsyklapedyia*, 12 vols, Minsk, 1969–75, XI, 1974, p. 522.
52 Bona Sforza also features in some of the works of the major Soviet-era Belarusian novelist Uladzimir Karatkevich (1930–84). Karatkevich, the pioneer of Belarusian-language historical fiction, wrote about the pre-Soviet past in a manner that plainly contrasted with the official version of history. His work can thus be seen as a precursor to the post-Soviet revival of memory about the Jagiellonians.
53 Most of the sources cited in the first part of this essay were printed in the early 1990s.
54 K. Tarasau, *Pamiats' pra lehendy. Postatsi belaruskai minuushchyny*, Minsk, 1990.
55 A medieval Polish military unit. The Belarusian text has *kharuhvy*, a loan word which the author explains to readers using a parenthesis.
56 Tarasau, *Pamiats' pra lehendy*, p. 65.
57 Tarasau, *Pamiats' pra lehendy*, p. 71. For 1410 as a victory of the people (not the Jagiellonians) in twentieth-century Poland, see Nowakowska, above, p. 59.
58 Kastsiuk et al., *Narysy historyi Belarusi: u 2-kh*, 2 vols, I, Minsk, 1994.
59 Kastsiuk et al., *Narysy historyi Belarusi*, pp. 3–4.
60 Kastsiuk et al., *Narysy historyi Belarusi*, p. 120.
61 Kastsiuk et al., *Narysy historyi Belarusi*, p. 118.
62 Kastsiuk et al., *Narysy historyi Belarusi*, pp. 121–2.
63 D. R. Marples, *Belarus: A Denationalized Nation*, London and New York, 1999; N. Leshchenko, 'A Fine Instrument: Two Nation-Building Strategies in Post-Soviet Belarus', *Nations and Nationalism* 10, 2004, pp. 333–52 (p. 333); N. Bekus, *Struggle over Identity. The Official and the Alternative 'Belarusianness'*, Budapest and New York, 2010; A. Goujon, 'Memorial Narratives of WWII Partisans and Genocide in Belarus', *East European Politics and Societies* 24, 2010, pp. 6–25.
64 Ia. K. Novik and G. S. Martsul', eds, *Historyia Belarusi: u dvukh chastkakh*, 2 vols, Minsk, 1998, I, *Chastka 1: Ad starachytnykh chasou – pa liuty 1917*, p. 110.
65 Novik and Martsul', *Historyia Belarusi*, I, p. 102.
66 V. A. Mel'nik, *Osnovy ideologii belorusskogo gosudarstva*, Minsk, 2009.

67 H. Sahanovich, 'Contra tyranos', in A. Dziarnovich, ed., *Naiias'neishaia Rech Paspalitaia. Tsyvilizatsyia – Kul'tura – Relihiia – Palityka – Avantura – Heroika – Uspamin*, Mensk, 2007, pp. 17–23 (p. 17).
68 L. R. Kazlou, *Z dazvolu karalia i vialikaha kniazia*, Minsk, 1992, repr. Minsk, 1998. The 1998 edition is cited here.
69 Kazlou, *Z dazvolu karalia*, pp. 10–11, 27.
70 Kazlou, *Z dazvolu karalia*, p. 13.
71 V. Charopka, *Liosy u historyi*, Minsk, 2005, pp. 49–65, 74–8, 79–86, 87–98, 99–107 respectively.
72 Charopka, *Liosy u historyi*, pp. 49, 65.
73 Charopka, *Liosy u historyi*, pp. 55, 77, 78.
74 Charopka, *Liosy u historyi*, p. 78.
75 G. Lian'kevich and L. Soboleva, 'Podarivshie Evrope korolei', *Belaruskaia Dumka* 3, 2006, pp. 130–3 (p. 132).
76 Lian'kevich and Soboleva, 'Podarivshie Evrope korolei', p. 132.
77 Lian'kevich and Soboleva, 'Podarivshie Evrope korolei', p. 133.
78 A. A. Kavalenia et al., eds, *Iahelony: dynastyia, epokha, spadchyna: materyialy Mizhnarodnai navukova-praktychnai kanferentsyi, Hal'shany-Navahrudak, 8–10 verasnia 2006h.*, Minsk, 2007.
79 Kavalenia et al., *Iahelony*, p. 7. Similar phrases can be found on pp. 13, 22, 23, 27 and 172.
80 Kavalenia et al., *Iahelony*, p. 7.
81 Kavalenia et al., *Iahelony*, p. 122.
82 Kavalenia et al., *Iahelony*, pp. 183–95.
83 Kavalenia et al., *Iahelony*, p. 184.
84 Kavalenia et al., *Iahelony*, p. 233.
85 Kavalenia et al., *Iahelony*.
86 Kastsiuk does not provide any references to illustrate his claims about existing literature.
87 Kavalenia et al., *Iahelony*, p. 234.
88 P. I. Brigadin, *Istoriia Belarusi v kontekste evropeiskoi istorii*, Minsk, 2007, pp. 59–62, 70–1.
89 Brigadin, *Istoriia Belarusi*, p. 55.
90 For another example of a similar source that briefly describes the Jagiellonians, see V. I. Golubovich and Iu. N. Bokhan, eds, *Istoriia Belarusi v kontekste mirovykh tsivilizatsii. Uchebno-metodicheskoe posobie*, Minsk, 2011, pp. 67–79.
91 H. P. Pashkou et al., eds, *VKL: Vialikae Kniastva Litouskae. Entsyklapedyia*, 3 vols, Minsk, 2005–10, vol. 2, 2007, p. 776.
92 Pashkou et al., *VKL*, vol. 2, p. 780.
93 A. Butevich, *Raskidanoe hniazdo kryvitskai slavy: Nezvychainaia vandrouka pa Kreuskikh murakh*, Minsk, 2008.
94 A. Butevich, *Karaleva ne zdradzhvala karaliu, abo Karaleuskae shliubavanne u Novaharodku: zaimal'ny apoved pra kakhanne 17-hadovai belaruskai kniazeuny Sof'i Halshanskai i 70-hadovaha karalia pol'skaha Iahaily: raman*, Minsk, 2010; A. Butevich, *Pamizh Kniastvam i Karonai. Ad Kreva da Krakava: dakumental'ny pratsiah ramana 'Karaleva ne zdradzhvala karaliu'*, Minsk, 2013.
95 V. Ipatava, *Znak Vialikaha mahistra*, Minsk, 2009; A. Rukal', *Na sluzhbe kniazia Radzivila*, Minsk, 2010.
96 R. Baravikova, 'Kazimir – syn Iahaily + Nastsia z 8 "B"', in A. Badak, R. Baravikova and A. Navarych, *Adzinoki vas'miklasnik khocha paznaiomitstsa*, Minsk, 2008, pp. 35–86. A. Pashkevich, *Sim pobedishi*, Minsk, 2012.
97 A. Korsak, 'Zvezdy operetty predstavili miuzikl "Sof'ia Gol'shanskaia"', *Naviny.by*, 9 June 2013, http://naviny.by/rubrics/culture/2013/06/09/ic_media_video_117_7819/, accessed 3.12.14.

8

THE JAGIELLONIANS IN UKRAINIAN TRADITIONS

Tetiana Hoshko

The paradigm of every 'national history' is based on the romantic idea of a nation's uniqueness and cultural self-sufficiency. This pattern is typified by Ukrainian 'national history', which is seen most clearly in the historical scheme of Mykhailo Hrushevsky (1866–1934).[1] There the living space of the Ukrainians was imagined as a definite whole where '[t]he two major creative forces in the life of every people, nationality and territory, combined'.[2] Thus, everything non-Ukrainian that appeared in the nation's space was associated with an aggressor who desired to seize 'our' land, subordinate 'our' faith, 'our' people, etc.[3] It is clear that with such an approach to the dichotomy of 'ours' versus 'alien', Poland and the Poles always played the role of the alien.[4]

In the fourteenth century, the southern and western lands of the former Kyivan Rus', including the territories of future Ukraine, were integrated into the Kingdom of Poland and the Grand Duchy of Lithuania (GDL). The Galicia-Volhynia Principality was split in two, with Galicia going to Poland and Volhynia to the GDL. In the middle of the century, the Rusian lands along the Dnipro River, including the Kyiv land, fell under the rule of the Grand Duke of Lithuania, Algirdas (Olgerd, d.1377), son of Gediminas. At the same time, Lithuanian princes captured Podolia. From this moment to the Union of Lublin (1569), the lands of future Ukraine were divided between the two states – the Kingdom of Poland and the Grand Duchy of Lithuania. In March 1569, during the Lublin Sejm negotiation of the real, legal, previously personal, union between the two states, King Sigismund Augustus issued a decree according to which the Podlachia and Volhynia Palatinates were to be included in the Polish Crown. In May, the king issued a similar decree concerning the Kyiv and Bratslav Palatinates. After the signing of the Union of Lublin, these territories belonged to the new union state – the Commonwealth. Thus, from the very beginning and until the end of the Jagiellonian dynasty the Ruthenian/Ukrainian lands were a part of its possessions.[5]

In the paradigm of Ukrainian national historiography, which tried to establish the idea of the nation-state, the Polish state was clearly alien. Therefore, according to Hrushevsky, in describing the 'stateless' period of Ukrainian history

> the main weight must be moved from the history of the state to the history of the people and society. The political, state life is, of course, an important factor, but next to it there are other factors – economic, cultural, with sometimes less, sometimes more significance than the political, but in any case they should not remain in the shadow outside of it.[6]

It is clear that under such conditions the Jagiellonians were not, and are not, among the priorities of Ukrainian scholars. Not a single work, or even a short article, exists where the main subject is a particular member of the Jagiellonian dynasty. Ukrainians never saw the Jagiellonians as their own dynasty. Moreover, historically lacking their own state, Ukrainians needed to legitimise the idea of such a state, to construct a consolidating nation-building myth. The Jagiellonians could not be a core of this myth, because their dynastic history did not coincide with the history of the Ukrainian state. They personified a state which was not perceived by Ukrainians as their own and against which the blade of the Cossack uprisings was directed.

The eighteenth-century Partitions of the Polish-Lithuanian Commonwealth had placed the far west of the Ukrainian lands under Austro-Hungarian rule, as the province of Galicia, but most became part of imperial Russia. It was Polish historians in the late nineteenth and early twentieth century who largely contributed to the rejection of the 'Jagiellonian myth' by Ukrainian historiography. At that time, the Poles were deprived of their own state and were searching for their own state-building myth. As Oksana Ruda writes, the Poles, like other European nations, attempted to 'cleanse' their glorious past of all shortcomings, because in it:

> the unrealised ideals of the contemporary epoch would be embodied. For the Polish people, it meant rebuilding a multinational Commonwealth within its alleged historical borders, the resolution of the Polish-Lithuanian and Polish-Ukrainian conflicts through the memory of a glorious coexistence in one state (the 'Jagiellonian idea'), and the exaltation of the Polish nation as a bearer of Western civilisation and culture. These myths led to the formation of such a Polish historical consciousness, which perceived the Ukrainians as a less culturally and socially developed nation. Basing themselves on these myths, turn of the century Polish historians and politicians insisted on the inclusion of ethnic Ukrainian lands in the future Polish Commonwealth.[7]

Accordingly, the 'Jagiellonian idea' became synonymous with a state alien to Ukrainians and with their enslaved status within it. This essay will first set out the broad frameworks within which historians of Ukraine have viewed the Jagiellonians, before examining a number of key themes in this historiography more closely.

Frameworks: Poland and Lithuania in the Ukrainian historical narrative

Poland and the Poles became enemy number one in the Ukrainian nation-building narrative.[8] The stereotype of the 'centuries-old struggle of Rus' against Poland' – the 'main enemy' of Ukrainian independence and the carrier of 'hostile Western values and Catholicism' – was entrenched in the minds of Ukrainian patriots by the first national historical works.[9] Perhaps the biggest contribution was made by Hrushevsky (active in Austrian-ruled Galicia, revolutionary Russia, in exile, and finally in the USSR) who in his foundational multi-volume *History of Ukraine-Rus'* (1898–1936) first traced the history of the Ukrainian people in a manner uninterrupted spatially or temporally, proving the continuity of national existence. His work was 'a classic example of how academic activity became the basis of the formation of a national ideology'.[10] During his lifetime, and for many years after his death, Hrushevky's concepts were canon for Ukrainian historiography. At the very beginning of the *History of Ukraine-Rus'*, Hrushevsky noted that 'from the middle of the fourteenth century onward, the Ukrainian people became part of other states, at times constituting a passive subject of foreign rule and of foreign law formed on foreign foundations',[11] so that national death and complete economic ruin threatened the Ukrainian people.[12] In Hrushevsky's opinion, this was a period of 'enslaving the Ukrainian people to the Polish nationality, not only in the cultural or political sphere but also in the social and political one, turning the Ukrainian population into a subservient, subject, exploited nationality'.[13]

The anti-Polish sentiments in Hrushevsky's works are often mixed with anti-Western passages. The historian rejected Western innovations, beginning with the 'cultural changes in Galician Rus'' in the fourteenth century, which he called the 'fatal break', and ending with the German law in the Ruthenian towns, in which he saw the reason for their decline, because the German law replaced 'old local relations', turning true self-government into a 'miserable parody of self-government'.[14] According to Natalia Yakovenko, such anti-Polish and associated anti-Western views of Hrushevsky indicate the impact of the 'Slavophile sentiments of the Russian historiography' on Hrushevsky,[15] because 'liberals and conservatives, Slavophiles and Ukrainophiles united on a common Polonophobic platform' in contemporary Russian society.[16] At the turn of the nineteenth century, the formation of the Ukrainian grand narrative was based upon the Russian historical narrative,[17] borrowing the key approaches of the latter, including the othering of Poland and the Poles. Thus, the image of an external enemy became one of the components of the national myth.[18] Moreover, according to Yakovenko, these concepts 'can be considered "fully formed" and even stable and virtually unmodified since at least the late nineteenth century'.[19]

Yakovenko links Hrushevsky's favouring of the Grand Duchy of Lithuania (GDL) over the Polish kingdom with his Slavophile sentiments. When Ukrainian historians do write about Jagiellonians, they mention[20] them as the grand dukes of Lithuania, rather than as Polish kings, because Hrushevsky had given the GDL the status of an almost proto-Ukrainian state, 'more Ruthenian than Lithuanian'.[21] In his monograph *Unmaking Imperial Russia*, Serhii Plokhy analysed in detail Hrushevsky's programmatic reasons for his different assessments of the 'Lithuanian' and 'Polish' pages of Ukrainian history.[22] These differences became 'canonical' in Ukrainian national historiography. Passages about the 'Ruthenianness' of the GDL (language, religion, culture, law, etc.) have been reproduced from textbook to textbook. However, Hrushevsky argued that 'if the Grand Duchy of Lithuania can (and should) be regarded as to some extent a Slavonic state, the successor of the Kyivan state, in any case, it was not Ukrainian, but Belarusian first of all, and its history in whole, as well as the history of the Grand Duchy of Moscow, cannot be included into the Ukrainian history'.[23]

For Hrushevsky, as well as for many later Ukrainian historians, the period from the middle of the fourteenth to the end of the sixteenth century was merely a 'transitional time'. According to Hrushevsky's disciple Ivan Krypiakevych[24] (1886–1967), the epoch lasting from the 1540s to the 1640s 'was not a time of breaking events, but a time of humdrum, daily work'; however, that very epoch 'laid the foundation for the national culture and made possible the development of the national revolution'.[25] And precisely this 'national revolution' (the Khmelnytsky Uprising against/within the Polish-Lithuanian Commonwealth, 1648–57) was valuable for constructing the narrative that affirmed Ukrainian national distinctiveness. This explains the fact that the 'Lithuanian-Polish period' long remained underexplored in national Ukrainian historiography. As the Russian Empire gave way to the Soviet Union, Ukrainian historiography within the USSR from 1919 was even less interested in this piece of history. The Lithuanian-Polish epoch was treated by the Ukrainian Soviet historians as the 'dark ages', an interim period of history and of no interest.[26]

In the post-World War II years, the study of the late medieval and early modern era gradually became marginalised. For example, the main professional periodical *Ukrainian Historical Journal* covered the Lithuanian-Polish period in 20 per cent of all publications between 1957 and 1966, whilst from 1967 to 1987 the proportion fell to 11 per cent. This is unsurprising, as in the late medieval and early modern period the Ukrainian lands had lost their connection with the territories that later became Russia, and it was thus difficult to represent the 'friendship of peoples' and the 'desire for reunification' that were the cornerstones of Soviet Ukrainian historiography. The Polish historian Tomasz Stryjek was generally right in calling the Soviet scheme of Ukraine's history merely a 'regional' version of Russian-Soviet history that combined ethnic and class visions of the historical process and thus contributed to the formation of the 'national consciousness of the Ukrainians in its Soviet version'.[27] In this context, the representation of the Lithuanian-Polish era in Kost' Huslysty's 1939 historical synthesis was quite typical. He wrote that the Grand Duchy of Lithuania's domination over Ukraine was not as severe as that of the medieval Golden Horde, but that with the 1569 Union of Lublin 'there arises a new large multinational state – the Polish-Lithuanian Commonwealth, in which the oppression of the Ukrainian nationality was especially heavy'.[28] Such were the guidelines for scholars during almost the entire Soviet era in Ukraine.

The Soviet epoch had interrupted the development of Ukrainian national historiography, but Ukrainian historians returned to this paradigm after Ukraine gained its independence in 1991. The new state now needed a historical justification for its right to exist. The old concepts of the 'populist' and 'statist' schools provided this well. Thus, on the verge of the 1980s and 1990s a process of 'remembering' the true 'national' history began. According to Andrii Blanutsa, it was precisely at that time that the revival of Lithuanian studies also began in Ukraine.[29] The term 'Polish-Lithuanian period' was also revived. However, some prominent historians actively deny this term's right to existence. Leontii Voitovych[30] offers his own periodisation of the history of Ukraine and singles out an 'appanage period' or 'epoch of appanage principalities', which began in the twelfth century and formally ended in 1492. He proposes to abandon the term 'Lithuanian-Polish era' because the period of the Ukrainian (Ruthenian) principalities' belonging to the Lithuanian-Ruthenian state was not allegedly fundamentally different from the period of their belonging to Kyivan Rus'.[31] However, most Ukrainian historians have not supported Voitovych's concepts.

Finally, it is worth mentioning that even the notion of dynasty is not sufficiently represented in Ukrainian historiography. The genealogical works of Leontii Voitovych, who emphasises the importance of studying dynastic history, are almost the only exception. The historian recognises the importance of studying not only the Rurikids' dynasty, traditionally considered 'ours', but also that of the Gediminids (including the Jagiellonians), as a dynasty that played a crucial role in the history of Ukraine and Europe in general.[32] It is very illustrative that in his synthesis of Ukrainian history, *The Gates of Europe*, the Harvard professor Serhii Plokhy devoted only a small chapter to the Lithuanian-Polish period, which lasted almost three centuries. The period functions in his work as a bridge, between the history of Rus' and the history of the Cossacks.[33]

Cossack myth versus Jagiellonian myth and Russian historical mythology

Against the Jagiellonian myth that has been elaborated and developed by Polish historiography, Ukrainian historiography has put forward a Cossack myth. Its beginnings were laid by the author(s) of the *History of the Rus'*.[34] Ever since this manuscript appeared in the early nineteenth century, the Cossack myth has become a cornerstone of modern Ukrainian historical identity. At first, describing the events of the fourteenth to sixteenth centuries, the author of the *History of the Rus'* briefly recounts the deeds of the Polish kings and grand dukes of Lithuania from Jagiełło to Sigismund I, but once 'Hetman Ruzhyns'kyi, on the permission of the King Sigismund the First, fighting self-will and disorder, [had] founded in Little Russia twenty standing Cossack regiments numbering two thousand each', the kings disappear from the pages of the book for a long time. Instead, the author lists in detail the Cossack hetmans, and considers the Cossacks' involvement in the foreign policy of the GDL and in the fight against the Tatars.

As Serhii Plokhy argues,

> the *History* [*of the Rus'*] was not a conscious manifesto of Russo-Ukrainian unity or of rising Ukrainian nationalism – the two opposing interpretations advanced by modern scholarship on the text – but an attempt on the part of the descendants of the Cossack officer elite to negotiate the best possible conditions for their incorporation into the empire.[35]

However, the fact that the *History of the Rus'*, which launched the Cossack myth, was created within the Russian imperial discourse has provoked ambivalent responses to the book. Taras Shevchenko perceived it as 'a call for freedom' and 'a call to arms in defense of the Ukrainian nation against its oppressors, the Russian tsars and nobles', while Alexander Pushkin

> regarded the author of the *History of the Rus'* as a fellow defender of the Russian Empire. For him the manuscript was not only a well-written work of history but also an indictment of Poland and the Catholic Church for their brutal rule over part of the Rus' lands in the not so distant past.[36]

Finally, Hrushevsky, who was an ardent advocate and promoter of the Cossack myth in Ukrainian historiography, 'refused to treat the Ukrainian past as part of a Russian or all-Russian historical narrative' on the conceptual level, which amounted to 'a major departure from the practice brought into modern Ukrainian historiography by the *History of the Rus'*'.[37] Interestingly, in 1991, on the eve of Ukraine's independence, when it became necessary to find historical legitimacy for the new state, Ukrainian intellectuals turned again to the *History of the Rus'*,[38] primarily because the Cossack times distinguished the history of Ukraine from the history of neighbouring countries and nations.

Thus, the genesis of the Cossacks and the formation of the Cossack social estate became the main themes for Ukrainian historiography from among the issues related to the Jagiellonians' reigns, from Jogaila to Sigismund Augustus (1370s to 1572). The largest contribution to the theme was made by Hrushevsky, who presented the most detailed analysis of the issue in the seventh volume of his *History of Ukraine-Rus'*, which included a study of the Cossack reforms carried out by the last Jagiellonians.

Kings and Cossacks

Hrushevsky concluded that sometime in the winter of 1523–24 or earlier, King and Grand Duke Sigismund I the Old had decided to organise a Cossack border corps.[39] In Hrushevsky's opinion, '[t]his was a rather bold idea: that of drawing into state service those steppe robbers whom the grand duke so recently ordered caught and condemned to death', even if this grand ducal order went unfulfilled.[40] According to Hrushevsky, in the early 1540s the grand duke's government contemplated the Cossack issue again, but 'all that was doomed to total failure'.[41] The real recruitment of the Cossacks for military service took place during the reign of King and Grand Duke Sigismund II Augustus (1548–72). Hrushevsky examined the king's Cossack reform, carried out in 1568–72, in detail.[42] He concluded that it

> was misleading and a failure when viewed in terms of its intended goals – curbing the Cossacks and establishing peace along southern borders – just as all the later reforms were. But, like subsequent ones, this reform was of great importance for the organization of the Cossacks and for their formation as a separate, semiprivileged social stratum that later gained a leading role in eastern Ukrainian affairs.[43]

In general, Hrushevsky tended to minimise the impact of the Polish kings on the early history of the Cossacks. According to him, the attempts of Sigismund the Old and the reforms of Sigismund Augustus and Stefan Batory (King and Grand Duke, 1576–85) only provided an impulse toward the transformation of the Cossacks into a new social estate, a shift which was accomplished by the Cossacks themselves. In this instance, as Serhii Plokhy noted, 'Hrushevsky remained faithful to the basic principle of his populist outlook, maintaining his belief in the creativity of popular masses in general and the Ukrainian Cossacks in particular.'[44]

Hrushevsky's estimations of the last Jagiellonians' policies on the Cossacks had a great influence on later Ukrainian historiography, which has until now repeated them with only minor variations. Borys Cherkas (2006), for example, ascribes the idea of the Cossacks' involvement in the state service to Sigismund I himself: 'Its essence was to settle several thousand Cossacks at the state expense on the islands in the Lower Dnieper . . .'[45] In another work, however, Cherkas supports Hrushevsky's opinion that all proposals concerning governmental organising of the Cossacks came one way or another from all of the Kyiv nobility.[46] Cherkas concludes that the Jagiellonians began to hire the Cossacks for military service not in the 1560s, as it was until recently accepted by historiography, but much earlier: 'Already the first mention of the Ukrainian Cossacks, dated 1489, clearly states that they were guides of Prince Jan Olbracht's troops, i.e. worked directly for the government and had the proper benefits in this from prey, if not from pay.'[47]

In his book *Ukrainian Cossacks: The Formation of a Social Estate*,[48] and the chapter 'Registered Cossacks in the State Service' in the *History of Ukrainian Cossacks*, Vitalii Shcherbak, in describing the measures of Sigismund I and Sigismund II Augustus to order the Cossacks, basically repeats Hrushevsky and comes to similar conclusions: 'Despite the small number of registered Cossacks the reform of Sigismund II Augustus in the early 1570s facilitated the organisation of Cossacks, their distinguishing from the other population strata. In fact, it started to constitute the Ukrainian Cossacks as a social estate.'[49] One can add that the

Cossacks themselves aspired to this, including *starshyna* (officers), who, as Yakovenko noted, tried to constitute their formation as the 'chivalrous (armed) population' even before the conclusion of the Union of Lublin in 1569.[50] In fact, the legitimation of the Cossacks through the creation of the Cossack register is perhaps the greatest merit of the Jagiellonians in the eyes of traditional Ukrainian historiography.

Polish-Lithuanian Unions

Besides the key topic of Cossack studies, other research areas related to the Jagiellonian era in Ukrainian history require mentioning. These are the studies of the Polish-Lithuanian Unions, of the foreign policy of the kings and great dukes, of their legislative and reform activity, granting of lands and privileges, and of their policies toward the Church.

The first Polish-Lithuanian Union, concluded in Krevo in 1385 (between Jogaila and Polish representatives), was one of the most important events in the history of Eastern Europe, and Ukrainian historians could not avoid it in their assessments. As Taras Hrynevych notes, Ukrainian scholars

> primarily considered the Union as an act of enslavement of the Ukrainian people, which interrupted the process of its state building and independent political and cultural life . . . Therefore, they often did not spare dark colours in the depiction of the process of joining of the Lithuanian-Ruthenian state to Poland . . .[51]

Hrushevsky was one of the first in Ukrainian historiography to try to interpret the implications of the Union:

> Modern historiography puts the history of purely dynastic relationship into the background and generally has a good reason for that. But sometimes purely dynastic facts so strongly interfere into the development of historical events and make such breaks in it that they themselves gain a paramount historic significance and become epochal facts. These undoubtedly include such a purely dynastic event as the marriage of the Grand Duke Yagailo of Lithuania with Queen Jadwiga (Hedwig) of Poland. Bringing with itself a union of the Grand Duchy of Lithuania with Poland, it became a starting point for the centuries' trend in the historical evolution of Eastern Europe, which still has not overcome the perturbations made by this union.[52]

For Hrushevsky, it was the 'unhappily set point' around which Poland and Lithuania then swirled for centuries. According to him, the Union was beneficial for Poland and promoted by the Polish nobility. However, Jogaila (Yagailo) also needed a union, and Hrushevsky describes his reasons in detail. Nevertheless, he doubted whether the Lithuanian princes and Jogaila himself fully understood the essence of the signed Union agreement, under which the GDL had to cease its existence as a state.[53] Let us not forget, however, that it was Jogaila and his descendants who took the greatest advantage of the results of the Union of Krevo.

Soviet historiography (1919–91) emphasised the negative consequences of the Union of Krevo for Ukraine and Belarus. For example, whilst describing the activities of the Jagiellonian dynasty founder Jogaila (Władysław II Jagiełło), Huslysty called him weak-willed, assigning him responsibility for the extremely difficult conditions in which the conclusion of the Union of Krevo placed Lithuania. Huslysty's assessment of the Union was ambivalent: it really did strengthen Poland and Lithuania, but at the same time led to the mutual alienation of Lithuania and Rus' (Belarus and Ukraine), and to the extension of Poland's expansion into Ukraine.[54]

The unification processes of the fourteenth to sixteenth centuries and the participation of the members of the Jagiellonian dynasty in them are poorly represented in Ukrainian historiography, but the same cannot be said of the Union of Lublin (1569), which concluded under the aegis of Sigismund II Augustus. Ukrainian historiography's perspectives on the Union were ambivalent and varied depending on political circumstances.[55] Notably, an interpretation of the Union of Lublin as an agreement between 'the free and the free, equal and equal' is found in the *History of the Rus'*.[56] The same interpretation was written by the members of the Brotherhood of Saints Cyril and Methodius in the *Books of the Genesis of the Ukrainian People* (1846).[57] In contrast, Hrushevsky criticised the Lublin Diet and the Union that concluded there: 'Celebrated later as an act of love, brotherhood, and sacrifice, in reality the diet was a chain of violence on others' beliefs and on others' rights committed by the pressure of state power and difficult political circumstances.'[58] This position was typical for most representatives of the 'populist' and 'statist' schools of Ukrainian historiography, who believed that the Union of Lublin had destroyed the remains of Ukrainian state traditions that had still existed in the GDL.[59] For its part, Soviet historiography emphasised both the advance of Polish lords deep into Ukraine and the increasing exploitation of the Ukrainian popular masses as results of the Union.[60]

This negative assessment of the results of the Union of Lublin long prevailed in Ukrainian and Ukrainian-Soviet historiography. Revision of this view was initiated by Yakovenko in particular, who wrote: 'One of the most striking consequences of the Union is the final turn of Ukraine's face to the West, particularly in education, the result of which was the emergence of the national school.'[61] She pointed to the pragmatism of the Ruthenian delegates at the Diet of Lublin, who not only agreed to the Union, but also actively participated in the preparation of the royal privilege.[62] Serhii Lep'iavko even argues that the position of the Ukrainian, primarily Volhynian nobility, who supported the incorporation, was crucial to the case of the Union: without their consent, Sigismund August would hardly have dared to aggravate his relationship with the Council of Lords of Lithuania. 'Despite the pressure of Poland, the choice of the Ukrainian nobility was voluntary. Unable to create their own state, they chose between two neighbours

[Poland and Muscovy] and the different models of social and political structure of the country.'[63]

The Union of Lublin single-handedly launched the creation of a separate Ukrainian identity. Yakovenko rightly wrote:

> Bridging the mutual detachment of the separate regions of Rus'-Ukraine due to the physical movement of population became one of the preconditions of separation of the conscious Ukrainian community from the Orthodox mass of the Commonwealth – the Belarusians and Ukrainians, which soon would begin to call itself an 'age-old Ruthenian people of Volodymyr's[64] root'.[65]

In fact, the Union of Lublin paved the way for the creation of early modern Ukraine, as Serhii Plokhy stressed in his new synthesis of Ukrainian history, arguing that the Orthodox princely elite gained in prestige, and their intellectual retainers began after 1569 to look back to the medieval past, in the process

> actually creating something new. Their invention would eventually become 'Ukraine', a term that appeared in the region for the first time during this sixteenth-century revival of princely power. It would take time for the name and the new space created by the Union of Lublin to become coterminous.[66]

The assessment of the Union of Lublin in historiography remains ambivalent, but the fact that in recent years a number of works which offer the Ukrainian reader new perspectives on this important event have appeared is one of the most important signs of the 'recovery' and modernisation of Ukrainian historiography.

Jagiellonians' foreign policy: the Ukrainian perspective

Attention to the Jagiellonian dynasty in Ukrainian historiography is particularly evident in an interest in the foreign policies of its individual representatives. Ivan Bartosh (2012), analysing the political situation in Central and Eastern Europe in the late fifteenth and early sixteenth century and the formation of an anti-Jagiellonian coalition at the time, also writes about the dynasty itself, appreciating its role and influence: 'In the beginning of the 1470s the Jagiellonian dynasty objectively become the most powerful force in Central and Eastern Europe.'[67] Noting Ladislaus II Jagiellon's acquisition of the Bohemian and Hungarian thrones in 1471 and 1490, Bartosh noted that this also galvanised opposition against the family.[68] This caused the formation of the so-called 'anti-Jagiellonian coalition', which Bartosh understands not as a one-time agreement of several states, but as a 'long-term phenomenon that arose objectively under the influence of the geopolitical situation in the last quarter of the fifteenth century in East Central Europe and of the strategic interests of the Moscow and Moldavian Principalities, the Crimean Khanate, and the Ottoman Empire'.[69] Following Hrushevsky,[70] Bartosh considers the Principality of Moscow the centre of the coalition.[71] Analysing the foreign policy of Casimir IV (grand duke 1440–92, king of Poland 1447–92), Bartosh notes that the king's desire to strengthen his control over the Danube trade routes and his access to the Black Sea was a major incentive for the extension of Jagiellonian authority to neighbouring areas.[72] During the creation of this broad anti-Jagiellonian coalition, the Muscovites tried to involve the Holy Roman Emperor Maximilian Habsburg in its orbit. The emperor pledged to help Ivan III seize 'the Grand Principality of Kiev, which is held by Casimir, the King of Poland, and his children'.[73] It is worth mentioning that, according to Olena Rusyna, this agreement was 'the first concrete step of Moscow toward "returning" the southern Rus' lands'.[74] However, this anti-Jagiellonian alliance of Muscovy with the Habsburgs was not completed, because in 1491 Ladislaus II signed his own agreement with the Emperor Maximilian.[75] In order to better describe the Jagiellonians' role in Europe at that time, Bartosh writes about a meeting of the dynasty members in Levoča, in which all of the brothers except Alexander, whose foreign policy was at that time concentrated on Moscow, participated. Rather than assessing the policies of individual dynasty members in the late 1490s, Bartosh instead focuses on the successes and failures of the Jagiellonian dynasty coalition. It is interesting that the author of this article has not discarded the Ukraine-centric vision of European history characteristic of traditional Ukrainian historiography. Focusing on the foreign policy of members of the Jagiellonian dynasty and their opponents, he reduces everything to the question of 'the Ukrainian lands in the GDL, which became a bargaining chip for the conclusion of this or that alliance', when in fact this was just one of the vectors of the wide-ranging confrontation in Central and Eastern Europe at the dawn of the sixteenth century. Further, his assertion that 'Kyiv continued to play a significant ideological and strategic role in the policies of the states'[76] of the region is not entirely accurate, to say the least.

Oleksii Balukh has also devoted an article to the foreign relations of the Kingdom of Poland in the late fifteenth century, namely regarding the Polish-Moldovan war of 1497–99, when King Jan Olbracht of Poland challenged Hungarian authority by marching into the princedom of Moldavia.[77] The only passage of the article in which the author indirectly assesses the crucial role of the Jagiellonians in the region in the late fifteenth century is the assertion that 'the main purpose of the Ottoman invasion of the Polish dominion was to weaken the Jagiellonians' influence in Eastern and North-Eastern Europe'.[78] Foreign policy issues are also discussed in the articles of Vladyslav Hulevych. In the 2013 article '"Kyiv Tragedy" of 1482: Myths and Facts', he tries to understand the causes and consequences of the Crimean Tatars' attack on Kyiv in 1482. This article once again confirms that Ukrainian authors are interested only in those Jagiellonian foreign policy activities that relate specifically to Ruthenian lands. Significantly, despite the fact that in 1482 the Kyiv region was a part of the GDL, whose grand duke was Casimir IV Jagiellon, the duke does not even feature in the list of keywords to the article (while Mengli Giray and Ivan III are mentioned) nor in the abstract.[79] Hulevych does not follow the received narrative, in which Ivan

III is blamed for the destruction of Kyiv by the Tatars in 1482, as part of Moscow's alliance with the Crimean khanate.[80] Instead, Hulevych asserts that with 'the destruction of the town [Kyiv] the khan sought to cause the maximum possible damage, under such conditions, to Casimir Jagiellon'. In other words, the responsibility is indirectly translated to the Polish king and grand duke of Lithuania, who held possession of Kyiv. If we add to this the fact that, according to Hulevych, 'Kyiv was not ready for the attack of the Tatars'[81] and the previous Tatars' campaigns against the Ruthenian lands 'did not cause a significant reaction from Casimir IV',[82] the author's negative attitude towards the king becomes clear. That, after all, is quite traditional for Ukrainian national historiography.

Legislation and reforms

The next important area of scholarly literature on the Jagiellonians includes the studies of the legislative and reform activities of the dynasty's individual members. It was during the Jagiellonians' reign that the codification of law in the GDL, including the Ruthenian lands (Casimir's Code, the First and Second Lithuanian Statutes), the agrarian reform of 1557, known in Ukrainian historiography as the 'voloka measurement' (*volochna pomira*), and the administrative reforms of the 1560s that opened the way to the conclusion of the Union of Lublin, were carried out. Ukrainian scholars have contributed interesting work to each of these areas.

The tradition of studying the Code of Casimir IV (1468) is extensive. Casimir's Code was founded and published in 1826 by Ignacy Daniłowicz (Ignatii Danilovich).[83] It was Daniłowicz who launched a tradition that views the law of the GDL as the Lithuanian-Ruthenian law that, in the middle of the nineteenth century, contributed to the crystallisation of the concept of the Lithuanian-Ruthenian state. Mikhail Vladimirsky-Budanov also did much to explore this monument of law. The scholar published the Code in his *Anthology of the History of Russian Law*, which remains one of the best legal history anthologies to this day. Vladimirsky-Budanov was the first to point out the similarity of the many clauses of the Code to those of the Justice of the Rus' (Ruskaia Pravda) and to the regional privileges of the GDL, concluding that the Code is a monument of Russian (Ruthenian) law.[84]

In Ukrainian historiography, the tradition of genuine scholarly study of the Code of 1468 has been continued only recently by modern historians and historians of law.[85] It is worth mentioning the works of Yu. Sen'kiv[86] and N. Yefremova.[87] Svitlana Kovaliova gave the Code most attention in her monograph, publishing it in both old Ruthenian and translated into modern Ukrainian.[88] Kovaliova considers the origin, nature and purpose of the Code in the context of the general tendencies of Casimir's policy, so she devotes several pages of her work to his activities as the king and grand duke. In her opinion, during his reign the form of government of the GDL evolved from an early feudal monarchy to an estates-representative system.[89] Kovaliova acknowledges the privilege of 2 May 1447, with which Casimir tried to secure the support of the social elite of the GDL:

The privilege granted by Casimir expanded the rights of princes, knights, nobles, boyars, and townspeople of both the Catholic and Orthodox religions. The equalisation of the Orthodox and Catholics contributed to the removal of social tensions, to the expanding social support for the sovereign, and to the consolidation of the social elite.[90]

The loyalty of the Kyiv region and Volhynia populations was important to the grand duke, so their new status was enshrined in regional privileges.[91] According to Kovaliova, the foundation of the privileges is to be found in norms of old Rus' origin. But a number of norms in these privileges repeat the privilege of 1447 and are new for the Ruthenian law. Acknowledging the efforts of Casimir IV in strengthening the state and the royal power, the author notes that the Code of 1468 was the last accord in the settlement of the legal framework of the GDL.[92]

The agrarian reform introduced to the GDL by the Statute on Volokas (*Ustava na voloki*) of Sigismund II Augustus (1557) has also attracted the attention of Ukrainian scholars. Hrushevsky supported the idea of this reform.[93] The reform was approved in the domains of Queen Bona Sforza (d.1557), as Hrushevsky also indicated: 'The figures that created the reform of 1557 and brought it into life largely come from her school.'[94] Hrushevsky himself did not devote much attention to this reform. This may be why the agrarian reform of the mid-sixteenth century has not often been studied by Ukrainian historians. The 'voloka measurement' was studied by Belarusian historian Uladzimir Picheta,[95] the Ukrainian scholar Dmytro Pokhylevych,[96] and more recently by Andrii Hurbyk,[97] who challenges the Soviet historiographical argument about the destruction of the peasant community and the abolition of public land tenure by the 'voloka measurement'.[98] In his studies, Hurbyk drew attention to the role of Bona Sforza, in whose domains some elements of reform were first approved.[99] Some studies devote themselves to her customs reform of 1536.[100] Bona Sforza is the only member of the Jagiellonian dynasty who both makes appearances in Ukrainian histories and has had entire studies dedicated to her.[101] This applies not only to agrarian reform – Ukrainian historians associate some Western European influences in culture and politics with the name of Queen Bona.[102] In general, the reformatory and legislative activity of the Jagiellonian dynasty members in both the GDL and the Kingdom of Poland remains underestimated in Ukrainian historiography.

The granting of lands and privileges

Land investiture by the Gediminids-Jagiellonians also attracts the attention of Ukrainian scholars. Historiography in this field has a relatively long tradition, beginning with the works of Matvei Liubavsky[103] and Mitrofan Dovnar-Zapolsky in the 1890s and early 1900s.[104] In recent decades, some progress has been made on this topic in Olena Rusyna's monograph *Siverian Land in the Grand Duchy of Lithuania* (1998). In one of its chapters, Rusyna considers, among other things, the investitures of lands by Alexander Jagiellon.[105] Vitaii Mikhailovsky studied the distribution of land performed by Polish and Lithuanian rulers in Podolia (2000s).[106] Andrii Blanutsa is the most active in this field. He has studied the granting of lands by Casimir IV, Alexander Jagiellon, Sigismund I the Old, and Sigismund II Augustus, and published a number of their privileges.[107] An article by Yurii Zazuliak is devoted to Jagiellonian mortgages in Galician Rus' in the fifteenth century.[108] He argues that 'in the middle of this century mortgages became the main instrument of the Jagiellonian dynasty's giving policy . . . Władysław III's (1434–44) large-scale giving policy considerably intensified the transfer of royal domain estates to the hands of the nobles and facilitated their quick promotions.'[109] He also points to the symbolic significance of the mortgages: 'Providing loans or gifts to the king was seen as an important sign of social prestige, which strengthened ties and obligations of both parties . . . and played an important symbolic function in social communication between the ruler and his subject.'[110]

The granting of privileges by the Jagiellonians in Ukrainian lands has also been analysed in studies of the customs system, the cohabitation of ethnic communities in the town of Lviv, the privileges for fairs and markets, and, of course, the location policies of the Polish kings and grand dukes of Lithuania (the founding of towns and the granting of urban law). The tradition of studying towns with German law in Ukrainian historiography is quite long, although not very rich.[111] The origins of this tradition go back to Volodymyr Antonovych and Mykhailo Hrushevsky, Dmytro Bahalii, Mikhail Vladimirsky-Budanov and Fedir Taranovsky. But only since the 1990s have these studies become active and gained depth. The urban policies of the grand dukes and kings have rarely been investigated directly. For the most part, Ukrainian historians explore the functioning of German law in specific towns,[112] in a region (Andrii Zaiats's study on Volhynia),[113] or in the towns of Ukraine in general,[114] and pay considerable attention to the investiture policies of the kings and grand dukes. In general, it can be argued that the granting of lands and privileges by the Polish kings and grand dukes of Lithuania in the fourteenth to sixteenth centuries is poorly studied. 'Spot' and sporadic studies do not make it possible to form a comprehensive synthesis of these activities performed by members of the Jagiellonian dynasty, on a statewide scale, or with specific regard to Ruthenian lands.

The Jagiellonians' Church policy

The Jagiellonian era in Ukrainian history is also associated with attempts to implement a Church union between the Latin and Orthodox Churches, which culminated in the Union of Brest in 1596 after the end of the dynasty. However, the Union was not achieved in a single day, and members of the Jagiellonian dynasty were in one way or another engaged in the matter. This has been reflected in the works of some Ukrainian historians.[115]

Under the Treaty of Krevo (1385), Catholicism was to be disseminated in the Grand Duchy of Lithuania, and its pagan populace converted, and this is what Jogaila tried to do. But even after his privilege of 1387, which awarded nobles who converted to Catholicism new rights, most of the population of the GDL (the vast majority of whom were already Orthodox) continued to be baptised into the Orthodox faith, as the Grand Master of the Teutonic Knights, Konrad von Jungingen, wrote in one of his letters.[116] Therefore it was necessary to seek compromise between the two faiths in uniting Poland and Lithuania, a fact with which Jogaila himself was concerned. Historians have associated his active planning of a church and communication with Cyprian, Metropolitan of Kyiv and All Rus', with this preoccupation. As Viktoriia Liubaschenko notes, 'It was the Polish-Lithuanian side that initiated the negotiations regarding the church union, and Władysław Jogaila was its main promoter.'[117] Liubaschenko has moved away from traditional Ukrainian historiography's treatment of Jogaila as a zealous champion of Catholicism (as opposed to Vytautas and especially Švitrigaila (Svidrigailo)) and tries to understand and demonstrate the Polish king's policy of ambivalence.

These events, amongst many others related to the participation of Polish and Lithuanian rulers in religious affairs and conflicts, are discussed in Borys Gudziak's 2001 monograph[118] and numerous articles. Ihor Skochylias has analysed the policies of the Polish kings regarding the Orthodox Church, balancing negative and positive assessments of these policies and describing, on the one hand, numerous harassments of the Orthodox and, on the other, the royal privileges that guaranteed their rights at the state level, including the diploma of Sigismund I from 23 October 1539 on the opening of the Ruthenian Orthodox Cathedral in Lviv, and the nomination of the first Bishop of Lviv, Macarius Tuchapsky.[119] He rightly noted that 'the governance of the Eastern Church in the Crown of Poland and Grand Duchy of Lithuania was based on the rights and privileges obtained by the Ukrainian-Belarusian bishops from the rulers of both states in the mid-fifteenth century'.[120] That is why an analysis of the Jagiellonians' policies toward the Church is essential for a complete picture of not only the period of their reign, but also the following historical epoch.

Jagiellonians in encyclopaedias and cultural memory

One of the best reflections of interest in a particular historical topic is its representation in reference books, primarily in dictionaries and encyclopaedias, which reflect the trends and achievements of academic historical work in popular terms. After World War II, two parallel encyclopaedic projects – Soviet Ukrainian and diaspora Ukrainian – established themselves as competitors. In some ways, however, they were very similar, especially in the lack of attention paid to the Lithuanian-Polish period of Ukrainian history and a negative, albeit to varying degrees, attitude towards Jagiellonians. Consequently, where entries about the Jagiellonians are to be found in the Ukrainian encyclopaedias, they are short and have negative connotations.

The diaspora encyclopaedic narrative was quite consistent with the conception of the history of Ukraine presented by Hrushevsky, including the negative connotations of Western influence in general. For example, a short article about the

Jagiellonian dynasty in the diaspora *Encyclopedia of Ukraine* (1988) ends with the words:

> In Ukraine, Jagiellon rule was marked by the liquidation of the last independent (appanage) Lithuanian-Ruthenian principalities, the consolidation of Polish rule in the western Ukrainian lands, intensive Polonisation, the imposition of Roman Catholicism and Germanic and Magdeburg law, urban growth, significant economic development, and the enserfment of the peasantry.[121]

The *Soviet Encyclopaedia of the History of Ukraine* (four volumes), published in Kyiv in 1969–72, virtually mirrored the work of the *Soviet Historical Encyclopaedia* published in Moscow. As in the Moscow *Encyclopaedia*, entries about the Jagiellonians were very schematic and devoid of authorship and references, which made it difficult for readers to get better acquainted with the topic.[122]

Contemporary Ukrainian historiography is trying to change the discourse and eliminate the gaps that emerged in the study of certain aspects of Ukraine's history through the focus on purely ethnic problems and the vitality of populist historical myths. The new *Encyclopaedia of the History of Ukraine* (2013) contains a thorough article on the Jagiellonians accompanied by a dynastic table. Interestingly, there is no Ukrainian item among the recommended literature in the article due to a complete lack of special studies on the topic in Ukrainian historiography.[123]

Interest in the Jagiellonian dynasty and the era of their rule remains low in Ukraine, however. The web portal of the Institute of History of Ukraine introduced a rating system for the articles in the *Encyclopaedia of the History of Ukraine* – the top 100[124] – that allows the most popular articles to be tracked in real time. The articles from the top 100 have at least a few thousand views, which generally indicates that an article is reasonably popular among its Ukrainian audience; none of the articles about the Jagiellonians are to be found in this list. The Jagiellonians are virtually absent from both cultural memory and public space in Ukraine. Only a few historical events of the period of their rule are present in the politics of cultural memory, namely the 1410 Battle of Grünwald, the granting of Magdeburg Law to Kyiv, and, more recently, the Battle of Orsha (1514) where the allied forces of the GDL and Poland defeated the Muscovite army. To memorialise these events a series of commemorative coins were released in Ukraine: for the 500th anniversary of the granting of Magdeburg Law to Kyiv (1 November 1999),[125] the 600th anniversary of the Grünwald victory (14 November 2010), and the 500th anniversary of the victory of Orsha (15 October 2014).[126] Additionally, several Ukrainian cities – Lviv, Ivano-Frankivsk, and Drohobych – have streets named after Ruthenian troops who served at the Battle of Grünwald.[127] The Jagiellonian (Lithuanian-Polish) era of Ukrainian history fits poorly into a historical discourse focused on the Ukrainian state and nation. As a result there are virtually no movies, plays, or radio or television programmes about the Jagiellonians, or their era as a whole, in Ukraine. In fact, the Jagiellonian era remains pretty much non-existent outside academic historical writings.

Conclusions

Thus, Ukrainian historiography, both in the early days of its formation and today, is not interested in the history of the Jagiellonian dynasty. Searching for the framework of a national grand narrative, Ukrainian scholars, following Hrushevsky, have found it in the Old Rus' and Cossack periods, not in the Polish-Lithuanian era. The idealisation of Old Rus' statehood was interwoven with notions of the Polish state as alien and expansionist. The approach to the Grand Duchy of Lithuania was slightly different, because it has traditionally been viewed as a state that had early on adopted the elements of Old Rus' culture and customs, and is even viewed as the 'latent era of Ukrainian statehood'. That is why Ukrainian historians were more interested in the history of the Lithuanian state and the members of the Lithuanian ruling house than in the history of the Polish Crown. Thus Ukrainian historiography has paid more attention to the Gediminids, and engaged with the Jagiellonians primarily as one of the Gediminid branches when it has considered them at all. As a result, despite the important role it played in Ruthenia between the fourteenth and sixteenth centuries, the Jagiellonian dynasty is poorly and inadequately represented in the Ukrainian historical narrative. In recent years, however, some positive shifts have occurred in Ukrainian historiography. In particular, the image of Poland has ceased to be completely negative, with the old historiographical formulations slipping away into oblivion. As Yakovenko optimistically believes, a generational change in Ukrainian historiography will lead to the rejection of the 'ghosts of the past' and to the emergence of a new paradigm.[128]

Notes

1 Mykhailo Hrushevsky (29.9.1866–24.11.1934) – Ukrainian historian, civic and political leader. Hrushevsky established the continuity of Ukrainian historical processes, even throughout the periods of Ukrainian statelessness. See more: O. Ohloblyn and L. Wynar, 'Hrushevsky Mykhailo', in V. Kubijovyč, ed., *Encyclopedia of Ukraine*, vol. II, Toronto, Buffalo, London, 1988, pp. 250–3.
2 M. Hrushevsky, *History of Ukraine-Rus'*, M. Skorupsky, trans., vol. 1, Edmonton, 1997, p. 7.
3 N. Yakovenko, 'Early Modern Ukraine between East and West: Projectures of an Idea', in K. Matsuzato, ed., *Regions: A Prism to View the Slavic-Eurasian World. Towards a Discipline of "Regionology"*, Sapporo, 2000, p. 50.
4 See more: N. Yakovenko, 'Pol'scha ta poliaky v shkil'nykh pidruchnykakh istorii, abo vidlunnia davn'oho i nedavn'oho mynuloho', in N. Yakovenko, *Paralel'nyi svit. Doslidzhennia z istorii uiavlen' ta idei v Ukraini XVI–XVII st.*, Kyiv, 2002, pp. 366–79.
5 See more: O. Subtelny, *Ukraine: A History*, 3rd edn, Toronto, Buffalo, London, 2000, pp. 67–80; P. R. Magocsi, *A History of Ukraine: The Land and Its Peoples*, 2nd edn, Toronto, Buffalo, London, 2010, pp. 133–49.

6 M. Hrushevs'kyi, 'Zvychaina skhema "rus'koi" istorii y sprava ratsionalnoho ukladu istorii skhidnoho slov'ianstva', http://litopys.org.ua/hrs/hrs02.htm, accessed 29.8.17.
7 O. Ruda, 'Beresteis'ka uniia u doslidzhenniakh l'vivs'kykh pol's'kykh istorykiv (1890–1914)', *Problemy slov'ianoznavstva* 57, 2008, p. 65.
8 N. Yakovenko, 'Skil'ky istorykiv – stil'ky unii (z nahody 440-littia Liublins'koi unii)', *Ukrains'kyi humanitarnyi ohliad* 14, 2009, p. 27.
9 L. Zashkil'niak, 'Obraz Pol'schi i poliakiv u suchasnii Ukraini', *Problemy slov'ianoznavstva* 60, 2011, p. 69.
10 N. Yakovenko, *Narys istorii seredn'ovichnoi ta rann'omodernoi Ukrainy*, Kyiv, 2005, p. 2.
11 Hrushevsky, *History of Ukraine-Rus'*, vol. I, p. 13.
12 Hrushevsky, *History of Ukraine-Rus'*, vol. I, p. 17.
13 Hrushevs'kyi, *Istoriia Ukrainy-Rusy*, vol. IV, Kyiv, 1993, p. 4.
14 Hrushevs'kyi, *Istoriia Ukrainy-Rusy*, vol. V, Kyiv, 1994, p. 233.
15 See more: N. Yakovenko, 'Koho ta yak inshuie Mykhailo Hrushevs'kyi v "Istorii Ukrainy-Rusy"', in *Obraz inshoho v susidnikh istoriiakh: mify, stereotypy, naukovi interpretatsii. Materaly mizhnarodnoi naukovoi konferentsii*, Kyiv, 15–16 hrudnia 2005 roku, Kyiv, 2008, pp. 95–102.
16 Yakovenko, 'Skil'ky istorykiv – stil'ky unii', p. 26.
17 See more: A. Tolochko, 'Dlinnaia istoriia Ukrainy', in A. Tolochko, *Kievskaia Rus' i Malorossiia v XIX veke*, Kyiv, 2012, pp. 9–46.
18 On Ukrainian historical myths see: A. Wilson, 'Myths of National History in Belarus and Ukraine', in G. Hosking and G. Schopflin, eds, *Myths and Nationhood*, London, 1997, pp. 182–97; D. Sudyn, 'Natsional'ni mify v suchasnii Ukraini', http://uamoderna.com/md/sudyn-national-myths, accessed 29.8.17.
19 Yakovenko, 'Koho ta yak inshuie Mykhailo Hrushevs'kyi v "Istorii Ukrainy-Rusy"', p. 90.
20 Serhii Plokhy (Plokhii, b.23.5.1957) – Mykhailo Hrushevs'kyi Professor of Ukrainian History at Harvard University (since 2007), Director of Harvard Ukrainian Research Institute (since 2013). Before 2007, he lived and taught in Ukraine and then in Canada (www.huri.harvard.edu/main/people/huri-personnel/65-plokhii.html, https://en.wikipedia.org/wiki/Serhii_Plokhii).
21 M. Hrushevs'kyi, *Istoriia Ukrainy-Rusy*, vol. III, Kyiv, 1992, p. 139.
22 S. Plokhy, *Unmaking Imperial Russia: Mykhailo Hrushevsky and the Writing of Ukrainian History*, Toronto, Buffalo, New York, 2005, pp. 153–211.
23 Hrushevs'kyi, *Istoriia Ukrainy-Rusy*, vol. IV, pp. 8–9. See also Lewis, on Belarus, in this volume.
24 Ivan Krypiakevych (25.6.1886–21.4.1967) – Ukrainian historian, began his career as a historian under the tutelage of M. Hrushevsky. Krypiakevych is an author of over 500 works on historiography, archaeography, sphragistics, cultural history (O. Ohlobyn, 'Krypiakevych Ivan', in Kubijovyč, *Encyclopedia of Ukraine*, vol. II, p. 682).
25 I. Kryp'iakevych, *Istoriia Ukrainy*, Lviv, 1990, p. 155.
26 See more: V. Vasylenko, *Politychna istoriia Velykoho kniazivstva Lytovs'koho (do 1569 r.) v skhidnoslov'ians'kykh istoriohrafiiakh XIX – persha tretyna XX st.* Avtoreferat na zdobuttia naukovoho stupenia doktora ist. nauk, Kyiv, 2007, p. 3. See also Vitalii Vasylenko's book: *Politychna istoriia Velykoho kniazivstva Lytovs'koho (do 1569 r.) v skhidnoslov'ians'kykh istoriohrafiiakh XIX – pershoi tretyny XX st.*, Dnipropetrovsk, 2006.
27 T. Stryjek, *Jakiej przeszłości potrzebuje przyszłość? Interpretacje dziejów narodowych w historiografii i debacie publicznej na Ukrainie 1991–2004*, Warsaw, 2007, p. 261.
28 K. Huslystyi, *Narysy z istorii Ukrainy*, issue II: *Ukraina pid lytovs'kym panuvanniam i zakhoplennia yii Pol'scheiu (z XIV st. po 1569 r.)*, Kyiv, 1939, pp. 3–5.
29 A. Blanutsa, 'Lytuanistychni studii v instytuti istorii Ukrainy (1936–2011 rr.): osnovni tendentsii', *Istoriohrafichni doslidzhennia v Ukraini*, 22, 2012, p. 317.

30 Leontii Voitovych (b.16.5.1951) – Ukrainian historian, head of the Department of History of Middle Ages and Byzantine Studies, Ivan Franko National University of Lviv (http://clio.lnu.edu.ua/en/employee/voytovych-leontiy-viktorovych).
31 L. Voitovych, *Kniazivs'ki dynastii Skhidnoi Yevropy (kinets' IX – pochatok XVI st.): sklad, suspil'na i politychna rol'*, Lviv, 2000, p. 7; L. Voitovych, *Kniazha doba: portrety elity*, Bila Tserkva, 2006, p. 13.
32 Voitovych, *Kniazivs'ki dynastii Skhidnoi Yevropy (kinets' IX – pochatok XVI st.)*, pp. 5–6, 283–356.
33 S. Plokhy, *The Gates of Europe: A History of Ukraine*, New York, 2015, pp. 66–72.
34 On the *History of the Rus'* and its hypothetical authors, see S. Plokhy, *The Cossack Myth: History and Nationhood in the Age of Empires*, Cambridge, 2012.
35 Plokhy, *The Cossack Myth*, p. 6.
36 Plokhy, *The Cossack Myth*, pp. 51, 53.
37 Plokhy, *The Cossack Myth*, p. 90.
38 In the months leading up to independence, Ivan Drach, the leader of *Rukh*, the largest pro-independence Ukrainian movement of the late 1980s and early 1990s, took it upon himself to translate the *History of Rus'* into modern Ukrainian (Plokhy, *The Cossack Myth*, pp. 4–5).
39 M. Hrushevsky, *History of Ukraine-Rus'*, vol. 7, Edmonton, 1999, pp. 68–80.
40 Hrushevsky, *History of Ukraine-Rus'*, vol. 7, pp. 80–1.
41 Hrushevsky, *History of Ukraine-Rus'*, vol. 7, pp. 83–4.
42 Hrushevsky, *History of Ukraine-Rus'*, vol. 7, pp. 109–10.
43 Hrushevsky, *History of Ukraine-Rus'*, vol. 7, p. 110.
44 Plokhy, *Unmaking Imperial Russia*, p. 199.
45 B. Cherkas, 'Ukrains'ke kozatstvo naprykintsi XV – u pershii polovyni XVI st.', in V. Smolii, ed., *Istoriia ukrains'koho kozatstva: Narysy*, vol. 1, Kyiv, 2006, p. 60.
46 B. Cherkas, 'Ukrains'ke kozatstvo u viis'kovo-politychnykh protsesakh Velykoho kniazivstva Lytovs'koho (20–30-ti rr. XVI st.)', in *"Istynu vstanovliuie sud istorii": Zbirnyk na poshanu Fedora Pavlovycha Shevchenka*, vol. 2, Kyiv, 2004, p. 161.
47 Cherkas, 'Ukrains'ke kozatstvo naprykintsi XV – u pershii polovyni XVI st.', pp. 64–5.
48 V. Shcherbak, *Ukrains'ke kozatstvo: formuvannia sotsial'noho stanu, druha polovyna XV – seredyna XVII st.*, Kyiv, 2000.
49 V. Shcherbak, 'Reiestrovi kozaky na derzhavnii sluzhbi', in Smolii, *Istoriia ukrains'koho kozatstva*, vol. 1, Kyiv, 2006, p. 75.
50 N. Yakovenko, *Ukrains'ka shliakhta z kintsia XIV do seredyny XVII st.: Volyn' i Tsentral'na Ukraina*, Kyiv, 2008, p. 245.
51 T. Hrynevych, 'Krevs'ka uniia v dyskusiiakh pol's'kykh istorykiv mizhvoiennoho chasu', *Studii z arkhivnoi spravy ta dokumentoznavstva* 18, 2010, p. 150.
52 Hrushevs'kyi, *Istoriia Ukrainy-Rusy*, vol. IV, p. 125.
53 Hrushevs'kyi, *Istoriia Ukrainy-Rusy*, vol. IV, pp. 125–30.
54 Huslystyi, *Ukraina pid lytovs'kym panuvanniam i zakhoplennia yii Pol'scheiu*, pp. 34–9.
55 Yakovenko, 'Skil'ky istorykiv – stil'ky unii', pp. 9–42.
56 *Istoriia Rusiv*, trans. I. Drach, http://litopys.org.ua/istrus/rusiv1.htm.
57 'Spysky "Knyhy buttia ukrains'koho narodu", vylucheni zi sprav Kyrylo-Mefodiivs'koho tovarystva', http://litopys.org.ua/index.html.
58 Hrushevs'kyi, *Istoriia Ukrainy-Rusy*, vol. IV, p. 414.
59 N. Polons'ka-Vasylenko, *Istoriia Ukrainy*, vol. 1, Kyiv, 1992, pp. 343–4.
60 Huslystyi, *Ukraina pid lytovs'kym panuvanniam i zakhoplennia yii Pol'scheiu*, p. 169.
61 N. Yakovenko, 'Zdobutky i vtraty Liublins'koi unii', *Kyivs'ka starovyna* 3, 1993, p. 82.
62 Yakovenko, 'Skil'ky istorykiv – stil'ky unii', p. 10.
63 S. Lep'iavko, 'Politychna systema Ukrainy doby Rechi Pospolytoi', in V. Lytvyn, ed., *Politychna systema dlia Ukrainy: istorychnyi dosvid i vyklyky suchasnosti*, Kyiv, 2008, p. 84.

64 A reference to Grand Prince Volodymyr (Volodimer) of Kyiv, the baptiser of the Rus'.
65 Yakovenko, *Narys istorii seredn'ovichnoi ta rann'omodernoi Ukrainy*, pp. 206–9.
66 Plokhy, *The Gates of Europe*, p. 72.
67 I. Bartosh, 'Antyiahellons'ka koalitsiia na terenakh Skhidnoi Yevropy naprykintsi XV – pochatku XVI st.', *Ukrains'kyi istorychnyi zbirnyk* 15/16, Kyiv, 2012, p. 18.
68 Bartosh, 'Antyiahellons'ka koalitsiia na terenakh Skhidnoi Yevropy naprykintsi XV – pochatku XVI st.'.
69 Bartosh, 'Antyiahellons'ka koalitsiia na terenakh Skhidnoi Yevropy naprykintsi XV – pochatku XVI st.', pp. 18–19.
70 Hrushevs'kyi, *Istoriia Ukrainy-Rusy*, vol. IV, p. 56.
71 Bartosh, 'Antyiahellons'ka koalitsiia na terenakh Skhidnoi Yevropy naprykintsi XV – pochatku XVI st.', p. 19.
72 Bartosh, 'Antyiahellons'ka koalitsiia na terenakh Skhidnoi Yevropy naprykintsi XV – pochatku XVI st.', p. 20.
73 Bartosh, 'Antyiahellons'ka koalitsiia na terenakh Skhidnoi Yevropy naprykintsi XV – pochatku XVI st.', p. 22.
74 O. Rusyna, *Studii z istorii Kyieva ta Kyivs'koi zemli*, Kyiv, 2005, pp. 74–5.
75 Bartosh, 'Antyiahellons'ka koalitsiia na terenakh Skhidnoi Yevropy naprykintsi XV – pochatku XVI st.', pp. 25–6.
76 Bartosh, 'Antyiahellons'ka koalitsiia na terenakh Skhidnoi Yevropy naprykintsi XV – pochatku XVI st.'.
77 O. Balukh, 'Pol's'ko-moldavs'ka viina 1497–1499 rr.', *Naukovi zoshyty istorychnoho fakul'tetu L'vivs'koho universytetu: Zbirnyk naukovykh statei* 9, 2008, pp. 57–66.
78 Balukh, 'Pol's'ko-moldavs'ka viina 1497–1499 rr.', p. 65.
79 V. Hulevych, '"Kyivs'ka trahediia" 1482 r.: mify i fakty', *Ukrains'kyi istorychnyi zhurnal* 5, 2013, p. 88.
80 Huleyych, '"Kyivs'ka trahediia" 1482 r.: mify i fakty'.
81 Huleyych, p. 97.
82 Huleyych, '"Kyivs'ka trahediia" 1482 r.: mify i fakty', p. 98.
83 See more: S. Koval'ova, *Sudebnyk velykoho kniazia Kazymyra Yahailovycha 1468 roku*, Mykolaiv, 2009, p. 4; *Khrestomatiia z istorii Ukrainy lytovs'ko-pol's'koi doby*, compiled by T. Hoshko, Lviv, 2011, p. 58.
84 M. Vladimirskii-Budanov, *Khrestomatiia po istorii russkogo prava*, vol. II, St Petersburg, 1901, pp. 32–41. See also: M. Vladimirskii-Budanov, *Ocherki po istorii Litovsko-Russkogo prava*, vol. 1, Kyiv, 1889.
85 For historiography of the Code see: I. Starostina, 'Sudebnik Kazimira IV', *Drevneishie gosudarstva na territorii SSSR. Materialy i issledovaniia*, 1988–89, Moscow, 1991, pp. 175–88; Koval'ova, *Sudebnyk velykoho kniazia Kazymyra Yahailovycha 1468 roku*, pp. 4–9; O. Vovk, 'Istoriohrafiia Sudebnyka Kazymyra IV 1468 roku', *Visnyk Kyivs'koho natsional'noho universytetu imeni Tarasa Shevchenka* 72, 2006, pp. 41–3.
86 Yu. Sen'kiv, 'Sudebnyk 1468 roku, yoho struktura, zmist ta znachennia', *Visnyk L'vivs'koho universytetu. Seriia yurydychna* 46, 2008, pp. 59–64.
87 N. Yefremova, 'Rozrobka Sudebnyka Kazymyra IV 1468 r. ta problemy vyznachennia yoho dzherel'noi bazy', *Visnyk L'vivs'koho universytetu. Seriia yurydychna* 44, 2007, pp. 83–9.
88 Koval'ova, *Sudebnyk velykoho kniazia Kazymyra Yahailovycha 1468 roku*.
89 Koval'ova, *Sudebnyk velykoho kniazia Kazymyra Yahailovycha 1468 roku*, pp. 11–15.
90 Koval'ova, *Sudebnyk velykoho kniazia Kazymyra Yahailovycha 1468 roku*, p. 14.
91 Koval'ova, *Sudebnyk velykoho kniazia Kazymyra Yahailovycha 1468 roku*, p. 16.
92 Koval'ova, *Sudebnyk velykoho kniazia Kazymyra Yahailovycha 1468 roku*, p. 23.
93 Hrushevs'kyi, *Istoriia Ukrainy-Rusy*, vol. V, pp. 206–7.
94 Hrushevs'kyi, *Istoriia Ukrainy-Rusy*, vol. V, p. 209.
95 V. Picheta, *Agrarnaia reforma Sigizmunda Avgusta v Litovsko-Russkom gosudarstve*, Moscow, 1958; V. Picheta, *Istoriia sel'skogo khoziaistva i zemlevladeniia v Belorussii*, vol. 1, Minsk, 1927, etc.

96 D. Pokhilevich, 'Dvizhenie feodal'noi zemel'noi renty v Velikom kniazhestve Litovskom v XV–XVI vv.', *Istoricheskie zapiski* 31, 1950, pp. 194–221; D. Pokhilevich, *Krest'ianstvo Belorussii i Litvy v XVI–XVIII vv*, Lviv, 1957, etc.
97 A. Hurbyk, *Ahrarna reforma v Ukraini XVI st.*, Kyiv, 1997; A. Hurbyk, *Evoliutsiia sotsial'no-terytorial'nykh spil'not v seredn'ovichnii Ukraini (volost', dvorysche, selo, siabrynna spilka)*, Kyiv, 1998; A. Hurbyk, 'Typolohiia terytorial'noi hromady v Ukraini XIV-XVIII st.', *Ukraina v Tsentral'no-Skhidnii Yevropi* 1, 2000, pp. 75–96; A. Hurbyk, 'Wspólnota wiejska na Ukrainie w XIV–XVIII w. Ewoljucja podstawowych form spoleczno-terytorianych', *Przegląd Historyczny* XC, 1, 1999, pp. 1–18, etc.
98 Hurbyk, 'Typolohiia terytorial'noi hromady v Ukraini XIV–XVIII st., p. 85.
99 A. Hurbyk, 'Ahrarna reforma seredyny XVI st.', in V. Smolii, ed., *Istoriia ukrains'koho selianstva: Narysy*, vol. 1, Kyiv, 2006, p. 119. See also: A. Blanutsa, 'Hospodars'ka polityka korolevy Bony u Velykomu kniazivstvi Lytovs'komu (za materialamy 32 knyhy zapysiv Lytovs'koi metryky)', *Ukraina v Tsentral'no-Skhidnii Yevropi*, Kyiv, 2011, pp. 191–206.
100 L. Zherebtsova, 'Deiaki aspekty praktychnoi roboty mytnoi sluzhby na zemliakh Velykoho kniazivstva Lytovs'koho', in *Ukraina Lithuanica: studii z istorii Velykoho kniazivstva Lytovs'koho*, vol. II, Kyiv, 2013, pp. 209–27.
101 The Third International Conference 'Bar Land of Podilia' was dedicated to the 520th anniversary of Bona Sforza. See: *Bars'ka zemlia Podillia: yevropeis'ka spadschyna ta perspektyvy staloho rozvytku. Do 520-richchia z dnia narodzhennia Bony Sfortsy ta 120-richchia vykhodu u svit pratsi M.S.Hrushevs'koho "Bars'ke starostvo. Istorychni narysy XV – XVIII st."*. *Materialy III Mizhnarodnoi naukovo-praktychnoi konferentsii*, editorial board M. Dmytriienko et al., Kyiv and Bar, 2014.
102 O. Kryzhanivs'kyi, 'Zakhidnoievropeis'ki tradytsii pravlinnia dynastii Sfortsiv v epokhu italiis'koho Vidrodzhennia ta yikh vplyv na formuvannia sotsiokul'turnykh utvoren' na zemliakh Podillia v pershii polovyni XVI st.', in *Bars'ka zemlia Podillia*, pp. 190–6; Ye. Mesniankin, 'Bona Sfortsa i epokha Vidrodzhennia v Podil's'komu Bari', in *Bars'ka zemlia Podillia*, pp. 198–201.
103 M. Liubavskii, *Oblastnoe delenie i mestnoe upravlenie Litovsko-Russkogo gosudarstva ko vremeni izdaniia pervogo Litovskogo statuta*, Moscow, 1892.
104 M. Dovnar-Zapol'skii, *Gosudarstvennoe khoziaistvo Velikogo kniazhestva Litovskogo pri Yagellonakh*, vol. 1, Kyiv, 1901.
105 O. Rusyna, *Sivers'ka zemlia u skladi Velykoho kniazivstva Lytovs'koho*, Kyiv, 1998, pp. 150–2.
106 V. Mykhailovs'kyi, *Nadavcha pozemel'na polityka volodariv Zakhidnoho Podillia (1402–1506 rr.)*. Avtoref. dys. na zdobuttia nauk. stupenia kand. ist. nauk, Kyiv, 2004; V. Mykhailovs'kyi, *Elastychna spil'nota. Podil's'ka shliakhta v druhii polovyni XIV – 70-kh rokakh XVI stolittia*, Kyiv, 2012, etc.
107 A. Blanutsa, *Zemel'ni volodinnia Volyns'koi shliakhty v druhii polovyni XVI st.*, Kyiv, 2007; A. Blanutsa, *Zemel'na polityka Yahelloniv na ukrains'kykh terenakh Velykoho kniazivstva Lytovs'koho (1440–1572 rr.)*, Kyiv, 2017.
108 Yu. Zazuliak, 'Zastavy yak element rozdavnychoi polityky Yahelloniv u Halyts'kii Rusi XV st.', *Visnyk L'vivs'koho universytetu. Seriia istorychna* 35–6, 2000, pp. 43–57.
109 Zazuliak, 'Zastavy yak element rozdavnychoi polityky Yahelloniv u Halyts'kii Rusi XV st.', p. 56.
110 Zazuliak, 'Zastavy yak element rozdavnychoi polityky Yahelloniv u Halyts'kii Rusi XV st.', p. 45.
111 See more: T. Hoshko, *Mahdeburz'ke pravo Tsentral'no-Skhidnoi Yevropy XIII-XVIII st. v ukrains'kii ta pol's'kii istoriohrafii*. Avtoref. dys. na zdobuttia nauk. stupenia kand. ist. nauk, Kyiv, 1999.
112 N. Bilous, *Kyiv naprykintsi XV – u pershii polovyni XVII stolittia. Mis'ka vlada i samovriaduvannia*, Kyiv, 2008.
113 A. Zaiats', *Urbanizatsiinyi protses na Volyni v XVI – pershii polovyni XVII st.*, Lviv, 2003.

114 T. Hoshko, *Narysy z istorii magdeburz'koho prava v Ukraini XIV – pochatku XVII st.*, Lviv, 2002; M. Kobylets'kyi, *Magdeburz'ke pravo v Ukraini: (XVI – persha polovyna XIX st.): istoryko-pravove doslidzhennia*, Lviv, 2008, etc.
115 See, e. g., Hrushevs'kyi, *Istoriia Ukrainy-Rusy*, vol. V, ch. VII.
116 V. Liubaschenko, 'Halych u tserkovno-uniinykh planakh Vladyslava Yahaila i mytropolyta Kypriiana', *Ukraina: kul'turna spadschyna, natsional'na svidomist', derzhavnist'. Zbirnyk naukovykh prats'* 20, 2011, p. 442.
117 Liubaschenko, 'Halych u tserkovno-uniinykh planakh Vladyslava Yahaila i mytropolyta Kypriiana', pp. 441–2.
118 B. Gudziak, *Crisis and Reform: The Kyivan Metropolitanate, the Patriarchate of Constantinople, and the Genesis of the Union of Brest*, Cambridge, MA, 2001; Ukrainian translation: B. Gudziak, *Kryza i reforma: Kyivs'ka mytropoliia, Tsarhorods'kyi patriarkhat i heneza Beresteis'koi unii*, Lviv, 2000.
119 I. Skochylias, *Halyts'ka (L'vivs'ka) yeparkhiia XII–XVIII st.*, Lviv, 2010, pp. 325–34.
120 Skochylias, *Halyts'ka (L'vivs'ka) yeparkhiia XII–XVIII st.*, p. 326.
121 'Jagiellon dynasty', in Kubijovyč, *Encyclopedia of Ukraine*, vol. II, p. 378.
122 A. Skaba, B. Babii, A. Borodin et al., eds, *Radians'ka entsyklopediia istorii Ukrainy*, vol. 2, Kyiv, 1972, pp. 91, 292; vol. 4, Kyiv, 1972, p. 550.
123 V. Mykhailovs'kyi, 'Iahellony', in V. Smolii, ed., *Entsyklopediia istorii Ukrainy*, vol. 10, Kyiv, 2013, pp. 722–3.
124 http://history.org.ua/?searchByPart&termin_hit, accessed 30.8.17.
125 https://uk.wikipedia.org/wiki/500-річчя_Магдебурзького_права_Києва_(монета), accessed 30.8.17; https://uk.wikipedia.org/wiki/500-річчя_Магдебурзького_права_Києва_(срібна_монета), accessed 30.8.17.
126 https://uk.wikipedia.org/wiki/500-річчя_битви_під_Оршею_(монета), accessed 30.8.17.
127 https://uk.wikipedia.org/wiki/Грюнвальдська_битва, accessed 30.8.17.
128 Yakovenko, *Paralel'nyi svit. Doslidzhennia z istorii uiavlen' ta idei v Ukraini XVI–XVII st.*, pp. 378–9.

9
THE JAGIELLONIAN DYNASTY IN RUSSIAN HISTORIOGRAPHY AND MEMORY

Olga Kozubska-Andrusiv

As grand dukes of Lithuania (1377–1596), the Jagiellonians' relations with the principalities of Rus' that would later form the core of the Russian state were rich and multi-faceted. The founder of the dynasty, Jogaila (Jagiełło/Yogaila, d.1434), was the son of Juliana, a daughter of Alexander, the grand duke of the Tver' Principality (d.1339). Moreover, Juliana negotiated a marriage between Jogaila and the daughter of Dmitriy (Donskoy, d.1389), Duke of Moscow, which, however, never came to fruition. The consequences of the choice made by Jogaila in 1385 were felt by his successors in the fifteenth century, when the conflicts between Lithuania and Moscow developed a character that was not only political, but also partially religious.[1] The Jagiellonians ruled over vast territories inhabited by Eastern Slavs and dominated by the Orthodox Church; that is, the lands of former Kievan Rus' annexed by Lithuania. At its height, the Grand Duchy of Lithuania stretched from the Baltic to the Black Sea, and from Polish borders to the region of Moscow: the lands of Rus' amounted to nine-tenths of the whole territory of the Duchy, and were inhabited by the predecessors of modern Ukrainians, Belarusians and Russians.[2] Since both Lithuania and the Duchy of Moscow were growing at the expense of their new territories, their borders edged closer and interests collided, resulting in numerous military conflicts. The so-called Russian-Lithuanian 'border wars', for instance, were conducted in 1487–94 during the reigns of Ivan III, the grand duke of Moscow (r.1462–1505), known as a 'gatherer of Russian lands', and Casimir Jagiellon (grand duke of Lithuania, 1440–92, king of Poland from 1447). A peace agreement was concluded in 1494, two years after Casimir's death, and was ensured by the marriage of Casimir's son Alexander (grand duke, 1492–1506) to Elena (Helena of Muscovy), a daughter of Ivan III. Nevertheless, this did not put an end to disagreements between the two countries, as later wars clearly demonstrated.[3] Taking the long history of political, military and dynastic contacts and interactions into account, this essay considers the treatment of the

Jagiellonian dynasty in Russian-language scholarship from the nineteenth century to the present, tracing three main periods (imperial, Soviet and post-Soviet) as well as accounting for the place of the Jagiellonians in the present-day public memory of the Russian Federation.

Historiography of the imperial period

Modern non-chronicle historical writing emerged in Russia in the eighteenth century. Starting with Karamzin's *History of the Russian State*,[4] the most important subject in Russian historiography of the nineteenth century became the formation of the state or the 'gathering of Russian lands' with its centre in Moscow.[5] At that time, many educated Russians supported the view that Russian empire-building was largely the process of collecting the indigenous Russian lands.[6] The incorporation of Lithuanian, Ukrainian, Polish and Belarusian lands into the Russian empire that had occurred after the Partitions of the Polish-Lithuanian Commonwealth in the late eighteenth century drew the attention of Russians to this region and its history. Because there was practically no book in Russian on the history of Poland, the translation of Bandtke's *Dzieje narodu polskiego (The Deeds of Polish People)* was highly welcomed.[7]

Armed rebellions in the recently incorporated territories became a subject of concern for intellectuals of the empire. Alexander Pushkin (1799–1837), arguably Russia's greatest poet, became highly sensitive to the issue of imperial geography after the Polish uprising of 1830–31; he depicted the imperial space (called the 'Russian lands') as extending from Finland to China, so that Poland, too, was an integral part of Russian imperial geography.[8] Simultaneously, historians realised the necessity of incorporating the annexed lands into the Russian historical grand narrative and of producing 'historical justifications' for political developments and territorial expansions. One of the first responses to this challenge came from N. Ustryalov, whose works were seminal for the following generation of Russian historians. Ustryalov raised questions about the location of the Grand Duchy of Lithuania (GDL) in Russian history.[9] For him, the Grand Duchy consisted of Lithuania proper (Gedimin's patrimony) and the 'native Russian lands' annexed by Lithuanians, where this pagan folk became 'dissolved' in the mass of Russian people.[10] The union of 1385 (called 'accidental circumstances') changed the situation, when the grandson of Gedimin, Jogaila, turned to Catholicism and united the Lithuanian Duchy with Poland, despite the desire of his subjects to live under an Orthodox Tsar.[11] Thus the author constructed a dichotomy of 'faithful ordinary people' versus 'treacherous rulers' that would be often repeated in later works. For Ustryalov, the Jagellonians were primarily members of a Lithuanian dynasty ('the house of Gedimin'), and as such connected to Russian history. At the same time, the name of Jogaila became connected to the beginning of Polish/Catholic expansion into the 'Russian lands' of Lithuania.

S. Soloviev (1820–79) and V. Klyuchevsky also shared the view that large parts of Russia's western borderlands were actually indigenous Russian lands, dispersed from the fall of medieval Kievian Rus', after Tatar-Mongol attacks and the annexations conducted by Poland and Lithuania.[12] Both historians supported the idea that the Russian empire was a Russian nation-state, attempting to apply the Western European concept of a nation to Russian reality.[13] Yet the newly self-proclaimed nation was an empire – a multi-ethnic conglomerate of numerous races, cultures and peoples gathered together by the power of the Muscovite tsars, who had now become Russian emperors.[14] As the case of the Polish-Lithuanian Commonwealth demonstrated, Russian historians preferred to view the subjugated territories as 'primordial Russian lands' inhabited by an 'indigenous Russian population' that were finally 'gathered' in one state.

According to Soloviev, both Moscow dukes in the north-east and Lithuanian dukes in the south-west were 'gathering' Russian lands, thus creating two states that soon entered into conflict with each other.[15] In Soloviev's view, by concluding the Union of Kreva/Krewo in 1385, 'Jogaila betrayed his own people, sacrificing their interests for the interest of aliens'.[16] In this way, Jogaila, the founder of the dynasty, was represented by Soloviev (as by Ustryalov) as a national traitor who, contrary to the wish of 'his own people', joined the union with Catholic Poland.

After the January insurrection of 1863–64 was crushed, Russian authorities initiated a number of policies to increase their control and reduce Polish cultural influence: the Commonwealth lands were to be re-claimed by the Russian nation and cleansed of Polish and Catholic influences.[17] The military expeditions of Russian troops undertaken against Polish and Lithuanian patriotic insurgents became a source of historical reminiscence in the book by G. Karpov.[18] Focusing on the confrontations between the two states in the past, the author viewed the Jagiellonians adversarially, as conquerors and problem makers.

After 1863–64, historians intensified their search for persuasive arguments and justifications for the right of the empire on these territories. The view that Lithuania was, in fact, the lands of western Rus' (sometimes termed as 'West-Russism' – *zapadnorussism*) emerged, a perspective which saw Lithuanians, Belarusians and Ukrainians as branches of one 'western Russian folk'. M. Koyalovich (1828–91), the main proponent of 'West-Russism', combined his interest in history with active participation in political discussions in Russian periodicals. Of Belarusian origin, he concentrated on the history of the Grand Duchy of Lithuania and published a collection of documents with a foreword[19] and his *Lectures on the History of Western Russia*.[20] Despite his political sentiments, which are easily discernible from his writing, Koyalovich was one of the first to provide a rational explanation for the Union of Krewo in 1385 without seeing it as an 'accident' resulting from Jogaila's personal ambitions. This, however, did not stop the tendency to present a negative picture of Jogaila, visible for instance in the work of M. Smirnov.[21]

Discussing personal features of Jogaila became a commonplace in the nineteenth century, as for instance in the work of A. Barbashev: the author contrasted the 'extraordinary personality of Vytovt' with the 'primitive Jogaila' (1885).[22] Since Polish scholars 'stubbornly and unjustifiably emphasised the Polish elements in Lithuanian history and hid the Russian ones', the immediate duty of Russian historians should be to disclose this bias and to raise the Russian element to its rightful position. These statements of Barbashev demonstrate once more how historical writing served an important element in the imperial policy of the 'elimination of Polish influences from Russian lands'.

P. Batyushkov, a high official in the imperial administration in Kaunas, dealt extensively with the 'historical destinies' of Lithuania and Belarus, supporting the idea of Lithuania as 'another Russian state' (1890).[23] As a result, his text states that the Russian empire incorporated 'Russian-Lithuanian regions' in 1772–93 and that 'this land is clearing itself from the deposits left by the Polish-Catholic yoke'.[24] The term 'clearing' is symptomatic for a member of the Russian bureaucracy authorised to carry out imperial assimilation policy. This policy was not limited to the restoration and strengthening of Orthodoxy and the 'original Russian character': a general and thorough de-Polonisation was necessary for the elimination of alien 'deposits'.[25]

S. Ilovayskiy dedicated a whole chapter of his *History of Russia* to Jogaila ('Jogaila and the Beginning of Polish-Lithuanian Union').[26] Speculating about Jogaila's personality, he repeated characteristics mentioned by earlier authors such as cruelty, immorality and cunning, adding also laziness and a passion for hunting.[27] Nevertheless, such speculations became rare in the increasingly sophisticated and rational Russian historiography of the late nineteenth century. By the end of the nineteenth century, most scholars had stopped talking about Jogaila's personal motives for the union. Instead, they turned to rational explanations of historical events, focusing on the economic and political factors of the union. This meant that less attention was paid to the founder of the Jagiellonian dynasty, even though the image of Jogaila as a traitor remained.

The status of the Lithuanian-Russian state in the Polish-Lithuanian Commonwealth and its social and political order were the main questions in *The GDL during the Time of the Lublin Union and until the Death of Stephan Bathory* by I. Lappo.[28] In Lappo's opinion, the history of the Russian people exceeds the history of the Russian state, and the Partitions of the Commonwealth were a unification of the 'two Russian states' (1901), Muscovy and the GDL.[29] In his evaluation of the deeds of the Jagiellonian dynasty, Lappo followed the lead of another Russian scholar – A. Trachevsky.[30] Trachevsky himself had assessed the ascent of the Jagiellonian dynasty to the Polish throne negatively, seeing it as a golden age of the 'disastrous nobility': that 'ugly historical anomaly – the noble republic or noble democracy' (1869).[31] Lithuania, 'with its powerful aristocracy and strong stately order, its attraction to Russian civilisation and eastern Orthodoxy', represented a striking contrast to 'chaotic noble Poland subjected to influences from the West with its Catholicism'.[32] Indeed, seeing a strong centralised monarchy as an ideal stately order, Russian historians were suspicious with regard to the far more pluralist Polish-Lithuanian Commonwealth. Similarly, A. Presnyakov in his *Lithuanian-Russian State*[33] emphasised the 'national and cultural-historical differences' between the Lithuanian-Russian state and Poland: this argument, repeated many times, had aimed to demonstrate the unstable character of the Polish-Lithuanian unions.

Summarising a century-long period of Russian imperial historiography, one has to admit that the Jagiellonian dynasty did not represent a separate topic for research: the members of the dynasty were mentioned when relevant to the events of Russian history (even if this was a history of the 'Lithuanian-Russian state'). Jogaila, the founder of the dynasty, received most scholarly attention. He was seen primarily as a Lithuanian ruler[34] and a member of the Gedimin dynasty, whose connections to Rus' were emphasised in every relevant context. In contrast to his grand ducal predecessors (like Mindovg or Gedimin), who were understood as participants in the Russian cultural and political sphere, Jogaila and his 1385 union with Poland represented a clear deviation. In Russian historiography of the period, Jogaila was typically depicted as a traitor who deceived his own people and brought them under Polish influence.

The territorial gains of the late eighteenth century, and a pressing need to incorporate annexed territories into the Russian imperial/national narrative, resulted in the concept of 'indigenous Russian lands' that having once been seized by neighbouring powers were now united again under Russian rule, and had become an integral part of the imperial 'Us'. By stressing the 'Russian character' of Lithuanians and seeing the GDL as 'primordial Russian lands', historians constructed the notion of a 'Lithuanian-Russian state', which evolved from Kievan Rus' and existed until the end of the Jagiellonian dynasty. However, members of the dynasty that led 'Russian lands' and the 'Russian people' away from unity with Moscow could not be an attractive subject for imperial historiography.

If Lithuania became a part of a bigger 'Us' in the historiography, Poland was doubtlessly seen as an aggressive and expansionist 'Other' who alienated and despoiled the Lithuanian part of 'Us'.[35] Unsurprisingly, many historians aimed to minimise Polish influences, and treated the history of Lithuania in a certain isolation from Poland. Moreover, the overriding emphasis was on the 'historical incorporation' of lands and peoples into the empire, but certainly not their rulers. Ignoring the dynasty as 'agents of alien powers', historians focused on the idea of the 'Russian people of Lithuania' who remained faithful to their cultural heritage and resisted the foreign (that is Polish) influences, which were violently introduced by their deceiving rulers. In the next, Soviet period, this concept of 'folk masses struggling for liberation' and 'wishing to unite themselves with the Russians' would be developed further and fully exploited in historical writing.

The Soviet period

At the beginning of the twentieth century, the GDL was a research subject in several universities in the Russian empire, with many scholars actively engaging with its history. The situation changed dramatically in the Soviet period, with the 1920s as a turning point in the study of the GDL. Many members of the older generation of historians had to leave Russia and continue their work in exile; Moscow, St Petersburg and Kiev ceased to be centres of Lithuanian/West Russian studies as Soviet historians showed little interest in the subject. After 1918, the borders of the Russian state changed once more, and 'western Rus'' became external once again – as Poland and Lithuania (and very briefly Belarus and Ukraine) became independent republics, which cut them away from a Russian national and stately narrative.

After the Second World War (1939–45), the situation changed yet again: the Soviet Union annexed western Ukraine and the Baltic states, and the task of the Soviet scholar became to incorporate their histories into a general concept of the history of the USSR.[36] As in the previous century, it was also necessary to justify this incorporation, and to construct a historical perspective for the 'common destiny' of these 'gathered lands'. However, the situation differed from that of the nineteenth century: in contrast to the Russian empire, which had annexed parts of the Polish-Lithuanian Commonwealth, the USSR (and earlier Soviet Russia) had to deal with nation-states. Thus the concept of 'gathering of primordial Russian lands' was substituted by the idea of the 'liberation' of 'brotherly republics' and their willing unification in 'one family of the USSR'. The concept that the Slavic people of the GDL aspired to be united with the Russian state was repeated in all Soviet grand narratives and in the national narratives of individual republics, such as the voluminous 'official' histories of the Lithuanian Soviet Socialist Republic (SSR), Belarusian SSR, or Ukrainian SSR.[37]

Moreover, Marxist history writing in its Soviet version focused on class struggle, oppressed nationalities, and the history of the popular masses, dismissing the importance of individual actors in historical processes, with few opportunities for the exploration of subjects like the Jagiellonians.[38] The first work on Lithuanian history written at this time – *The Formation of the Lithuanian State* by V. Pashuto – can be seen as an attempt to present the history of the GDL from a Marxist point of view, as well as to provide a necessary adaptation of Lithuanian history to new circumstances.[39] The author noted that the development of the GDL was essential to the general history of the Lithuanian SSR as well as 'for the evaluation of political development in the national states of Russia, Poland and the Baltics [*Pribaltika* in the original]'.[40] Pashuto critically assessed the previous 'bourgeois' scholarship that 'saw the emergence of the Lithuanian state as a result of the activity of Lithuanian dukes'.[41] As a result, everything connected to the dynastic history of Lithuanian dukes (or the Polish kings) was deemed irrelevant. The work also demonstrates a change in the attitude towards Lithuania: it was pictured as an aggressor occupying Belarusian and Ukrainian lands, so that 'peoples oppressed by Lithuania were seeking support from the fraternal Russian folk and from the centralised Russian state'.[42] Moreover, the growth of the centralised/heterogeneous Russian state meant a simultaneous decline of 'feudal Lithuania'.[43]

In the Soviet as well as in the imperial historiography, a centralised unified state was recognised as the ideal political order and the main goal of any political formation: the success or failure of a ruler is often measured against the 'fullness' of this centralisation. Whilst castigating abstract Lithuanian or Polish feudal lords, Pashuto nevertheless appreciated the deeds of the medieval Lithuanian dukes (Mindovg, Keystut, Olgerd, etc.), whom he called 'not only distinguished statesmen, but also talented military leaders'.[44] Additionally, the author expressed a 'deep respect' for Lithuanian and Belarusian peoples in their liberating wars against the 'aggression of German feudal lords', i.e. Teutonic Knights.[45] Indeed, the Teutonic Order (as a historical echo of the recently defeated Nazi Germany) became the archenemy in Soviet medieval scholarship of that time, taking the role Catholic Poland had held in the old historiography. For Pashuto, the union between Poland and Lithuania (1385) was an urgent political necessity in the face of German aggression, an important factor in the liberation struggle of the people, a position which constituted an obvious break from an older historiographic tradition.[46]

Even if Poland lost its role of aggressive 'Other', both Poland and Lithuania were treated ambivalently by Soviet historians: on the one hand, Polish or Lithuanian 'folk masses' were viewed positively; on the other, Polish or Lithuanian feudal lords – oppressors and exploiters – were not. The presentation of the 'people's masses' as a decisive historical agent was commonplace in school textbooks too.[47] However, both the 'masses' and their 'oppressors' (landowners, nobility, dukes, Polish kings, etc.) usually remained abstract and anonymous. A shared history was an important unifying element in the USSR, and every nation's goal was final unification with the 'fraternal Russian people' (as 'unification' under an Orthodox Russian ruler had been in the imperial period). Therefore, the Communist party urged historians not to emphasise the historical conflicts between the nations of the Soviet Union. As a result, other schemes of Lithuanian history were constructed, emphasising the need for Russian aid and Russians as 'the only true allies' in the struggle of the Lithuanians against German aggressors.[48]

B. Floria, writing in 1978, shifted the accent from 'feudal occupation' to 'feudal colonisation', and for him Jogaila's 1385 union had meant access to new land: 'establishing Jogaila on the Polish throne, the Polish ruling class strived to open Eastern Europe to their feudal colonisation'.[49] However, these plans did not come to fruition, because of the 'formation of the centralised Russian state and its program of the complete elimination of the political lordship of Polish and Lithuanian "feudals" in Belarusian and Ukrainian lands'.[50] This emphasis on land colonisation probably reflected a general interest in different aspects of the social history of the GDL, as peasants, urban life, the social elite, and law became subjects of study.[51] One more distinctive feature of the works of Floria: he avoided the geographical constructs of imperial scholarship such as 'western Rus'' or 'south-western Rus''. In those rare cases where a notion from 'imperial geography' was employed (like Russian lands/*russkie zemli* in Lithuania), he expressed it with quotation marks.

The research agenda of Marxist historiography was not a suitable environment for the emergence of a study of the Jagiellonians. Even the declining ideological and methodological restrictions of the late 1980s did not bring great change. The paradigm of national/statist historiography, methodological conservatism, and a lack of information about the research directions of Western scholarship (historical anthropology and study of royal rituals, prosopography, or gender studies, etc.) obstructed the chance of seeing the royal dynasties in a new light.

The post-Soviet period

The release of the ideological pressure on history writing in the USSR felt at the end of the 1980s did not reduce the pressure on the past. Facing the collapse of the existing order, historians were among those who felt obliged to assess the current situation and eventually to suggest a direction for further development. 'What is Russia?' asked research papers; round table discussions and conferences searched carefully for flaws, for schisms, for cultural or even genetic traits — anything that could explain the perceived failure to be prosperous, democratic, truly European. This intellectual mood of self-punishing introspection, although not new, had clearly been affected by political and economic uncertainty.[52]

The fall of the Soviet Union demonstrated that a strong centralised power, praised by Soviet ideologists, was not a guarantee of success. In this context, the image of the Grand Duchy of Lithuania and the Polish-Lithuanian Commonwealth as religiously and ethnically pluralistic states, as 'another Rus'' which was able to implement cultural, democratic and legal conventions of Europe (in contrast to Muscovite Rus'), and which enjoyed a more tolerant and democratic model of development (again, unlike autocratic Moscow), started to emerge.[53] This view was expressed by S. Dumin: 'the experience of the Great Lithuanian and Russian Duchy demonstrates that not only the Asian despotism of Ivan the Terrible could be created in the east-Slavic lands, but also an effective functioning of the democratic institutions of a multi-national state'.[54] In this context, a re-evaluation of the role of Jogaila ('the oldest son of a Tver' Princess') and his union with Poland looks quite logical. For Dumin, the unification with Poland changed the situation in the Grand Duchy in a positive way: 'Lithuania faced the West . . . this time west-European cultural influences, which were channelled through *friendly* [sic!] Poland, became much stronger and left more durable and visible results, than all the raids of Teutonic Knights.'[55] Indeed, any aspects of 'facing the West' or 'European cultural influence' discovered in past centuries were an integral part of Russian (and post-Soviet) political rhetoric in the early 1990s. Dumin revised widely spread Russian historiographical clichés such as the 'Catholic expansion' and the 'wish of Ukrainian and Belarusian folks to be united with Russians', and commented ironically on the contemporary belief among historians that the inhabitants of southern and western Rus' shared Moscow's program of unification.[56]

A gradual process of strengthening national sentiments and a preference for the national problematics of historical writing can be observed as early as the Soviet period, especially towards its end. This process became particularly intense after the collapse of the Soviet Union (1991) and in the national republics, which now became independent states. The 'nationally selective' approach also affected the study of the GDL, while more and more works were published in languages other than Russian. S. Polekhov noted that topics on the history of the GDL became popular in those states that emerged on the Duchy's territory (i.e. Lithuania, Belarus and Ukraine), and that its history was incorporated into the picture of the national past of these states.[57]

Topics on the 'Russian lands' of the Grand Duchy of Lithuania continued to appear in Russian scholarship.[58] A. Dvornichenko, for instance, published on social and political structures in the 'Russian lands of the Grand Duchy of Lithuania', focusing primarily on towns.[59] Relations with Rus' and the formation of the Lithuanian state became the subject of D. Alexandrov's research.[60] Following the 'cultural turn' in historiography, M. Krom (1997) dealt with the mindsets of different social groups (social elite, burghers, clergy) in the borderlands of the late fifteenth and early sixteenth centuries in his book 'Between Rus' and Lithuania'.[61] Krom posed the problem of political loyalty among different groups of urban dwellers in the towns on the border, forced to choose between Moscow and Lithuania, as a central question of his work. In contrast to the stereotypes spread by Soviet historiography, Krom demonstrated that this choice did not always favour Moscow. M. Bychkova compared the governmental institutions, social structures, and political ideologies of the Russian state and the Grand Duchy of Lithuania.[62] Applying a multi-disciplinary approach and analysing written, archaeological and cartographical sources, V. Yanin investigated the relationships between Novgorod and Lithuania in the fifteenth century.[63] I. Starostina continued to study legal sources from the GDL.[64] Amongst the scholarly texts dealing, whether directly or indirectly, with the Jagiellonian dynasty in the 2000s, the Russian-language articles of Belarusian scholar Z. Nekrashevich-Korotkaya, whose research area is the history of early modern Latin poetry in the GDL, must be mentioned.[65] The model of the Lithuanian state, rather than the Jagiellonian dynasty, attracted the interest of the editors of 'Istoricheskiy Vestnik', when they invited scholars from not only Russia but Ukraine, Belarus, Lithuania, and Poland to present their views on the subject.[66] S. Polekhov's book on the Lithuanian dynastic wars, *Vitovt's Heirs: The Dynastic War in the Grand Duchy of Lithuania in the 1430s*, was published in 2015.[67]

However, in the late 1990s, interest in the history of the GDL started to decline in Russian historiography. Discussing this tendency, A. Filyushkin offered the following explanations: first, there were no academic research centres dealing with the history of the GDL; second, numerous dissertations defended in post-Soviet times had not led to the formation of distinctive research schools in Russian scholarship.[68] Earlier, reviewing the recent historiography on the GDL in Russia, Filyushkin had stated that in most cases the study of the Grand Duchy of Lithuania and Polish-Lithuanian Commonwealth was a result of private interests and the initiatives of individual scholars dealing with the history of Eastern Europe. Moreover, the GDL had not, in his opinion, developed into a separate subject of research, but had been investigated in the context of more comprehensive problems such as international politics, Eastern European wars, cultural and religious life, or general Russian history.[69] Filyushkin did not, however, offer an explanation of this phenomenon. Why had the initial enthusiasm and interest in the GDL in the early 1990s declined in the 2000s? Why had there been no proper study of the Jagiellonian dynasty? A closer look at the general situation of history and memory in post-Soviet Russia can potentially give more answers.

The decade after the collapse of communism was notable for the absence of any official ideology. In the 1990s, the memory politics of Boris Yeltsin's government followed a model of 'cultural patriotism', emphasising not so much Russia's imperial glory but rather its cultural achievements, especially in the eighteenth and nineteenth centuries, which many Russians consider as at the very least comparable to those of the West. The situation began to change drastically under Putin: the greatness of the Russian empire replaced its culture as the key theme of the new memory politics.[70] The cult of the state became the core of the 'new Russian ideology', which aims to justify the immense increase of the president's power and the return to a neo-imperial stance in foreign policy.[71] Tracing the reflection of these developments in scholarship, one notices that the focus of researchers in the 1990s was on the notion of the nation, whereas the following decade saw a renewed interest in the notion of empire in what has been termed the 'imperial turn'.[72]

In the 2000s, the evolution of Vladimir Putin's regime was accompanied by a new revision of history that has again become central to the new 'Russian ideology' whose proponents proclaim that, after the collapse of the traditional ideologies, the 'politics of history is the only possible form of politics' and have integrated history into a strategy of self-assertion.[73] The Second World War became central to the new 'history politics' (or the new 'memory politics'). Contemporary Russian authorities pretend that Poland, Ukraine and the Baltic countries initiated memory wars against Russia.[74] In order to 'defend the memory of the Great Patriotic War', the Russian government initiated an impressive memorial campaign. In May 2009, President Dmitri Medvedev summoned a commission to address the 'falsifications of history to the detriment of Russia's interests'. Simultaneously, the governing United Russia party proposed a law against the 'rehabilitation of Nazism', making it a culpable offence to 'violate the historical memory of events which took place during the Second World War'.[75] Investigating Russian historical memory and related legislation, N. Koposov noted ironically that one has to appreciate the uniqueness of the proposed law: memory laws as they exist in the West defend the memory of those who suffered crimes committed by the government. In contrast, the Russian law intends to defend the memory of the state.[76]

In Russia, the desire to be recognised as a great world power seems inseparable from national identity. There is also a deep-rooted sense of why Russia has so often fallen short of realising its supposedly preordained potential as a great power: just like in the paradigmatic case of the *smuta* (Time of Troubles, 1598–1613), difficulties can only be overcome by a joint popular effort and by a resourceful leader who unites the people and restores order.[77] The idealisation of a strong leader and a centralised power equal to that of the Stalinist era led to glorification of Stalin and his politics, and to neo-Stalinism. As N. Adler observed, in Russia, two decades after the collapse of the Soviet Union, Stalin's popularity has soared in nationwide polls, reflecting a popular longing for the country's former prestige and the accompanying sense of security.[78]

It is obvious that under the new Russian ideology, which proclaimed a consolidated (centralised) state and its 'greatness' the highest priority, anything that is associated with plurality, tolerance and various degrees of decentralisation will struggle to find favour. Even historically, when Lithuania and parts of Poland belonged to the empire, the Jagiellonians did not become a part of the Russian historical 'Us'. They are unlikely to become so now. The Jagiellonian epoch and the social order associated with it are of no appeal to contemporary 'memorial politics' in Russia.

The Jagiellonian dynasty in literature and media

Radio and TV programs

Radio programs about Lithuanian and Polish history in Russian are rare, but two podcasts from the radio station 'Ekho Moskvy' deserve our attention. The first program, *Jogaila, the Grand Duke of Lithuania*, was broadcast on 7 January 2007, with history professor N. Basovkaya as a guest speaker.[79] Starting with the question 'What do our school pupils know about Jogaila?' the guest and the journalist (A. Venediktov) delivered a somewhat chaotic discussion of the duke's personality ('he was a hero in history, but a terrible person in private life'), the Kulikovo (1380) and Grünwald (1410) battles, the paintings of Jan Matejko (d.1893), and the beginning of Lithuania and its relationship with the Teutonic Order. *The Grand Duchy of Lithuania*, aired from 16 March 2013, was a discussion with historian Igor Danilevskiy, who stressed that the history of the GDL belonged to Russian history as well as to the histories of modern Lithuania, Belarus, Ukraine, and Poland.[80] He also mentioned Jogaila as the founder of the Jagiellonian dynasty 'that ruled Poland for a long time', but generally focused on a different set of questions (language, religion, the GDL as another model of a Rus' state, etc.). TV programs such as *The Grand Duchy of Lithuania. Another Rus'* (19 March 2014)[81] and *Gordon's Program: The Grand Duchy of Lithuania* (16 January 2015) with Dvornichenko as a speaker[82] worked to popularise the idea of the GDL as an alternative Rus', but with practically no reference to the Jagiellonians.

The Jagiellonian dynasty in urban memory: a website of the town of Trubchevsk

Trubchevsk, a town in the Briansk region of Russia, has its own website ('informational portal') with a detailed history of the settlement. The compiler dedicated a lengthy part of the history ('Trubetskiye and Jogailans or how long does a dynasty last?') to the dynasties that were important to the town.[83] The two dynasties are taken as a pretext for thoughts on destinies of the historical personages: 'why are children born from the same parents so diametrically opposed in their behaviour?' asked the author. This introduction defined the way in which the narrative developed, creating a sharp contrast between the founder of the Trubetskiye dynasty, Dmitriy Olgerdovich, on the one hand, and the founder of the Jagiellonian dynasty on the other.

The former (Dmitriy) was known for 'shedding his blood on Kulikovo field', while the latter (Jogaila) 'attacked powerless Russian troops'; the former was 'a decent Orthodox Christian', while the latter, 'born as pagan, became a Catholic in order to gain the crown, but remained a pagan in his essence'; Dmitriy had only one wife, while Jogaila 'had four wives and his behaviour violated invisible spiritual laws'. Dmitriy was 'so noble in his conduct' due to his Orthodox faith, and consequently 'his genealogical tree grew, in contrast to that of Jogaila'. It is difficult to determine the cause of such a negative, xenophobic attitude towards the Jagiellonians. As a private initiative, this history of Trubchevsk reflected the private views of its compiler. At the same time, it remains on the website (the only website containing a history of the town), so it may reveal the 'popular memory' of the Jagiellonians in Briansk.

Electronic media have demonstrated another tendency of Russian 'commemorative strategies': an attempt to 'nationalise' important events in the history of the GDL, such as the Grünwald battle of 1410. The website of the Russian Military-Historical Society, funded by Putin in 2012 and designed to investigate and produce propaganda for Russian military history, states that 15 July 1410 should be commemorated as the day when 'Russian troops and their allies . . . defeated German knights . . .'[84] Paradoxically, Soviet historiography, which was often accused of distortion and the falsification of historical facts, called the battle 'a victory of Polish and Lithuanian people'. Contemporary Russian 'historical policy makers' went much further and unequivocally attributed the victory to 'Russian troops'.

Cinema

Films related to the history of the Jagiellonians in the Russian language have been produced by Belarusian filmmakers. The earliest, *Trap for a Zubr. Vitovt* (1995), was produced by the National TV and Radio Company of Belarus, and depicted 'not only the facts of the bygone times of the GDL, but also the deeds of the people who strived for power and glory', representing Vitovt (Vytautas) as 'the leader of Belarusian feudal lords in the struggle for independence', as well as his antagonist Jogaila. *Legends of the Grand Duchy* (2005) is a documentary dedicated to the 595th anniversary of the Grünwald battle, and includes Jogaila and Vitovt as representatives of Poland and the Grand Duchy respectively. Film production is a much more costly enterprise than fiction writing, the creation of a website, or even the organisation of a radio interview: it is usually a state or commercially sponsored process. At the same time, film is a powerful medium that shapes collective memories of the past and therefore cannot be ignored by those who form the national 'memory policy'. In the process of creating its own national historical narrative, Belarus turned to the subject of the GDL and the Jagiellonians, seeing the Grand Duchy as a predecessor of the Belarusian state, and medieval Lithuanians as future Belarusians.[85] Russia, on the other hand, selected different topics to animate its national history, and a lack of Russian films on the Jagiellonians does not mean that Russian film producers have ignored the historical genre. On the contrary: patriotic culture dominated Russia's movie screens; and, starting from the late 1990s, the American practices of blockbuster productions were adopted to make Russian historical epics.[86] Movies about Prince Vladimir, the pre-Kievan past, Russian tsars (e.g. Ivan the Terrible), the Time of Troubles etc., all attempted to provide myths about the Russian nation, its heroic values, and sources of rebirth after 1991. The cartoon *Prince Vladimir* (2006) serves as a good example: organised on a big scale, this project was supported by academic D. Likhachov, assisted by famous archaeologist V. Yanin, and even blessed by the Patriarch Alexy II (for the first time in the history of animation).[87] Because historical film 'performs' the national historical narrative, often interpreting and reinforcing it, topics for filming are carefully selected in accordance to their relevance for national historiography and the current political moment.

As is discussed above, the Russian leadership routinely reinforces the memory of the Second World War as 'pre-eminently a Russian national symbol' and encourages Soviet nostalgia.[88] In this context, the film industry has contributed to the propaganda of Russian glory and heroism during 'the Great Patriotic War'. A vivid illustration of this trend is a new film, *Panfilov's 28 Men* (2016): showing Red Army soldiers outnumbered by invading Germans but battling on heroically, it has become part of Putin's campaign to restore Russian pride. Even though the film is based on a Communist myth, the themes of the story chime with the Kremlin's worldview: the Second World War as a heroic victory that united the Soviet state against fascism, and still unites today's Russia against a similar threat that has, they claim, resurfaced in Ukraine.[89] G. Carleton rightly remarked that war narratives would seem to be the optimum vehicle to reclaim or revitalise Soviet cultural mythologies.[90] Not only are they eminently well suited for the re-enactment and display of ideo-historical conceits, the aesthetic imperatives typically associated with them recall canonical standards of socialist realism: the 'binary opposition' between good and evil, the protagonist reflecting 'heroic (or epic) archetypes', the subordination of female characters to the 'male superior' and, last but not least, the victorious resolution of conflict.[91]

It is possible to conclude that, in modern Russia, the Jagiellonians belong to the domain of world history (and not national history) and are seldom discussed on TV or in radio programs. They do not have a place in the national memory and rare references to the dynasty or Jogaila himself reveal a rather negative attitude that could be explained by the clichés of schoolbooks and by the view of the Polish-Lithuanian Commonwealth as an enemy of the Russian state. Despite a clear interest in filming national historical epics, film producers in modern Russia have paid little attention to the Jagiellonian dynasty, dealing with subjects more directly related to national history and national glory.

Summary

'Academic history has rhythms and priorities of its own, but its tone and overall agenda, at least in Russia, derive in obvious ways from the society it serves.'[92] These words of Merridale were written about post-Soviet realities, but they are easily applicable to the whole, more than two hundred year long period of Russian historiography. Even though its subject matter relates to the distant past, historiography is also linked by hidden threads to the present, to current historical/political situations, to 'history in the making', and to its reflection in the minds of historians, who are themselves part of historiography.

The imperial period (that is the nineteenth until the early twentieth century) was the height of scholarly interest in the Jagiellonians. Nevertheless, the dynasty and its individual members did not usually represent a subject of study per se, but were mentioned in the context of the history of Russia or the GDL. Imperial Russia's annexation of part of the Polish-Lithuanian Commonwealth in the late eighteenth century, and the subsequent uprisings of the 1830s and 1860s, demonstrated a pressing need for a historically grounded justification of the territorial gains of the empire, and for the incorporation of these territories into the Russian 'national state'. As a result, a concept of the 'western part of Rus'' or the 'Lithuanian-Russian state' inhabited by 'Russian people' was constructed and developed in the second half of the nineteenth century. The 'Lithuanian-Russian state' as an alternative 'gathering of Rus' lands' became a subject of research for many Russian historians. The Union of Krewo (1385), when the Lithuanian grand duke Jogaila united his Duchy with Poland, was understood as a turning point, enabling Polish cultural and religious influences, and endangering the 'primordial Russian character' of the land. The name of Jogaila, the founder of the dynasty, became associated with negative (from a Russian point of view) tendencies such as the spread of Catholicism, Polonisation, and the gradual elimination of the political autonomy of the state. Jogaila became the most investigated member of the dynasty, and his deeds and personal qualities were examined and evaluated (usually in a negative way). At the same time, there is only one study dedicated entirely to Jogaila (or the Jagiellonians). The annexed territory and its population, rather than its former rulers, represented the main interest for the Russian empire. Thus it was more important for Russian historians to concentrate on the history of a broadly-defined 'Russian nation' and the past of the territories of its empire. The dynasty, which opened 'the western part of Rus'' to alien influences and contributed to the decline of the 'Lithuanian-Russian state', found little appreciation in a historiography shaped by the stately/national paradigm.

The Soviet times brought important changes to the political geography of Eastern Europe and Russian historiography. Lithuania became independent (1918–39) and situated outside the Russian state as well as outside its historiography. Later, the annexation of Lithuania by the USSR was followed by the emergence of studies about the Lithuanian past. However, spheres of investigations defined by the Marxist methodology and Soviet ideology excluded the Jagiellonians from the recognised research subjects.

The end of the Soviet era (1991) and the release of ideological pressure led to the revival of concepts from the imperial historiography: the 'Lithuanian-Russian state' was understood again as 'another Rus'', but this time its usefulness as a model of alternative development was taken into account. Fascination with the plurality and tolerance associated with the GDL soon declined under the pressure of the new Russian ideology, which declared the centralised state and its 'greatness' the highest priority. The 'new historical policy' left little space for topics such as the Jagiellonian dynasty. The Jagiellonians are now seen as a part of an alien grand narrative and as belonging to general world history. With some insignificant exceptions, the Jagiellonian dynasty has not constituted a separate research subject in Russian historical scholarship. Similarly, the Russian sphere of 'popular history and memory', especially that of recent decades, does not reveal any particular fascination with the Jagiellonians, focusing instead on those subjects that have the potential to raise patriotic sentiments and to unite the Russian people around the state and a strong national leader.

Notes

1. S. Dumin, Drugaya Rus': Velikoye kniazhestvo Litovskoye i Russkoye), *Istoriya Otechestva: lyudi, ideyi, resheniya: ocherki istorii Rossii IX – nachala XX v.*, Moscow, Politizdat, 1991, pp. 76–126; quoted after: www.rulit.me/books/drugaya-rus-velikoe-knyazhestvo-litovskoe-i-russkoe-read-362609-1.html accessed 25.9.17.
2. Ibid.
3. More on the subject: K. Bazilevich, *Vneshnyaya politika Russkogo tsentralizovannogo gosudarstva. Vtoraya polovina XV veka*, Moscow, 1952; D. Alexandrov and D. Volodikhin, *Bor'ba za Polotsk mezhdu Litvoy i Rus'yu v XII-XVI vekakh*, Moscow, Avanta, 1994; Yu. Alexeyev, *Pokhody russkikh pri Ivane III*, St Petersburg, 2007; M. Krom, *Starodubskaya vojyna 1534–1537*, Moscow, 2008.
4. N. Karamzin, *Istoria gosudarstva Rossiyskogo v 12 t.*, St Petersburg, Izdaniye brat'ev Sleninykh, 1816–29.
5. T. Sanders, ed., *Historiography of Imperial Russia: The Profession and Writing of History in a Multinational State*, New York, 1999, pp. 18–19.
6. V. Tolz, *Russia: Inventing the Nation*, London, 2001, p. 161.
7. G. Bandtke, *Istoriya gosudarstva Pol'skogo*, vols 1–2, St Petersburg, 1830.
8. S. Bilenky, *Romantic Nationalism in Eastern Europe. Russian, Polish, and Ukrainian Political Imaginations*, Stanford, CA, 2012, p. 45.
9. N. Ustrialov, *O Litovskom kniyazhestve. Issledovaniye voprosa, kakoye mesto v Russkoy istorii dolzhno zanimat' Velikoye kniazhestvo Litovskoye?*, St Petersburg, 1839.
10. Ibid., p. 17.
11. Ibid., pp. 18, 24.
12. Tolz, *Russia*, p. 172.
13. Ibid., p. 16.
14. S. Plokhy, *Unmaking Imperial Russia: Mykhailo Hrushevsky and the Writing of Ukrainian History*, Toronto, 2005, p. 17.
15. S. Solovyev, *Istoriya Rossii s drevnejshikh vremen*, St Petersburg, 1851–79.
16. Ibid., 2: 1054–1462, vol. 4.
17. T. Weeks, 'Word and Practice 1863–1914', *Proceedings of the American Philosophical Society*, 148, 4, 2004, p. 475.
18. G. Karpov, *Istoriya bor'by Moskovskogo gosudarstva s Pol'sko-Litovskim. 1462–1508*, Moscow, 1867.

19 M. Koyalovich, *Istoricheskoye issledovaniye o Zapadnoj Rusi*, St Petersburg, 1855.
20 M. Koyalovich, *Lektsii po istorii Zapadnoj Rusi*, Moscow, 1864.
21 M. Smirnov, *Yagiello-Yakov-Vladislav I pervoye soyedinenie Litvy s Pol'shej*, Odessa, 1868.
22 A. Barbashev, *Vitovt i yego politika do Grunval'dskoj bitvy (1410)*, St Petersburg, 1885, V–VI.
23 N. Batiushkov, *Belorussiya i Litva. Istoricheskiye sud'by Severo-Zapadnogo kraya*, St Petersburg, Obshchestvennaya pol'za, 1890.
24 Ibid.
25 For more on the subject, see T. Weeks, 'Russification and the Lithuanians, 1863–1905', *Slavic Review*, 60, 1, 2001, pp. 96–114; M. Dolbilov, 'Russian Nationalism and the Nineteenth-Century Policy of Russification in the Russian Empire's Western Region', in K. Matsuzato, ed., *Comparative Imperiology*, Sapporo, 2010, pp. 141–58; M. Staliunas, *Making Russians: Meaning and Practice of Russification in Lithuania and Belarus after 1863*, Amsterdam, Rodopi, 2007.
26 S. Ilovajskij, *Istoriya Rossii*, vol. 2, Moscow, 1896, pp. 87–153.
27 Ibid., p.167.
28 I. Lappo, *Velikoe knyazhestvo Litovskoye za vremya ot zaklyucheniya Lyublinskoj unii do smerti Stefana Batoriya: Opyt issledovaniya politicheskogo i obschestvennogo stroya*, vol. 1, St Petersburg, Tipografiya Mattisena, 1901.
29 Ibid., p. 5.
30 Ibid., p. 91.
31 A. Trachevsky, *Pol'skoe bezkorolev'e po prekrashchenii dinastii Yagellonov*, Moscow, 1869, XV.
32 Ibid., pp. xxxv–xxxvi.
33 A. Presnyakov, *Litovsko-Russkoye gosudarstvo v 13–16 vv.*, St Petersburg, 1910.
34 Russian authors seldom called him Władysław II Jagiełło, as is usual in Polish historiography.
35 For Jagiellonians as 'Them' to a national 'Us', see also Lewis and Mickūnaitė in this volume.
36 As S. Plokhyi pointed out, the year 1934 witnessed a major turn in the development of Soviet historiography: the period of autonomous (if not completely independent) development of national historiographies was over, and their amalgamation into the Russocentric 'history of the USSR' was about to begin. See Plokhy, *Unmaking Imperial Russia*, p. 13.
37 B. Grekov, ed., *Ocherki istorii SSSR. Period feodalizma. Konets XV – nachalo XVII vv*, Moscow, 1955, pp. 147–54; B. Ponomariov, ed., *Istoriya SSSR s drevnejshikh vremen do nashikh dnej*, 12 vols., vol. 2, Moscow, 1966; L. Abetsedarskij, *Istoriya belorusskoj SSR*, T. I., Minsk, 1961; A. Kasymenko et al., *Istoriya Ukrainskoj SSR*, T. I., Kyiv, 1969; Yu. Yurginis et al., *Istoriya Litovskoy SSR*, Vilnius, SSR, 1978.
38 Nevertheless, the fascination of Marxist historians with the 'working masses' did not obstruct the increasing popularity of 'national monarchs' such as Ivan IV the Terrible in Russian historiography of the Soviet period. In line with the Communist party's preoccupation with state-building and legitimacy, a number of figures previously denigrated as representatives of the old regime were popularised as models of decisive leadership (e.g. Ivan IV, Peter the Great and Alexander Nevskiy). This phenomenon was analysed by D. Brandenberger and K. Platt. Disputing the facile reduction of Ivan the Terrible's rehabilitation to a mere symptom of Stalin's cult of personality, they examined the campaign from the perspective of the Russocentric etatist ideological line. See D. Brandenberger and K. Platt, 'Terribly Pragmatic: Rewriting the History of Ivan IV's Reign, 1937–1956', in *Epic Revisionism: Russian History and Literature as Stalinist Propaganda*, Madison, University of Wisconsin Press, 2006, pp. 157–78.
39 V. Pashuto, *Obrazovaniye litovskogo gosudarstva*, Moscow, 1959.
40 Ibid., p. 3. It is necessary to note that Soviet medievalists united the people (and countries) of the south-eastern Baltic in one category, 'Pribaltica', which was considered

a single unit on the Soviet mental map. See M. Megem, 'Syuzhety srednevekovoj litovskoj istorii i politika konstruirovaniya proshlogo v sovetskoj istoriografii', *Vestnik MGOU* 3, 2013, p. 12.
41 Pashuto, *Obrazovaniye*, p. 4.
42 Ibid., p. 389.
43 Ibid., p. 398.
44 Ibid., p. 234.
45 Ibid.
46 Ibid., p. 426.
47 History textbooks have long played an unusually political role in Russo-Soviet society, serving as a mechanism for indoctrination from above. See David Brandenberger, 'A New Short Course? A. V. Filippov and the Russian State's Search for a "Usable Past"', *Kritika: Explorations in Russian and Eurasian History* 10, 4, 2009, pp. 825–33, https://muse.jhu.edu/article/369901.
48 E. Gundavichus, *Istoriya Litovskoj SSR: S drevnejshikh vremen do 1861 goda*, part 1, Vilnius, 1953, p. 63.
49 B. Florya, *Russko-pol'skiye otnosheniya i politicheskoye razvitiye Vostochnoj Evropy vo vtoroj polovine XVI – nachale XVII vv.*, Moscow, Nauka, 1978, pp. 11–12.
50 Ibid., pp. 19–20.
51 D. Pokhilevich, *Krest'yane Belorussii i Litvy vo vtoroj polovine XVIII v.*, Vilnius, Akademiya Nauk Litov., SSR, 1966; V. Otamanosvkij 'Razvitiye gorodskogo stroya na Ukraine v XIV–XVIII vv. i magdeburgskoye pravo', *Voprosy Istorii*, 3, 1958, pp. 122–35; P. Sas, *Feodal'nye goroda Ukrainy v kontse XV – 60 godakh XVI v.*, Kyiv, 1989; Z. Kopysskij, *Sotsialno-politicheskaya istoriya gorodov Belorussii XVI – pervoy poloviny XVII v*, Minsk, 1975.
52 C. Merridale, 'Redesigning History in Contemporary Russia', *Journal of Contemporary History* 38, 1, 2006, p. 13.
53 A. Dvornichenko and Yu. Krivosheyev, '"Feodal'nye vojny" ili demokraticheskiye alternativy', *Vestnik Sankt-Peterburgskogo gosudarstvennogo universiteta Seriya* 2: Istoriya. Yazykoznaniye. Literaturovedeniye, 3, 1992, pp. 3–12; M. Krom, 'Rossiya i Velikoye Knyazhestvo Litovskoye: dva puti v istorii', *Anglijskaya Naberezhnaya*, 4, 2000, pp. 73–100; D. Aleksandrov *Politsentrizm obyedinitelnykh tendentsij v Yuzhnoj, Yugo-Vostochnoj, Yugo-Zapadnoj i Zapadnoj Rusi (XIII–XIV veka)*, doctoral dissertation, Moscow, 2001.
54 Dumin, *Drugaya Rus'*.
55 Ibid.
56 Ibid.
57 S. Polekhov, *Vnutripoliticheskij krizis v Velikom knyazhestve Litovskom v 30-e gody XV veka*, doctoral dissertation, Moscow, 2011, p. 3. On this process, see also Lewis in this volume.
58 Plokhy aptly commented that, regarding the 'Russian lands/people/language' of the GDL, the effort to identify Westernised 'Russians' in the history of the Grand Duchy, coupled with the inability of scholars writing in Russian to distinguish the 'Russians' of the Grand Duchy terminologically from those inhabiting the modern Russian nation, will continue to hinder research on the political and cultural history of the region. This observation is probably even more applicable to contemporary English-language historiography. Slavic studies in the West continue to be influenced by the imperial-era view that the Grand Duchy of Lithuania belongs to 'Russian' history. Textbooks on Russian history repeat this: the author of the best known of them (*History of Russia*), Riasanovsky, refers to the Grand Duchy of Lithuania as a 'Lithuanian-Russian state' and to its East Slavic population as 'Russians'. See S. Plokhy, *The Origins of the Slavic Nations: Premodern Identities in Russia, Ukraine, and Belarus*, Cambridge, Cambridge University Press, 2006, p. 88.
59 A. Dvornichenko, *Russkiye zemli Velikogo knyazhestva Litovskogo (do nachala XVI v.). Osnovnye cherty sotsial'nogo i politicheskogo stroya*, St Petersburg, 1993.

60 D. Aleksandrov, *Yuzhnaya, yugo-zapadnaya i tsentralnaya Rus' v XIII-XIV i obrazovaniye Litovskogo gosudarstva*, Moscow, 1994.
61 M. Krom, *Mezhdu Rus'yu i Litvoj: Zapadnorusskiye zemli v sisteme russko-litovskikh otnoshenij kontsa XV-pervoj treti XVI v.*, Moscow, 1997.
62 M. Bychkova, *Russkoye gosudarstvo i Velikoye knyazhestvo Litovskoye s kontsa XV v. i do 1569 g.: Opyt sravnitelno-istoricheskogo izucheniya politicheskogo stroya*, Moscow, 1996.
63 V. Yanin, *Novgorod i Litva: Pogranichnye situatsii XIII-XV vv.*, Moscow, Moscow University Press, 1998.
64 I. Starostina, *Pravo Velikogo knyazhestva Litovskogo XV v. v kontekste kulturno-istoricheskikh sviazej Pol'shy, Litvy i Rusi*, in T. Dzhakson and E. Melnikova, eds, *Vostochnaya Evropa v istoricheskoj retrospective: K 80-letiyu V.T. Pashuto*, Moscow, Yazyki russkoj kultury, 1999, pp. 237–44.
65 Zh. Nekrashevich-Korotkaya, 'Gosudarstvennaya i dinasticheskaya kontseptsiya poemy "Prusskaya vojna" Yana Vislitskogo', *Studia linguistica*, 3, 2009, pp. 231–6; Zh. Nekrashevich-Korotkaya, 'Pobeda v Grunval'dskoj bitve kak *omen faustum* dinastii Yagiellonov v epopeye "Prusskaya voyna" (1516) Yana Vislitskogo', *ŽALGIRIUI – 600, Istoriniaimūšiai Lietuvos Didžiosios Kunigaikštystėsraštijoje. VII Jurgio Lebedžioskaitymai. Pranešimų santraukos*, Vilnius, Vilniaus universiteto leidykla, 2010, pp. 20–1.
66 A. Titkov, ed., 'Litva, Rossiya, Pol'sha (XIII–XVI vv.)', *Istoricheskijy Vestnik*, 154, 2014.
67 S. Polekhov, *Nasledniki Vitovta. Dinasticheskaya vojna v Velikom knyazhestve Litovskom v 30-e gody XV veka*, Moscow, Indrik, 2015.
68 A. Filyushkin, '"Drugaya Rus"' v russkoj istoriografii', *Lietuvos Didžiosios Kunigaikštijos tradicija ir Paveldo "Dalybos"*, Vilnius, Vilniaus universiteto leidykla, 2008, p. 112.
69 Ibid.
70 This tendency is reflected in the polls of 'Levada-Tsentr' (March 2016): answering the question 'What should Russia be proud of?', 76 per cent of Russians indicated the territorial gains of the Russian empire and the annexations of Siberia, Far East, Kazakhstan and Central Asia, Caucasus, Ukraine, Byelorussia, Poland and Finland. See: www.levada.ru/2016/06/30/natsionalnaya-gordost/, accessed 25.9.17.
71 N. Koposov, 'The Armored Train of Memory: The Politics of History in Post-Soviet Russia', *Perspectives on History*, January 2011, www.historians.org/publications-and-directories/perspectives-on-history/january-2011/the-armored-train-of-memory-the-politics-of-history-in-post-soviet-russia, accessed 25.9.17.
72 A. Dialla, 'Between Nation and Empire: Revisiting the Russian Past Twenty Years Later', *Historein*, 13, 2013, www.historeinonline.org.
73 J. Prus, 'Russia's Use of History as a Political Weapon', *The Polish Institute of International Affairs. Policy Paper*, 12/114, 2015, pp. 1–8.
74 See O. Bertelsen, 'A Trial in Absentia: Purifying National Historical Narratives in Russia', *Kyiv-Mohyla Humanities Journal*, 3, 2016, http://kmhj.ukma.edu.ua/article/view/73942, accessed 25.9.17 Bertelsen analysed contemporary Russian memory politics and the ideological underpinnings of the 2011 Moscow court verdict that criminalised a Ukrainian scholarly publication, *ChK-GPU-NKVD in Ukraine: People. Facts. Documents*, by Yurii Shapoval, Volodymyr Prystaiko and Vadym Zolotariov (1997). This case study demonstrates how a state-sponsored historical narrative in Russia has been reinforced by silencing competing historical interpretations. The author concluded that by reintroducing Stalinist practices, Russia attempts to block the voices of historians in neighbouring states and to restore a common ideological and cultural space that once had been Soviet.
75 N. Koposov, *Pamyat' v zakone, Russ.ru*, August 2014, www.russ.ru/Mirovaya-povestka/Pamyat-v-zakone, accessed 25.9.17.
76 Koposov, 'The Armored Train of Memory'.
77 Ibid.

78 N. Adler, 'Reconciliation with – or Rehabilitation of – the Soviet Past?', *Memory Studies* 5, 3, 2012, p. 328. The sociological survey presented by 'Levada-Tsentr' made it clear: for the first time the percentage of positive evaluations of Stalin was substantially higher than negative ones (40 per cent positive against 19 per cent negative). See: www.levada. ru/2016/03/25/figura-stalina-v-obshhestvennom-mnenii-rossii/., accessed 25.9.17. The same centre noted the rise in popularity of other odious figures of the Soviet past like Dzerzhinsky: the percentage of respondents who support the idea of restoration of Dzerzhinsky's monument in Moscow (destroyed in 1991) is 51 per cent in the capital, and 49 per cent in the provinces. See: www.levada.ru/2015/07/24/pamyatnik-dzerzhinskomu-i-knyazyu-vladimiru/, accessed 25.9.17.
79 'Velikij knyaz' Litovskij Yagajlo' [radio program], 'Ekho Moskvy', http://echo.msk.ru/programs/vsetak/48697/, accessed 25.9.17.
80 'Velikij knyaz' Litovskij Yagajlo' [radio program], "'Ekho Moskvy', http://echo.msk.ru/programs/netak/1031364-echo/, accessed 25.9.17.
81 'Velikoye knyazhestvo Litovskoye. Drugaya Rus', S. Polekhov. Moderator A. Mozzhukhin, 2014, www.youtube.com/watch?v=EdGNlmjIXOE, accessed 25.9.17.
82 'Grand Duchy of Lithuania', A. Dvornichenko. Moderator A. Gordon, 2015, http://statehistory.ru/519/Gordon--Velikoe-knyazhestvo-Litovskoe/, accessed 25.9.17.
83 'Trubchevsk. Informatsionnyj portal', Part 5, 'Trubetskiye, Yagelloni ili skolko dlitsya dinastiya?', http://trubchevsk.pro/index.php?option=com_content&view=article&id=74:2011-11-27-09-08-15&catid=9:9-&Itemid=30, accessed 25.9.17. In this context, one can mention another victory (on 4 November), which replaced the commemoration of the so-called Great October social revolution on 7 November: 4 November – the day when a Russian popular uprising expelled the troops of the Polish-Lithuanian Commonwealth from Moscow in 1612 – became the National Unity Day in 2005. The idea of this state holiday is to commemorate Russian people 'of different social standing, nationalities and religion', united in their efforts to preserve the state and to liberate the capital from foreign invaders. Even though this historical episode has nothing to do with the Jagiellonian dynasty, commemorating the 'liberation of Moscow and Russia from Poles' clearly demonstrated the 'borders' of Russian national memory and the impossibility for a foreign dynasty to be a part of the national 'Us'.
84 'Grunval'dskaya bitva 15.07.1410', Pamyatnaya data voyennoy istorii Rossii, 15.07.2015, http://histrf.ru/rvio/activities/news/item-1850, accessed 25.9.17. See also a short video produced by the Russian Military-Historical Society in 2015: www.youtube.com/watch?t=30&v=LPkkwRAfxs0, accessed 25.9.17.
85 See also Lewis in this volume.
86 S. Norris, *Blockbuster History in the New Russia: Movies, Memories and Patriotism*, Bloomington, IN, 2012, p. 5.
87 Ibid., p. 212.
88 Bertelsen, 'A Trial', p. 76. A Levada-Tsentr survey from 5 December 2016 demonstrated the effectiveness of the pro-Soviet rhetoric: more than half of Russians (56 per cent) still have nostalgic feelings about the USSR. 'Raspad SSSR: prichiny i nostalgiya', *Levada-Tsentr*, May 2015, www.levada.ru/2016/12/05/raspad-sssr-prichiny-i-nostalgiya/, accessed 25.9.17. Moreover, 78 per cent of Russian citizens are proud of the Soviet period in the history of the country. See 'Natsionalnaya gordost', *Levada-Tsentr*, June 2016, www.levada.ru/2016/06/30/natsionalnaya-gordost/, accessed 25.9.17.
89 H. Bone, 'Putin backs WW2 myth in new Russian film', *BBC News*, October 2016, www.bbc.com/news/world-europe-37595972, accessed 25.9.17.
90 G. Carleton, 'History Done Right: War and the Dynamics of Triumphalism in Contemporary Russian Culture', *Slavic Review* 70, 3, 2011, p. 615.
91 Ibid.
92 Merridale, 'Redesigning History in Contemporary Russia', pp. 13–28.

BIBLIOGRAPHY

Archival sources

Kungliga och furstliga personers enskilde egendom, vol. 3, Stockholm, Royal Palace Archives, 1556–1594

ÖNB, Vienna Codex MS 8043

Státní oblastní archiv v Třeboni, Historica Třeboň 4834

T. Narbutt, 'Dzieje narodu litewskiego przez Teodora Narbutta. Tom dziesiąty. Część 1-sza. Dodatki, poprawy, odmiany, autorowie i dzieła przytoczone, tudziej i regestr układowy, z ryciną, Wilno: nakładem i drukiem Antoniego Marcinowskiego, 1842', Wroblewski Library of the Lithuanian Academy of Sciences, Manuscript Department, MS F. 18, B. 206/2/7

Printed works

Aarnipuu, P., *Turun linna kerrottuna ja kertovana tilana*, Helsinki, Finnish Literature Society, 2008

Abedetsedarskii, L. S., ed., *Istoriia belorusskoi SSR v dvukh tomakh*, 2 vols, 2nd edn, Minsk, Izdatel'stvo Akademii Nauk Belorusskoi SSR, 1961

Abetsadarski, L. *Istoriya belorusskoy SSR*, T. I., Mensk, Akademiya Nauk BSSR, 1961

Acta Tomiciana, Poznań, Władysław Pociecha, Wacław Urban, Andrzej Wyczański et al., eds, 18 vols, n.p., 1852–1999

Adla, Z., J. Černý and J. Kalousek, *Obrázky z českých dějin a pověstí*, Prague, Albatros, 1979

Adler, N., 'Reconciliation with – or Rehabilitation of – the Soviet Past?', *Memory Studies*, 5, 3, 2012, p. 328

Afanas'ev, Iu. N., 'Fenomen sovetskoi istoriografii', in Iu. N. Afanas'ev, ed., *Sovetskaia istoriografiia*, Moskva, Rossiiskii gosudarstvennyi gumanitarnyi universitet, 1996, pp. 7–41

Åkerman, S., 'Queen Christina and Messianic Thought', in *Sceptics, Millenarians, and Jews*, D. S. Katz, J. I. Israel, eds, Leiden, Brill, 1999, pp. 142–60

Alekna, A., *Lietuvos istorija*, Šv. Kazimiero draugijos leidinys Nr. 106, Kaunas, Saliamono Banaičio spaustuvė, 1911
Aleksaitė, I., ed., *Lietuvių teatro istorija*, bk 3, *1970–1980*, Vilnius, KFMI, 2006, pp. 162–5
Aleksandravičius, E. and A. Kulakauskas, *Carų valdžioje: XIX amžiaus Lietuva*, Vilnius, Baltos lankos, 1996
Aleksandrov, D., *Politsentrizm obyedinitelnykh tendentsiy v Yuzhnoy, Yugo-Vostochnoy, Yugo-Zapadnoy i Zapadnoy Rusi (XIII–XIV veka)*, doctoral dissertation, Moscow, 2001
—— *Yuzhnaya, yugo-zapadnaya i tsentralnaya Rus' v XIII-XIV i obrazovaniye Litovskogo gosudarstva*, Moscow, Rossiyskaya Akademiya estestvennykh nauk, 1994
Alexandrov, D. and D. Volodikhin, *Borba za Polotsk mezhdu Litvoy i Rusyu v XII–XVI vekakh*, Moscow, Avanta, 1994
Alexeyev, Yu., *Pokhody russkikh pri Ivane III*, St Petersburg, Izdatelstvo Peterburgskogo Universiteta, 2007
Almgren, H. and H. Albin Larsson, *Alla tiders historia*, Malmö, Bas. Interaktiv. Gleerups Utbildning AB, 2013–16
Anderson, B., *Imagined Communities: Reflections on the Origins and Spread of Nationalism*, London, Verso, 1983
Andersson, I., *Gripsholm, slottet och dess samlingar*, Stockholm, Nordisk rotogravyr, 1937
Andriulytė, A., 'Šv. Kazimiero relikvijų pagerbimas Vilniuje 1922 metais', in Subačius, *Šventasis Kazimieras istorijos vyksme*, pp. 66–74
—— 'Karališkųjų palaikų atradimas Vilniaus Arkikatedroje 1931 m.: atvaizdų kolekcija', *Acta Academiae Artium Vilnensis*, vol. 65/66, *Lietuvos kultūros karališkasis dėmuo: įvaizdžiai, simboliai, reliktai*, Vilnius, VDA leidykla, 2012, pp. 327–60
Appela, W. and E. Ulčinaitė, eds, *Inscriptiones eccleasiarum Vilnensium / Inskrypcje z Wileńskich kościołów / Vilniaus bažnyčių įrašai*, vol. 1, Vilnius, Aidai, 2005
Armitage, D., 'What's the Big Idea? Intellectual History and the Longue Durée', *History of European Ideas*, 38, 2012, pp. 493–507
Assmann, A., *Cultural Memory and Western Civilisation: Functions, Media, Archive*, Cambridge, Cambridge University Press, 2011
Assmann, J., *Cultural Memory and Early Civilisation: Writing, Remembrance and Political Imagination*, Cambridge, Cambridge University Press, 2011
—— *Erinnerungsräume: Formen und Wandlungen des kulturellen Gedächtnisses*, Munich, Beck, 1999
—— *Das kulturelle Gedächtnis. Schrift. Erinnerung und politische Identität in frühen Hochkulturen*, Munich, Beck, 1992
—— *Kollektives Gedächtnis und kulturelle Identität*, Frankfurt am Main, Suhrkamp, 1988
Augé, M., 'Les formes d'oubli', Paris, Payot & Rivages, 1998
Augustynowicz, A., *Die Kandidaten und Interessen des Hauses Habsburg in Polen-Litauen während des Zweiten Interregnums, 1574–1576*, Vienna, WUV, Universitätverlag, 2001
Baár, M., *Historians and Nationalism: East Central Europe in the Nineteenth Century*, Oxford, Oxford University Press, 2010
Baczkowski, K., *Walka Jagiellonów z Maciejem Korwinem o koronę czeską w latach 1471–1479*, Kraków, Jagiellonian University Press, 1980
—— *Zjazd wiedeński 1515: geneze, przebieg i znaczenie*, Warsaw, Państwowe Wydawnictwo Naukowe, 1975
Bak, J. M., 'Good King Polish Ladislas: History and Memory of the Short Reign of Władysław Warneńczyk in Hungary', in J. M. Bak, *Studying Medieval Rulers and Their Subjects: Central Europe and Beyond*, Balázs Nagy and Gábor Klaniczay, eds, Variorum Collected Studies Series, 956, Farnham, UK, and Burlington, VT, Ashgate, 2010, pp. 182–3

—— 'Hungary: Crown and Estates', in C. Allmand, ed., *New Cambridge Medieval History*, vol. 7, c.1415–c.1500, Cambridge, Cambridge University Press, 1998, pp. 707–26

Bakó, Zs., 'Adatok a Székely Bertalan életmű kutatásához', in Székely Bertalan (1835–1910), kiállítása: Magyar Nemzeti Galéria 1999. szeptember 30–2000. január 30. / Ungarische Nationalgalerie 30. September 1999–30. Januar 2000, Zs. Bakó, A. Kiséry, H. Schmőr-Weichenhain, S. Vadasi, eds, Budapest, Magyar Nemzeti Galéria, 1999, pp. 13–58

Baksay, S., *Dáma. Történeti körkép Kimnach László rajzaival*, Budapest, Franklin-Társulat, 1899

Balbín, B., *Miscellanea historica Regni Bohemiae; Liber Regalis VII*, Prague, n.p., 1687

Baliński, M., *Pamiętniki o królowej Barbarze, żonie Zygmunta Augusta*, 2 vols, Warsaw, J. Glücksberg, 1837–40

Balukh, O., 'Pol's'ko-moldavs'ka viina 1497–1499 rr.', *Naukovi zoshyty istorychnoho fakul'tetu L'vivs'koho universytetu: Zbirnyk naukovykh statei*, 9, 2008, pp. 57–66

Bałuś, W., 'Wawel dziewiętnastowieczny: poziomy interpretacji', *Waweliana* III, 1994, pp. 11–18

Bandtke, G., *Istoriya gosudarstva Polskogo*, vols 1–2, St Petersburg, Imperatorskaya Rossiyskaya Akademiya, 1830

Bárány, A., *Dr. Várkonyi Tibor: Négy király, egy szultán. Tarsoly Kiadó*, Budapest, 2014, Turul, 2015, vol. 88, pp. 33–5

Baravikova, R., 'Kazimir – syn Iahaily + Nastsia z 8 "B"', in A. Badak, R. Baravikova and A. Navarych, *Adzinoki vas'miklasnik khocha paznaiomitstsa*, Minsk, Litaratura i mastatstva, 2008, pp. 35–86

Barbashev, A., *Vitovt i yego politika do Grunvaldskoy bitvy (1410)*, St Petersburg, Tipografiya Skorokhodova, 1885

Baronas, D. and S. C. Rowell, *The Conversion of Lithuania: From Pagan Barbarians to Late Medieval Christians*, Vilnius, Lithuanian Institute of Folkore and Literature, 2016

Barta, G. and A. Fekete Nagy, *Parasztháború 1514-ben*, Budapest, Gondolat, 1973

Bartlová, M., 'Světec, král a skutečný vládce: Nástěnné malby v kapli sv. Václava za vlády Jagellonců', *Dějiny a současnost*, 4, 2012, pp. 32–5

Bartolomeides, L., *Rozmlauwánj Jozefa Druhého s Matěgem Prwnjm Korwýnus řečeným, w Králowstwj Zemřelých Při Přjtomnosti některých giných Vherských Králů držané*, Praha, n.p., 1789

Bartosh, I., 'Antyiahellons'ka koalitsiia na terenakh Skhidnoi Yevropy naprykintsi XV – pochatku XVI st.', *Ukrains'kyi istorychnyi zbirnyk*, 15, Kyiv, Instytut istorii Ukrainy, 2012, pp. 18–26

Bartoszewicz, K., *Księga pamiątkowa obchodu pięćsetnej rocznicy zwycięstwa pod Grunwaldem*, Kraków, F. Terakowski, 1911

Batiushkov, N., *Belorussia i Litva. Istoricheskiye sud'by Severo-Zapadnogo kraya*, St Petersburg, Obshchestvennaya polza, 1890

Bauer, T. A., *Feiern unter den Augen der Chronisten. Die Quellentexte zur Landshuter Fürstenhochzeit von 1475*, Munich, Herbert Utz Verlag, 2008

Bazilevich, K., *Vneshniaya politika Russkogo tsentralizovannogo gosudarstva. Vtoraya polovina XV veka*, Moscow, Izdatelstvo Moskovskogo Universiteta, 1952

Bekus, N., *Struggle over Identity. The Official and the Alternative 'Belarusianness'*, Budapest, New York, Central European University, 2010

—— 'Nationalism and Socialism: "Phase D" in the Belarusian Nation-Building', *Nationalities Papers*, 38, 2010

Bengtsson, H., *Uppsala domkyrka 6. Gravminnen*, Uppsala, Upplandsmuseet, 2010

Berend, N., 'The Mirage of East Central Europe: Historical Regions in a Comparative Perspective', in G. Jaritz and K. Szende, eds, *Medieval East Central Europe in a*

Comparative Perspective: From Frontier Zones to Lands in Focus, Abingdon, Routledge, 2016, pp. 9–23

Berger, S., L. Eriksonas and A. Mycock, eds, *Narrating the Nation. Representations in History, Media and the Arts*, Oxford, New York, Berghahn Books, 2008

Bergius, B., ed., *Konung Carl den IX:des rim-chrönika*, Stockholm, Hesselberg, 1759

Bernhard, M. H. and J. Kubik, *Twenty Years after Communism: The Politics of Memory and Commemoration*, Oxford, Oxford University Press, 2014

Berowska, M. and M. Grądzka, *Skarbiec Baśni i Legend Polskich*, Warsaw, Foksal, 2014

Biaudet, H., *Documents concernant les relations entre le Saint-Siège et la Suède durant la seconde moitié du XVIe siècle*, Paris, Plon-Nourrit, 1907

—— *Le Saint-Siège et la Suède durant la seconde moitié du XVIe siècle: études politiques. 1, 1*, Paris, Plon-Nourrit, 1907

Bibó, I., 'Ha a zsinati mozgalom a 15.században győzött volna . . . Bibó István címzetes váci kanonok beszélgetései apósával, Ravasz László bíboros érsekkel a római katolikus egyház újkori történetéről, különös tekintettel a lutheránus és kálvinista kongregációkra. Egyház-, kultúr-és politikatörténeti uchrónia', in I. Bibó, *Válogatott tanulmányok*, vol. 4, Budapest, Magvető, 1990, pp. 265–82

—— 'A magyar társadalomfejlődés és az 1945.évi változás értelme', in I. Bibó, *Válogatott tanulmányok*, vol. 3, Budapest, Magvető, 1986, pp. 5–124

Bilenky, S., *Romantic Nationalism in Eastern Europe. Russian, Polish, and Ukrainian Political Imaginations*, Stanford, CA, Stanford University Press, 2012

Biliński, P. and P. Plichta (eds), *Krakowska szkoła historyczna a Polskie Towarzystwo Historyczne*, Kraków, Jagiellonian University Press, 2017

Bilous, N., *Kyiv naprykintsi XV – u pershii polovyni XVII stolittia. Mis'ka vlada i samovriaduvannia*, Kyiv, Vydavnychyi dim 'Kyievo-Mohylians'ka akademiia', 2008

Birnbaum, M., *Humanists in a Shattered World. Croatian and Hungarian Latinity in the Sixteenth Century*, Columbus, OH, Slavica Publishers, 1986

Biskup, M., 'Die dynastische Politik der Jagiellonen um das Jahr 1475 und ihre Ergebnisse', *Österreichische Osthefte* 18, 3, 1976, pp. 203–17

Blacker, U., A. Etkind and J. Fedor, eds, *Memory and Theory in Eastern Europe*, New York, Palgrave, 2013

Blanutsa, A., *Zemel'na polityka Yahelloniv na ukrains'kykh terenakh Velykoho kniazivstva Lytovs'koho (1440–1572 rr.)*, Kyiv, Instytut istorii Ukrainy, 2017

—— 'Lytuanistychni studii v instytuti istorii Ukrainy (1936–2011 rr.): osnovni tendentsii', *Istoriohrafichni doslidzhennia v Ukraini*, 22, Kyiv, Instytut istorii Ukrainy, 2012, pp. 313–29

—— 'Hospodars'ka polityka korolevy Bony u Velykomu kniazivstvi Lytovs'komu (za materialamy 32 knyhy zapysiv Lytovs'koi metryky)', *Ukraina v Tsentral'no-Skhidnii Yevropi*, 11, Kyiv, Instytut istorii Ukrainy, 2011, pp. 191–206

—— *Zemel'ni volodinnia Volyns'koi shliakhty v druhii polovyni XVI st.*, Kyiv, Instytut istorii Ukrainy, 2007

Bobrzyński, M., *Dzieje Polski w zarysie*, Warsaw, Gebethner & Wolff, 1879

—— *O ustawodawstwie nieszawskim Kazimierza Jagiellończyka*, Kraków, Jagiellonian University Press, 1873

Böckl, M., *Die Braut von Landshut. Das tragische Leben von Herzogin Hedwig*, Bayerland, Landshut, 2001

Boia, L., *History and Myth in Romanian Consciousness*, New York, Central European University Press, 2001

Borkowska, U., *Dynastia Jagiellonów w Polsce*, Warsaw, Wydawnictwo Naukowe PWN, 2011

Bourin, M. and P. Chareille, eds, *Genèse médiévale de l'anthroponomie moderne*, 2, 2: Persistances du nom unique. Désignation et anthroponomie des femmes. Méthodes statistiques pour l'anthroponymie. Etudes d'anthroponymie médiévale, IIIe et IVe Rencontres, Azay-le-Ferron, 1989–90, Tours, 1992

Brandenberger D. and K. Platt, 'Terribly Pragmatic: Rewriting the History of Ivan IV's Reign, 1937–1956', *Epic Revisionism: Russian History and Literature as Stalinist Propaganda*, Madison, University of Wisconsin Press, 2006, pp. 157–78

Brassicanus, J. L., *Phoenix sive luctus Austriae ob mortem incomparabilis heroinae D. Annae Quiritium, Pannonum ac Bohemorum Reginae, etc.*, Vienna, n.p., 1547

Brigadin, P. I., *Istoriia Belarusi v kontekste evropeiskoi istorii*, Minsk, GIUST BGU, 2007

Brodericus, S., *De conflictu hungarorum cum Solymano Turcarum Imperatore ad Mohach historia verissima*, P. Kulcsár, ed., Budapest, Akadémiai Kiadó, 1985

Brook, M., *Popular History and Fiction: The Myth of August the Strong in German Literature, Art and Media*, Bern, Peter Lang, 2013

Brouka, P. et al., eds, *Belaruskaia Savetskaia Entsyklapedyia*, 12 vols, Minsk, n.p., 1969–75, XI, 1974

Bruun, J. et al., *Ritari*, Helsinki, Sanoma Pro Oy, 2015

Bues, A., *Die Jagiellonen: Herrscher zwischen Ostsee und Adria*, Urban-Taschenbücher 646, Stuttgart, W. Kohlhammer, 2010

Bumblauskas, A., *Lietuvos istorijos modeliai XIX–XX a. istoriografijoje*, Vilnius, VU leidykla, 2007

—— *Senosios Lietuvos istorija, 1009–1795*, Vilnius, R. Paknio leidykla, 2005

Butevich, A., *Pamizh Kniastvam i Karonai. Ad Kreva da Krakava: dakumental'ny pratsiah ramana 'Karaleva ne zdradzhvala karaliu'*, Minsk, Zviazda, 2013

—— *Karaleva ne zdradzhvala karaliu, abo Karaleuskae shliubavanne u Novaharodku: zaimal'ny apoved pra kakhanne 17-hadovai belaruskai kniazeuny Sof'I Hal'shanskai i 70-hadovaha karalia pol'skaha Iahaily: raman*, Minsk, Litaratura i mastatsva, 2010

—— *Raskidanoe hniazdo kryvitskai slavy: Nezvychainaia vandrouka pa Kreuskikh murakh*, Minsk, Belaruskaia navuka, 2008

Bychkova, M., *Russkoye gosudarsvo i Velikoye kniazhestvo Litovskoye s kontsa XV v. i do 1569 g.: Opyt sravnitelno-istoricheskogo izucheniya politicheskogo stroya*, Moscow, Rossiyskaya Akademiya Nauk, 1996

Carlén, O., *Gripsholm slott, dess historia, tafvelsamling, m.m.*, Stockholm, Albert Bonniers förlag, 1877

Carleton, G., 'History Done Right: War and the Dynamics of Triumphalism in Contemporary Russian Culture', *Slavic Review*, 70, 3, 2011

Čechura, J., *České země v letech 1437–1526. II. Díl. Jagellonské Čechy (1471–1526)*, Prague, Libri, 2012

Cermanová, P., R. Novotný and P. Soukup, eds, *Husitské Století*, Prague, Nakladatelství Lidové noviny, 2014

Charopka, V., *Liosy u historyi*, Minsk, Belarus', 2005

Cherkas, B., 'Ukrains'ke kozatstvo naprykintsi XV – u pershii polovyni XVI st.', in V. Smolii, ed., *Istoriia ukrains'koho kozatstva: Narysy*, vol. 1, Kyiv, Vydavnychyi dim 'Kyievo-Mohylians'ka akademiia', 2006, pp. 57–65

—— 'Ukrains'ke kozatstvo u viis'kovo-politychnykh protsesakh Velykoho kniazivstva Lytovs'koho (20–30-ti rr. XVI st.)', in *'Istynu vstanovliuie sud istorii': Zbirnyk na poshanu Fedora Pavlovycha Shevchenka*, vol. 2, Kyiv, Instytut istorii Ukrainy, 2004, pp. 158–64

—— *Šv. Kazimiero gyvenimo ir kulto istorijos šaltiniai / Casimiriana. Fontes vitae et cultus S. Casimiri, Fontes ecclesiastici historiæ Lithuaniæ* 3, Vilnius, Aidai, 2003

Chrościcki, J., *Sztuka i polityka: funkcje propagandowe sztuki w epoce Wazów, 1587–1668*, Warsaw, Państwowe Wydawnictwo Naukowe, 1983
Chrzanowski, T., *Działalność artystyczna Tomasza Tretera*, Warsaw, Państwowe Wydawnictwo Naukowe, 1984
Chyczewska, A., *Marcello Bacciarelli, 1731–1818*, Wrocław, Ossolineum, 1973
Činátl, K., *Naše české minulosti, aneb, jak vzpomínáme*, Prague, Nakladatelství Lidové noviny, 2014
—— 'Palackého dějiny a historická paměť národa', *Dějiny – teorie – kritika*, 6, 2009
Čiurinskas, M., ed., *Ankstyvieji šv. Kazimiero 'Gyvenimai' / Casimiriana II. Vitae antiquiores S. Casimiri, Fontes ecclesiastici historiæ Lithuaniæ* 4, Vilnius, Aidai, 2004
Čornej, P., *Historici, historiografie a dějepis*, Prague, Univerzita Karlova v Praze, nakladatelství Karolinum, 2016
Čornej, P. and M. Bartlová, *Velké dějiny zemí Koruny české*, Prague, Paseka, 2007
—— *Dějiny a současnost*, 4, 2012
Corswant-Naumburg, I., *Greve Erik Dahlbergh: kungligt råd, fältmarskalk och generalguvernör: 'hiärtan alldra kiäreste herr far'*, Visby, Liberans förlag, 2008
Crownshaw, R., 'Introduction', *Parallax* 17, 4, 2011, pp. 1–3
Csorba, D., 'II. Lajos király halála historiográfiai nézőpontból', in Farkas et al., *'Nekünk mégis Mohács kell'*, pp. 160–1
Czarnecka, R., *Barbara i król*, Poznań, Wydawnictwo 'Książnica', 2013
—— *Signora Fiorella: kapeluszniczka królowej Bony*, Kraków, Skrzat, 2010
Czerny, H., *Der Tod der bayerischen Herzöge im Spätmittelalter und in der frühen Neuzeit (1347–1579). Vorbereitungen – Sterben – Trauerfeierlichkeiten – Grablegen – Memoria*, München, C. H. Beck, 2005
Dabrowski, P., *Commemorations and the Shaping of Modern Poland*, Bloomington, Indiana University Press, 2004
Daukantas, S., *Istorija žemaitiška*, 2 pts, B. Vanagienė, ed., *Lituanistinė biblioteka*, Vilnius, Vaga, 1995.
—— *Lietuvos istorija*, 2 vols, Plymouth, 1893–97
—— *Budą senowęs-lëtuwiû kalnienû ir żamajtiû iszraszczę pagał senowęs rasztû Jokyb's Łaukys*, St Petersburg, C. Hintze, 1845
Deák, I., 'Historiography of the Countries of Eastern Europe: Hungary', *American Historical Review*, 94, 1992, pp. 1041–63
Decius, J. Ludovicus, *De Jagiellonum familia, De Sigismundi regis temporibus*, Kraków, Hieronymus Wietor, 1521
Dixon, C. Scott and M. Fuchs, eds, *The Histories of Emperor Charles V: Nationale Perpspektiven von Persönlichkeit und Herrschaft*, Münster, Aschendorff, 2005
Długosz, J., *Annales seu cronicae incliti Regni Poloniae*, vols 10–12, Warsaw, Wydawnictwo Naukowe PWN, 1985–2005
Dmytriienko, M. et al., eds, *Bars'ka zemlia Podillia: yevropeis'ka spadschyna ta perspektyvy staloho rozvytku. Do 520-richchia z dnia narodzhennia Bony Sfortsy ta 120-richchia vykhodu u svit pratsi M.S.Hrushevs'koho 'Bars'ke starostvo. Istorychni narysy XV – XVIII st.'. Materialy III Mizhnarodnoi naukovo-praktychnoi konferentsii*, Kyiv, Bar, Bars'kyi raionnyi istorychnyi muzei, 2014
Dolbilov, M., 'Russian Nationalism and the Nineteenth-Century Policy of Russification in the Russian Empire's Western Region', in K. Matsuzato, ed., *Comparative Imperiology*, Sapporo, Slavic Research Center, Hokkaido University, 2010, pp. 141–58
Donath, M., ed., *Die Grabmonumente im Dom zu Meissen*, Leipzig, Leipziger Universitätsverlag, 2004

Dounar-Zapol'ski, M., *Historyia Belarusi*, Minsk: Belaruskaia entsyklapedyia im. Petrusia Brouki, 1994
Dovnar-Zapol'skii, M., *Gosudarstvennoe khoziaistvo Velikogo Kniazhestva Litovskogo pri Iagellonakh, T. 1*, Kiev, Tipografiia Imperatorskago Universiteta sv. Vladimira, 1901
Dubravius, J., *Historia Bohemica, ab origine gentis . . .*, Hanau, 1602
—— *Historiae Regni Boiemiae, de rebus memoria dignis, in illa gestis, ab initio Boiemorum, qui ex Illyria venientes, eandem Boiemiam, in medio propemodum superioris Germanie sitam, occupauerunt*, Prostannae, 1552
—— *Jo. Dubravii Olomuzensis episcopi Historia Bohemica a Thoma Jordano . . .*, Francofurti, Impensis Johannis Georgii Steck, 1687
Ducreux, M. É., 'Nation, état, education. L'enseignement de l'histoire en Europe centrale et orientale', *Histoire de l'education*, 86, 2000 [Histoire et Nation en Europe centrale et orientale XIXe–XXe siecles], pp. 5–36
Duczmal, M., *Jagiellonowie: Leksykon biograficzny*, Kraków, Wydawnictwo Literackie, 1996
Dumin, S., '"Drugaya Rus": Velikoye kniazhestvo Litivskoye i Russkoye', *Istoriya Otechestva: liudi, ideyi, resheniya: ocherki istorii Rossii IX – nachala XX v.*, Moscow, Politizdat, 1991, pp. 76–126
Dvornichenko, A., *Russkiye zemli Velikogo kniazhestva Litovskogo (do nachala XVI v.). Osnovnyie cherty sotsialnogo I politicheskogo stroya*, St Petersburg, University of St Petersburg Press, 1993
Dvornichenko, A. and Yu. Krivosheyev, '"Feodalnyie voyny" ili demokraticheskiye alternativy', *Vestnik Sankt-Peterburgskogo gosudarstvennogo universiteta Seriya 2: Istoriya. Yazykoznaniye. Literaturovedeniye*, 3, 1992, pp. 3–12
Dvorský, Fr., ed., 'Truchlivá pisen o zahynuti Ludvika krále Českého', *Časopis českého musea*, 38, 1864, pp. 389–92
Eiden, M., *Das Nachleben der schlesischen Piasten: dynastische Tradition und moderne Erinnerungskultur vom 17. bis 20. Jahrhundert*, Cologne, Böhlau, 2012
Elridge Carney, J., *Fairy Tale Queens: Representations of Early Modern Queenship*, New York, Palgrave Macmillan, 2012
Engel, P., *The Realm of Saint Stephen: A History of Medieval Hungary, 895–1526*, London, New York, I. B. Tauris, 2001
Englund, P., *Silvermasken: En kort biografi över drottning Kristina*, Stockholm, Bonnier, 2006
Eötvös, J., *Magyarország 1514-ben. Regény*, Pest, 1847, available online at http://mek.oszk.hu/04700/04774/, accessed 14.10.17
Erben, K. J., ed., *Výbor z literatury české*, 2 vols, Prague, W kommissí u Kronbergra i Řiwnáče, 1868
—— *Bartošova Kronika pražská od léta páně 1524 až do konce léta 1530*, Prague, J. G. Kalve: Bedřich Tempský, 1851
Erdélyi, G., 'Tales of a Peasant Revolt: Taboos and Memories of 1514 in Hungary', in Kuijpers et al., *Memory before Modernity*, pp. 93–109
Ericson, L., *Johan III. En biografi*, Lund, Historiska media, 2004
Erll, A., 'Travelling Memory', *Parallax* 17, 4, 2011, pp. 4–18
—— 'Regional Integration and (Trans)cultural Memory', *Asia Europe Journal* 8, 2010, pp. 305–15
Erős, V., 'A Mohács-vita', *Magyar Szemle* 23, 5–6, 2014, pp. 55–76
Eskelinen, R. and M. Troberg, *Matkalippu historiaan*, Helsinki, Edita, 2008
Evans, R. J. W., 'The Politics of Language in Hungary', in H. Scott and B. Simms, eds, *Cultures of Power in Europe during the Long Eighteenth Century*, Cambridge, Cambridge University Press, 2007, pp. 200–24

Fajt, J., ed., *Europa Jagellonica. Kunst und Kultur Mitteleuropas unter der Herrschaft der Jagiellonen 1386–1572. Ausstellungskatalog / Exhibition Guide*, Potsdam, Haus der Brandenburgisch-Preußischen Geschichte, 2013
—— 'Ein Bandt von freuntschaft und lieb'. Eheverbindungen der Jagiellonen: Die jagiellonischen Prinzessinnen Hedwig d.Ä., Sophia, Barbara, Anna, Hedwig d.J., in *Europa Jagellonica*.
—— 'Das Zeitalter der Jagiellonen in den Ländern der Böhmischen Krone und die tschechische Historiographie', in E. Wetter, ed., *Die Länder der Böhmischen Krone und ihre Nachbarn zur Zeit der Jagiellonenkönige (1471–1526): Kunst, Kultur, Geschichte*, Ostfildern, Thorbecke, 2004, pp. 15–30
Falkdalen, K. T., *Vasadöttrarna*, Lund, Historiska Media, 2015
Fancev, F., 'Mohacka tragedija od god. 1526. suvremenoj hrvatskoj pjesmi', *Nastavni Vjesnik*, 43, 1934/35, pp. 18–28
Farkas, F. G., 'II. Lajos rejtélyes halála II.', *Magyar Könyvszemle*, 117, 2001, pp. 33–66
—— 'II. Lajos rejtélyes halála I.', *Magyar Könyvszemle*, 116, 4, 2000, pp. 443–63
Farkas, F. G., Zs. Szebelédi and B. Varga, eds, *'Nekünk mégis Mohács kell . . .' II. Lajos király rejtélyes halála és különböző temetései*, Budapest, MTA BTK – OszK, 2016
Feindt, G., F. Krawatzek, D. Mehler, F. Pestel and R. Trimçev, 'Entangled Memory: Towards a Third Wave in Memory Studies', *History and Theory* 53, 2014, pp. 24–44
Feliński, A., *Barbara Radziwiłłówna: tragedya w 5 aktach*, Krakow, 1820
Fichtner, P. S., *Ferdinand I. Wider Türken und Glaubensspaltung*, Wien, Verlag Styria, 1986
Fijałek, J. and W. Semkowicz, eds, *Codex diplomaticus Ecclesiae Cathedralis necnon dioeceseos Vilnensis / Kodeks dyplomatyczny Katedry i diecezji Wileńskiej*, vol. 1, *1387–1507*, Krakow, PAU, 1948, no. 564, pp. 676–79
Filyushkin, A., '"Drugaya Rus"' v russkoy istoriografii', *Lietuvos Didžiosios Kunigaikštijos tradicija ir Paveldo 'Dalybos'*, Vilnius, Vilniaus universiteto leidykla, 2008
Finnish National Board of Education, *National Core Curriculum for Basic Education 2014*, Helsinki, Finnish National Board of Education, 2016
Flik, J., *Poczet królów polskich w zbiorach Muzeum Okręgowego w Toruniu*, Toruń, Muzeum Okręgowe, 2nd edn, 2000
Florya, B., *Russko-polskiye otnosheniya i politicheskoye razvitiye Vostochnoy Yevropy vo vtoroy polovine XVI – nachale XVII vv.*, Moscow, Nauka, 1978, pp. 11–12
Fodor, P., 'Hollók évadja. Gondolatok a mohácsi csatáról és következményeiről', in Farkas et al., *'Nekünk mégis Mohács kell . . .'*
Fógel, J., *II. Lajos udvartartása*, Budapest, Hornyánszky Viktor, 1917
—— *II. Ulászló udvartartása (1490–1516)*, Budapest, Hornyánszky Viktor, 1913
Fraknói, V., *A magyar királyválasztások története*, Budapest, Athenaeum, 1921
—— *Werbőczy István élete*, Budapest, Franklin Társulat, 1899
—— 'A Hunyadiak és a Jagellók kora (1440–1526)', in Sándor Szilágyi, ed., *A magyar nemzet története*, Budapest, Athenaeum, 1896, vol. 4
—— 'Werbőczy István a mohácsi vész előtt', *Századok*, 1896, vol. 10, pp. 437–69, 597–639
—— 'II. Ulászló királlyá választása', *Századok* 1885, vol. 19
—— *Magyarország a mohácsi vész előtt*, Budapest, Szent-István Társulat, 1884
—— *A magyar nemzet története*, ed. Sándor Szilágyi, Budapest, Athenaeum, 1896, vol. 4
—— ed., *Relationes oratorum pontificiorum. Magyarországi pápai követek jelentései 1524–26, Monumenta Vaticana Historiam regni Hungariae illustrantia* II/1, Budapest, 1884, reprinted Budapest, METEM, 2001
Franaszek, A., ed., *Testament Zygmunta Augusta*, Kraków, Ministry of Art and Culture, 1975

Frost, R. I., *The Oxford History of Poland-Lithuania*, vol. I, Oxford, Oxford University Press, 2015
—— 'Obsequious Disrespect: The Problem of Royal Power in the Polish-Lithuanian Commonwealth under the Vasas, 1587–1668', in R. Butterwick, ed., *The Polish-Lithuanian Monarchy in European Context*, Basingstoke, Palgrave, 2001, pp. 150–71
Fryxell, A., *Handlingar rörande Skandinaviens historia* 3, Stockholm, Elmén, 1817
Füetrer, U., *Bayerische Chronik*, München, 1909
Galavics, G., 'Dorffmaister István történeti képei', in L. Kostyál and M. Zsámbéky, eds, *'Stephan Dorffmaister pinxit'. Dorffmaister István emlékkiállítása*, Szombathely, Szombathelyi Képtár, 1997, pp. 85–6
Gałęziowska, M., 'Świętowanie wybranych rocznic bitwy pod Grunwaldem formą komunikacji rytualnej państwa i narodu', *Kultura i Społeczeństwo* 4, 2012, pp. 83–108
Gardberg, C. J., *Turun linnan kolme Katariinaa*, trans. Irma Savolainen, Helsinki, Otava, 1993, pp. 48–116
—— *Turku Castle. A Tour of the Stronghold*, Turku, The Historical Museum, 1980
—— 'Åbo slott under den äldre vasatiden. En byggnadshistorisk undersökning', Helsinki, Suomen muinaismuistoyhdistys, 1959
Garstein, O., *Rome and the Counter-Reformation in Scandinavia until the Establishment of the S. Congregatio De Propaganda Fide in 1622*, vols I–II, Oslo, Universitetforlaget, 1963, 1968
Gąsior, A., 'Dynastische Verbindungen der Jagiellonen mit den deutschen Fürstenhäusern', in M. Omilanowska and T. Torbus, eds, *Tür an Tür. Polen – Deutschland 1000. Jahre Kunst und Geschichte. Katalog der Ausstellung im Martin-Gropius-Bau Berlin, 23. September 2011–9. Januar 2012*, Köln, DuMont Buchverlag, 2011
—— 'Stufungen bildlicher Repräsentation. Die Darstellungen des Markgrafen Friedrich d. Ä. von Brandenburg-Ansbach und seiner Gemahlin Sophie von Polen', in U. Borkowska and M. Hörsch, eds, *Hofkultur der Jagiellonendynastie und verwandter Fürstenhäuser / The Culture of the Jagiellonian and Related Courts*, Studia Jagellonica Lipsiensia 6, Ostfildern, Jan Thorbecke, 2010, pp. 314–17
Genii Serenissimorum Principum Philippi Wilhelmi Comitis Palatini Rheni . . . sponsi, et Annae Catharinae Constantiae, augustissimorum regum Sigismundi III filiae . . . Collegium Societas Iesu, Coliniae Agrippinae, Ex typographia Henrici Krafft, 1642
Gieysztor, A., 'Przedmowa', in *Polska Jagiellonów, 1386–1572*, Warsaw, Zamek Królewski, 1987
Gillgren, P., *Vasarenässansen: konst och identitet i 1500-talets Sverige*, Stockholm, Signum, 2009
Girs, A., *Konung Johan den III:des chrönika*, A. A. von Stiernman, ed., Stockholm, Grefing, 1745
Głuchowski, J., *Icones książąt y królów polskich*, Krakow, Jan Januszowski, 1605
Gołaszewski, Z., *Aleksander i piękna Helena*, Warszaw, Bellona, 2014
Golubovich, V. I., and Iu. N. Bokhan, eds, *Istoriia Belarusi v kontekste mirovykh tsivilizatsii. Uchebno metodicheskoe posobie*, Minsk, Ekoperspektiva, 2011
Górny, M., *The Nation Should Come First: Marxism and Historiography in East Central Europe*, Antoni Górny, trans., Aaron Law, ed., *Warsaw Studies in Contemporary History* 1, Dariusz Stola and Machteld Venken, eds, Frankfurt am Main, Peter Lang, 2013
Górny M. and K. Kończal, 'The (Non-)Travelling Concept of les Lieux de Mémoire: Central and Eastern European Perspectives', in Pakier and Wawrzyniak, *Memory and Change*.
Górska, H., 'Restauracja katedry na Wawelu przez Sławomira Odrzywolskiego na przełomie XIX I XX wieku', *Waweliana* III, 1994, pp. 123–41

Goujon, A., 'Memorial Narratives of WWII Partisans and Genocide in Belarus', *East European Politics and Societies*, 24, 2010, pp. 6–25
Graus, Fr. et al., eds, *Přehled československých dějin. Díl. I. Do roku 1848*, Prague, Nakl. Československé akademie věd, 1958
Grekov, B., ed., *Ocherki istorii SSSR. Period feodalizma. Konets XV – nachalo XVII vv.*, Moscow, Akademiya Nauk SSSR, 1955
de Groot, J., *The Historical Novel*, Abingdon, Routledge, 2010
Grušas, J., *Barbora Radvilaitė*, Vilnius, Vaga, 1972
Grzesiuk-Olszewska, I., *Polska rzeźba pomnikowa w latach 1945–1995*, Warsaw, Neriton, 1995
Gudavičius, E., *Lietuvos istorija*, vol. 1, *Nuo seniausių laikų iki 1569 metų*, Vilnius, LRS leidykla, 1999
Gudavičius, E. and A. Bumblauskas, *Būtovės slėpiniai*, A. Švedas, ed., vol. 1, *Nuo Netimero iki . . .*, vol. 2, *Užmiršta Lietuva*, Vilnius, Alma littera, 2014–16
Gudavičius, E. and A. Nikžentaitis, eds, *Popiežių bulės dėl kryžiaus žygių prieš prūsus ir lietuvius XIII a.*, Vilnius, Mintis, 1987
Gudziak, B., *Crisis and Reform: The Kyivan Metropolitanate, the Patriarchate of Constantinople, and the Genesis of the Union of Brest*, Cambridge, MA, Ukrainian Research Institute, Harvard University: distributed by Harvard University Press, 2001 / *Kryza i reforma: Kyivs'ka mytropoliia, Tsarhorods'kyi patriarkhat i heneza Beresteis'koi unii*, Lviv, Instytut Istorii Tserkvy L'vivs'koi Bohoslovs'koi Akademii, 2000
Guenée, B., *Histoire et culture historique dans l'Occident médiéval*, Paris, Aubier-Montaigne, 1980
Gumowski, M., 'Trzy serie portretów Jagiellońskich', *Wiadomości Numizmatyczno-Archaeologiczne* XIX, 1937, pp. 41–66
Gundavichus, E., *Istoriya Litovskoy SSR: S drevneyshikh vremen do 1861 goda*, pt 1, Vilnius, Akademiya Nauk Litov, SSR, 1953
Gustaitė, G., 'Šv. Kazimiero 400 metų kanonizavimo sukakties minėjimas 1922', *Lietuvių katalikų mokslų akademijos metraštis*, 21, 2002, pp. 388–406
Gyáni, G., 'Changing Relationship between Collective Memory and History Writing', *Colloquia*, 19, 2012, pp. 138–41
—— 'Elbeszélhető-e egy csata hiteles története? Metatörténeti megfontolások', *Hadtörténelmi közlemények*, 119, 1, 2006, pp. 121–33
Hadler, S., 'Europe's Other? The Turks and Shifting Borders of Memory', *European Review of History* 24, 4, 2017, pp. 507–26
Hahr, A., *Drottning Katarina Jagellonica och Vasarenässansen: studier i vasatidens konst och svensk-polsk-italienska förbindelser*, Uppsala, Almqvist & Wiksell, 1940
—— *Katarina Jagellonicas gravvård i Uppsala domkyrka. Särtryck ur Uppländsk bygd*, Stockholm, Nordisk Rotogravyr, 1940
Hájek z Libočan, V., *Kronika česká*, J. Linka and P. Voit, eds, Prague, Academia, 2013
Halbwachs, M., *On Collective Memory*, trans. L. A. Coser, Chicago, University of Chicago Press, 1992
—— *Les cadres sociaux de la mémoire*, Paris, F. Alcan, 1925
Halecki, O., 'Idea Jagiellońska', *Kwartalnik Historyczny* 51, 1937, pp. 486–510
Hamann, B., ed., *Die Habsburger. Ein biographisches Lexikon*, Vienna, Verlag Carl Ueberreuter, 1988
Härtl-Kasulke, C., *Karl Theodor Piloty (1826–1886): Karl Theodor Pilotys Weg zur Historienmalarei, 1826–55*, Munich, Stadtarchiv München, 1991
Hartung, A., *Joachim II und sein Sohn Johann George. Ein Historisches Gemählde aus der brandenburgischen Geschichte*, Berlin, Wilhelm Dieterici, 1798

Hausen, R., *Förteckning öfver Hertig Johans af Finland och hans gemål Katarina Jagellonicas lösegendom 1563*, Helsinki, Kejserliga Senatens tryckeri, 1909

Häutle, C., *Genealogie der erlauchten Stammhauses Wittelsbach*, München, Wilhelm Dieterici, 1870

Hedwig, die schöne Königstochter aus Polen, Gemahlin Herzogs Georg des Reichen von Bayern-Landshut, und die Schatzkammern auf dem Schlosse zu Burghausen historisches Trauergemälde aus d. 15. Jahrhundert; für theilnehmende Herzen geschrieben, Burghausen, J. Lutzenberger, 1860

'Hedwig, Hedwig!', *Burghauser Anzeiger*, Nr. 19, 18 February 1902

Heiss, G., Á. v. Klimó, P. Kolář and D. Kováč, 'Habsburgs' Difficult Legacy: Comparing and Relating Austrian, Czech, Magyar and Slovak National Master Narratives', in S. Berger and C. Lorenz, eds, *The Contested Nation: Ethnicity, Class, Religion and Gender in National Histories*, Basingstoke, New York, Palgrave Macmillan, 2008, pp. 367–404

Heltai, G., *Krónika az magyaroknak dolgairól*, ed. M. Kulcsár, introduction by P. Kulcsár, Budapest, Magyar Helikon, 1981

Hiereth, S., *Herzog Georgs Hochzeit zu Landshut im Jahre 1475. Eine Darstellung aus zeitgenossischen Quellen*, Landshut, Verkehrsverein Landshut, 1988

—— 'Die Landshuter Hochzeit als Organisationsproblem. Landshuter Hochzeit 1475–1975', *Österreichische Osthefte* 18, 1976

—— 'Zeitgenossische Quellen zur Landshuter Furstenhochzeit 1475', *Verhandlungen des Historischen Vereins fur Niederbayern* 85, 1959, pp. 1–64

Historia critica regum Hungariae. Ex fide domesticorum et exterorum scriptorum concinnata, 42 vols, Pest, n.p., 1779–1817

Historia pragmatica Hungariae concinnata a Stephano Katona . . ., 2 vols, Buda, n.p., 1782–84

Hóman, B. and G. Szekfű, *Magyar történet*, Budapest, Királyi magyar egyetemi nyomda, 1928

Homolicki, M., *Wizerunki i roztrząsania naukowe, Poczet nowy drugy*, Vilnius, 1844, vol. 24

Horvat, R., 'Rat kralja Vladislava II. na Lovru Iločkoga', *Vienac*, XXVIII, 2, 1896, pp. 30–1

Horváth, A., *Krúdy Gyula Mohács-trilogiája. Egy történelmi tényregény születése*, PhD dissertation, Budapest: Eötvös Loránd Tudományegyetem, Bölcsészettudományi Kar, 2010, available online http://doktori.btk.elte.hu/lit/horvathanna/diss.pdf, accessed 13.10.17

Horváth, M., *Magyarország történelme*, vol. 3, Pest, Heckenast Gusztáv, 3rd edn, 1871

Hoshko, T., ed., *Khrestomatiia z istorii Ukrainy lytovs'ko-pol's'koi doby*, Lviv, Vydavnytstvo Ukrains'koho Katolyts'koho Universytetu, 2011

Hoshko, T., *Narysy z istorii magdeburz'koho prava v Ukraini XIV – pochatku XVII st.*, Lviv, Afisha, 2002

—— *Mahdeburz'ke pravo Tsentral'no-Skhidnoi Yevropy XIII-XVIII st. v ukrains'kii ta pol's'kii istoriohrafii*. Avtoref. dys. na zdobuttia nauk. stupenia kand. ist. nauk, Kyiv, Instytut ukrains'koi arkheohrafii ta dzhereloznavstva im. M. Hrushevs'koho NAN Ukrainy, 1999.

Hrushevsky, M., *History of Ukraine-Rus'*, trans. M. Skorupsky, vols 1, 7, Edmonton, Canadian Institute of Ukrainian Studies Press, 1997

Hrušovský, F., *Slovenské dejiny*, Turčiansky Sv. Martin, Matica slovenská, 3rd edn, 1939

Hrynevych, T., 'Krevs'ka uniia v dyskusiiakh pol's'kykh istorykiv mizhvoiennoho chasu', *Studii z arkhivnoi spravy ta dokumentoznavstva*, 18, 2010, pp. 149–56

Hübner, J., *Bibliotheca Genealogica, Das ist: Ein Verzeichniß aller Alten und Neuen Genealogischen Bücher von allen Nationen in der Welt: den Liebhabern der Politischen Wissenschafften zur Bequemlichkeit gesammlet, und In eine richtige Ordnung gebracht*, Hamburg, Brandt, 1729
Hulevych, V., '"Kyivs'ka trahediia" 1482 r.: mify i fakty', *Ukrains'kyi istorychnyi zhurnal*, 5, 2013, pp. 88–100
Hultmark, E., *Kungliga Akademiens för de fria konsterna utställningar 1794–1887 – Förteckning över konstnärer och konstverk*, Stockholm, A-B Hasse W. Tullbergs boktryckeri, 1935
Hurbyk, A., 'Ahrarna reforma seredyny XVI st.', in V. Smolii, ed., *Istoriia ukrains'koho selianstva: Narysy*, vol. 1, Kyiv, Naukova dumka, 2006
—— 'Typolohiia terytorial'noi hromady v Ukraini XIV–XVIII st.', *Ukraina v Tsentral'no-Skhidnii Yevropi*, 1, 2000, pp. 75–96
—— 'Wspólnota wiejska na Ukrainie w XIV–XVIII w. Ewoljucja podstawowych form społeczno-terytorianych', *Przegląd Historyczny*, XC, 1, 1999, pp. 1–18
—— *Evoliutsiia sotsial'no-terytorial'nykh spil'not v seredn'ovichnii Ukraini (volost', dvorysche, selo, siabrynna spilka)*, Kyiv, Instytut istorii Ukrainy, 1998
—— *Ahrarna reforma v Ukraini XVI st.*, Kyiv, Naukova dumka, 1997
Huslystyi, K., *Narysy z istorii Ukrainy*, issue II: *Ukraina pid lytovs'kym panuvanniam i zakhoplennia yii Pol'scheiu (z XIV st. po 1569 r.)*, Kyiv, Vydavnytstvo AN URSR, 1939
Ihnatouski, U., *Karotki narys historyi Belarusi. Lektsyi, chytanyia nastaunikam pachatkovykh shkol Menshchyny*, Mensk, Drukarnia Ia. Hrynbliata, 1919
Ihnatsenka, I. M. et al., eds, *Historyia Belaruskai SSR u piatsi tamakh*, 5 vols, Minsk, Navuka i tekhnika, 1972–75; vol. 1, *Tom I: Pershabytnaabshchynny lad na terytoryi Belarusi. Epokha feadalizmu*, 1972
Ijäs, M., 'Katariina Jagellonica – vaimo, kuningatar, diplomaatti', *Genos. Journal of the Genealogical Society of Finland* 2, 2009, pp. 52–9
Illik, P., *A Mohács-kód. A csatavesztés a magyar köztudatban*, Budapest, Unicus Műhely, 2015
Ilovayskiy, S., *Istoriya Rossiyi*, vol. 2, Moscow, Kushnerev i Ko, 1896
Iorga, N., *Istoria lui Ştefan cel Mare pentru poporul roman*, Bucureşti, Minerva, 1904
Ipatava, V., *Znak Vialikaha mahistra*, Minsk, Knihazbor, 2009
Istoriia Ukrainy-Rusy, vols III–V, Kyiv, Naukova dumka, 1992–94
Ivinskis, Z., 'Jogaila valstybininkas ir žmogus', in A. Šapoka, ed., *Jogaila*, Kaunas, Švietimo m-jos knygų leidybos komisija, 1935
—— 'Karalienės Barboros Radvilaitės drama', *Naujoji Vaidilutė*, 10, 1935
—— 'Jogaila Lietuvos istorijoje ir mes. Jo mirties 500 metų proga', *Naujoji Romuva*, 171, 1934
Jagiellon, C., 'Letter to the stadtholder (*ståthållare*) of Stockholm Castle', Gripsholm, 17 May 1567. Kungl. Samfundet för utgivande av handskrifter rörande Skandinaviens historia, *Handlingar rörande Skandinaviens historia*, vol. 4, Stockholm, Elmén och Granberg, 1817, pp. 52–3
Janicki, K., *Vitae Regum Polonorum elegiaco carmine descriptae*, Kraków, Łazarz Andrysowicz, 1565
Jankevičiūtė, G., 'Šv. Kazimiero atvaizdas XX a. Lietuvos dailėje ir 1943 m. konkursas', in Subačius, *Šventasis Kazimieras istorijos vyksme*, pp. 75–84
—— *Dailės gyvenimas Lietuvos Respublikoje 1918–1940*, Kaunas, NMKČDM, 2003
Janonienė, R., 'Vilniaus Žemutinės pilies ikonografiniai šaltiniai', in R. Ragauskienė, ed., *Vilniaus Žemutinė pilis XIV a.–XIX a. pradžioje. 2002–2004 m. istorinių šaltinių paieškos*, Vilnius, Lietuvos pilys, 2006, pp. 11–43

Jasienica, P., *Jagiellonian Poland*, trans. Alexander Jordan, Miami, American Institute of Polish Culture, 1978

Jászay, P., *A magyar nemzet napjai a Mohácsi vész után*, Pest, Hartleben Konrád Adolf, 1846

Jefferson, J., *The holy wars of King Wladislas and Sultan Murad: The Ottoman-Christian Conflict from 1438–1444*, Leiden, 2012

Jeschke, I., *Eine bemerkenswerte Frau: Anna von Polen, Gemahlin Herzog Bogislaws X*, in *Stettiner Hefte* 9, 2003

Jiroušek, B., *Josef Macek: mezi historií a politikou*, Prague, Výzkumné centrum pro dějiny vědy, 2004

Johnson, U. G., *Gripsholm Castle*, Stockholm, The Swedish National Museum of Fine Arts, 2nd edn, 1989

Jókai, M., *Fráter György*, Budapest, Akadémiai Kiadó, 1972

Joutard, P., *La Légende des Camisards. Une sensibilité au passé*, Paris, Gallimard, 1977

Kákošová, Z., 'Podoby zobrazenia Turka a tureckých reálií v slovenskej literatúre 16. a 17. storočia', *Bohemica Litteraria*, 13, 1–2, 2010, pp. 31–45

Kałamajska-Saeed, M., *Ostra Brama w Wilnie*, Warsaw, PWN, 1990

Kalous, A., *Matyáš Korvín, 1443–1490: uherský a český král*, České Budějovice, n.p., 2009

Kamusella, T., *The Politics of Language and Nationalism in Modern Central Europe*, Basingstoke, Palgrave Macmillan, 2009, pp. 346–430

Kansteiner, W., 'Finding Meaning in Memory: A Methodological Critique of Collective Memory Studies', *History and Theory*, May 2002, pp. 179–97

Karpov, G., *Istoriya bor'by Moskovskogo gosudarstva s Polsko-Litovskim. 1462–1508*, Moscow, n.p., 1867

Kastsiuk, M. et al., *Narysy Historyi Belarusi: u 2-kh*, 2 vols, Minsk, Belarus', 1994

Kasymenko, A. et al., *Istoriya Ukrainskoy SSR*, T. I., Kyiv, Akademiya Nauk Urk SSR, 1969

Kasza, P., '*Mert látom, hogy néhányan . . . az eseményeket másképp mesélik, mint megtörténtek . . .*' *Brodarics István tevékenysége irodalomtörténeti megközelítésben*, PhD dissertation, Szeged, Szegedi Tudományegyetem. Irodalomtudományi Doktori Iskola, 2007

Katariina Jagellonica. Puolan prinsessa, Suomen herttuatar, Ruotsin kuningatar. 1526–1583: puolalaisten museoiden järjestämä näyttely Turun linnassa, 11.6. – 6.7.1965, Turku, Turun kaupungin historiallinen museo, 1965

Kavalenia, A. A. et al., eds, *Iahelony: dynastyia, epokha, spadchyna: materyialy Mizhnarodnai navukova-praktychnai kanferentsyi, Hal'shany-Navahrudak, 8–10 verasnia 2006h.*, Minsk, Belaruskaia navuka, 2007

Kazlou, L. R., *Z dazvolu karalia i vialikaha kniazia*, Minsk, Polymia, 1992, repr. Minsk, Arty-feks, 1998

Kéky, L., *Baksay Sándor*, Budapest, Franklin-Társulat, 1917

Kelemen, Z., *Történelmi emlékezet és mitikus történet Krúdy Gyula műveiben*, Budapest, Argumentum Kiadó, 2005

Keller, K., 'Frauen und dynastische Herrschaft. Eine Einführung', in B. Braun, K. Keller and M. Schnettger, eds, *Nur die Frau des Kaisers? Kaiserinnen in den Frühen Neuzeit*, Böhlau, Wien, 2016, pp. 13–26

Kerepeszki, R., 'Horthy Miklós mohácsi beszéde, 1926. Emlékezethely a politikai gondolkodásban és a nemzetközi kapcsolatok történetében', in M. Takács, ed., *A magyar emlékezethelyek kutatásának elméleti és módszertani alapjai*, Loci Memoriae Hungaricae 2, P. S. Varga, O. Száraz, Debrecen, Debreceni Egyetemi Kiadó, 2013, pp. 309–20

Kiaupienė, J., ed., *Lietuvos istorija*, vol. 3, A. Dubonis, ed., *XIII a. – 1385 m.: valstybės iškilimas tarp Rytų ir Vakarų*; vol. 4, J. Kiaupienė, ed., *Nauji horizontai: dinastija, visuomenė, valstybė. Lietuvos Didžioji Kunigaikštystė 1386–1529 m.*; vol. 5, J. Kiaupienė, ed., *Veržli Naujųjų laikų pradžia. Lietuvos Didžioji Kunigaikštystė 1529–1588 metais*, Vilnius, Baltos lankos, 2011, 2009, 2013
—— 'Lietuvos Didžiosios Kunigaikštystės kaitos laikas – 1529–1588 metai', in Kiaupienė, *Lietuvos istorija*, vol. 5
Kiaupienė, J., Z. Kiaupa and A. Kuncevičius, *The History of Lithuania before 1795*, Vilnius, Arlila, 2000
—— *Lietuvos istorija iki 1795 m.*, Vilnius, Valstybinis leidybos centras, 1995
Kirchner, E., *Die Churfürstinnen und Königinnen auf dem Throne der Hohenzollern*. Theil I und II. Berlin, Wiegandt & Grieben, 1866–67
Klaniczay, T., 'Mi és miért veszett Mohácsnál?' in *Hagyományok ébresztése*, Budapest, Szépirodalmi, 1976, pp. 200–6
Klapisch-Zuber, C., *L'arbre des familles*, Paris, Éditions de la Martinière, 2003
Klebelsberg, K., 'Preface' to I. Lukinich, ed., *Mohácsi emlékkönyv 1526*, Budapest, Magyar Királyi Egyetemi Nyomda, 1926
Klein, K. Lee, 'On the Emergence of Memory in Historical Discourse', *Representations*, 69, 2000, pp. 127–50
Knöfel, A. S., *Dynastie und Prestige: Die Heiratspolitik der Wettiner*, Dresdner Historische Studien, vol. 9, Köln, Böhlau, 2009
Kobylets'kyi, M., *Magdeburz'ke pravo v Ukraini: (XVI – persha polovyna XIX st.): istoryko-pravove doslidzhennia*, Lviv, PAIS, 2008
Kohler, A., *Ferdinand I. 1503–1564. Fürts, König und Kaiser*, München, C. H. Beck, 2003
Kolankowski, L., *Polska Jagiellonów: dzieje polityczne*, Lwów, Gubrynowicz i Syn, 1936
Kölcsey, F., 'Nemzeti hagyományok', in F. Toldy, ed., *Kölcsei Kölcsey Ferencz minden munkái*, vol. 3, Pesten, Heckenast Gusztav, 1860, pp. 5–34
Kónya, P. et al., *Dejiny Uhorska*, Bratislava, Trio Publishing, 2014
Kopysskiy, Z., *Sotsialno-politicheskaya istoriya gorodov Belorussii XVI – pervoy poloviny XVII v*, Mensk, Nauka i Tekhnika, 1975
Kopysskii, Z. Iu. and M. F. Zaloga, eds, *Belorussiia v epokhu feodalizma. Sbornik dokumentov i materialov*, 4 vols, Minsk, Izdatel'stvo Akademii nauk BSSR, 1959–79; vol. 1, *Tom pervyi: S drevneishikh vremen do serediny XVII veka*, 1959
Koreň, J., *Dejiny československého národa. Dejepis pre slovenské ľudové školy (a pre opakovacie školy)*, Prešov, Nákladom Štehrovho kníhkupectva, 1921
Körner, F., ed., *Vaterländische Bilder aus Ungarn und Siebenbürgen, der Woiwodina und dem Banat, Kroatien, Slawonien, der Militärgrenze sowie Dalmatien: in Schilderungen aus Natur, Geschichte, Industrie und Volksleben*, Leipzig, Spamer, 1858, vol. 3
Körner, G. and P. Lindberg, *PULS Historia*, Grundbok, Natur och Kultur, 2012
Kosáry, D., *Magyar külpolitika Mohács előtt*, Budapest, Magvető, 1978
Kosman, M., 'Zygmunt August w opinii współczesnych i potomnych', *Pamiętnik Biblioteki Kórnickiej* 19, 1982, pp. 19–76
Kossányi, B., *A Báthory-Sobieski emlékkiállitás katalogusa: Catalogue de l'exposition commémorative Báthory-Sobieski*, Budapest, Sárkány-Nyomda Részvénytársasá, 1933
Kováč, D., *Dejiny Slovenska*, Praha, Nakladatelství Lidové noviny, 1998
Kovács, G. 'A mohácsi történelmi emlékhely. Szimbolikus harc a történelmi emlékezetért', in T. Hofer, ed., *Magyarok Kelet és Nyugat közt. A nemzettudat változó jelképei*, Budapest, Néprajzi Múzeum, 1996, pp. 283–303
—— 'Változatok a történelemre. Tanulmányok Székely György tiszteletére', in G. Erdei and B. Nagy Balázs, eds, Budapest, Budapesti Történeti Múzeum, 2004

Koval'ova, S., *Sudebnyk velykoho kniazia Kazymyra Yahailovycha 1468 roku*, Mykolaiv, Vydavnytstvo Chornomors'koho derzhavnoho universytetu im. Petra Mohyly, 2009

Kőváry, L., *A millennium lefolyásának története s a millennáris emlékalkotások*, Budapest, Athenaeum Társulat, 1897

Koyalovich, *Lektsii po istorii Zapadnoy Rusi*, Moscow, n.p., 1864

—— *Istoricheskoye issledovaniye o Zapadnoy Rusi*, St Petersburg, n.p., 1855

Kozák, P., 'Zikmund Jagellonský: králův bratr na knížecím stolci', *Vlastivědné listy Slezska a severní Moravy*, 37, 2011, pp. 6–10

—— 'Zástavní pán nebo 'freyer Fürst'? několik poznámek k opvské vládě Zikmunda Jagellonského', *Acta historica Universitatis Silesianae Opaviensis*, 1, 2008, pp. 87–97

Krausen, E., ed., *Germania Sacra*, Neue Folge 11. Die Bistümer der Kirchenprovinz Salzburg. Das Erzbistum Salzburg I. Die Zistersienserabtei Raitenhaslach, Berlin, New York, Walter de Gruyter, 1977

Krawyczyk, J., *Matejko i historia*, Warsaw, Instytut Sztuki Polskiej Akademii Nauk, 1990

Krieger, K. F., *Die Habsburger im Mittelater*, Stuttgart, Berlin, Köln, Kohlhammer, 1994

Krom, M., *Starodubskaya voyna 1534–1537*, Moscow, Rubezhi XXI, 2008

—— 'Rossiya i Velikoye Kniezhestvo Litovskoye: dva puti v istorii', *Angliyskaya Naberezhnaya*, 4, 2000, pp. 73–100

—— *Mezhdu Rus'yu i Litvoy: Zapadnorusskiye zemli v sisteme russko-litovskikh otnosheniy кontsa XV-pervoy treti XVI v.*, Moscow, Arkheograficheskiy Tsentr, 1997

Krúdy, G., *Királyregények: Mohács, Festett király, Az első Habsburg*, Budapest: Szépirodalmi kiadó, 1979

Kryp'iakevych, I., *Istoriia Ukrainy*, Lviv, Svit, 1990

Krzyżaniakowa, J. and J. Ochmański, *Władysław II Jagiełło*, Wrocław, Ossolineum, 1990

Kryzhanivs'kyi, O., 'Zakhidnoievropeis'ki tradytsii pravlinnia dynastii Sfortsiv v epokhu italiis'koho Vidrodzhennia ta yikh vplyv na formuvannia sotsiokul'turnykh utvoren' na zemliakh Podillia v pershii polovyni XVI st.', in Dmytriienko et al., *Bars'ka zemlia Podillia*, pp. 190–6

Kubijovyč, V., ed., *Encyclopedia of Ukraine*, vol. II, Toronto, Buffalo, London, University of Toronto Press, 1988

Kubík, V., ed., *Doba jagellonská v zemích české koruny (1471–1526): konference k založení Ústavu dějin křest'anského umění KTF UK v Praze*, České Budějovice, nakl. Tomáš Halama, 2005

Kubinyi, A., 'A Jagelló-kori Magyar állam', *Történelmi szemle*, 48, 3–4, 2006, pp. 287–307

—— 'Historische Skizze Ungarns in der Jagiellonenzeit', in A. Kubinyi, *König und Volk im spätmittelalterlichen Ungarn*, Herne, Tibor Schäfer, 1998

—— 'Alltag und Fest am ungarischen Königshof der Jagellonen 1490–1526', in Kubinyi, *König und Volk im spätmittelalterlichen Ungarn*, pp. 184–206

—— 'The Road to Defeat: Hungarian Politics and Defense in the Jagiellonian Period', in J. M. Bak and B. Király, eds, *From Hunyadi to Rákóczi: War and Society in Later Medieval and Early Modern Hungary*, New York, Brooklyn, 1982, pp. 159–78

Kučera, M., *Slovenské dejiny I. Od príchodu Slovanov do roku 1526*, Literárne informačné centrum, 2011, pp. 306–12

Kulin, F., *Hódíthatatlan szellem. Dózsa György és a parasztháború reformkori értékelésérol*, Budapest, Akadémiai Kiadó, 1982

Kuthan, J., *Královské dílo za Jiřího z Poděbrad a dynastie Jagellonců. Díl první. Král a šlechta*, Prague, Nakladatelství Lidové noviny, 2010

Kuthen, M., *Catalogus ducum Regumque Bohaemorum in quo summatim gesta singulorum singulis Distichis continentur. In super additae sunt eorum facies Iconicae & ad viuum deliniatae*, Prague, 1540

Labuda, G., *Szkice z dziejów Pomorza*, vol. I, Warsaw, Książka i Wiedza, 1958
Lahtinen, A., *Pohjolan prinsessat. Viikinkineidoista renessanssiruhtinattariin*, Jyväskylä, Atena, 2009
—— '"There's No Friend Like a Sister": Sisterly Relations and the Rhetoric of Sisterhood in the Correspondence of the Aristocratic Stenbock Sisters', in A. Korhonen and K. Lowe, eds, *The Trouble with Ribs: Women, Men and Gender in Early Modern Europe*, Helsinki, Helsinki Collegium for Advanced Studies, 2007, pp. 180–200
Lapinskas, D., *Dux Magnus*, libretto by Kazys Bradūnas, English translation by John G. Paton, Chicago, 1984
Lappo, I., *Velokoye kniazhestvo Litovskoye za vremia ot zakliuchenia Liublinskoy unii do smerti Stefana Batoriya: Opyt issledovaniya politicheskogo I obschestvennogo stroya*, vol. 1, St Petersburg, Tipografiya Mattisena, 1901
Lastouski, V., *Karotkaia historyia Belarusi*, Vil'nia, Drukarnia Martsina Kukhty, 1910; repr. Minsk, Universitetskae, 1992
—— *Shto treba vedats' kazhnamu belarusu?*, Mensk, Drukarnia A. Ia Hrynbliata, 1918; repr. Berlin, n.p., 1944
Laužikas, R., *Istorinė Lietuvos virtuvė. Maistas ir gėrimai Lietuvos Didžiojoje Kunigaikštystėje*, Vilnius, Briedis, 2014
Leino, E., *Juhana Herttuan ja Catharina Jagellonican lauluja*, 1919; 6th edn, Helsinki, Otava, 2001
—— *Pieśni księcia Jana i Katarzyny Jagiellonki*, trans. J. Litwiniuk, Helsinki, Ahjo, 1981; Warszawa, Państwowy Instytut Wydawniczy, 1981
Lelewel, J., *Polska: dzieje i rzeczy jej*, 20 volus, Poznań, J. K. Żupański, 1858–86
Leshchenko, N., 'A Fine Instrument: Two Nation-Building Strategies in Post-Soviet Belarus', *Nations and Nationalism*, 10, 2004
Levandauskas, V. and R. Vaičekonytė-Kepežinskienė, *Napoleonas Orda: senosios Lietuvos architektūros peizažai*, Vilnius, VDA leidykla, 2006
Lévi-Strauss, C., *Anthropologie structurale*, Paris, Plon, 1985, 1st edn, 1958
Levy, D. and N. Sznaider, *The Holocaust and Memory in the Global Age*, trans. A. Oksiloff, Philadelphia, Temple University Press, 2006
Lewicki, A. and A. Sokołowski, eds, *Codex epistolaris saeculi decimi quinti*, vol. I, Kraków, Akademia Umiejętności, 1876
Lian'kevich, G. and L. Soboleva, 'Podarivshie Evrope korolei', *Belaruskaia Dumka*, 3, 2006, pp. 130–3
Lileyko, J., *Zamek Królewski w Warszawie*, Warsaw, Państwowe Wydawnictwo Naukowe, 3rd edn, 1986
—— 'Władysławowski pokój marmurowy na zamku królewskim w Warszawie i jego twórcy', *Biuletyn Historii Sztuki* 37, 1, 1975
Lilienthal, A., *Die Fürstin und die Macht. Welfische Herzoginnen im 16. Jahrhundert. Elisabeth, Sidonia, Sophia*, Quellen und Darstellungen zur Geschichte Niedersachsens 127, Hannover, Hahnsche Buchhandlung, 2007, pp. 241–84
Lindberg, B., 'Introduktion: nationalism och nationell identitet i 1700-talets Sverige', in A. Karlsson and B. Lindberg, eds, *Nationalism och nationell identitet i 1700-talets Sverige*, Uppsala, Uppsala universitet, 2002, pp. 7–15
Lindner, R., *Historiker und Herrschaft. Nationsbildung und Geschichtspolitik in Weißrußland*, München, R. Oldenbourg, 1999
—— *Karotkaia Historyia Belarusi*, Vil'nia: Drukarnia Martsina Kukhty, 1910; repr. Minsk, Universitetskae, 1992
Liske, X., *Studia z dziejów wieku XVI*, Poznań, Jan Konstanty Żupański, 1867

Liubaschenko, V., 'Halych u tserkovno-uniinykh planakh Vladyslava Yahaila i mytropolyta Kypriiana', *Ukraina: kul'turna spadschyna, natsional'na svidomist', derzhavnist'. Zbirnyk naukovykh prats'*, 20, 2011, pp. 434–52

Liubavskii, M., *Oblastnoe delenie i mestnoe upravlenie Lytovsko-Russkogo gosudarstva ko vremeni izdaniia pervogo Litovskogo statute*, Moscow, Universitetskaia tipografiia, 1892

Ljunggren, P., *Upptäck historia*, Stockholm, Liber, 2015

Losontzi, I., *Hármas kis tükör, melly I. A' szent históriát, II. Magyar Országot, III. Erdély Országot, annak földével, polgári – állapatjával, és históriájával, gyenge elmékhez alkalmazott módon a' nemes tanulóknak summásan, de világosan elö-adja és ki mutatja*, Pozsony, n.p., 1777

Łowmiański, H., *Polityka Jagiellonów*, ed. Krzysztof Pietkiewicz, Poznań, Wydawnictwo Poznańskie, 1999

Lüthi, M., *The European Folk Tale: Form and Nature*, trans. John D. Niles, Bloomington, Indiana University Press, 1986

Macek, J., *Jagellonský věk v českých zemích: 1471–1526*, 4 vols, Prague, Academia, 1992–99

Maciej of Miechów, *Chronica Polonorum*, Kraków, n.p., 1519 and 1521

Maciejowski, S. and M. Kromer, *De Sigismundo Primo Rege Poloniae etc Duo Panegyrici funebres, dicti Cracoviae in eius funere, Nempe Sermo Samuelis Episcopi Cracoviensis & Regni Poloniae Cancellarij. Oratio Martini Cromeri, Canonici Cracoviensis & Oratoris Regij*, Mainz, 1550

Mačiulis, D., 'Vytauto Didžiojo metų (1930) kampanijos prasmė', *Lituanistica*, 2, 2001, pp. 54–75

Magocsi, P. R., *A History of Ukraine: The Land and Its Peoples*, 2nd edn, Toronto, Buffalo, London, Toronto University Press, 2010

Magyar Márs avagy Mohách mezején történt veszedelemnek emlékezete, Vienna, Cozmerovius, 1653

Maironis, J., *Lietuvos istorija. Su kunigaikščių paveikslais ir žemėlapiais*, St Petersburg, 1906

Mănicută, C., 'Ștefan cel Mare – evocare istorică și mit romantic', *Codrul Cosminului* 10, 2004, pp. 81–2

Marcell, B., 'A Mohács = centenárium regényei', *Korunk*, May 1927

Marcinkevičius, J., *Raštai*, vol. 3, *Poemos, dramos*, Vilnius, Vaga, 1982, pp. 110–413.

Marczali, H., ed., *Nagy képes világtörténet*, Budapest, Révai Testvérek, vol. 6, ed. J. Csuday and Gyula Schonherr, electronic edition online at www.elib.hu/01200/01267/html/06kotet/06r05f31.htm, accessed 23.10.17

Markauskaitė, N., 'Lietuvos jėzuitų provincijos statybinė veikla: Vilniaus profesų namų Šv. Kazimiero bažnyčia XVII–XVIII amžiais', unpublished PhD dissertation, Vilnius, Vilnius Academy of Arts, 2004

Markauskaitė, N. and S. Maslauskaitė, eds, *Šventojo Kazimiero gerbimas Lietuvoje*, Vilnius, LNM, 2009

Márki, S., *Dósa György*, Magyar Történeti Életrajzok, Budapest, Athenaeum, 1913

Marples, D. R., *Belarus: A Denationalized Nation*, London and New York, Routledge, 1999

Márton, E. S., *Magyar gyász; vagy-is Második Lajos magyar királynak a mohátsi mezőn történt veszedelme*, Pesten, Landerer Mihály, 1792

Masaryk, T. G., *The Meaning of Czech History*, Chapel Hill, University of North Carolina Press, 1974

Maslauskaitė, S., ed., *Vilniaus katedros požemiai. Vadovas*, Vilnius: BPM, 2013

—— *Šventojo Kazimiero atvaizdo istorija XVI–XVIII a.*, Vilnius, LNM, 2010
Matejko, L., *Poczet królów i książąt polskich*, with text by Stanisław Smolka i August Sokołowski, Vienna, Maurycy Perles, 1893
Maternicki, J., 'Miejsce i rola "Kwartalnika Historycznego" w dziejach historiografii polskiej', *Kwartalnik Historyczny* 95, 1, 1988, pp. 3–20
Matulaitis, J., 'Jurgis Matulevičius, Dievo ir Apaštalų Sosto malone . . .', *Vilniaus garsas*, 28 May 1922, no. 19, pp. 2–3
—— 'List pasterski. Jerzy Matulewicz . . .', *Nasza ziemia*, 21 May 1922, no. 16, pp. 3–4
Matušakaitė, M., *Karalienė Barbora ir jos atvaizdai*, Vilnius, Versus aureus, 2008
—— *Vilniaus Žemutinės pilies rūmai*, 5 pts, Vilnius, LII, 1989–2003
Matušakaitė, M. and A. Bumblauskas, eds, *Lietuvos Didžiosios Kunigaikštystės valdovų rūmų atkūrimo byla. Vieno požiūrio likimas*, Vilnius, VU leidykla, 2006
Mazower, M., *Salonica, City of Ghosts: Christians, Muslims and Jews, 1430–1950*, London, HarperCollins, 2004
Megem, M., 'Siuzhety srednevekovoy litovskoy istorii i politika konstruirovaniya proshlogo v sovetskoy istoriografii', *Vestnik MGOU* 3, 2013
Mel'nik, V. A., *Osnovy ideologii belorusskogo gosudarstva*, Minsk, Vysheishaia shkola, 2009
Mérai, D., 'Memory from the Past, Display for the Future: Early Modern Funeral Monuments from the Transylvanian Principality', doctoral thesis, Central European University, 2017
Merridale, C., 'Redesigning History in Contemporary Russia', *Journal of Contemporary History*, 38, 1, 2006
Mesenhöller, M., 'Ein früher Traum von Europa', *Die Zeit*, 7 March 2013
Mesniankin, Ye., 'Bona Sfortsa i epokha Vidrodzhennia v Podil's'komu Bari', in Dmytriienko et al., *Bars'ka zemlia Podillia*, pp. 198–201
Messenius, J., *Suomen riimikronikka*, Harry Lönnroth, Martti Linna, trans. and eds, Helsinki, Finnish Literature Society, 2004
—— *Scondia Illustrata*, vol. 7, Stockholmiae, Enaeus, 1702
—— *Genealogia Sigismundi*, Dantisci Ex molybdographia Viduae Guillemothanae, 1608
Micke-Broniarek, E., *Gallery of Polish Painting: Guide*, Warsaw, Muzeum narodowe w Warszawie, 2006
Mickūnaitė, G., *Making a Great Ruler: Grand Duke Vytautas of Lithuania*, New York, CEU Press, 2005
Mihály, I., *'Magyarország panasza': a Querela Hungariae toposz a XVI–XVII. század irodalmában*, Debrecen, Kossuth, 1995
—— Nemeskürty, I., *Krónika Dózsa György teteiról*, Budapest, Kossuth, 1972
—— *Ez történt Mohács után: Tudósítás a magyar történelem tizenöt esztendejéről 1526–1541*, Budapest, Szépirodalmi, 1966
Moeglin, J. M., 'Dynastisches Bewusstsein und Geschichtsschreibung. Zum Verständnis der Wittelsbacher, Habsburger und Hohenzollern im Spätmittelalter', *Historische Zeitschrift* 256, 1993, pp. 593–635
Mór, B. and A. Fazekas, *Mohács Kommandó*, Budapest, Corvina, 2013
Morison, M. and J. Bell, 'A Narrative of the Journey of Cecilia, Princess of Sweden to the Court of Queen Elizabeth', *Transactions of the Royal Historical Society* 12, 1898, pp. 181–224
Mrozowski, P., 'Europa Jagiellonica – z warszawskiej perspektywy', in *Europa Jagiellonica, 1386–1572. Sztuka i kultura w Europie Środkowej za panowania Jagiellonów*, Warsaw, Muzeum Narodowe we Warszawie, 2012

Mykhailovs'kyi, V., *Elastychna spil'nota. Podil's'ka shliakhta v druhii polovyni XIV – 70-kh rokakh XVI stolittia*, Kyiv, Tempora, 2012
—— *Nadavcha pozemel'na polityka volodariv Zakhidnoho Podillia (1402–1506 rr.)*. Avtoref. dys. na zdobuttia nauk. stupenia kand. ist. nauk, Kyiv, n.p., 2004
—— 'Iahellony', in V. Smolii, ed., *Entsyklopediia istorii Ukrainy*, vol. 10, Kyiv, Naukova dumka, 2013, pp. 722–3
Nagy, A. F., V. Kenéz, L. Solymosi and G. Érszegi, eds, *Monumenta rusticorum in Hungaria rebellium anno MDXIV*, Budapest, Akadémiai Kiadó, 1979
Naidziuk, I. and I. Kasiak, *Belarus' uchora i sian'nia. Papuliarny narys z historyi Belarusi*, original publication details unknown, 1943; repr. Minsk, Navuka i tekhnika, 1993
'A Napkelet és a Hölgyfutár című lap polemiája Than Mór mohácsi vész című képéről, 1857', in Szabó, *Mohács*, pp. 500–4
Narbutt, T., *Dzieje starożytne narodu litewskiego*, 9 vols, Vilnius, Nakładem Marcinowskiego, 1835–41
Nekrashevich-Korotkaya, Zh., 'Pobeda v Grunvaldskoy bitve kak *omen faustum* dinastii Yagiellonov v epopeye "Prusskaya voyna" (1516) Yana Vislitskogo', *ŽALGIRIUI – 600, Istoriniaimūšiai Lietuvos Didžiosios Kunigaikštystėsraštijoje. VII Jurgio Lebedžioskaitymai. Pranešimų santraukos*, Vilnius, Vilniaus universiteto leidykla, 2010, pp. 20–1
—— 'Gosudarstvennaya i dinasticheskaya kontseptsiya poemy "Prusskaya voyna" Yana Vislitskogo', *Studia linguistica*, 3, 2009, pp. 231–6
Neubauer, J., 'General Introduction', in M. Cornis-Pope and J. Neubauer, eds, *History of the Literary Cultures of East-Central Europe: Junctures and Disjunctures in the 19th and 20th Centuries*, vol. 3: *The Making and Remaking of Literary Institutions*, Amsterdam, Philadelphia, John Benjamins, 2007
Neugebauer, S., *Icones et vitae principum ac regum Poloniae omnium*, Frankfurt, n.p., 1620
Neumann, T., 'A "Dobzsekirályról" egy kicsit másképp – Ötszáz éve halt meg II. Ulászló', online article published 1 April 2016: http://ujkor.hu/content/dobzsekiralyrol-egy-kicsit-maskepp-otszaz-eve-halt-meg-ii-ulaszlo, accessed 5.8.16
—— 'Királyi aláírás és pecséthasználat a Jagelló-kor elején', *Turul* 83, 2, 2010, pp. 33–53
—— 'II. Ulászló koronázása és első rendeletei (Egy ismeretlen országgyűlésről és koronázási dekrétumról)', *Századok* 142, 2, 2008, pp. 315–37
Neville, K., 'The Land of the Goths and Vandals: The Visual Presentation of Gothicism at the Swedish Court, 1550–1700', *Renaissance Studies*, 27, 2013, pp. 435–59
Niehoff, B., 'Es war Einmal . . . Die Landshuter Hochzeit für Kinder', in B. Niehoff, ed., *In Eren liebt sie: die Landshuter Hochzeit 1903–2005: Annäherungen an das Jahr 1475*, Landshut, Museen der Stadt Landshut, 2005, p. 47
Niehoff, F., '"Landshuter Hochzeit" als "experimentelles Mittelalter"', in F. Niehoff, ed., *Das Goldene Jahrhundert der Reichen Herzöge*, Landshut, Museen der Stadt Landshut, 2014
—— ed., *Landshuter Hochzeit seit 1475*, Landshut, Museen der Stadt Landshut, 2013
—— ed., *Die Landshuter Hochzeit 1903–2005. Annäherungen an das Jahr 1475*, Landshut, Museen der Stadt Landshut, 2005
—— 'Von Zauber, den der Rost des Alten auf das Gemüt des Menschen ausübt . . . Der Landshuter Rathaussaal als Erinnerungsort', in Niehoff, *In Eren liebt sie*.
Nikžentaitis, A., *Vytauto ir Jogailos įvaizdis Lietuvos ir Lenkijos visuomenėse*, Vilnius, Aidai, 2002
—— *Witold i Jagiełło: Polacy i Litwini we wzajemnym stereotypie*, Poznań, Poznańskie Towarzystwo Przyjaciół Nauk, 2000

Nolte, C., *Familie, Hof und Herrschaft. Das verwandtschaftliche Beziehungs- und Kommunikationsnetz der Reichsfürsten am Beispiel der Markgrafen von Brandenburg-Ansbach (1440–1530)*, Stuttgart, Thorbecke, 2005

Nora, P. et al., *Les Lieux de mémoire*, 3 vols, Paris, Gallimard, 1984–92

—— 'Between Memory and History: Les Lieux de Mémoire', *Representations*, 26, Special Issue: Memory and Counter-Memory, Spring, 1989, pp. 7–24

Norris, S., *Blockbuster History in the New Russia: Movies, Memories and Patriotism*, Bloomington, Indiana University Press, 2012

Novik, Ia. K. and G. S. Martsul', eds, *Historyia Belarusi: u dvukh chastkakh*, 2 vols, Minsk, Universitetskae, 1998, vol. 1, *Chastka 1: Ad starachytnykh chasou – pa liuty 1917*

Nowakowska, N., *Church, State and Dynasty: The Career of Cardinal Fryderyk Jagiellon (1468–1503)*, Basingstoke, Ashgate, 2007

—— 'Jagiellonians and Habsburgs: The Polish Historiography of Emperor Charles V', in S. C. Dixon and Martina Fuchs, eds, *The Histories of Emperor Charles V*, Münster, Aschendorff, 2005

Nowakowska, N., I. Afanasyev, S. Kuzmová, G. Mickūnaitė, S. Niiranen and D. Zupka, *Dynasty in the Making: The Jagiellonians, c. 1380–1650*, forthcoming

Nyman, M., *Förlorarnas historia: Katolskt liv i Sverige från Gustav Vasa till drottning Kristina*, Uppsala, Katolska bokförlaget, 1997

Obodziński, A., *Pandora starożytna monarchów polskich*, Kraków, n.p., 1640

Oborni, T. and Sz. Varga, 'A béke mint a hatalmi propaganda eszköze Jagelló (II.) Ulászló és Szapolyai (I.) János uralkodása idején', in *A történettudomány szolgálatában. Tanulmányok a 70 éves Gecsényi Lajos tiszteletére*, Budapest, Győr, 2012, pp. 251–65

Ochman, E., *Post-Communist Poland: Contested Pasts and Future Identities*, Abingdon, Routledge, 2013

Ohlobyn, O., 'Krypiakevych Ivan', in Kubijovyč, *Encyclopedia of Ukraine*, vol. II, p. 682

Ohloblyn, O. and L. Wynar, 'Hrushevsky Mykhailo', in Kubijovyč, *Encyclopedia of Ukraine*, vol. II, pp. 250–3

Okoń, J., K. Gara and J. Rzegocka, eds, *Żywot Świętego Kazimierza królewicza polskiego i książęcia litewskiego w Wilnie Roku 1606 przez Mateusza Chryzostoma Wołodkiewicza przełożony*, Warsaw, Muzeum Historii Polski, 2016

Orda, N., *Album widoków historycznych Polski*, Warsaw, Maksymilian Fajans, 1873–83

Ortutay, Gy., 'Mohács emlékezete. Elhangzott a Mohácsi Történelmi Emlékhely felavatásán', in Szabó, *Mohács*, pp. 537–42

Ortvay, T., *Mária, II. Lajos magyar király neje 1505–1558*, Magyar Történeti Életrajzok, Budapest, Athenaeum, 1914

Orzechowski, S., *Ornata et copiosa oratio*, Venezia, 1548

Orzelski, Ś., *Bezkrólewia ksiąg ośmioro, czyli, dzieje Polski od zgonu Zygmunta Augusta, 1572 aż do r. 1576*, Warsaw, Wydawnictwo Artystyczne i Filmowe, 1980

Otamanosvkiy, V., 'Razvitiye gorodskogo stroya na Ukraine v XIV–XVIII vv. i magdeburgskoye pravo', *Voposy Istorii*, 3, 1958, pp. 122–35

Paasivirta, J., *Finland and Europe. The Period of Autonomy and the International Crises, 1808–1914*, Minneapolis, University of Minnesota Press, 1962

Pakier, M. and J. Wawrzyniak, *Memory and Change in Europe: Eastern Perspectives*, New York, Berghahn Books, 2016

Palacký, F., *Dějiny národu českeho v Čechách a v Moravě*, 5 vols, Prague, Nakladatel L. Mazáč, 1937 [1836–67], vol. 5

Pálffy, G., *The Kingdom of Hungary and the Habsburg Monarchy in the Sixteenth Century*, Boulder, CO, Center for Hungarian Studies and Publications, 2009

Paliušytė, A., ed., *Lietuvos dailininkų žodynas*, vol. 2, *1795–1918*, Vilnius, LKTI, 2012
Palmén, E. G., 'Puolan kirjallisuudesta poimittuja tietoja Suomen historiaan', *Historiallinen Arkisto* XVIII, Helsinki, Suomen Historiallinen Seura, 1903, pp. 336–61
Papánek, J., J. Fándly and J. Sklenár, eds, *Compendiata historia gentis Slavae*, Tyrnaviae, Typis Wenceslai Jelinek, 1793
Papeé, F., *Aleksander Jagiellończyk*, Kraków, Polska Akademia Umiejętności, 1949
—— *Jan Olbracht*, Kraków, Polska Akademia Umiejętności, 1936
Pärnänen, J. A., *Le premier séjour de Sigismond Vasa en Suède 1593–1594*, Annales academiae scientiarum Fennicae B XXVIII, 1933
Pashkevich, A., *Sim' pobedishi*, Minsk, Knihazbor, 2012
Pashkou, H. P. et al., eds, *VKL: Vialikae Kniastva Litouskae. Entsyklapedyia*, 3 vols, Minsk, 'Belaruskaia Entsyklapedyia', 2005–10, vol. 2, 2007
Pashuto, V., *Obrazovaniye litovskogo gosudarstva*, Moscow, Akademiya Nauk, 1959
Peringskiöld, J., *Monumenta Ullerakerensia cum Upsalia nova*, Stockholm, Joh. L. Horrn, 1719
Perjés, G., *The Fall of the Medieval Kingdom of Hungary, 1526–41*, Boulder, CO, Social Science Monographs, 1989
—— *Az országút szélére vetett ország*, Budapest, Magvető, 1975
Pestel, F., G. Feindt, F. Krawatzek, D. Mehler and R. Trimçev, 'Promise and Challenge of European Memory', *European Review of History* 24, 4, 2017, pp. 495–506
Péter, K., 'Mohács nemzeti tragédiává válik a magyar történetben', in András Kiss and Veronka Dáné, eds, '"... éltünk mi sokáig 'két hazában' ...", Tanulmányok a 90 éves Kiss András tiszteletére', *Speculum Historiae Debreceniense* 9, Debrecen, 2012, pp. 17–27
Peters, C., *Women in Early Modern Britain 1450–1640*, Basingstoke, Palgrave, 2003
Petráň, J., 'Stavovské království a jeho kultura v Čechách (1471–1526)', in J. Homolka, J. Krása, V. Mencl, J. Pešina and J. Petráň, eds, *Pozdně gotické umění v Čechách (1471–1526)*, Prague, Odeon, 1978, pp. 14–24
Petrauskas, R., 'Valdančioji dinastija: iškilimas, išnykimas, vidiniai konfliktai ir jų sprendimas', in Kiaupienė, *Lietuvos istorija*, vol. 3, pp. 334–61
—— 'Lietuvos Didžiosios Kunigaikštystės valdymo struktūra ir institucijos', in Kiaupienė, *Lietuvos istorija*, vol. 4, pp. 254–5
Petrus, A., 'Fundusz centowy Aleksandry z Borkowskich Ulanowskiej na odnowienie Zamku Królewskiego na Wawelu (1894–1939)', *Waweliana* III, 1994, pp. 109–22
Picheta, U., *Historyia Belarusi, chastka pershaia*, Maskva, Leningrad, Dziarzhaunae vydavetstva, 1924
Picheta, V. I., *Belorussiia i Litva XV – XVI vv. (issledovaniia po istorii sotsial'no ekonomicheskogo, politicheskogo i kul'turnogo razvitiia)*, Moskva, Izdatel'stvo Akademii Nauk SSSR, 1961
—— *Agrarnaia reforma Sigizmunda Avgusta v Litovsko-Russkom gosudarstve*, 2nd edn, Moskva, Izdatel'stvo Akademii Nauk SSSR, 1958
—— *Istoriia sel'skogo khoziaistva i zemlevladeniia v Belorussii*, vol. 1, Minsk, Narkomzem, 1927
—— *Istoriia litovskogo gosudarstva do liublinskoi unii*, Vil'no, Izdatel'stvo 'Litvy', 1921
Pieśni nowe o królu polskim Stefanie Pierwszym ... wespółek y o Krolewnie Annie, Kraków, n.p., 1576
Pirożyński, J., *Die Herzogin Sophie von Braunschweig-Wolfenbüttel aus dem Hause der Jagiellonen (1522–1575) und ihre Bibliothek. Ein Beitrag zur Geschichte der deutsch-polnischen Kulturbeziehungen in der Renaissancezeit*, trans. Kordula Zubrzycka, Wolfenbütteler Schriften für Geschichte des Buchwesens 18, Wiesbaden, Harrassowitz, 1992
Piszczatowska, M., 'Pochód na Wawel', *Spotkania z Zabytkami* 8, 2008, pp. 38–9

Plokhy, S., *The Gates of Europe: A History of Ukraine*, New York, Basic Books, 2015
—— *The Cossack Myth: History and Nationhood in the Age of Empires*, Cambridge, Cambridge University Press, 2012
—— *The Origins of the Slavic Nations: Premodern Identities in Russia, Ukraine, and Belarus*, Cambridge, Cambridge University Press, 2006
—— *Unmaking Imperial Russia: Mykhailo Hrushevsky and the Writing of Ukrainian History*, Toronto, Buffalo, New York, University of Toronto Press, 2005
Pociecha, W., *Królowa Bona, 1494–1557: ludzie i czasy Odrodzenia*, 4 vols, Poznań, Poznańskie Towarzystwo Przyjaciel Nauk, 1948–59
—— *Geneza hołdu pruskiego, 1467–1525*, n.p., Instytut Bałtycki, 1937
Pokhilevich, D., *Krestyane Belorussii i Litvy vo ctoroy polovine XVIII v.*, Vilnius, Akademiya Nauk Litov., SSR, 1966
—— *Krest'iane Belorussii i Litvy v XVI–XVIII vv.*, Lviv, Izdatelstvo Lvovskogo universiteta, 1957
—— 'Dvizhenie feodal'noi zemel'noi renty v Velikom kniazhestve Litovskom v XV–XVI vv.', *Istoricheskie zapisk*, 31, 1950, pp. 194–221
Polekhov, S., *Nasledniki Vitovta. Dinasticheskaya voyna v Velikom kniazhestve Litovskom v 30-e gody XV veka*, Moscow, Indrik, 2015
—— *Vnutripoliticheskiy krizis v Velikom kniazhestve Litovskom v 30-e gody XV veka*, doctoral dissertation, Moscow, 2011
Polívka, M. and F. Šmahel, eds, *In Memoriam Josefa Macka (1922–1991)*, Prague, Historický ústav, 1996
Pollmann, J., *Memory in Early Modern Europe, 1500–1800*, Oxford, Oxford University Press, 2017
Pollmann, J. and E. Kuijpers, 'Introduction', in E. Kuijpers, J. Pollmann, J. Muller and J. Steen, eds, *Memory before Modernity: Practices of Memory in Early Modern Europe*, Leiden, Brill, 2013
Polnische Zeitung. Von der Wahl und Krönunge dess Königs in Polen Sigmunds III. Printzen auss Schweden. Desgleichen. Wie Ertzhertzog Maximilian auss Osterreich auch erwehlter König in Polen . . . Neben einer richtigen Geburts Liny des Jagellonischen Stammes . . . etc., s.l., n.p., 1588
Polnischer Königs- Stammen oder Beschreibung des Gross-Hertzoglichen Littauischen Geschlechts, Aus welchem bey fast dreyhundert Jahren her, Zwölf daraus geborene oder demselben anverwandte Fürsten, Zu Königen in Polen erwehlet worden . . .Mit Einführung Des Neu-erwehlten Königs Michael Thomas Koribut geboren Hertzogs von Wissnowetz, Etc. Littauischer . . ., Nuremberg, Stuttgart, 1669
Polons'ka-Vasylenko, N., *Istoriia Ukrainy*, vol. 1, Kyiv, Naukova dumka, 1992
Ponomariov, B., ed. *Istoriya SSSR s drevneyshikh vremen do nashikh dney*, 12 vols, vol. 2, Moscow, Akademiya Nauk SSSR, 1966
Porter, B., *When Nationalism Began to Hate: Imagining Modern Politics in Nineteenth Century Poland*, New York, Oxford University Press, 2000
Presniakov, A., *Litovsko-Russkoye gosudarstvo v 13–16 vv.*, St Petersburg, n.p., 1910
Prohászka, J., 'A lacikonyha mivoltának és nevének kérdéséhez', *Magyar Nyelv*, 61, 1, 1965, pp. 96–100
Prus, J., 'Russia's Use of History as a Political Weapon', *The Polish Institute of International Affairs. Policy Paper*, 12, 114, 2015, pp. 1–8
Przeździecki, A., ed., *Jagiellonki polskie, w XVI. wieku: obrazy rodziny i dworu Zygmunta I i Zygmunta Augusta Królów polskich*, Kraków, W drukarni Uniwersytetu Jagiellońskiego, pod zarządem Konst. Mańkowskiego, 1868–78

Przydacz, M., 'Polityka zagraniczna wobec Białorusi', in Paweł Musiałka, ed., *Główne kierunki polityki zagranicznej rządu Donalda Tuska w latach 2007–11*, Kraków, Wydawnictwo eSPe, 2012, pp. 279–94

Purš, J. and M. Kropilák, eds, *Přehled dějin Československa. Díl I/1. Do roku 1526*, Prague, Academia, 1980

Rady, M., *The Habsburg Empire: A Very Short Introduction*, Oxford, Oxford University Press, 2017

—— 'Rethinking Jagiello Hungary (1490–1526)', *Central Europe*, 3, 1, 2005, pp. 3–18

Ragauskas, A., 'Ar istorikas Teodoras Narbutas (1784–1864) buvo istorijos šaltinių falsifikuotojas?', *Acta humanitarica universitatis Saulensis*, 9, 2009

Ragauskienė, R., 'The Marriage of Catherine Jagiellon and John III Vasa in Vilnius (1562)', in E. Saviščevas and M. Uzorka, eds, *Lithuania-Poland-Sweden. European Dynastic Unions and Historical-Cultural Ties. Studies of the Palace of the Grand Dukes of Lithuania*, vol. XXI, Vilnius, National Museum – Palace of the Grand Dukes of Lithuania, 2014, pp. 102–19

Rajala, P., *Unio mystica. Mika Waltarin elämä ja teokset*, Helsinki, Otava, 2011

Rajić, J., *Istorija raznih slavjanskih narodov, naipače Bolgar, Horvatov i Serbov*, Saint Petersburg, 1795

Rangström, L., *En brud för kung och fosterland: kungliga svenska bröllop från Gustav Vasa till Carl XVI Gustaf*, Stockholm, Livrustkammaren och Atlantis, 2010

Réthelyi, O. et al., eds, *Mary of Hungary: The Queen and Her Court 1521–1531*, Budapest, Budapest History Museum, 2005

Révész, E., 'Történeti kép mint sajtóillusztráció 1850–1870', in Á. Mikó and K. Sinkó, eds, *Történelem – Kép, Múlt és művészet kapcsolata Magyarországon. Kiállítási katalógus*, Budapest, Magyar Nemzeti Galéria, 2000, pp. 580–97

Rogge, J., 'Nur verkaufte Töchter? Überlegungen zu Aufgaben, Quellen, Methoden und Perspektiven einer Sozial- und Kulturgeschichte hochadeligen Frauen und Fürstinnen im deutschen Reich während späten Mittelalters und Beginn der Neuzeit', in *Principes. Dynastien und Höfe im späten Mittelalter*, Thorbecke, Stuttgart, 2002, pp. 235–76

Rolker, C., *Das Spiel der Namen: Familie, Verwandschaft und Geschlecht im spätmittelalterlichen Konstanz*, Konstanzer Geschichts- und Rechtsquellen 45, Ostfildern, Jan Thorbecke Verlag, 2014

Rousso, H., *Le syndrome de Vichy (1945–198..)*, Paris, Éditions du Seuil, 1987

Różek, M., 'Uzupełnienie do fundacji królewskiej kaplicy Wazów', *Biuletyn Historii Sztuki*, XXXVI, 2, 1974, pp. 393–6

—— 'Źródła do fundacji i budowy królewskiej kaplicy Wazów przy katedrze na Wawelu', *Biuletyn Historii Sztuki* XXV, 1, 1973, pp. 3–9

Ruda, O., 'Beresteis'ka uniia u doslidzhenniakh l'vivs'kykh pol's'kykh istorykiv (1890–1914)', *Problemy slov'ianoznavstva*, 57, 2008

Rudling, P. A., *The Rise and Fall of Belarusian Nationalism, 1906–1931*, Pittsburgh, University of Pittsburgh Press, 2015

Rukal', A., *Na sluzhbe kniazia Radzivila*, Mensk, kampaniia 'Tvorchasts'', 2010

Rüsen, J., 'Was ist Geschichtskultur? Überlegungen zu einer neuen Art, über Geschichte nachzudenken', in K. Füssmann, H. T. Grütter and J. Rüsen, eds, *Historische Faszination. Geschichtskultur heute*, Köln, Weimar and Wien, Böhlau, 1994, pp. 3–26

Rusyna, O., *Sivers'ka zemlia u skladi Velykoho kniazivstva Lytovs'koho*, Kyiv, n.p., 1998

Ruszczycówna, J., 'Nieznanie portrety ostatnich Jagiellonów', *Rocznik Muzeum Narodowego w Warszawe* 20, 1976, pp. 5–119

Ryszkiewicz, A., *Malarstwo Polskie: romantyzm, historyzm, realism*, Warsaw, Auriga, 1989

Sahanovich, H., 'Contra tyranos', in A. Dziarnovich, ed., *Naiias'neishaia Rech Paspalitaia. Tsyvilizatsyia – Kul'tura – Relihiia – Palityka – Avantura – Heroika – Uspamin*, Mensk, Lohvinau, 2007, pp. 17–23

Sakcinski, I. Kukuljević, ed., *Chronicon breve Regni Croatiae. Joannis Tomasich Minoritae – Kratak ljetopis hrvatski Ivana Tomašića malobraćanina*, Arkiv za povjestnicu jugoslavensku, no. 9, 1868, pp. 1–34

Sanders, T., ed., *Historiography of Imperial Russia: The Profession and Writing of History in a Multinational State*, New York, M. E. Sharpe, 1999

Sapetowa, I., *Malarski poczet królów i książąt polskich według rysunków Jana Matejki w sali obrad Rady Powietowej w Mielcu*, Warsaw, Wydawnictwo Naukowe PWN, 1992

Sapkowski, A., *Lux Perpetua*, Warsaw, Supernowa, 2006

—— *Boży bojownicy*, Warszaw, Supernowa, 2004

—— *Narrenturm*, Warsaw, Supernowa, 2002

Šapoka, A., ed., *Lietuvos istorija*, Kaunas, Šviesa, 1936

Sas, P., *Feodalnyie goroda Ukrainy v kontse XV – 60 godakh XVI v.*, Kyiv, Naukova Dumka, 1989

Sasinek, F. V., *Dejiny kráľovstva uhorského*, vol. 2, Turčiansky Sv. Martin, Knihtlačiarsko-učastinársky spolok, 1871

Schröder, J. H., *Testamentum Catharinae Jagellonicae, Reginae Sveciae*, Uppsala, 1831

Sebők, F., 'Hungarian Priest Historians on the Jagellonian Era', in L. Löb, I. Petrovics and Gy. Szőnyi, eds, *Forms of Identity: Definitions and Changes*, Szeged, József Attila Tudományegyetem, 1994, pp. 89–95

—— 'Új törekvések a Jagelló-kori rendiség kutatásában a XX. század elején', *Acta historica*, 96, 1992, pp. 47–53

Seifertová, L., *Dějiny udatného českého národa*, Prague, Petr Prchal, 2003

Seifridus, G., *Genealogia Illustrissimorum Principum Marchionum Brandenburgensium*, Witebergæ, 1555

Sen'kiv, Yu., 'Sudebnyk 1468 roku, yoho struktura, zmist ta znachennia', *Visnyk L'vivs'koho universytetu. Seriia yurydychna*, 46, 2008, pp. 59–64

Shcherbak, V., *Ukrains'ke kozatstvo: formuvannia sotsial'noho stanu, druha polovyna XV – seredyna XVII st.*, Kyiv, Holovna redaktsiia ukrains'koi radians'koi entsyklopedii, 2000

—— 'Reiestrovi kozaky na derzhavnii sluzhbi', in V. A. Smolii, ed., *Istoriia ukrains'koho kozatstva: Narysy*, vol. 1, Kyiv, Vydavnychyi dim 'Kyievo-Mohylians'ka akademiia', 2006, pp. 73–86

Shkialionak, M., *Belarus' i susedzi. Histarychnyia narysy*, Belastok, Belaruskae Histarychnae Tavarystva, 2003

Sigismundi III . . . Poloniae et Sueciae Regis . . . Cracoviam ingressus, Kraków, n.p., 1587

Signori, G. and C. Rolker, *Konkurrierende Zugehörigkeit(en): Praktiken der Namengebung im europäischen Vergleich*, Konstanz, UVK-Verl.-Ges, 2011

Sihvo, H., 'Eino Leino: runo ja elämä', in H. Mäkelä, ed., *Elämän kirja. Valikoima Leinon tuotannosta*, Helsinki, Otava, 1980, pp. 15–35

Sinkó, K., 'Historizmus-Antihistorizmus', in Mikó and Sinkó, *Történelem – Kép*, pp. 103–15

—— 'A Mohácsnál elesett II. Lajos testének feltalása', in Mikó and Sinkó, *Történelem – Kép*, pp. 600–2

—— 'Kontinuitás vagy hagyomány újrateremtése? Történeti képek a 19. században (Részlet)', in Szabó, *Mohács*, pp. 471–8

—— 'II. 1. 17. Székely Bertalan (1835–1910). II. Lajos király holttestének föltalálása a mohácsi csatatéren', in I. Nagy, ed., *Aranyérmek, ezüstkoszorúk. Művészkultusz és műpártolás magyarországon a 19. században*, A Magyar Nemzeti Galéria kiadványai 1995/1, Budapest, Magyar Nemzeti Galéria, 1995, p. 234

—— 'A művészi siker anatómiája 1840–1900', in Nagy, *Aranyérmek*, pp. 15–47

Sirmiensis, G., *Epistola de perditione regni Hungarorum*, Monumenta Hungariae Historica, Series 2, Scriptores, vol. 1, ed. Gustáv Wenzel, Pest, 1857

Skaba, A., B. Babii, A. Borodin et al., eds, *Radians'ka entsyklopediia istorii Ukrainy*, vols 2, 4, Kyiv, Holovna redaktsiia ukrains'koi radians'koi entsyklopedii, 1972

Skochylias, I., *Halyts'ka (L'vivs'ka) yeparkhiia XII–XVIII st.*, Lviv, Vydavnytstvo Ukrains'koho Katolyts'koho Universytetu, 2010, pp. 325–34

Skolverket, *Läroplan för grundskolan, förskoleklassen och fritidshemmet 2011 (reviderad 2016)*, historia, Stockholm, Wolters Kluwer, 2016

Smirnov, M., *Yagiello-Yakov-Vladislav i pervoye soyedinenie Litvy s Polshey*, Odessa, n.p., 1868

Snyder, T., *The Reconstruction of Nations. Poland, Ukraine, Lithuania, Belarus, 1569–1999*, New Haven and London, Yale University Press, 2003

Solovyev, S., *Istoriya Rossii s drevneyshikh vremen*, St Petersburg, Obshchestwennaya polza, 1851–79

Sołtys, A., 'Pomniki Antoniego Madeyskiego na tle problemu restauracji katedry krakowskiej', *Studia Waweliana* III, 1994, pp. 157–67

Sroka, S., *Z dziejów stosunków polsko-węgierskich w późnym średniowieczu: szkice*, Kraków, Universitas, 1995

Sruoga, B., *Milžino paunksmė: trilogiška istorijos kronika*, Kaunas, Tulpė, 1932

Stachoń, B., *Polityka polska wobec Turcji i akcji anty-tureckiej w wieku XV do utraty Kilii i Białogrodu, 1484*, Lwów, Towarzystwo Naukowe [we Lwowie], 1930

Stahleder, E., 'Die Landshuter Hochzeit von 1475 nach dem widerentdeckten Bericht des "Markgrafschriebers"', in H. Bleibrunner, ed., *Beitrage zur Heimatkunde von Niederbayern*, Passau, Landshut Regierung von Niederbayern, 1976

—— *Landshuter Hochzeit 1475. Ein bayerische-europäisches Hoffest aus der Zeit der Gotik*, Ottobrunn-Riemerling, Hornung, 1984

Staliunas, M., *Making Russians: Meaning and Practice of Russification in Lithuania and Belarus after 1863*, Amsterdam, Rodopi, 2007

Stangier, T., 'Hochzeitsgeschichte(n) – Eine Annäherung auf Umwegen', in Niehoff, *In Eren liebt sie*, pp. 29–31

Stankevich, A., 'Raskazy z historyi Belarusi dlia shkolau i narodu', reprinted in A. Stankevich, *Z boham da Belarusi*, Vil'nia, Instytut belarustyki, 2008, pp. 63–72

—— *Vitaut Vialikì i Belarusy (referat, chytany na urachystai akademii u Vil'ni u sali 'Apollo' 27.X. 1930h., u dzen' 500-lets'tsia s'mertsi Vitauta, Vialik. Kniazia Litouska-Belaruskaha*, Vil'nia, Belaruskaia drukarnia im. Fr. Skaryny, 1930

Starostina, I., 'Pravo Velikogo kniazhesta Litovskogo XV v. v kontekste kulturno-istoricheskikh sviazey Polshy, Litvy i Rusi', in T. Dzhakson and E. Melnikova, eds, *Vostochnaya Yevropa v istoricheskoy retrospective: K 80-letiyu V.T. Pashuto*, Moscow, Yazyki russkoy kultury, 1999, pp. 237–44

—— 'Sudebnik Kazimira IV', in *Drevneishie gosudarstva na territorii SSSR. Materialy i issledovaniia, 1988–1989*, Moscow, Nauka, 1991, pp. 175–88

Stauber, R., 'Herrschaftsrepräsentation und dynastische Propaganda bei den Wittelsbachern und Habsburgern um 1500', in *Principes. Dynastien und Höfe im späten Mittelalter*, Stuttgart, Thorbeke, 2002, pp. 371–402

Stenroos, M. et al., *Turkulaisen veden pitkä matka Halistenkoskelta Turun keskuspuhdistamolle*, Turku, Turun Vesilaitos, 1989

Stryjek, T., *Jakiej przeszłości potrzebuje przyszłość? Interpretacje dziejów narodowych w historiografii i debacie publicznej na Ukrainie 1991–2004*, Warsaw, Instytut Studiów Politycznych PAN; Oficyna Wydawnicza Rytm, 2007

Subačius, P., ed., *Šventasis Kazimieras istorijos vyksme: įvaizdis ir refleksija*, Vilnius, LNM, 2006

Subtelny, O., *Ukraine: A History*, 3rd edn, Toronto, Buffalo, London, University of Toronto Press, 2000

Sucheni-Grabowska, A., *Zygmunt August: król polski i wielki książę litewski: 1520–1562*, Warsaw, Krupski, 1996

—— 'Jagiellonowie i Habsburgowie w pierwszej połowie XVI w.', *Sobótka* 4, 1983, pp. 449–67

Suchodolska, E. and M. Wredet, *Jana Matejki dzieje cywilizacji w Polsce*, Warsaw, Zamek Królewski, 1998

Sulimczyk, 'W Bazylice Wilenskiej', *Słowo*, 14 August 1931, no. 193

Szabados, Gy., 'Jezsuita "sikertörténet" (1644–1811). A magyar történettudomány konzervatív megteremtőiről', in G. Tóth, ed., *Clio inter arma. Tanulmányok a 16–18. századi magyarországi történetírásról*, Budapest, MTA, 2014, pp. 203–26

—— 'The Annals as a Genre of Hungarian Jesuit Historiography in the 17th–18th Centuries. From the State History to the History of the State', in A. Steiner-Weber, ed., *Acta Conventus Neo-Latini Upsaliensis: Proceedings of the Fourteenth International Congress of Neo-Latin Studies*, Leiden, Brill, 2012, pp. 1067–75

Szabó, D., *Küzdelmeink a nemzeti királyságért 1505–1526 (A magyar nemzet önállóságáért és függetlenségéért vívott küzdelmek története az 1505-iki rákosi országgyűléstől a Rákoczi-emigratio kihaltáig*, vol. 1, Budapest, Franklin, 1917

—— *A magyar országgyűlések II. Lajos korában*, Budapest, Hornyánszky Viktor, 1909

Szabó, G. Szentmártoni, '"Romulidae Cannas", avagy egy ál-Janus Pannonius-vers utóélete, eredeti szövege és válodi szerzője', in E. Békés and E. Tegyey, eds, *Convivium Pajorin Klára 70.születésnapjára*, Debrecen and Budapest, Debreceni Egyetem sokszorosítóüzemében, 2012, pp. 183–94

Szabó, J. B., 'Mohács', *Rubicon*, 8, 2013, pp. 4–19

—— 'Mohács legendáink nyomában', *Korunk*, 3, 2012, pp. 27–33

—— 'A mohácsi csata és a "hadügyi forradalom". II. rész. A magyar hadsereg a mohácsi csatában', *Hadtörténelmi közlemények*, 118, 2005, pp. 573–627

—— 'A mohácsi csata és a "hadügyi forradalom ». I. rész.', *Hadtörténelmi közlemények*, 117, 2004, pp. 443–78

—— ed., *Mohács*, Budapest, Osiris, 2006

Szajnocha, K., *Jadwiga i Jagiełło 1374–1413: opowiadanie historyczne*, 2 vols, Lwów, Karol Wild, 1855

Szakály, F., *A mohácsi csata*, Budapest, Akadémiai, 1975

Szakály, F., ed., *Mohács Tanulmányok a mohácsi csata 450. évfordulója alkalmából*, Budapest, Akadémiai, 1986

Szathmáry, K. P., *Sirály*, 3 vols, Pest, Müller Gyula, 1855

Szczekocka-Mysłek, K., *Jasnogórski poczet królów i książąt polskich*, Warsaw, Wydawnictwo Spółdzielcze, 1990

Szűcs, J., *Nemzet és történelem*, Budapest, Gondolat, 1973

Tagebuch des Erich Lassota von Steblau: Nach einer Handschrift der von Gersdorff-Weicha'schen Bibliothek zu Bautzen herausgegeben und mit Einleitung und Bemerkungen begleitet von Reinhold Schottin, Halle, G. Emil Barthel, 1866

Tamošiūnienė, I., *Šv. Jurgio prospektas: nuo vizijos iki tikrovės*, Vilnius, LNM, 2012
Tarasau, K., *Pamiats' pra lehendy. Postatsi belaruskai minuushchyny*, Minsk, Polymia, 1990
Tarashkevich, B., *Belaruskaia hramatyka dlia shkol*, Vil'nia, Vydan'ne Belaruskaha Kamitetu, 1918
Tawaststjerna, E., *Sibelius: 1865–1905*, vol. 1, trans. R. Layton, Berkeley and Los Angeles, University of California Press, 1976
Tewes, M., 'Die Landshuter Fürstenhochzeit 1475', in Niehoff, *In Eren liebt sie*, pp. 20–5
—— 'Die Landshuter Hochzeit 1903–2005. Annäharungen an ein mittelalterliches Fest', in Niehoff, *In Eren liebt sie*, pp. 40–5
Thomas, B., 'Der Knabenharnisch Jorg Seusenhofers fur Sigmund II. August von Polen', *Zeitschrift des deutschen Vereins für Kunstwissenschaft* 6, 1939, pp. 221–34
Titkov, A., ed., 'Litwa, Rossiya, Polsha (XIII–XVI vv.)', *Istoricheskiy Vestnik*, 154, 2014.
Tkalčić, I. K., *Hrvatska povjestnica*, Zagreb, Dragutin Albrecht, 1861
Tolochko, A., 'Dlinnaia istoriia Ukrainy', in A. Tolochko, *Kievskaia Rus' i Malorossiia v XIX veke*, Kyiv, Laurus, 2012, pp. 9–45
Tolz, V., *Russia: Inventing the Nation*, London, Arnold, 2001
Tota, A. L. and T. Hagen, *Routledge International Handbook of Memory Studies*, London, Routledge, 2015
Tóth, Z., *The Making of Mohács . . . Occurrence, Regional Discourse and the Building of the 'National Past' in Comparative History. A Case Study*, available online at: www.academia.edu/3847061/The_Making_of . . .Mohacs, pp. 1–17, accessed 21.3.14
—— 'The Hungarian Peculiarities of National Remembrance: Historical Figures with Symbolic Importance in Nineteenth-Century Hungarian History Paintings', *AHEA: E-Journal of the American Hungarian Educators Association*, 5, 2012, pp. 1–16
Traba, R. and H. Henning Hahn, eds, *Polsko-niemieckie miejsca pamięci*, 5 vols, Warsaw, Wydawnictwo Naukowe Scholar, 2012–15
Trachevskiy, A., *Polskoye bezkorolevie po prekrashchenii dinastii Yagellonov*, Moscow, 1869
Trencsényi, B., 'Writing the Nation and Reframing Early Modern Intellectual History in Hungary', *Studies in Eastern European Thought*, 62, 2010, pp. 135–54
Trencsényi, B. and M. Kopeček, eds, *Discourses of Collective Identity in Central and Southeast Europe (1770–1945)*, vol. 1: *Late Enlightenment. Emergence of the Modern, National Idea*, Budapest, 2006
Tresp, U., 'Eine "famose und grenzenlos mächtige Generation." Dynastie und Heiratspolitik der Jagiellonen im 15. und zu Beginn des 16. Jahrhundert', *Jahrbuch für Europäische Geschichte* 8, 2007, pp. 3–28
Treter, T., *Regum Poloniae Icones*, Rome, n.p., 1591
Trimonienė, R. R., *Lietuvos Didžioji Kunigaikštystė ir Vidurio Europa XV–XVI a. sandūroje*, Šiauliai, ŠPI, 1996
—— 'Triukšmas dėl karališkų karstų atradimo Vilniuje', *Mūsų Vilnius*, 28, 1931
Tringli, I., 'Kosáry Domonkos és a Mohács-vita', *Magyar Tudomány*, 12, 2013, pp. 1437–41
—— *Mohács felé 1490–1526*, Magyarország története 8, Budapest, Kossuth Kiadó, 2009
Troebst, S., 'Halecki Revisited: Europe's Conflicting Cultures of Remembrance', in M. Pakier and B. Stråth, eds, *European Memory? Contested Histories of Politics and Remembrance*, New York, Berghahn, 2016, pp. 56–63
Twardoch, S., *Wieczny Grunwald*, Warszaw, Narodowe Centrum Kultury, 2010
Ustrialov, N., *O Litovskom kniazhestve. Issledovaniye voprosa, kakoye mesto v Russkoy istorii dolzhno zanimat' Velikoye kniazhestvo Litovskoye?* St Petersburg, Ekspeditsiya zagotovleniya gosudarstvennykh bumag, 1839

Bibliography 251

Vaičekonis, P., 'Šv. Kazimiero palaikų tremtis Vilniaus Šv. Apašt. Petro ir Povilo bažnyčioje (1952–1989)', in Subačius, *Šventasis Kazimieras istorijos vyksme*, pp. 157–64
Vaitkevičius, B., M. Jučas and V. Merkys, eds, *Lietuvos TRS istorija*, vol. 1, *Nuo seniausių laikų iki 1917 metų*, Vilnius, Mokslas, 1985
Valančius, M., *Raštai*, B. Vanagienė, ed., vol. 2, Lituanistinė biblioteka 12, Vilnius, Vaga, 1972
—— *Žemajtiu wiskupistę aprasze k. Motiejus Wołonczewskis (1413–1841 m. istorija)*, 2 pts, Vilnius, J. Zawadzki, 1848
Vardy, S. B., 'The Changing Image of the Turks in Twentieth Century Hungarian Historiography', in *Clio's Art in Hungary and Hungarian America*, New York, Columbia University Press, 1985, pp. 147–70
—— *Modern Hungarian Historiography*, Boulder, CO, East European Quarterly, 1976
—— 'The Social and Ideological Make-up of Hungarian Historiography in the Age of Dualism (1867–1918)', *Jahrbücher Für Geschichte Osteuropas*, Neue Folge, 24, 2, 1976, pp. 208–17
Varga, I. and M. Z. Pintér, *Történelem a színpadon. Magyar történelmi tárgyú iskoladrámák a 17.–18. században*, Budapest, Argumentum, 2000
Varga, K., ed., *1896: A Millenniumi Országos Kiállítás és az ünnepségek krónikája*, Budapest, Atlasz Kiadó, 1996
Várkonyi, T., *Négy király, egy szultán*, Budapest, Tarsoly Kiadó, 2014
Vasylenko, V., *Politychna istoriia Velykoho kniazivstva Lytovs'koho (do 1569 r.) v skhidnoslov'ians'kykh istoriohrafiiakh XIX – pershoi tretyny XX st.*, Avtoreferat na zdobuttia naukovoho stupenia doktora ist. nauk, Kyiv, n.p., 2007
—— *Politychna istoriia Velykoho kniazivstva Lytovs'koho (do 1569 r.) v skhidnoslov'ians'kykh istoriohrafiiakh XIX – pershoi tretyny XX st.*, Dnipropetrovsk, Natsional'nyi hirnychyi universytet, 2006
Vávra, J., *Gindelyho učebnice dějepisu pro školy měštanské*, Prague, Nákladem F. Tempského, 1895, vol. 2
Veleslavína, Daniel Adam z, *Kalendař hystorycký, krátké poznamenánj wssechněch dnůw gednohokaždého měsýce přes celý rokI*, Prague, 1590
Veress, E., *Izabella királyné*, Magyar Történeti Életrajzok, Budapest, Athenaeum, 1901
Verzhbovsky, F., *Dve kandidatury na polskii prestol Vilgelma iz Rozenberga i erzgerzoga Ferdinanda, 1574–1575. Po neizdannym istochnikam*, St Petersburg, n.p., 1889
Viliūnė, G., *Vilniaus Madona*, Vilnius, Alma Littera, 2014
—— *Vorläuffig Historich-Politische Einleitung Zu der Hauptfrage, ob Die von König Ferdinand I. mit Seiner Gemahlin Anna Jagelonica, Königin zu Böheim, etc. etc. Durch L. s.l. 1745*, n.p.
Vladimirskii-Budanov, M., ed., *Khrestomatiia po istorii russkogo prava*, vol. II, St Petersburg, n.p., 1901
Voitovych, L., *Kniazha doba: portrety elity*, Bila Tserkva, Vydavets' Oleksandr Pshonkivs'kyi, 2006
—— *Kniazivs'ki dynastii Skhidnoi Yevropy (kinets' IX – pochatok XVI st.): sklad, suspil'na i politychna rol'*, Lviv, Instytut ukrainoznavstva im. I. Kry'iakevycha NAN Ukrainy, 2000
Vovk, O., 'Istoriohrafiia Sudebnyka Kazymyra IV 1468 roku', *Visnyk Kyivs'koho natsional'noho universytetu imeni Tarasa Shevchenka*, 72, 2006, pp. 41–3
Wecowski, P. (ed.), *Jagellonský i ich Świat*, ed. Piotr Węcowski, Kraków, Societas Vistulana, 2016
Yakovenko, N., 'Skil'ky istorykiv – stil'ky unii (z nahody 440-littia Liublins'koi unii)', *Ukrains'kyi humanitarnyi ohliad*, 14, 2009, pp. 9–42

—— *Ukrains'ka shliakhta z kintsia XIV do seredyny XVII st.: Volyn' i Tsentral'na Ukraina*, Kyiv, Krytyka, 2008

—— 'Koho ta yak inshuie Mykhailo Hrushevs'kyi v "Istorii Ukrainy-Rusy"', in *Obraz inshoho v susidnikh istoriiakh: mify, stereotypy, naukovi interpretatsii. Materaly mizhnarodnoi naukovoi konferentsii*, Kyiv, 15–16 hrudnia 2005 roku, Kyiv, Instytut istorii Ukrainy, 2008, pp. 95–102

—— *Narys istorii seredn'ovichnoi ta rann'omodernoi Ukrainy*, Kyiv, Krytyka, 2005

—— *Paralel'nyi svit. Doslidzhennia z istorii uiavlen' ta idei v Ukraini XVI–XVII st.*, Kyiv, Krytyka, 2002

—— 'Pol'scha ta poliaky v shkil'nykh pidruchnykakh istorii, abo vidlunnia davn'oho i nedavn'oho mynuloho', in Yakovenko, *Paralel'nyi svit*, pp. 366–79

—— 'Early Modern Ukraine between East and West: Projecturies of an Idea', in K. Matsuzato, ed., *Regions: A Prism to View the Slavic-Eurasian World. Towards a Discipline of 'Regionology'*, Sapporo, Slavic Research Center, Hokkaido University, 2000

—— 'Zdobutky i vtraty Liublins'koi unii', *Kyivs'ka starovyna*, 3, 1993

Yanin, V., *Novgorod i Litva: Pogranichnyie situatsii XIII–XV vv.*, Moscow, Moscow University Press, 1998

Yefremova, N., 'Rozrobka Sudebnyka Kazymyra IV 1468 r. ta problemy vyznachennia yoho dzherel'noi bazy', *Visnyk L'vivs'koho universytetu. Seriia yurydychna*, 44, 2007, pp. 83–9

Yurginis, Yu. et al. *Istoriya Litovskoy SSR*, Vilnius, Akademiya Nauk Litov. SSR, 1978

Wallerstein, I., 'Does India Exist?', in Wallerstein, *The Essential Wallerstein*, New York, New Press, 2000

Waltari, M., *Kaarina Maununtytär*, 6th edn, Porvoo and Helsinki, WSOY, 1947

Wandycz, P., 'Poland's Place in Europe in the Concepts of Piłsudski and Dmowski', *East European Politics and Societies* 4, 3, 1990, pp. 451–68

Weeks, T., 'Russification: Word and Practice 1863–1914', *Proceedings of the American Philosophical Society*, 148, 4, 2004, p. 475

—— 'Russification and the Lithuanians, 1863–1905', *Slavic Review*, 60, 1, 2001, pp. 96–114

Wehrmann, M., *Genealogie des pommerschen Herzogshauses*, Stettin, Saunier, 1937

—— 'Der Tod der Herzogin Anna (1503)', *Monatsblätter der Gesellschaft für Pommersche Geschichte und Alterthumskunde* 15, 1901, pp. 171–3

Werner, E., ed., *Landshuter Stadtgeschichte, Band III. Die Landshuter Hochzeit von 1475*, Landshut, Stadt Landshut, 2008

Westenrieder, L., *Beiträge zur vaterländischen Historie, Geographie, Statistik und Landwirtschaft*, München, n.p., 1789

Wheatcroft, A., *Habsburgs: Embodying Empire*, London, Viking, 1995

Wiivk Koialowicz, A., *Historiae Lithuaniae*, 2 vols, Gdansk, 1655; Antwerp, 1669

Wilson, A., 'Myths of National History in Belarus and Ukraine', in G. Hosking and G. Schopflin, eds, *Myths and Nationhood*, London, Taylor & Francis, 1997, pp. 182–97

Winter, J., *Remembering War: The Great War between History and Memory in the 20th Century*, New Haven, CT, Yale University Press, 2006

Wojciechowscy, M. and Z. Wojciechowscy, *Polska Piastów, Polska Jagiellonów*, Poznań, Drukarnia Św. Wojciecha, 1946

Zaiats', A., *Urbanizatsiinyi protses na Volyni v XVI – pershii polovyni XVII st.*, Lviv, Vydavnytstvo 'Dobra sprava', 2003

Zarycki, T., *Ideologies of Eastness in Central and Eastern Europe*, London, Routledge, 2014

Zashkil'niak, L., 'Obraz Pol'schi i poliakiv u suchasnii Ukraini', *Problemy slov'ianoznavstva*, 60, 2011, pp. 68–80

Zazuliak, Yu., 'Zastavy yak element rozdavnychoi polityky Yahelloniv u Halyts'kii Rusi XV st.', *Visnyk L'vivs'koho universytetu. Seriia istorychna*, 35–6, Lviv, n.p., 2000, pp. 43–57

Xenopol, A. D., *Istoria românilor din Dacia Traiană*, Editura Stiinţifică şi Enciclopedică, Bucharest, 1888–93

Zerling-Konopka, A., *Izabela Jagiellonka: Los tak chciał*, Warsaw, Rytm, 2015

Zherebtsova, L., 'Deiaki aspekty praktychnoi roboty mytnoi sluzhby na zemliakh Velykoho kniazivstva Lytovs'koho', *Ukraina Lithuanica: studii z istorii Velykoho kniazivstva Lytovs'koho*, vol. II, Kyiv, Instytut istorii Ukrainy, 2013, pp. 209–27

Zhyugzhda, Y., ed., *Istoria Litovskoi SSSR*, pt 1, *S drevneishykh vremen do 1861 g.*, Vilnius, Gos. izd. politicheskoi i nauchnoj literatury, 1953

Zíbrt, Č. and Z. Nejedlý, eds, 'Dvě písně o bitvě u Moháče 1526', *Časopis Musea Království českého*, 79, 1905, pp. 370–4

Zins, H., *Ród Ferberów i jego rola w dziejach Gdańska w XV i XVI wieku*, Lublin, Towarzystwo Naukowe Katolickiego Uniwersytetu Lubelskiego, 1951

Žiugžda, J., ed., *Lietuvos TSR istorija. Nuo seniausių laikų iki 1861 metų*, pt 1, Vilnius, Valstybinės politinės ir mokslinės literatūros leidykla, 1953; 2nd edn, 1957

Zottmayr, F. X., *Genealogie des königlichen Hauses Baiern*, Stuttgart, Füssen, 1834

Zygulski, Z., *Broń w dawnej Polsce na tle uzbrojenia Europy i Bliskiego wschodu*, Warsaw, PWN, 1975

Other media

'500-richchia Mahdeburz'koho prava Kyieva (moneta)', https://uk.wikipedia.org/wiki/500-річчя_Магдебурзького_права_Києва_(монета), accessed 30.8.17

'500-richchia Mahdeburz'koho prava Kyieva (sribna moneta)', https://uk.wikipedia.org/wiki/500-річчя_Магдебурзького_права_Києва_(срібна_монета)

'500-richchia bytvy pid Orsheiu (moneta)', https://uk.wikipedia.org/wiki/500-річчя_битви_під_Оршею_(монета)

Altmann, C., 'Das unbekannte Herrschergeschlecht Mitteleuropas', Deutschlandfunk 7.3.13, www.deutschlandfunk.de/das-unbekannte-herrschergeschlecht mitteleuropas.1148.de.html?dram:article_id=239699, accessed 13.3.17

Augustinas, Ž., 'The Case of IN', www.augustinas.lt/in_atvejis_en.html, accessed 26.1.17

Bačiulis, V., 'Barbora Radvilaitė', pt 1, www.lrt.lt/mediateka/irasas/11144; pt 2, www.lrt.lt/mediateka/irasas/11145, accessed 7.12.16

Bán, Z. A., *The Knight of Mist. Gyula Krúdy (1878–1933): A Portrait* [painting], available online at www.hlo.hu/news/the_knight_of_fogginess, accessed 13.10.17

Bertelsen, O., 'A Trial in Absentia: Purifying National Historical Narratives in Russia', *Kyiv-Mohyla Humanities Journal*, 3, 2016, http://kmhj.ukma.edu.ua/article/view/73942, accessed 25.9.17

Billmark, C. J., 'Johan III:s fängelse på Gripsholm. Hertig Karls kammare', Stockholm, National Museum, NMH A 450/1982

Bleichner, S. M., *Die landshuter Füsternhochzeit 1475. Immaterielles Kulturerbe und Re-Inszenierung – ein axiologisches Phänomen*, Lehmanns Media, 2015 [eBook]

Bone, H., 'Putin backs WW2 myth in new Russian film', *BBC News*, October 2016, www.bbc.com/news/world-europe-37595972, accessed 25.9.17

von Bredow, V., 'Poland's New Golden Age: The Second Jagiellonian Age', *The Economist*, June 2014, http://superseriale.se.pl/newsy/zloty-wiek-nowy-serial-o-jagiellonach-w-tvp-zastapi-klan_786752.html, accessed 1.12.16

'Būtovės slėpiniai' (1993–2004), accessible at www.lrt.lt/paieska/#/content/Būtovės slėpiniai, accessed 3.11.16

'Catherine Jagiellon', Swedish Queens in the sixteenth century, Stockholm, National Archive, K73 [microfilm]

Cholina, A., dir., 'Barbora Radvilaitė', Lithuanian National Opera and Ballet Theatre, 2011

Cholina, A., dir., K. Mašanauskas, comp., 'Žygimanto Augusto ir Barboros Radvilaitės legenda', premiered in December 2014, Ach Theatre production on various stages, www.ach.lt/lt/spektakliai/carmen-22/#home, accessed 14.12.16

City with Which My Heart Lies, Panevėžys Tourism Centre, www.panevezysinfo.lt/upload/1204/files/PANEVEZYSknyga.pdf, accessed 5.11.17

'Czesi popsują plany PiS na Trójmorze? Nie chcą być częścią anyniemieckiego paktu', *Newsweek Polska*, 19 June 2017, www.newsweek.pl/swiat/polityka/trojmorze-pomysl-polskiego-rzadu-na-antyniemiecka-koalicje-w-ue,artykuly,412012,1.html, accessed 9.17

Dahlbergh, E., '59', *Suecia Antiqua et Hodierna* I, Stockholm, 1667–1705

Dialla, A., 'Between Nation and Empire: Revisiting the Russian Past Twenty Years Later', *Historein*, 13, 2013, https://ejournals.epublishing.ekt.gr/index.php/historein/article/viewFile/2257/2091.pdf

Europa Jagiellonica website, https://research.uni-leipzig.de/gwzo/index.php?option=com_content&view=article&id=678&Itemid=567, accessed 6.11.17

'Figura Stalina v obshchestvennom mnenii Rossii', *Levada-Tsentr*, March 2016, www.levada.ru/2016/03/25/figura-stalina-v-obshhestvennom-mnenii-rossii/, accessed 25.9.17

The Finnish Literature in Translation database, Finnish Literature Society, http://dbgw.finlit.fi/kaannokset/index.php?lang=ENG, accessed 23.12.16

Galamb, Z. and K. Keserű, *Orlai Petrics Soma*, available online at www.munkacsy.hu/dokumentumok/dir6/2211_491_Orlai_Petics_Soma_kiallitasi_kalogus.pdf, accessed 14.10.17

Gerő, A., 'A National Fable: The Case of the House of Árpád', available online at http://geroandras.hu/en/blog/2016/03/24/national-fable/, accessed 13.10.17

Górski, A., 'Idea jagiellońska', 'Niezależna', December 2013, http://niezalezna.pl/49037-idea-jagiellonska

'Grand Duchy of Lithuania', A. Dvornichenko. Moderator A. Gordon, 2015, http://statehistory.ru/519/Gordon--Velikoe-knyazhestvo-Litovskoe/

'Grunvalskaya bitva 15.07.1410', Pamiatnaya data voyennoy istorii Rossii, 15.07.2015, http://histrf.ru/ru/rvio/activities/news/item-1850, accessed 25.9.17

'Grunvalskaya bitva 15.07.1410', [online video], 2015, Russian military history society, www.youtube.com/watch?t=30&v=LPkkwRAfxs0, accessed 25.9.17

Grušas, J., 'Barbora Radvilaitė, www.lrt.lt/mediateka/irasas/14304, accessed 7.12.16

Hampl, Petr, 'Pevnost Česká republika nebo kavárna Česká republika?', http://petrhampl.com/pevnost-nebo-kavarna, accessed 10.11.17

Harrison, D., 'Kungliga svenska bröllop från Gustav Vasa till Carl XVI Gustaf. Ett stycke kunglig populärhistoria, *Svenska Dagbladet*', 19 June 2010, www.svd.se/kultur/litteratur/ett-stycke-kunglig-popularhistoria_4886905.svd, accessed 16.5.16

'Hriunvalds'ka bytva', https://uk.wikipedia.org/wiki/Грюнвальдська_битва

Hrushevs'kyi, M., 'Zvychaina skhema "rus'koi" istorii y sprava ratsionalnoho ukladu istorii skhidnoho slov'ianstva', http://litopys.org.ua/hrs/hrs02.htm, accessed 29.8.17

'Instytut istorii Ukrainy', http://history.org.ua/?searchByPart&termin_hit, accessed 30. 8.17

'Iškilmės Vilniuje: 1562 m. Kotrynos Jogailaitės ir Suomijos kunigaikščio Jono III vestuvės', www.ldkistorija.lt/#iskilmes-vilniuje-1562-m-kotrynos-jogailaites-ir-suomijos-kunigaikscio-jono-iii-vestuves_fact_1564, accessed 5.11.16

Istoriia Rusiv, trans. I. Drach, http://litopys.org.ua/istrus/rusiv1.htm, accessed 29.8.17
'Istorijos detektyvai', *LRT Mediateka*, www.lrt.lt/mediateka/irasai#/program/171, accessed 3.11.16
Jankauskas, R., 'Barboros Radvilaitės kūno rekonstrukcija – antropologinės charakteristikos šaltinis', www.ldkistorija.lt/#barboros-radvilaites-kuno-rekonstrukcija-antropologines-charakteristikos-saltinis_fact_244, accessed 5.11.16
Jurašas, J., dir., 'Barbora Radvilaitė', Kaunas National Drama Theatre, 2014
'Katarina Jagellonica', Swedish National Archives (Riksarkivet), Stockholm, Royal Archives, Swedish queens, 16th century SE/RA/710003/02/001/K 73 [microfilm]
Klösz, G., Műtárgyfotó - II. Lajos páncélja és egyéb magyar vonatkozású tárgyak az 1876. évi műipari kiállításon az ambrasi Kunstkammerből, [online photograph]: http://gyujtemeny.imm.hu/gyujtemeny/mutargyfoto-ii-lajos-pancelja-es-egyeb-magyar-vonatkozasu-targyak-az-1876-evi-muipari-kiallitason-az-ambrasi-kunstkammerbol/6857, accessed 14.10.17
Koposov, N., '"The Armored Train of Memory": The Politics of History in Post-Soviet Russia', *Perspectives on History*, January 2011, www.historians.org/publications-and-directories/perspectives-on-history/january-2011/the-armored-train-of-memory-the-politics-of-history-in-post-soviet-russia, accessed 25.9.17
—— *Pamyat v zakone*, Russ.ru, August 2014, www.russ.ru/Mirovaya-povestka/Pamyat-v-zakone, accessed 25.9.17
Korsak, A., 'Zvezdy operetty predstavili miuzikl "Sof'ia Gol'shanskaia"', *Naviny.by*, 9 June 2013, http://naviny.by/rubrics/culture/2013/06/09/ic_media_video_117_7819/, accessed 3.12.14
Krobová, A., 'Jagellonci a Kutná Hora', *Český rozhlas*, 8 July 2012, www.rozhlas.cz/leonardo/historie/_zprava/jagellonci-a-kutna-hora-1-cast--1080908, accessed 20.9.17
Kürti, P., 'Mohács. Krúdy Gyula regénye Pantheon-kiadás', in *Nyugat*, 1927, vol. 8, online http://epa.oszk.hu/00000/00022/00417/13025.htm, accessed 13.10.17
Kuśmierczyk, M., 'Trójmorze: czym jest koncepcja forsowana przez Prezydenta Andrzeja Dubę?', Onet news website, 4 July 2017, http://wiadomosci.onet.pl/kraj/trojmorze-czym-jest-koncepcja-forsowana-przez-prezydenta-andrzeja-dude/7mmjm4f, accessed 9.17
Landshuter Hochzeit, produced Jürgen Binder, Landshut, Studio SRI and studio 5, 2013 [CD]
Landshuter Hochzeit 1475 Treffpunkt Europas - einst und jetzt, dir. Claus Zettl, Landshut, 'Die Förderer', 2009 [DVD]
Landshuter Hochzeit Programme, 2017, www.landshuter-hochzeit.de/files/pdf/auffuehrung2017/programme_2017_en.pdf, accessed 4.9.17
'LDK didikai 1515m. Jogailaičių ir Habsburgų susitikime Vienoje', www.ldkistorija.lt/#ldk-didikai-1515-m-jogailaiciu-ir-habsburgu-susitikime-vienoje_fact_495U, accessed 5.11.16
The Legend of Suriyothai, dir. Chatrichalerm Yukol, Sahamongkol Film International and Sony Pictures Classics, 2001
Lietuvos Respublikos Lietuvos Didžiosios Kunigaikštystės valdovų rūmų atkūrimo ir paskirties įstatymas, 17 October 2000, no. VIII-2073, https://e-seimas.lrs.lt/portal/legalAct/lt/TAD/TAIS.111863, accessed 8.11.16
Marcos, F. Sánchez, *Historical Culture*, www.culturahistorica.es/historical_culture.html, trans. Philip Banks, accessed 7.2.16
Mattson, E., 'No one but death', in cooperation with the Royal Armoury, the Polish Institute and the Polish Embassy in Stockholm, www.bringtolife.se/jagellonica.html, accessed 17.2.16 [dramatic monologue]

Męclewska, M., 'Prawda i legenda o medalierskiej serii królów Polskich z czasów Stanisława Augusta', 2004, conference paper published online, http://mazowsze.hist.pl/files/Kronika_Zamkowa/PDF_bez_tytulowych/Kronika_Zamkowar2005-t1_2_(49_50)/Kronika_Zamkowa-r2005-t1_2_(49_50)-s29-43/Kronika_Zamkowa-r2005t1_2_(49_50)-s29-43.pdf, accessed 12.10.14

Messenhöler M., 'Die Jagiellonen – nie gehört?', *Die Zeit*, 7 March 2013, www.zeit.de/2013/11/Jagiellonen-Ausstellung-Potsdam, accessed 4.9.17

Národní archiv Archiv České koruny (1158–1935) 1962, monasterium.net: http://monasterium.net/mom/CZ-NA/ACK/1962/charter, accessed 19.9.17

'Natsionalnaya gosdost', *Levada-Tsentr*, June 2016, www.levada.ru/2016/06/30/natsionalnaya-gordost/, accessed 25.9.17

Neumann, T., 'King Wladislaus II: Weak Ruler or Victim of Circumstances?', unpublished lecture, Prague, 2011, available online at www.academia.edu/5627572/King_Wladislaus_II_Weak_Ruler_or_Victim_of_Circumstances_Unpublished_the_written_version_of_a_lecture_held_in_Prague_2011_, accessed 5.8.16

Nykvarn city council, www.nykvarn.se/upplevaochgora/kultur/drottningkallan.4.3652860f14ade737119898c.html, accessed 24.11.15

O bitvě Moháčské čili o porážce krále Ludvíka II., http://zlatyfond.sme.sk/dielo/1078/Kollar_Narodnie-spievanky-1-Spevy-historicky-pamatne/25, accessed 23.10.17

'Orbis Lithuaniae. Lietuvos Didžiosios Kunigaikštystės istorijos', www.ldkistorija.lt, accessed 5.11.16

'Pamyatnik Dzerzhinskomu i knyazyu Vladimiru', *Levada-Tsentr*, July 2015, www.levada.ru/2015/07/24/pamyatnik-dzerzhinskomu-i-knyazyu-vladimiru/, accessed 25.9.17

'Paskutinis valdovas Vilniuje: Aleksandras Jogailaitis', www.ldkistorija.lt/#paskutinis-valdovas-vilniuje-aleksandras-jogailaitis_fact_302, accessed 5.11.16

Petrauskas, R., 'Karalių motina ir senelė: Sofija Alšėniškė', www.ldkistorija.lt/#karaliu-motina-ir-senele-sofija-alseniske_fact_294, accessed 5.11.16

The Picture Collections of National Board of Antiquities of Finland, HK10000, 2008, www.kuvakokoelmat.fi/pictures/view/HK10000_2008, accessed 25.11.16

Pollmann, J., plenary lecture, 'Remembering the Reformation' Conference, Cambridge, September 2017

Portraits of members of the Jagiellon family, workshop of Lucas Cranach the Younger, 1553–1556, in the Princes' Czartoryski Museum in Cracow, Fundacja XX Czartoryskich przy Muzeum Narodowym, XII-536 XII-545 [painting]

Ragauskienė, R., 'Mitai apie Barborą Radvilaitę', www.ldkistorija.lt/#mitai-apie-barbora-radvilaite_fact_265, accessed 5.11.16

'Raspad SSSR: prichiny i nostalgiya', *Levada-Tsentr*, May 2015, www.levada.ru/2016/12/05/raspad-sssr-prichiny-i-nostalgiya/, accessed 25.9.17

'Regions of Memory' Project conference website, Warsaw University, 2016, http://enrs.eu/en/news/1337-regions-of-memory-ii-memory-regions-as-discourse-and-imagination, accessed 5.11.17

Salmson, H., 'Katarina Jagellonica uppvisar sin vigselring för Jöran Persson', Stockholm, Stockholm Auktionsverk, 1865 [painting]

Sienkiewicz, H., 'O Powieści Historycznej', *Słowo*, 1889, nr. 98–101, re-published at http://hamlet.edu.pl/sienkiewicz-opowiesci, accessed 20.9.17

Simmler, J., 'Katarzyna Jagiellonka w więzieniu w Gripsholmie', Warsaw, National Museum of Warsaw, 1859 [painting]

Sjöberg-Pietarinen, S., 'Kun Katariina Jagellonica rautaesiripun puhkaisi', 18 May 2005, *Turun Sanomat*, www.ts.fi/mielipiteet/paakirjoitukset/1074044966/Solveig+SjobergPietarisen+aliokirjoitus+Kun+Katarina+Jagellonica+rautaesiripun+puhkaisi, accessed 22.2.16

Ślązak, R., 'Polityka piastowska, czy jagiellońska', *3obieg.pl*, November 2013, http://3obieg.pl/polityka-piastowska-czy-jagiellonska, accessed 23.11.16

Spysky 'Knyhy buttia ukrains'koho narodu', vylucheni zi sprav Kyrylo-Mefodiivs'koho tovarystva', http://litopys.org.ua/index.html, accessed 29.8.17

'The statue of King Louis II by Imre Varga', anon., www.kozterkep.hu/~/1126/II_Lajos_szobra_Mohacs_2006.html, accessed 5.11.17

Sudyn, D., 'Natsional'ni mify v suchasnii Ukraini', http://uamoderna.com/md/sudyn-national-myths, accessed 29.8.17

'Tales of the Revolt. Oblivion, Memory and Identity in the Low Countries, 1556–1700' Project, led by Judith Pollmann, 2008–13, https://vre.leidenuniv.nl/vre/tales/emm/tales-of-the-revolt/Pages/startPage.aspx, accessed 5.11.17

'Trubchevsk. Informatsionnyi portal', Part 5, 'Trubetskiye, Yagiellonu ili skolko dlitsia dinastiya?', http://trubchevsk.pro/index.php?option=com_content&view=article&id=74:2011-11-27-09-08-15&catid=9:9-&Itemid=30, accessed 25.9.17

'Velikiy kniaz Litovskiy Yagaylo' [radio program], 'Ekho Moskvy', http://echo.msk.ru/programs/vsetak/48697/, accessed 25.9.17

'Velikiy kniaz Litovskiy Yagaylo' [radio program], 'Ekho Moskvy', http://echo.msk.ru/programs/netak/1031364-echo/, accessed 25.9.17

'Velikoye kniazhestvo Litovskoye. Drugaya Rus', S. Polekhov. Moderator A. Mozzhukhin, 2014, www.youtube.com/watch?v=EdGNlmjIXOE, accessed 25.9.17

Visegrad Group website, www.visegradgroup.eu/about, accessed 7.11.17

'Vlast' fakta. Velikoye Kniazhestvo Litovskoye', O. Nemenskiy, A. Gronskiy, 2016, https://tvkultura.ru/video/show/brand_id/20903/episode_id/1380611/video_id/1535208/

'Western Balkans top of the agenda', Polish Foreign Ministry Press Release, November 2013, www.msz.gov.pl/en/news/western_balkans_top_of_the_agenda_during_v4_ministers__meeting_in_budapest_, accessed 5.11.17

'Widok zamku Jagiellońskiego, raozwalonego do szczętu przez Gubernatora Fryzla i część Katedry Wilenskiej w roku 1802', *Vilniaus Žemutinės pilies ikonografiniai šaltiniai*, pp. 38–9, figs 15–17 and pp. 42–3, fig. 20, Czartoryski Library, Krakow

Wojas, J., 'Idea jagiellońska w XXI wieku', *Portal Spraw Zagranicznych*, June 2009, www.psz.pl/122-opinie/idea-jagiellonska-w-xxi-wieku, accessed 23.11.16

INDEX

Alexander Jagiellon (1461–1506) 165–6, 196, 205
Alexander, Prince of Tver (1301–1339) 205
Anna Jagiellon (1476–1503) 131, 178
Anna Jagiellon, Queen of Poland (1523–1569) 126, 128, 145
Anna of Bohemia and Hungary (1503–1547) 105–7, 109–10, 123, 124–5, 129
Anna Vasa of Sweden (1568–1625) 144
architecture: Colyn Mausoleum, St Vitus Cathedral, Prague 123–4; Gripsholm Castle 147–8; Marble Room, Warsaw Castle 51–2; Prague 116; Raitenhaslach monastery 130; Royal Mausoleum, Prague Cathedral 106–7; Schöningen 123; St Mary's Church, Wolfenbüttel 124; Turku Castle 150–2, 156; funerary chapel, Uppsala Cathedral 144–7; Vilnius 30–1, 40–1; Vilnius Cathedral 34–6; Vladislav Hall, Prague Castle 115

Barbara Jagiellon (1478–1534) 124–5
Báthory, Stephen (1533–1586) 126, 188
battle: of Grunwald 5, 17, 58–9, 62–3, 173, 198, 215–16; of Mohács 7, 11, 73, 76–7, 83, 86–90, 102, 116; of Varna 81
Bohemia: Kingdom of 104–9
Bona Sforza (1494–1557) 123, 156, 177, 194

cartoons: Czech 112–14; German 135
Casimir I, saint (1458–1484) 29, 34–6

Casimir IV (1427–1492) 6, 121, 162, 165–6, 193–4, 196, 205
Catherine (Catharina) Jagiellon (1526–1583) 126, 141–56
Charles IX, King of Sweden (1550–1661) 145
Christina, Queen of Sweden (1626–1689) 156
Corvinus, Matthias (1443–1490) 75, 77, 81, 85, 89, 90
Cossack, identity 187–90

drama: about Barbara Radziwiłł 27–38, 41; about Catherine Jagiellon 149
dynasty, concept of 20–1, 41, 64, 102–4, 107–9, 116, 187

education: Belarusian 174, 178; Czech 109–10, 114–15; Finnish 115; Hungarian 75–6; Swedish 149
Elizabeth I, Queen of England (1533–1603) 154
Elizabeth of Austria (1526–1545) 34
encyclopaedia: Belarusian Soviet 172; Ukrainian 197–8
engraving, of Uppsala Jagiellonian tomb 145, 147
Eric XIV, King of Sweden (1533–1577) 147–8, 154
Europe 39–40, 60, 90, 116
exhibition: 'Catherine Jagiellon', 152; 'Europa Jagellonica' 114, 131–2; 'Jagiellonian Poland' 62; 'Vienna

Index

Congress 1515: Turning Point for Central Europe' 132; world exhibition, London 81

Ferdinand I, Archduke of Austria, King of Bohemia and Hungary, Holy Roman Emperor (1503–1564) 124, 126
festival: celebrating Grunwald 58; recreating Landshut wedding, *see* Landshut
film: Belarusian 162; Lithuanian 38; Polish 62; Russian 216–17
Finland: Duchy of 142–3
folklore *see* popular culture
Frederick III, Holy Roman Emperor (1415–1493) 133

George the Rich, Duke of Bavaria (1455–1503) 132
golden age: Hungarian 78, 90; Polish 55–9, 62
Grunwald *see* battle: Grunwald
Gustav I, King of Sweden (1496–1560) 144, 148, 150

Habsburg, dynasty 77, 81–2, 90, 124–7, 193
Hedwig of Anjou, Queen of Poland 162, 174–5
Hedwig of Brandenburg (1540–1602) 129–30, 132–5
Helena of Moscow (1476–1513) 205
Henry II, Duke of Brunswick-Wolfenbüttel (1489–1568) 123
historical scholarship: Belarusian 164–7, 172–9; Bohemian *see* Czech; Croatian 12, 16, 79; Czech 104–5, 107–9, 112, 109–12, 114; Finnish 151–2; German-language 127–9, 131–2; Hungarian 81–3, 85–6, 87–90; Lithuanian 31–4, 38–40, 41; Polish 54–5, 59; Russian 212–14, 219; Russian imperial 168–70, 206–9, 218; Serbian 12; Slovak 84–5, 90; Soviet 36–7, 59–60, 168, 170–2, 186, 191, 194, 209–12, 218; Swedish 145, 149–50; Ukrainian 183–97
Hohenzollern, dynasty 123–4
Holy Roman Empire 121–3, 125–7
Hungary: First Republic of, 85–7; Kingdom of 71–85; People's Republic of 87–8; Third Republic of 88–90

Isabella of Aragon (1470–1524) 156
Ivan III, Grand Prince of Moscow (1440–1505) 193, 205

Ivan IV, Tsar of All Rus' (1530–1584) 212
Ivan, the Terrible *see* Ivan IV

Jadwiga of Anjou *see* Hedwig of Anjou
Jogaila (Jagiełło) (c. 1362–1434) 5, 33–4, 128, 142, 163–5, 167–9, 172–3, 174–6, 178, 188, 190, 193, 196–7, 205–8, 210, 215–16, 218
John II Casimir Vasa, King of Poland (1609–1672) 156
John III Vasa, King of Sweden and Finland (1537–1592) 126, 141–56
Juliana of Tver (c. 1325–1391) 205

Kraków 51–2, 56–8

Ladislaus I, king of Poland and Hungary (1424–1444) 5, 75
Ladislaus II, king of Bohemia and Hungary (1456–1516) 6, 73, 75–6, 81–3, 85, 87–9, 102–3, 105–6, 107–8, 112–14, 121, 125
Ladislaus IV, king of Poland-Lithuania (1632–1648) 51–2, 156
Ladislaus Jagiełło *see* Jogaila
Landshut: wedding 132; wedding recreation 132–5
literary representation: of Anna Jagiellon 56; of Catherine Jagiellon and John III 153–4; Czech historical novels 114–15; of Hedwig of Brandenburg 129–30, 134–5; Hungarian historical novels 87; of Jogaila 56, 178–9; of Ladislaus II 78; of Louis II 83–4; of Matthias Corvinus 76, 81–4, 86; of Mohács 76, 83, 86; Polish historical novels 56, 61; of Sigismund II 56; of Sophia of Halshany 178–9
Lithuania: Grand Duchy of 4–5, 28, 38–9, 165, 169, 183, 185–6, 193–4, 196–7, 206–9, 212–15, 218–19; Republic of 10–11, 32–3, 39–40
Louis II (1506–1526) 11, 73–7, 79–84, 89, 102–10, 116, 123, 126; armour of 76–7

magazine illustration, of Louis II 83
Maximilian I, Holy Roman Emperor (1459–1519) 109, 126, 132, 193
Maximilian II, Holy Roman Emperor (1527–1576) 106–7
Maximilian III, Archduke of Austria (1558–1516) 126
memorabilia: of Hedwig of Brandenburg 135; Polish representations of

Jagiellonians 61; of Sophie of Halshany 176; Ukrainian commemorative coins 198
memory studies and theory 1–4, 16–17, 50, 103, 115–16
Mohács *see* battle: Mohács
monument *see* sculpture *and* architecture
music: about Barbara Radziwiłł 41; about Catherine Jagiellon 152–3; about Ladislaus I 78; about Louis II 104; about Mohács 78, 104; about Sophie of Halshany 179

painting: of Anna of Bohemia and Hungary and family 124; of Bohemian rulers 106; of Casimir I 35; of Catherine Jagiellon in miniature 146–7; of cells in Gripsholm Castle 147–8; Hungarian historical, of Jagiellonians 79–81; of Jagiellonian portraits 55; of Landshut wedding 132–3; of Louis II 42; of Mohács 79–81; Polish portrait cycles 76, 79–81
Poland: Third Republic of 11, 60–3; Third Partition of 53–9, 206
Polish-Lithuanian Commonwealth 29, 51–3
popular culture: Bavarian 133–5; Czech 112–15; Finnish 154–5; Lithuanian 40; Polish 61; Russian 214–17; Swedish 148; Ukrainian 198–9
print: of Czech rulers 106; of Triumphal Arch of Emperor Maximilian I 125; woodcuts of Sigismund III 51

radio: Czech historical programme 114; German national 121; Russian historical podcasts 215
Radziwiłł, Barbara (1520/1523–1551) 34, 37–8, 41–2
Rudolf II, Holy Roman Emperor (1552–1612) 107
Russia: Empire of 11–12, 206–9; Federation 212–18

sculpture: of Anna Jagiellon 59–60, 124; backgammon board 106; of Hedwig of Anjou and Jogaila 90; Heilsbronn altarpiece 124; of Jagiellonian dynasty 60–1; of Jogaila 58–9, 61; at Mohács 88; monument to Sophia of Halshany 176; of *Procession to the Wawel* 56–8
Sigismund I (1467–1548) 7, 121, 125, 141, 145, 162, 165–6, 188–9, 196
Sigismund II (1520–1572) 8, 28–9, 31–2, 37–8, 56, 107, 126, 141, 162, 165–6, 169–70, 178, 188–90, 194, 196
Sigismund III (1566–1632) 51, 107, 126, 141, 144, 150
Sigismund Augustus *see* Sigismund II
Sigismund the Old *see* Sigismund I
Sigismund Vasa *see* Sigismund III
Sophia of Halshany (c. 1405–1451) 161, 175–6
Sophie Jagiellon (1464–1512) 124
Sophie Jagiellon (1522–1575) 123, 145
sovereignty, loss of 29–30, 54–5, 74, 85, 184
Soviet Union 209–12
Steven I, King of Hungary (c. 975–1038) 82
Sweden: Kingdom of 142–3

Tannenburg *see* battle: Grunwald
tapestry, of Catherine Jagiellon and husband 151

Ukraine 11, 187
Union of Brest (1596) 196
Union of Krevo (1385–1386) 162, 190, 196, 207, 211
Union of Lublin (1569) 162, 166, 183, 191–2

Varna *see* battle: Varna
Vasa, dynasty 51–2, 126, 141–56
Vitovt *see* Vytautas
Vladimir the Great, Grand Prince of Kiev (c. 958–1015) 217
Vytautas (c. 1350–1430) 34, 163–8

wedding: double wedding of Anna of Bohemia and Hungary and Louis II 109, 125; Landshut *see* Landshut
Wettin, dynasty 123, 129
Wittelsbach, dynasty 123, 125, 128, 134
Wolfenbüttel *see* architecture: St Mary's Church, Wolfenbüttel

Printed in Great Britain
by Amazon